Contemporary Popular
Music

AMERICAN POPULAR MUSIC ON ELPEE:

Contemporary Popular Music

Other volumes:

- *Black Music*
- *Jazz*
- *Grass Roots Music*

Contemporary Popular Music

Dean Tudor

Chairman
Library Arts Department
Ryerson Polytechnical Institute
Toronto, Canada

Nancy Tudor

Head
Cataloguing Department
Toronto Public Library
Toronto, Canada

Libraries Unlimited, Inc. - Littleton, Colo. -1979

LIBRARIES UNLIMITED, INC.
P.O. Box 263
Littleton, Colorado 80160

Library of Congress Cataloging in Publication Data

Tudor, Dean.
    Contemporary popular music.

    (American popular music on Elpee)
    Includes index.
    1. Music, Popular (Songs, etc.)--United States--
Discography.   I. Tudor, Nancy, joint author.   II. Title.
III. Series.
ML156.4.P6T83   016.78'042'0973   78-32124
ISBN 0-87287-191-6

PREFACE

This book is a survey of one aspect of American commercial popular music on discs: contemporary popular music. The other three modes—jazz, grass roots, and black music—are detailed through three other books, all published by Libraries Unlimited. Coverage extends to all worthwhile discs since the advent of recorded sound, as presently available on long-playing records or tapes. Recently deleted items are included when they are still available from specialist stores, and the labels are international in scope, for many reissued records of American music are currently available in France, Scandinavia, West Germany, Japan, and in other countries. For this book, about 750 recordings have been pre-selected and annotated, representing relatively current thought expressed through thousands of reviews and articles, plus hundreds of books, that we have read (fully explained on p.15). Thus, the recordings selection librarian can base his or her choice upon informed evaluation rather than random choice. In some respects, then, this book is to contemporary popular music recordings as the H. W. Wilson *Standard Catalog* series are to books, or as Bill Katz's *Magazines for Libraries* is to periodicals. Our criteria have been noted through discographic essays and comments, mainly emphasizing musical development, "popularity," repertoire indexes, artistic merits of discs, and extra-musical developments. Our arrangement includes a division by anthologies, different stylings, different time periods, diverse instrumentation and vocal techniques, etc., along with explanatory narrative essays that present short musicological descriptions, definitions, brief histories, roots of development and progressions, and a discussion on the written literature (reviews, articles, books). Each album is numbered, and sometimes a few are grouped together for ease of discussion. All relevant order information is included: name of artists, title, label, last known serial number, and country of origin, with a directory of addresses at the rear of the book. Each annotation averages 300 words, and specifically states why the record and/or material is significant. In each grouping, anthologies have been collected together, "innovators" have been carefully separated into their own section, and important discs have been starred to indicate "a first purchase."

This book can be used by both libraries and individuals to build a comprehensive record collection reflective of contemporary popular music, within the constraints noted in each section. Other uses include the background of musical interactions found in the explanatory notes and annotations, an overview of the contemporary popular music field in general, and criteria on which to base *future* purchases. Obviously, this aid is only as current as are clearly defined musical developments; thus, while the physical discs are, for the most part, "in-print," the actual performed music is lagging behind this book's printing date because no one knows what "fresh" music of 1977 or 1978 will be the leader in the years to come. Other limitations include the placement of discs within all four books. Our intent has been to select recordings that are indicative of a style, regardless of the so-called classification of an artist or group. The over-riding condition for each selection has been its manner of presentation—whether a "pop" or a "jazz" item, a "country" or a "rock" item—with serious decisions on placement. But all classification schemes seem to have their exceptions. However, we are confident that in our four books, viewed as a whole, nothing has been overlooked.

For *Contemporary Popular Music*, this meant deciding what is jazz-oriented mood or pop music (or is it pop-oriented jazz music?). Thus, this particular book includes the so-called "breathy ballads" of Ben Webster and Stan Getz, while the main annotation for these two jazz artists will be found in *Jazz*. Similarly, here will be found pre-1950 "big bands" and "dance bands," while *Jazz* contains the modern era big bands of Stan Kenton, Maynard Ferguson, Woody Herman, which are no longer dance bands. Additionally, Benny Goodman is in both books—for his jazz combo and his swing band. "Jazz-rock" is here, but "pop jazz" is in *Jazz*. The placement of both sub-genres reflects more accurately the initial market and subsequent impact and influence. "Blues" belongs with *Black Music* (although some can be found in *Grass Roots* and *Jazz*), but "white blues" is a rock music phenomenon, and thus is in this book. "Country rock" is another sub-genre that is here, rather than in *Grass Roots Music*. Yet it made more sense to retain "troubador" music with the folk process, as well as the modern British electric folk movement (which is more rock-oriented than troubador music). For convenience, we list below the important troubador recordings that have influenced the rock world. The marketing patterns of cross-overs and fragmentation in the music world are, as indicated in the introduction, further examples of regional breakdowns in musical styles.

TROUBADOR DISCS INFLUENCING THE
ROCK MUSIC WORLD

Joan Baez. *Contemporary Ballad Book*. two discs. Vanguard VSD49/50.

Jackson Browne. *Late for the Sky*. Asylum 7E-1017.

Leonard Cohen. *Songs*. Columbia CS 9533.

Jim Croce. *Photographs and Memories—His Greatest Hits*. ABC ABCD835.

John Denver. *Greatest Hits*. RCA CPL1-0374.

Bob Dylan. *Basement Tapes*. two discs. Columbia C2-33682.

Bob Dylan. *Blonde on Blonde*. two discs. Columbia C2S 841.

Bob Dylan. *Bringing It All Back Home*. Columbia KCS 9128.

Arlo Guthrie. *Alice's Restaurant*. Reprise RS 6267.

Woody Guthrie. *Library of Congress Recordings*. three discs. Elektra EKL 271/2.

Kris Kristofferson. *Me and Bobby McGee*. Monument Z 30817.

Gordon Lightfoot. *The Very Best*. United Artists. UALA 243-G.

Joni Mitchell. *Blue*. Reprise MS 2038.

Van Morrison. *Moondance*. Warner Brothers WS 1835.

Fred Neil. *Everybody's Talkin'*. Capitol ST294.

Randy Newman. *Sail Away.* Reprise MS 2064.

Nilsson. *Nilsson's Aerial Ballet.* RCA LSP 3956.

Laura Nyro. *New York Tendaberry.* Columbia KCS 9737.

Tom Paxton. *Ramblin' Boy.* Elektra EKS 7277.

John Prine. *John Prine.* Atlantic SD8296.

Simon and Garfunkel. *Greatest Hits.* Columbia PC31350.

Cat Stevens. *Greatest Hits.* A & M SP 4519.

James Taylor. *Sweet Baby James.* Warner Brothers WS 1843.

Jerry Jeff Walker. *Mr. Bojangles.* Atco SD33-259.

ACKNOWLEDGMENTS AND THANKS

While this book is basically a summation and synthesis of existing thought about contemporary popular music (as revealed through books, periodical articles, record reviews, and the music itself), we sought guidance from collectors in the field through letters and conversations. All are knowledgeable critics; some are even librarians. In no way did they comment on the text itself; that was our responsibility alone. Our thanks, then, go to: Andrew Armitage (rock, troubador), John Arpin (piano, show music), Gordon Bean (stage and film), Paul Copeland (British dance bands, popular mainstream vocalists), Judy Davidson (rock and roll), Larry Ellenson (rock), Paul Hornbeck (troubador), Glen Hunter (stage and film), Fay Lando (stage and film, popular mainstream), and Paul Steuwe.

Our gracious thanks also to Nan Ward who typed a good part of the manuscript.

Dean Tudor
Nancy Tudor

1978

"Popular music in America never was taken seriously by anyone
other than the people who produced it or bought it."
—Mike Jahn, *Rock* (1973)

TABLE OF CONTENTS

Preface   5

Acknowledgments and Thanks   8

What This Book Is All About and How to Use It 13

Introduction to Popular Music 21

The Best of the Best: Anthologies of Popular Music
  on Records 29

MAINSTREAM POPULAR MUSIC

MAINSTREAM POPULAR MUSIC: Introduction 35
  History 35
  Literature 39

GENERAL POPULAR MUSIC 40
  Nineteenth Century American Popular Music 40
  Twentieth Century American Popular Music 41

VOCAL STYLISTS 45
  Male 45
    Innovators 45
    Standards 51
  Female 60
    Innovators 60
    Standards 64
  Groups 73
    Innovators 73
    Standards 75

INSTRUMENTAL ENSEMBLES 79

NOVELTY AND HUMOR 84
  Anthologies 84
  Standards 86

BIG BANDS 87
  Introduction 87
    Development 88
    Literature 89

BIG BANDS (cont'd)
Anthologies 90
Innovators 91
American Dance Bands 95
Pre-War 95
Post-War 103
British Dance Bands 110
Anthologies 110
Standards 110
Latin Dance Music 113

STAGE AND FILM 114
Introduction 114
Literature 115
Stage 116
Original Casts 116
Revivals and Studio Versions 122
Films 125
Anthologies 125
Individual Titles 127
Composers 130
Artists 133

ROCK MUSIC

ROCK MUSIC: Introduction 147
Techniques 147

ROCKABILLY 148
Introduction 148
Techniques 149
Literature 150
Anthologies 150
Innovators 153
Standards 155

ROCK 'N' ROLL 157
Introduction 157
Characteristics 158
Literature 159
Anthologies 160
Innovators 165
Standards 167
Revival 172

MODERN ROCK 'N' ROLL 173
    The Sixties and Seventies 173
    Anthologies 174
    Standards 174

ROCK 180
    Introduction 180
        Technical Effects 181
        Lyrics 183
        Literature 184
    Anthologies 185
    Innovators 186
    Standards 191

BLUES ROCK 198
    Introduction 198
    Anthologies 199
    Innovators 200
    Standards 203

ACID ROCK 206
    Introduction 206
    Innovators 207
    Standards 209

COUNTRY/FOLK ROCK 211
    Introduction 211
    Innovators 211
    Standards 214

HEAVY METAL (HARD ROCK) 217
    Introduction 217
    Innovators 218
    Standards 220

NOTABLE EXPERIMENTATION 223
    Introduction 223
    Recordings 224

CITATIONS, DIRECTORIES, INDEXES. 233
    Book Citations 235
    Periodical Citations 249
    Directory of Labels and Starred Records 251
    Directory of Specialist Record Stores 301
    Mainstream Popular Artists' Index 303
    Rock Artists' Index 309

WHAT THIS BOOK IS ALL ABOUT
AND HOW TO USE IT

"Of all the arts, music has always been nearest
to the hearts of Americans and the most expressive of their
essential needs, fears, and motivations."
—William O. Talvitie

"Music is music and that's it. If it sounds good,
it's good music and it depends on who's listening
how good it sounds."
—Duke Ellington

"It's all music, no more, no less."
—Bob Dylan (1965)

This reference tool offers a complete pre-selected evaluative guide to the best and most enduring recorded contemporary popular music (largely American) available on long-playing discs and tapes. It can be used by both libraries and individuals to build up a comprehensive collection reflective of every area of contemporary popular music. About 750 discs are annotated within a space of 300 (average) words each indicating musical influences, impact, and importance. This represents about a $7,500 investment. However, about 220 key albums are identified and suggested as a "first purchase" (about $1,000). These are seminal recordings. The interested individual can use the selection guide to buy first, for instance, the key big band or rock 'n' roll albums followed by the balance. Then this person could start purchasing all other discs by favorite vocal stylists, or perhaps move on to another field such as stage music or experimental rock music. The approach is by ever-widening circles.

This book also is concerned with the preservation of recorded popular music through the long-playing disc. The commercial disc, even though it does not adequately reflect the total characteristics of musical genres, is a very convenient way to scrutinize popular music and audience reactions in an historical perspective. A disc preserves exactly the manner of a performance, with absolutely no chance of change through future progression—except for the most recent materials that have been altered by remixing or tape dubbing (e.g., Hank Williams with strings or Simon and Garfunkel's "Sounds of Silence" with a soft rock background). Records are constantly available around the country; some may be difficult to acquire, but the waiting is worth the aggravation. By the 1970s, audiences for all types of music have been fully catered to in some form or another. However, at some point in the development of a genre, musical minorities can become cult fanatics who insist on having every single note a particular artist performed. At this point, the cult audience must seek out bootleg records, taped concerts, airshots, and so forth, most of which are outside the mainstream of the recording industry.

The discographic essays in this book provide information on the basic elements of musical genres, criticisms, and analysis, as well as literature surveys for book and magazine purchases. The introductory essay presents an overview of popular music generally; the bibliography lists core books and magazines dealing with popular music that were especially chosen to show broad historical trends of importance and influence. The narrative discographic essays head each category, beginning with musicological descriptions, definitions, and continuing with brief histories and roots of development, reasons why it succeeded, musical hybrids, recording company policies, leading proponents in the field, criteria for inclusion of records, a discussion on record critics, and the tendencies of specialist review magazines. A useful by-product of this mechanism is that significant data and criticism are presented on which the record librarian can base popular music phonodisc selection for future recorded issues and reissues. The *Annual Index to Popular Music Record Reviews* can serve to update this book for record purchasing.

ARRANGEMENT AND FORMAT

All records in this volume are arranged under such categories as anthologies, stylings, time periods, instrumentation, vocal techniques, and so forth, as laid out in the table of contents. Narrative essays not only introduce mainstream popular and rock music, but also head each category within. These essays include short musicological descriptions, definitions, brief histories, roots of development and progressions, the leading proponents in the field, general criteria for inclusion of the specific records that follow, and a discussion of relevant books and existing periodicals (plus some detail on record reviewing and critics).

Each album discussed is entered in abbreviated discographic style: an internal numbering scheme to pinpoint its location within the book; entry by group, individual or title (if anthology) with commonalities collected for comparison purposes; album title, the number of discs in the package, label and serial number; country of origin if *not* American. Prices have been omitted because of rapid changes, discounts, and foreign currencies. Annotations, which average 300 words, specifically state why the record and/or material is significant, with references to personnel and individual titles.

There are three clear special indications: one, the "innovators" have been carefully separated into their own section; two, important discs have been starred (*); and three, the anthologies have been collected (see the short essay on the anthology, page 29). In terms of budgets, the suggested order of purchasing is: 1) within each genre desired, the starred anthologies (approximately $250 total for each genre); 2) within each genre desired, the other anthologies (approximately $750); 3) within each genre desired, the starred recordings of the innovators (approximately $500); 4) within each genre desired, the rest of the innovators (approximately $500); 5) within each genre desired, the balance of the starred items (approximately $750); 6) within each genre desired, the rest of the recordings (approximately $4,750).

The repackaged anthology represents the best choice for even the smallest of libraries. This maximizes the dollar so that libraries can get a reasonable "flavoring" of the widest repertoires or themes in an attempt to manage on the smallest of budgets. Larger libraries which, for whatever reason, prefer not to collect in a particular genre could still supplement their collection by purchasing the worthwhile anthologies in those genres for about $250 a grouping. These books will not include "classical" music, spoken word and humor, children's, marching bands, foreign language, religious (except for gospel and sacred music, both exceptionally popular religious music), and non-commercial items such as instructional recordings, educational records if the commercial form co-exists on album, and field trips (except for significant folk music).

Additional information is provided after the text: a directory of latest known addresses for record companies, plus an indication of their albums that we have starred in label numerical order; a short list of specialist record stores; a bibliography of pertinent books and periodicals; and an artist index with entries for both musical performances in diverse genres and musical influences.

METHOD OF RATING

Written materials about important popular music phonodiscs exist in a variety of forms: scattered discographic essays; scattered citations as footnotes; short biographic essays of leading performers; books with lists of records; discographic "polls"; annual "best of the year" awards; "tops of the pops" lists and chart actions; and passing references in ordinary reviews. Written material about popular music genres in general—at an introductory level—exists mainly in books, but such books were not written with the intention of assembling a representative historical core collection of phonodiscs.

The basic method we have used is a manual version of citation analysis by consensus. Through the 1965-1976 period, we studied about 60 popular music periodicals, which contained over 50,000 relevant reviews and over 10,000 articles. We also read more than 2,000 books on popular music, some dating from the 1920s, and we actually listened to 14,000-plus long-playing albums. Although we didn't know it at the time, work began on this book in 1967—a decade ago. We started out by identifying, for personal use, *all* the important performers in popular music, and we then read widely and bought all of that person's material *before* going on to anyone else. The rationale here was that, since these performers are acknowledged as the *best*, even their "off" material might be considerably better than a second-generation or derivative imitator. By moving in ever-widening circles (somewhat akin to a Venn diagram), we then began to investigate influences, impacts, and importance—for whatever reasons. At the same time we began to categorize performers so that we could make some sense out of the profusion of records by time, place, and influence. Generally, the slotting of performers by genre does not really affect one's appreciation of them at all but rather produces common groupings for the novice listener. What has developed is the categorization of available records rather than of the performers. Thus, this book is about significant recordings rather than significant artists (although the two do coincide fairly often). By *not* first choosing artists and then seeking out important discs (which is what we started to do) but instead seeking important recordings first, we have neatly avoided the "star" approach, which has two main disadvantages: first, that individual reputations may rise and fall without reference to artistic merit; and second, that styles of performance rapidly change from fashionable to unfashionable.

Reading and listening widely, we developed several criteria for evaluation:

1. Musical development
    a) musical quality of the recording
    b) importance in relation to music history
    c) musical standards of musicians (soloists, sidemen, session artists)
    d) musical creativeness, inventiveness, devotion, drive
    e) each musical genre is considered on its own terms as being equally important

2. "Popularity"
    a) airplay listings since 1920s
    b) reviews of records
    c) purchases
    d) critics' notes
    e) amount of material available
    f) longevity of the artist
    g) music itself (words and/or melodies)
    h) indication of "influence on" and "influenced by"—the links in a chain

3. Index to repertoires
    a) the favorite tunes of the performers
    b) the tunes most recorded and performed constantly
    c) what was re-recorded and why
    d) what was best remembered by fans and friends
    e) sheet music and songbook availability
    f) the tunes still being performed by others

4. Artistic merit of a record
    a) the way the song or tune is structured
    b) the relation between its structure and meaning
    c) the manipulation of the medium
    d) the implications of its content
    e) art criticism

5. Extra-musical developments
    a) the record industry and media manipulation
    b) the concept album or one with a thematic or framing device (both original, long-playing recordings and reissued collections of singles)
    c) the impact of radio and regional breakdowns

5. Extra-musical developments (cont'd)
   d) the folklore process of oral transmission
   e) consideration of differences in listening appreciation between singles (78 and 45 rpm) and albums (33-1/3 rpm)

Citation analysis revealed that certain artists and tunes keep appearing, and hence any important record is important by virtue of its historical worth, influence, best-selling nature, trend setting, and so forth. We have deliberately restricted ourselves to long-playing discs, believing that most of the major records of the past (available only as single plays before 1948) are now available in this format.

We would not be honest, though, if we stated that we personally enjoyed every single album. Each individual's cultural upbringing places limits on what he can enjoy completely, and these restrictions can be overcome only by an extensive immersion into the society that created the genre of music. Attempting to understand what the artist is saying will help build a vocabulary of listening. For example, rockabilly has less impact on a British dance band, and British dance band music has less (or no) impact on a rockabilly fan. Thus, we must treat each musical genre as being equally important in terms of what it attempts to do, with an eye to cross-fertilization among different horizontal structures. It must be recognized that we are *not* rating an acid rock item against an innovative female vocalist (say Ella Fitzgerald). Rather, we are comparing similar genre recordings against each other, such as a country/folk rock music recording against another country/folk rock item.

One difficulty we faced was that there is no historical perspective for the recordings of the past decade; this is particularly noticeable for notable experimentation in rock music and some contemporary vocalists. We have no idea how this music will be accepted ten years from now, but we certainly know that these recordings should have a prominent place because of their current importance. It was a different world fifty, forty, thirty years ago; of course, the artists of a prior generation seem funny-strange today. Let us hope that the future will still remain kind.

PROBLEMS IN SELECTING FOR A COLLECTION

The selection of better pop recordings poses a problem because of the profusion of unannotated "best listings," the current trend toward reissuing and repackaging, and the unavailability of some records due to sudden deletions. Record librarians, most of whom lack a subject knowledge of popular music, usually select the most popular recordings without turning to evaluations. With the impact of the music and its general availability at low prices, the record librarians may end up with a current collection without an historical core. Where can record librarians turn for the back-up record evaluations of older discs? The same problems of continuity and historical perspective exist with respect to best-selling books. A disc that received rave reviews a decade ago might be consigned to the wastebasket today.

There is another reason that libraries end up with purely contemporary collections of popular music. Records do wear out and get lost or stolen; replacements may be sought. However, the original record could be deleted and the librarian lacks a source for locating an appropriate and perhaps better record by the same artists. For lack of a better alternative, the selector usually chooses an artist's latest recording, if that artist is still to be represented in the collection. This means a continually contemporary collection with no historical perspective.

The problem of choosing older records (or new reissues of older records) becomes one of selecting blindly from the *Schwann—1* or *Schwann—2* catalogs, or else hunting for the occasional discographic essay or lists in whatever periodicals are at hand. Fortunately, the librarian can also turn to *Popular Music Periodicals Index, 1973-* (Scarecrow, 1974-) or *Annual Index to Popular Music Record Reviews, 1972-* (Scarecrow, 1973-), but these are indexes only to the substance. Our book is a selection tool of that substance, enabling selectors to base their choices on informed evaluation rather than on random choice.

The balance of material in these books is not always in proportion to the importance of a genre or an artist, and this is mainly because there are so many examples of *good* music—"a good song is a good song." A greater proportion of materials is included for the minority offerings in blues, bluegrass, rockabilly, etc.—the same forms of music that laid the foundations for more commercial offerings in soul, country, rock music, respectively.

THE MARKET PLACE—IN BRIEF

The year 1977 was a very significant anniversary year for records. In 1877, Edison invented the phonograph by embossing sound on a piece of tinfoil wrapped around a *cylinder* and reproduced that sound through an acoustic horn. (Marie Campbell, the girl who recited "Mary Had a Little Lamb," died in 1974 at the age of 103.) Ten years after Edison's success, in 1887, Emile Berliner invented the gramophone for *flat* discs. In 1897 the first shellac pressings were created, and in 1907, the first double-sided record was created by Odeon, the record company. In 1917, the first jazz disc was recorded by Victor (original Dixieland Jazz Band, January 30), and ten years later, in 1927, the first modern country music was recorded (Jimmie Rodgers and the Carter Family, August 2). That same year saw two inventions: the first sequential recording device (magnetic paper tape, by J. A. O'Neill) and Edison's development of the long-playing record. Also in 1927 came the first record changer, the first transmission of television, and the first feature-length talking picture. This book, then, is about some of those events and the impact on modern popular music of today, and it appears at a time in which more discs from the past are currently available than in any other previous year.

Records have always been popular purchases, despite their original high costs. And the market has always been flooded with as many discs as it could hold. For instance, in 1929, about 1,250 old-time music 78 rpm discs were released; by 1976, this number was about 850 for 45 rpm discs (the modern equivalent of country and bluegrass music). In terms of 1929 dollars, though, this music now costs less than a dime. At that time, there were 10 million phonographs; now, there are about 70 million phonographs. In 1929, there were about 100 record companies, but by 1976, the industry numbered over 1,500.

During those years, four types of companies have developed. First, there are the *majors* (CBS, MCA, RCA, UA, Capitol, Mercury, etc.), who have shared the bulk of the market. The *independents* (King, Imperial, Arhoolie, Savoy, etc.) arose as an alternative source of music, catering to musical minorities; these companies were interested not in getting rich but in promoting good music. A third category is the quasi-legal *bootleg* outfits. Some of these are sincere companies interested in reissuing treasures of the past by performers long since dead or missing (e.g., Biograph, Yazoo, Old Timey), while some are dubious operations that issue taped concerts and other unpublished items they feel should not be withheld from fans (e.g., Bob Dylan's *White Wonder* set, Rolling Stones' concerts, jazz and dance music airshots). The fourth grouping consists of *pirates*, who reproduce in-print records and tapes in the lucrative rock and country fields, and who, by false and misleading claims, make a high profit since they pay no royalties and no studio costs are collected. The records included in this book were produced by an uncommonly high percentage of independent and bootleg labels. This is because the roots of each musical genre lie in the beginning steps taken by independent companies and by the innovative performers themselves, who first recorded for these labels early in their careers.

It should certainly be noted that the historical worth of disc recordings will increase even more in the years to come. One reason that older recordings have not been popular is that modern higher fidelity equipment amplifies the poorer reproduction of bygone years. An early compensation from the late 1950s was the "electronically processed stereo" disc, in which the highs went to one channel and the lows to the other. This suited stereo consoles but not the hi-fi components market. By 1976, though, RCA had developed its "sound stream" process, in which a computer reduces not only surface scratch from older discs but also faulty resonance and reverberation. This computer "justification" works on the same principles as NASA's clarification of the 1976 pictures of the surface of Mars. RCA's first such disc was of Caruso recordings; within the next few years, certain forms of popular music may be added.

POST-1974 RECORDINGS: POTENTIAL CLASSICS

Although the discographic information and availability of albums are current with this book's imprint, most of the music described here had been recorded before 1974. This lead time of five years allows for settling, to detect trends rather than fads, to let the jury, as it were, have sufficient time to deliberate and to arrive at decisions. Recognizing, however, that certain modern discs just *might* be significant in the long run, we list those recent innovative records of quality that have drawn exceptionally fine current reviews. These are:

Contemporary Pop

Charles Aznavour. *A Tapestry of Dreams.* RCA CPL1-0710.

Shirley Bassey. *Good, Bad but Beautiful.* United Artists UALA 542G.

Blossom Dearie. *Sings.* Daffodil BMD 101.

Eumir Deodato. *Prelude.* CTI 6021.

Ella Fitzgerald and Joe Pass. *Take Love Easy.* Pablo 2310.702.

Helen Humes. *Talk of the Town.* Columbia PC 33488.

Jack Jones. *Bread Winners.* RCA LSP 4092.

Bette Midler. *The Divine Miss M.* Atlantic SD 7288.

Maria Muldaur. *Maria Muldaur.* Reprise MS 2148.

Olivia Newton-John. *If You Love Me, Let Me Know.* MCA 411.

Gilbert O'Sullivan. *Back to Front.* MAM 5.

Rock

Jeff Beck and Jan Hammer. *Live.* Epic PE 34433.

Elvin Bishop. *Hometown Boy Makes Good.* Capricorn CP 0176.

Peter Frampton. *Frampton Comes Alive.* two discs. A & M SP 3703.

Iggy and the Stooges. *Raw Power.* Columbia KC 32111.

Jefferson Starship. *Red Octopus.* Grunt BFL1-0999.

Elton John. *Captain Fantastic and the Brown Dirt Cowboy.* MCA 2142.

Queen. *A Day at the Races.* Elektra 1091.

Queen. *A Night at the Opera.* Elektra 1053.

Lou Reed. *Berlin.* RCA APL 1-0207.

Bob Seeger. *Night Moves.* Capitol ST 11557.

Paul Simon. *There Goes Rhymin' Simon.* Columbia KC 30750.

Patti Smith. *Horses.* Arista AL 4066.

Southside Johnny and the Ashbury Dukes. *I Don't Want to Go Home.* Epic PE 34180.

Wet Willie. *Keep on Smilin'.* Capricorn CP 0128.

Wings. *At the Speed of Sound.* Capitol SW 11525.

REFERENCES AND INDEX

In the introductory comments to each section, reference will be made to the literature on the topic of mainstream popular or rock music. When a name appears followed by a number in parentheses—e.g., Ewen (32)—the reader should consult "Book Citations" for a full entry and a description of the book. When a title is followed by a number—e.g., *Creem* (3)—the "Periodical Citations" should be consulted. (Items such as "62a" represent updates or new entries and are filed in proper numerical sequence.)

The alphanumeric code preceding each entry first locates that item in the overall classification used for the four volumes (P here denotes mainstream popular music, and R denotes entries in the rock section, as B denotes entries in *Black Music*, etc.). The number immediately following the letter code then indicates the major section of this book in which an item/artist can be found. Additionally, the artists' index references all of the recordings listed in this book by that code number.

INTRODUCTION TO POPULAR MUSIC

"Time has a way of making the style stick out,
rather than the music, unless
that music is exceptional."
—Joe Goldberg

Popular music is a twentieth century art form made available to the masses through records, radio and, to a lesser extent, nightclubs, concerts, festivals, and television. As an art form, it is in a state of constant evolution in which each generation redefines its own music. One's perception of popular music is based only on what is heard or what is available to be heard. "Access," then, becomes a key word that was not found before either the breakdown of regional barriers or the advent of mass media. Previous to bulk production of commercial recordings (about 1920), different styles had arisen to meet the moods of geographic areas and of the times. All that these diverse styles had in common were the elements of rhythm, melody, harmony, and form; each style went its separate way in emphasizing one of these elements over the other. Sorting out the musical strains and streams is confusing, then, because of the vast number of musical and extra-musical influences shaping the styles. Some of these will be explored in the introductions to the various volumes on specific musical genres, but it should be noted that there are five general statements that appear to be incontrovertible when discussing styles of popular music:

1) Styles persist past their prime, and often they are revived by a new musical generation, perhaps in a series of permutations.

2) One development in a style leads to another development through constant evolution.

3) Each style and stream of music influences the other styles and streams through the artists' awareness of trends in all areas, this caused by the exposure that the mass media give to such a variety of artists.

4) Styles are as much shaped by extra-musical influences (such as the recording industry and radio) as by other styles themselves.

5) To the novice, all music performed in one particular style may sound the same, but each stream is a language or form of communication, and to become familiar with it, the listener must consciously learn this new language.

Each of these statements will be further explored in this section and with the appropriate genres of popular music.

Schoenberg once wrote (in a different context): "If it is art it is not for all; if it is for all it is not art." Popular music relates to the existing mores of an era, and it falls in step with a current culture by reflecting popular tastes. In this sense, popular music is relevant to its audience's interests. But listeners evolve with time, for society never stands still. Popular music changes in response to audience manipulation or demand; consequently, *all* popular music styles of the past may make little sense to a modern audience. There appears to be little need *today* for the sentimental ballads of the late nineteenth century, the New Orleans jazz sound, the Tin Pan Alley pop music of the 1920-1950 period, and so forth, in terms of what that music meant to *past* generations. However, it is important to note the older styles of popular music because these styles have revivals that show an interest in the past (for stability or nostalgia) and also show the evolution of modern streams of music. In recordings, for each genre there exist at least three types of similar music: the original recordings of by-gone days; a revival of the style reinterpreted in modern terms; and the modern equivalent that evolved from that early style. An example would be the slick group singing of the 1930s and 1940s, as exemplified by the Andrews Sisters (in the original form), the Pointer Sisters (in the revival), and the Manhattan Transfer (in the modern equivalent). Through the phonograph record, all three co-exist, and future singers in this genre could borrow a different emphasis from each of the three closely-related styles to project a fourth synthesis of, to continue the example, the vocal group singing slick, catchy lyrics.

Over a period of years, each style of popular music loses much of the original drive, mood, and inventiveness that came from its roots in tradition. As a minority music style catches on with wider audiences, and as this style becomes influenced by both other genres and urban cultures, the original excitement of the innovation becomes diminished considerably. This is inevitable as styles evolve and as performers add something "a little different" to distinguish themselves from the increasing number of other similar musicians interpreting the same genre. This creates permutations and sub-genres, resulting in the creation of yet other musical streams. As these styles become commercially successful, performers self-consciously appraise their music as found in shows, concerts, or on record, and they become concerned over their image and saleability. They are frightened that they might fall into a rut (or, more appropriately, a groove). However, seeking reappraisal by becoming observers defeats both the spontaneity and the emotional impact of the music, and no emerging musical sub-genre would long survive if it stayed with a narrow conception of its style. This is what happened to the Beatles, and, to their credit, they split up when they recognized that they could no longer develop musically as a group. An emerging style at its beginnings can offer real excitement, emotion, and exuberance, all of which tend to fade (or be jaded or tired) in its mature years. This, then, is a prime rationale for the preservation and retention of early and historical recordings that helped to produce fanatical enthusiasm among both the performers and the audiences who knew and recognized new, emerging popular music styles.

It was David Reisman who identified two groups of performers and listeners as early as 1950 ("Listening to Popular Music," *American Quarterly* 2:359-71). There was the majority audience, which accepted the range of choices offered by the music industry and made its selections from this range without considering anything outside of it. And there were also the "cults," or minority audiences, more active and less interested in words and tunes than in the arrangement, technical virtuosity, and elaborate standards for listening and analysis. This audience (now scattered among the forms of early country music, jazz, blues, musical shows, rockabilly, etc.) preferred "personal discovery" of the music, and usually arrived at such listening pleasures by painstakingly searching for the roots of modern popular music. Their outlook was international, and they had a sympathetic attitude to black musicians, whom they considered to be the prime source of material. It was the cults that promoted "early music," wrote the books and magazines, and produced reissues of original recordings and issues of rediscovered early performers. The latter were past their prime but still active and often better in the musical style than current interpreters. The recordings cited in this book are based on both the cult image and the emerging musical stylings.

On a personal basis, as members of the cult, we have found that one of the most maddening things about loving minority musical styles is the frustration we feel when we try to share that love with others who are both ignorant of the form and apathetic towards it ("I don't know and I don't care"). In addition, there is an equally disheartening feeling—when that favorite minority musical style either changes into another form of expression which becomes more popular than the original while still being imitative, or when it gets raped by enterprising producers and performers who then try to pass it off as theirs alone. The circle becomes complete and the frustrations compounded when we try to convince others that this more "popular" music is but a pale imitation of the originals. We admit, therefore, that there is a proselytizing tone to the construction of this book.

The most dramatic influence upon the popular music of the twentieth century has been black African music. Its characteristics have pervaded all forms (except perhaps most musical comedies). Jazz, blues, and soul, of course, have direct roots. But the important innovators in other fields have had direct contact with black musicians and had assimilated black sounds, such as Bill Monroe (bluegrass music), Woody Guthrie (folk and protest music), Bob Wills (western swing), Jimmie Rodgers and the Carter Family (country music), Benny Goodman (big bands), Elvis Presley (rockabilly), the Yardbirds and the Beatles (blues rock), and Led Zeppelin (heavy metal music). Without this assimilation, there would have been no popular music as we know it today.

All of this relates to the essential differences between European (Western) and African (black) music. Black music, in its components, prefers an uneven rhythm but in strict time, and with a loose melody that follows the *tone* of the words. This tone is explained by the fact that the same syllable of a word can connote different things depending on whether it is sung in a high, medium, or low pitch of voice. For the African singer or instrument, beauty resides in the *expression* of music (the *how* of performance). Western music, on the other hand, prefers an even rhythm (which explains why rhythm is the weakest element here) in loose time, with a strict melody that follows the *stress* of the words. For the Western performer, the music stands or falls on its own merits (the *what* of performance), and, ideally, the performance could be perfectly duplicated by others in another place and time.

Much has been written about the differences between Western and black music (see the bibliography section), but little about why white audiences did not accept black music. Three assumptions, however, have arisen. One involves social barriers denying white access to black music; that access was a phenomenon brought about by mass media. Another relates to the musical traditions of black music that were foreign to white audiences (e.g., sexuality, ghetto life). A third assumption is that basic differences in musical cultural upbringing produce preconceptions of what is music and what is not (for example, the white listener defines a tune by its melody, whereas a black listener thinks of it in terms of its chord progressions; white song lyrics are either sentimental or sophisticated, while black song lyrics are experiential and improvised).

As an incidental note, it appears that the state of Texas is actually the well-spring of much of today's popular music. Most of the significant innovators were born and raised in Texas, where they perfectly assimilated the diverse musical stylings of the blues, ethnic materials (Chicano, Caribbean, Cajun), jazz, and so forth, to create and fashion swing jazz, western swing, urban blues, country music, troubador songs, rhythm 'n' blues, rock and roll, and country rock music. No appropriate written materials have yet emerged to explain this complex cross-fertilization of musical ideas, but it is important to remember that the vertical separation of white and black music did not exist in Texas (i.e., both groups shared a common heritage) and that literally all kinds of musical influences were at work virtually simultaneously—a true melting pot.

It is not our intention to present a history of the recording industry or of radio (elementary surveys can be found in Schicke's *Revolution in Sound* [112] for records, and in Passman's *The Dee Jays* [91] for radio), but we view these industries as being equally important as the music itself towards the shaping of popular music. Both recordings and radio had the power to encourage and to deny by their manipulation of public tastes. A brief overview of the highlights follows:

1917-1925—limited retention of sound through the acoustic recording method. Many companies formed.

1925-1931—electric recordings begin, capturing the sounds of a piano and larger groups. 1929 was a peak year, with different markets for different recording styles of regional characteristics (largely ignored outside the geographic areas of marketing; no cross-fertilizations except by musicians who borrowed from other records).

1931-1934—The Depression meant fewer sales (in 1933, these were 7 percent of the 1929 peak), fewer recordings, and the rise of recorded sound on radio. This was the beginning of regional breakdowns.

1934-1941—This period saw cheaper records ($0.25 to $0.35), more recording activities, and the beginning of *professional* musicians who aided in the shifting of the geographic centers of recording activities (pop moved to Hollywood, swing jazz to the West and Midwest, western swing to the Midwest, folk to New York, etc.).

1942-1945—Musicians were drafted, shortage of shellac appeared, there was the ASCAP ban, and the musicians' union went on strikes. Very little new music recorded here, but this was also the beginning of independent companies.

1946-1950—The post-War era saw the establishment of hit parades, the popularity of juke boxes, records becoming full-time radio programming, a complete break in regional stylings, and expenses rising for touring groups.

1950-1959—This period brought a resurgence of *different* forms of music existing simultaneously for diversified but separate markets (blues, jump music, rhythm 'n' blues; jazz, swing, bop, cool; rock and roll; folk, country, bluegrass, etc.), this because of many competing independent companies. The situation is similar to the 1920s.

1959-1963—An age of imitation and derivative music, this was highlighted by a watered-down folk revival, the beginnings of soul music, and the decline of specialized markets in bluegrass, jazz, and rock 'n' roll.

1964-1970—An age of cross-overs, this period sees country music go pop and rock music emerge as a symbiotic co-existent through country-rock, blues-rock, jazz-rock, theatre-rock, soul-rock, folk-rock, etc.

1970-   —Now there is the simultaneous co-existence not only of separate musical styles, but also of merging styles and "roots" music. All three are widely known to a mass audience for the first time *ever*.

Recordings have had a troubled history, and it is a wonder at all that historically important recordings still remain. Many basic conflicts shaped audience appeal. First, it was the cylinder versus the disc, and then the conflict about early playing speeds that ranged from 60 to 85 revolutions per minute. Then, there were different types of materials used for the physical product (metal, shellac, paper, etc.). The method of reproduction varied from the "hill and dale" of the vertical groove cutting to the horizontal cutting, being compounded by the outward playing groove as against the inward playing groove. After World War II, further technological conflicts had to be resolved: tape versus disc; 45 rpm versus 33-1/3 rpm; ten-inch disc versus seven-inch disc; ten-inch disc versus twelve-inch disc; stereophonic sound versus monophonic sound; quadrophonic sound versus stereophonic sound; different configurations of quadrophonic sound (discrete, matrixed, compatible) and tapes (reel-to-reel, cartridge, cassette), and so forth. If an audience was expected to hear everything available and make judgments, then it would have to purchase a wide variety of equipment far too expensive for all but radio stations. Thus, unless recordings were issued and reissued in a variety of configurations, there would be music that people would simply never hear because they lacked the necessary play-back equipment.

Beyond the shape of the prime listening document, there were other conflicts. Various musician unions' strikes against the industry precluded hearing first-hand evidence of aural changes in music at crucial times. The various licensing bans called by ASCAP in the 1940s precluded listening to new records on radio and on the juke box. The rise of the disc jockey on radio led to an influence over what records the public could hear, which in turn resulted in scandals of "payola" and "drugola" for bribes that ensured that certain records were played (and others thus denied air time). And from time to time, there were various shortages of materials for reproducing the record, such as the wartime shellac crisis (to buy a new record, the customer had to turn in an old one for recycling) and the vinyl crisis of the 1970s. All of these slowed down the rate at which new music became acceptable.

The practices of the recording industry are also illuminating when trying to understand the popular music performer. The big schism in the industry occurred during World War II. Previous to this time, the type of singer the industry looked for was one who coupled low cost with better-than-average returns. Later, when the industry learned that it took money to make money, the shift would be to turn a fairly high investment into an astronomical return. Thus, the pre-war performers were largely middle-aged people who had already established for themselves a loyal fandom. These people were self-accompanied, and wrote or modified their own materials. Indeed, their major employment was not in records, or even in music. They were *not* "professional musicians," but simply better than adequate performers who were paid a flat recording fee and given no promotional tours for emphasizing any regional characteristics of their music. At this time, radio was viewed as a competitor, and each record was usually about 50 percent sold out within a year (and left in the catalog for up to 10 years or more). Post-war developments, taking into account the young returning servicemen and the later "war baby boom," concentrated on the under-30 performer, who then broke new ground with a solid financial investment behind him.

These singers and musicians usually performed other people's materials (except for the 1970s rock movement) and relied on great accompaniment from major studio session men. Their prime occupation was in music, especially records; they were "professionals" with a high profile from tours and promotions. They were paid royalties instead of a flat rate, no doubt as a result of collecting funds from radio stations that were now heavily dependent on records as a source of programming. As national markets were aimed for (there was obviously more money to be made here than in just one geographic or minority audience), the music's consistency became blander and more stylized. Tours and national exposure meant that record sales would peak in the first three months, and many records were generally withdrawn after a year. Economically, this meant that, of all elpees released in 1977, 85 percent *lost* money, with the remaining 15 percent being monster sellers that created the corporate profits.

Record companies are always quick to discover new audiences. The fast pace of the industry, plus the high failure rate, indicate which records sell and which do not. Whether they are *good* records or not is largely immaterial. Playlists of radio stations, and best-selling lists of trade magazines, provide an *index* to popular music rather than a *criterion*. This is in much the same way as lists of best-selling books, in that both reflect the interests of the time. Whether they are enduring or not is up to "history" to decide, and by tracing the development of musical styles, any record's impact and influence can be ascertained. As Robert Shelton (*Country Music Story*) has said: "Few popular music styles remain pure for long. Nothing can spread quite so quickly as a musical style that is selling." On this basis, each and every modern record must be regarded as a one-shot attempt. No matter what its popularity, just three months after its release few people appear to buy it. And if the record is successful, then it will generate hybrids and derivative imitations (in addition to making its originators duplicate their success with an exact follow-up copy). This is the determining factor in the preservation and continuation of music, despite the poor side effects caused by records.

There is a distinction that can be made between a *record*, a *broadside*, and the *oral tradition*. The latter is very limited, being based on one-to-one contact in a community, and changes in the music are prone to develop. The broadside, on the other hand, presents words only (it might have been sung at the time of sale), and the later "sheet music" added piano versions of the music. With a broadside, one had to find a tune. With sheet music, one had to find an accompanying instrument. Both, though, stabilized the texts. A record, on the other hand, has not only the words and melody but also the performance style: the text, tune, and style are together in one package, from one particular moment in time. It can be replayed and memorized, and the listener can learn from it—perhaps indicating variants in later performances—and also, of course, duplicate any of its success.

Not everybody could possibly buy all records. Originally, it was up to radio to provide a "free" service, which meant random selection until the days of "Top 40" playlists. Radio was the medium that not only transmitted older songs but also created the regional breakdown in styles, as one geographic area began to hear the songs of other adjoining areas. Radio used a lot of material, and because of its random nature, it created a demand for more and newer material. This was furnished by both new records and live performances. The latter were very important, for many programs were recorded off the air at home, and are now available via small reissue labels. Disc recordings have certainly never reflected any artist's entire repertoire, and it is questionable as to how many discs were actually favorites of the performer. It was up to the a. and r. men and producers to select the tunes for marketing, yet this interfered with the artist's natural choice of songs. This was the case with Uncle Dave Macon, who also never felt at home in the studio. With radio work, the performer could program what he or she liked to sing and usually (in the early days) performed in front of an audience. "Airshots," as they are called, could determine more about a performer's repertoire than discs, and they also plugged the gaps that existed when there were recording bans. This was absolutely crucial during the development of bop jazz because few people outside of New York were aware of the music (in its early period, it was not recorded because of the recording bans).

A graphic conceptual display of diverse major Western musical influences in the twentieth century is shown on page 28. There are, of course, many, many minor variations. (Relative size of boxes is not indicative of influence or importance.)

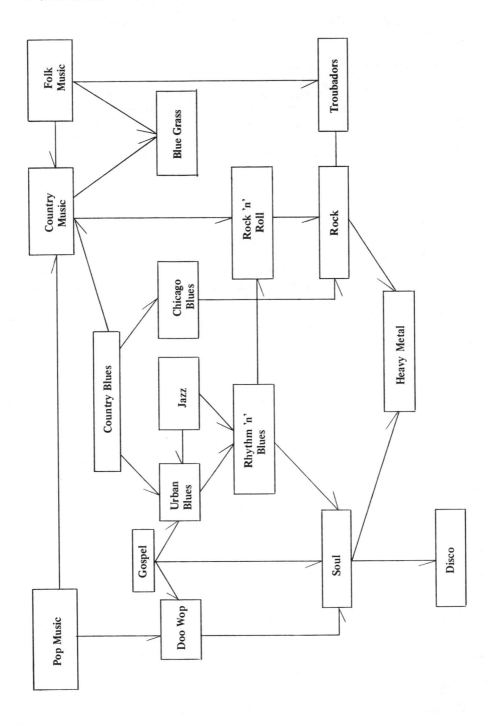

THE BEST OF THE BEST:
Anthologies of Popular Music on Records

"Anthology" is derived from Greek words meaning "flower gathering." Presumably, this means either the best that is available or a mixed bag, with some parts showing off the rest by means of contrast. Certainly the display should be stunning, for why else anthologize? In the music world, anthologies serve either as samplers or as introductions to a company's products. These collections of the works of popular performers sell to a captured audience that is used to having pre-selected convenience items before their eyes. At the same time, anthologies are invaluable for rapidly building up a music record library, or for fleshing out an area of music not already covered in the library. There will also be little duplication among the items in collections if the library does not already have the originals.

Within the past three years, aided by the soaring costs of studio time and performers' fees plus the recognized nostalgia fad, more anthologies and collections than ever before have been released. From a manufacturer's point of view, they are cheap to produce: the material has virtually paid for itself already; the liner notes are few (if any) or standardized; there is uniform packaging and design; a ready market exists, which the rackers and jobbers love, so little advertising is necessary; and anthologies act as samplers of the performer or to the catalog, hence promoting future sales. However, selection of the program depends on the cooperation of music publishers in granting reduced rates.

Personally, we are quite partial to anthologized performances. For a pure musical experience, there has been nothing quite like, say, on a hot and humid night, throwing on a pile of 45 rpm singles and sitting back guzzling beer while tapping to the rhythms. At this point, our attention span is about three minutes; thus a new record with a new voice comes on just as minds start to wander. With older records, the effect is one of familiarity, evoking fond, past memories. For the sake of convenience and better musical reproduction, though, a stack of anthologized long-play records makes this easier. Most new records today can be quite boring between the highlights, and it is not uncommon for a group to have an album with one hit single, fleshed out with nine duds. You really wouldn't want to hear it all again. Too, while most people might all like or remember one or two particular numbers, they also like other tracks individually. An anthology or "best" album attempts to take those most popular selections that we all enjoy and market them so that the most people might like the whole reissue album. One man's meat is not another man's poison in the case of the anthology.

Many reservations exist about compilations, especially with regard to trickery, motives, and shoddy packaging. Some of these are discussed here, but a few general comments are also necessary. In many instances, anthologies have only 10 tracks to a disc. This may be fewer tracks than the original albums had, and certainly it makes each number more expensive at a per selection cost. Yet, there are distinct advantages for a certain market that has low-fidelity equipment: the wider grooves give a full range of sound and increase the bass proportionately, thus making this particular type of disc virtually ideal for home stereo consoles and for older, heavier needle cartridges. Since these wider grooves don't wear out as quickly as compressed ones, the records may be played over and over again with less wear than on an "original" disc. In other instances, some "best" collections (especially multi-volume sets) almost equal the catalog material from which they are drawn and, hence, cost more in the long run.

Trickery involves a number of gimmicks, such as "electronic enhancement" for stereo, with its vast echoing sound being reminiscent of a train station lobby. These types are dying out, as it costs money to re-channel, some of the public are demanding original monophonic sound, and—the biggest marketing blow of all—these discs have been relegated to the semi-annual *Schwann—2* catalog with the mono discs. Sometimes the informative print is very small, or was printed say, yellow on orange, and the consumer virtually couldn't read the notice "enhanced for stereo." Some tricks are not solely for deception, though. Cute tricks include the title "The Worst of the Jefferson Airplane"—an obvious collection of best material. But what about an original first record by an unknown group that is titled "The Best of . . ." just to attract sales?

Another problem with the vinyl product is that anthologies are mostly regional pressings. Duplicate masters are used in factories not as careful as the home plant and are shipped directly to the regional distributor. Of course, a careless pressing sounds worse than a skillfully crafted product. And the polyvinyl chloride content can drop to below 85 percent. This is important, for the extender in a disc can be exposed to the stylus riding on the otherwise soft plastic and great harm can occur. Classical records are generally 95-99 percent vinyl, with pop recordings being around 90 percent. Anything lower than 90 percent can be detrimental to sound reproduction.

The material included in anthologies is another concern. It is usually selected by the producer or company, so that it may have no relation to what the performers themselves think is their best material. Many groups are anthologized *after* they leave one company for greener pastures, and the original manufacturer can keep churning out the reissues year after year, relying on the groups' future success to advertise the old reissued product. Some anthologies are shoddily passed off as memorials after a performer's death; others are issued if performers cannot produce an album in any one particular year, whether through accident (as in Bob Dylan's case), personal problems, laziness, or personnel changes. This keeps the name in front of the record-buying public, but too often the album is at full list price and the cover only mentions in passing that it is a reissue.

With the new packaging gatefold, is it likely that *all* notes on anthologies (as well as many others) will be inside the shrink-wrapped cellophane parcel. Thus, the consumer will not know what he is supposed to buy until he reads a review, ad, or opens the package (thus forfeiting a "return" if he already has the item). As these records rarely get reviewed or advertised, there is no certain way of knowing what is on them; Schwann does not often give track listings for them.

Anthologies are also notable for what they do not contain. The biggest performers are rarely anthologized while they are still under contract, and if they are, then the discs are sold at full price. There is no inexpensive introduction to the best material of Hank Snow, Charlie Pride, Elvis Presley, or the Rolling Stones.

When the latter group left Decca/London, the company released two anthologies at a full price of $10.98. Presley is available on a set of four discs, if you want virtually *all* of his better product. England is the best place to go for inexpensive reissues in all fields, particularly so if the reissue is not available on the North American market.

Mail order houses are a direct development from the recording companies, and some of the latter have gone into the business themselves. Being leased only for such a one-shot appearance, the selected items are pure gravy for the companies. Thus, with groove compression, 18 to 24 titles (2½ minutes long) can appear on some of these albums. Usually these discs are promoted only by television commercials or direct mail. Other reissue companies (prevalent in England) lease material from the original companies and repackage it as they see fit. Pickwick International is most successful at this, drawing on the large Capitol and Mercury catalogs (which is one reason why these two companies do not reissue many discs).

The anthologies listed in the musical genres herein consist of reissued material, either in the form of anthologies, "best" collections, or "live" versions of studio tracks that enjoy reasonably good sound. They are set apart as subsections entitled "anthologies." These records are offered as a pre-selected guide to really good performances, or as material that may lie outside of a library's main interest or collecting policy. For instance, a recorded sound library may want to capture a flavoring of the blues without exceptional expense and without culling lists of basic records, discographic essays, or even Schwann (which splits blues among "current popular" and "jazz"). Determining what records may be basic, essential, or important is not always an enjoyable listening experience; it is certainly expensive. What is being stressed here is quantity *with* quality: to get the best and most available at the cheapest price possible. In many instances, a well-rounded collection will result from buying anthologies, but not necessarily an in-depth collection.

Basic recordings are something else again—interesting for the derivative performers that will follow in the style, but mainly useful in a historical context. Such a collection is one to build on—to use the "basic" in its literal sense. These selections are listed to capture the whole field at once. The demise of the record shop's listening room has meant that the informed consumer can no longer hear an album before purchase; others might not have any real knowledge of music other than somewhat vague personal interests. How can they hear the "best" in another field? The same reasons for anthology production that are advanced by recording companies can be applied when libraries acquire such records: to introduce people to new listening pleasures (despite all the gimmicks of hard sell). Also, nearly all these records are also available on tape (except for most of the mono reissues).

Mainstream
Popular Music

MAINSTREAM POPULAR MUSIC:
INTRODUCTION

> "If you want to succeed, you've got to have
> a *sound* to distinguish yourself from
> everyone else."
> —Allan MacCrae,
> folksinger

Much of this section comprises what can be called derivative music. For "record" or "pop" music, most of it is reinterpretive, second generation sounds taken from the worlds of the other musical genres. The nasal twang of country has been dropped, the solo acoustic instrument of folk has been augmented by strings, the beat of rhythm and blues has been modified, the distortion of rock has been softened, the swing of jazz is missing, and the harshness of the blues has been softened. By the mid sixties, all of this music had been given a characteristic full, lush sound, suitable for home stereo consoles or middle-of-the-road (MOR) radio programming. Often, this music has been called the "music of Middle America," or of the silent majority. "Standards" (popular songs written many years ago but still in the repertoire of most singers) and ballads are its main repertoire, with borrowings from other fields (especially from the musical stage; see that section) for crooners and chanteuses. Usually the format is to create a specific sound for a specific entertainer and "bend" the selections chosen to that particular sound. With this method, it is possible for each vocalist to record several albums a year. The resulting mood music of the 1970s is a mixed bag of Latin themes, light cocktail jazz, soft rock, and soft country music. Characteristics include the fact that it can be regarded as background music and not taken seriously; can be listened to regularly by the automobile driver and the lonely housewife. It can be soothing, and incredibly beautiful if the melody and the arrangements are considered equally in a lush sort of way. And it is the bread-and-butter of the major recording companies, for these discs are guaranteed to make money.

HISTORY

Here is a brief overview of historical conditions. From the 1892 "After the Ball" success right through to the mid-1920s, audiences lacked the opportunity and facilities to capture popular music for replay. All musical pleasures at that time were *transitory*—live performances in the theater, the club or home. Once the final chord was performed, it was over. At this time, great importance was attached to sheet music so that at least the lyrics and composition would not be forgotten and could be resung over and over again at home. It was not until the development of the record that Tin Pan Alley existed; it was not until then that dance crazes really developed, such as the 1921 Shimmy, the 1923 Blues, the 1924 Charleston, the 1926 Black Bottom; and it was not until then that the catholicity of the public's musical tastes was called into question.

This latter point is exceptionally important, for there was little music interpretation or criticism at the time on any wide scale. There were no reference points to be gone over and over again by playing a "record." There were no definitive recordings by any major artists until later in the decade, and with them arrived criticism by means of the old "compare and contrast" method. Some of the most meaningless arguments in popular music were subsequently developed, and they have plagued us ever since. Then, with popular music recording well under way by 1930, the savage effects of the Depression caused record sales to drop by 94 percent in 1934 when compared to those of 1929. The most prominent performers continued to flourish, record, and make money for their companies, but most others disappeared—particularly in country music, old time music, jazz, and blues.

Most recording was done in New York City, through the Tin Pan Alley tunesmiths, but by 1925—with competition from radio, the development of the electrical recording system, and the catholic tastes of listeners—field trips were made, and sub-stations were established in Chicago, Los Angeles, San Antonio, Atlanta, Memphis, St. Louis, etc., to seek out newer voices. Competition became fierce among the companies, and many went bankrupt in the Depression. Not only were records *not* selling, but the air waves were full of "free" music. Later on, the juke box would be perfected, so that music could travel almost anywhere. But at the same time a blandness set in, for the basic premise in the late 1930s was to find a handful of artists who could sound like the stars (e.g., Bing Crosby) and to record them as economically as possible—using the same musicians over and over, and even the same song titles. This created a "studio sound" that was instantly recognizable. And this spread over to other musical fields as well. Sophistication and individuality were lacking in most recordings from 1943 or so onwards. The process had taken many years, but by thirty years later, it has spread to every form of commercial music.

This appeal to the lowest common denominator has two consequences: one, any innovations are immediately smothered by a glut of imitators on the market, thereby causing that specific sub-genre to be overworked and to disappear within the popular mainstream; and two, the popular mainstream absorbs all such music in its customary bland approach and regurgitates it as "mellowed" (as mentioned at the beginning of this section). Over the years, there have been fans of slow ballads and uptempo songs. The former have been here since before the turn of the century, with the sentimental ballad, and will be here for the next fifty years or so (based on observing the present 1978 generation)—tremendous staying power over the years. The latter, of a more frenetic nature, quickly burns out. It too, though, has dominated the market in ebbs and flows and has gone under different names, such as ragtime, jazz, the Charleston, swing, rhythm 'n' blues, rock and roll, and lastly, modern rock. We are not saying that these are all the same thing; but we are saying that when rock disappears, something else of a hectic pace will replace it. (There is a third category of widely popular songs, the novelty, which is essentially a fad and quickly loses currency.)

We can regard the 1935-1950 period as the Golden Age of American popular music. Records were becoming available as the Depression lessened; radio broke down regional barriers, the big bands had their start, and continued; the song stylist and studio sound emerged; most of the best American songwriters wrote in this period; and most people listened to and appreciated the same musical pieces (there was no "youth market," no "good music" programming, etc.). One of the keys to success in this time period was the network radio program. "Live" music counted most in those days to make a hit, for royalty payments were higher when all networks were monitored and the songs counted for performance rights payments. ASCAP (the American Society of Composers, Artists, and Publishers) did the collecting and instituted tight control to determine what was to be exposed for the public's aural consideration by restricting lyrics and music to the lowest common denominators of form, subject matter, vocabulary, and emotions.

But by the end of World War II, several changes occurred that were to have profound effect and thus end the Golden Age. An obvious one was cutbacks due to the poor economy. The first to go were superfluous musicians, especially with the advent of tape recording and the success with overdubbing. Tape recording also allowed for competition from smaller companies because it was so easy to do. Television caused the demise of network radio shows, especially live ones (or at least "freshly taped" recent shows). BMI (Broadcasters Music Incorporated) was set up as an alternative to ASCAP—and it had no controls. Being such a liberal competitive performing rights society, it very quickly—in the 1940s—got contracts with people performing r 'n' b, country, and jazz (and later, rock 'n' roll and rock music). With BMI there to collect royalties, such music also got on the radio, some of it for the first time ever. Another change was the rise of the a and r (artist and repertoire) man, employed by the record company to pick material for vocalists. This meant a decline in the publisher's business.

Then the baby boom created the "youth market" after 1955. Rock and roll and r 'n' b swept the nation (country music almost died; jazz went cool and modal), to be followed by folk music and then the British invasion of blues and rock. By this writing, the effectiveness of the older style "popular" mainstream music as a market leader had been over for twenty years. "Popular" mainstream still exists, but as MOR music plus musical show tunes (and there have not been many of these latter since 1960).

In any technical discussion on "popular" mainstream music, two facets have to be covered. One is the *popular song*; the other is the *popular singer*. First, the *song*. Hal Levy has said "the popular song . . . is a combination of interdependent words and music which, when sung, communicates idea and emotion . . . it appeals to a wide range of people." In the "popular" mainstream, this is the ballad, the uptempo song, and the novelty song alluded to earlier. In all cases, of course, the music should fit the lyrics and vice versa. The necessary components of a popular song include the following:

1) a theme or story that is interesting or provocative;

2) an emotion (romance, joy, sorrow, grief) that tends to be exaggerated in order to put the theme across in 200 seconds or so;

3) a viewpoint of "I," "you," or a third person who relates the singer to the listener;

4) a form, usually of 32 bars (four 8 bar segments in A - A - B - A stanza arrangement, which is the most common, and where B forms the release or bridge) and comprising two different melodic strains (here, A and B). Within this form, the lyricist has to develop the phrase, the theme

(a collection of phrases to advance the song), and the stanza of at least eight bars;

5) a basis for rhythm, which is the underpinning of the beat derived from accenting and repeating the downbeats. Both the lyrics and the music must match at this point;

6) the melody is comprised of rhythmic patterns that are effected by changes of tone. Melody comes from the music, and "inflection" is its partner in the lyric;

7) an overall sound to the song, created by harmonic structures, abstract sounds, rhymes, alliterations, consonance, assonance, etc., in the lyrics, plus various devices that relate to a particular singer (which is important when one is writing for an individual, as, for example, when Paul Anka writes for Frank Sinatra) such as the range of octaves, intervals and breathing space (open-throated sweet vowels for ballads and short vowels and consonants for uptempo songs), word choice and juxtaposition.

Second, the *singer*. The popular song singer accepts the song as a lyrical extension of speech, and is concerned with its text, meaning, melody, and rhythm. The singer also recognizes that the popular song is not frozen exactly as it was written, and some points should be considered:

1) a great popular song, exhibiting all of the characteristics noted above, will be all that is needed for a mediocre singer. There is no way that such a singer can improve on the song and how it is sung;

2) a good popular singer will use several devices in order to put across the song as an expression of communication. These heightening devices include: the turn, the slur, the appoggiatura (slight, brief dissonance in a chord), the melismatic (flowing) style, the mordent (ornamentation), the scat vocal, the portamento (swift slide between two notes), the rubato (taking liberties with rhythm), the vocal riff, and the falsetto (especially in non-"popular" genres as country, gospel, r 'n' b, soul, flamenco);

3) the popular singer interprets the song—all of the physical requirements of live or recording engagements focus on the singer—in a liberal manner by dropping or adding notes, creating a cadenza or even a coda built on a vocal riff (a concern given the 4 or 8 bar episodic quality of stanzas);

4) the popular singer utilizes the microphone to amplify not only the voice but other virtues as well: the refining of the melodic line and vocal inflection, subtle enunciation and phrasing, the stressing of good vocal or talking habits. All of this has created a warm intimacy in the popular song tradition, an intimacy lacking in the musical stage, and of course it is less wearing on the vocal chords and breathing apparatus. It has also created actors and actresses out of popular singers (through posture, gesture, facial expression);

5) not burdened by problems related to an unamplified voice (where powerful tone and tessitura [range] are needed), the popular singer can concentrate on intimate tones, such as consonantal tripping through *l, m, n, ng*, etc.; the *coupe de glotte* (glottis stroke), which emphasizes the separation of vowels from the rest of the word, especially the "e"; the raise of pitch (sometimes to falsetto); the free improvisation of the scat vocal; and melismatic ornamentation;

6) the popular singer is, above all, an entertainer who is an interpreter but is very rarely a creator, as in jazz singing where the singers tend to be interested in sophisticated, off-beat material, the beat, and the melody.

Many, many older performers have not yet turned up on long-playing records (either in solo albums or in anthologies). Reasons for this include: a) caution on the part of the recording company; b) the people are no longer "popular" singers; c) scratchy or older sound from acoustic recordings and cylinders; d) no one can find the metal parts and/or records; e) competition already exists from bootleg recording copies of radio shows on disc. Here is a list of some of the biggest, most prolific vocalists who have not been served well by reissues:

Frank Crumit	Merry Macs
Edith Day	Grace Moore
Cliff Edwards	Lee Morse
Chick Endor	Eddie Morton
Sammy Fain	Jack Normouth
Art Gillham	Will Oakland
Adelaide Hall	George O'Connor
Wendell Hall	Harry Richman
The Happiness Boys	Lanny Ross
Frances Langford	Jean Sablon
Ella Logan	Jack Smith
Nick Lucas	Aileen Stanley
Johnny Marvin	Arthur Tracy
James Melton	Trix Sisters

The *worst* omissions are the Revelers, a most popular group in the 1920s, and master vaudevillian Bert Williams.

LITERATURE

Material on "popular" mainstream is rather haphazard as so many sources in other musical genres have come together—in a toned down way—to create a great sprawling mainstream. Survey books outlining this great stream include Ewen (32, 34), Field (36), Howard (55), Lee (65, for British influences), Mellers (79), and Whitcomb (134, 135). Stambler's (121) encyclopedia covers songs, musicals, singers, and styles from 1925-1965.

Biographical material can be found in Kinkle's (59) massive work, Burton's (15) long reference epic, and Stambler (121). Composers and lyricists are given great prominence in popular music books. Ewen (33) covers 28 composers and thirteen lyricists. Wilk (137) adds more information on people from Jerome Kern to Stephen Sondheim. Wilder (136) studies both songs and their creators in the 1900-1950 period. Burton's (15) book is titled *Tin Pan Alley*, and Whitcomb (135) presents a pictorial history of that place, 1919-1939. Singers fare better as far as individual biographies go, but there are few analytical works. Pleasants (93) examines the vocal tradition through 22 innovators, while Barnes (3) concentrates on Frank Sinatra and the song stylists. Rust (106) wraps it all up with his "complete entertainment discography" from 1875 to 1942, a listing of every record made by popular singers during this time period.

Passman's (91) work presents information on the evolution and impact of the disc jockey. These were the men and women who played the hits located by Whitburn (130, 131, 132) in a series of books listing "top" popular records (1940-1955) and "top" easy listening records (1961-1974).

As far as periodicals go, there are none solely devoted to popular music (as was the case before 1960 for rock 'n' roll). *High Fidelity* (6) and *Stereo Review* (10) present the odd article on song writers or singers. *Melody Maker* (7), despite its being an English publication, actually gives more such coverage and includes dance bands. The British *Gramophone* did not have any articles, but presented good quality record reviews, especially of vintage works from before 1950. Biographical articles can be found in many general magazines (use the *Readers' Guide* index to retrieve these) and in the daily newspapers. What does exist in variant form in the many periodicals dealing with music can be located through the *Popular Music Periodicals Index* (94). The largest selection of "popular" music recordings can be located through the *Annual Index to Popular Music Record Reviews* (1) which lists about 750 that are reviewed each year.

GENERAL POPULAR MUSIC

NINETEENTH CENTURY AMERICAN POPULAR MUSIC

P1.1   Joan Morris and William Bolcom. After the Ball; A Treasury of Turn-of-the-Century Popular Songs. Nonesuch H71304.

Mezzo-soprano Morris and pianist Bolcom collaborate here on a very tasteful collection of pre-Tin Pan Alley popular songs, and just about every one of these fourteen songs would have been an RIAA gold winner if discs had existed. As it was, these best-sellers come from the era of sheet music. The first, and one of the biggest sellers, was "After the Ball" (by Charles K. Harris, 1892). It marked the first turning point in popular music by selling *five million* copies. (The largest selling song before that time was Stephen Foster's "Old Folks at Home," at around a mere 130,000.) As noted in the liner descriptions by Morris, a new concept had developed in music at the time: marketing. The push was on to sell more songs of every type; no longer would publishers sit and wait for sales. The period here runs from 1892 to 1909, and the gamut of songs includes such rich and wonderful items as "Good Bye, My Lady Love," the poignant "A Bird in a Gilded Cage," "On the Banks of the Wabash," and "Will You Love Me in December As You Do in May?" The lyrics are reproduced on the inside covers.

P1.2   **Nineteenth Century American Ballroom Music: Waltzes, Marches, Polkas and Other Dances.** Nonesuch H 71313.
This is an excellent reworking of the variety of ballroom music available to socially conscious Americans in the latter half of the nineteenth century. A number of styles are presented by the Smithsonian Social Orchestra and Quadrille Band, led by James Weaver, such as polkas, waltzes, mazurkas, reels, quickstep, quadrilles, and polonaises. Titles include stirring versions of the "Star Spangled Banner," "Mountain Belle Schottisch," the "Masonic March," "Sweet Home," and "Wood Up Quickstep." An exemplary performance, complete with the usual Nonesuch scholarly interpretive notes.

TWENTIETH CENTURY AMERICAN POPULAR MUSIC

P1.3   **Collector's Choice—Original Hits.** Rediffusion 01-173 (British issue).
The material on this anthology all comes from the Dot catalog of the 1950s. The American album has been out-of-print for a decade, and these tracks have not been anthologized anywhere else. Items here include Debbie Reynolds's successful "Tammy," the Mills Brothers' version of "Paper Doll," the 1956 remake of "So Rare" (originally recorded by Jimmy Dorsey in 1936), and a 1957 remake of the Andrews Sisters' "Bei Mir Bist Du Schon."

P1.3a   **Dancing Twenties.** Folkways RBF 27.
This generous anthology, complete with good notes, presents a wide-ranging collection of dance tunes from the 1920s, done in all of the styles that predominated throughout that decade. It is a very good sampler, with titles by Isham Jones, the Piccadilly Revels Orchestra, Gene Rodemich, George Olsen, Ray Miller, Ted Weems, Roseland Dance Orchestra, Tom Satterfield, early Frankie Carle, and the marvelous Scranton Sirens, among others in the eighteen track compilation.

P1.4*   **Encores from the 30s, v.1 (1930-1935).** two discs. Epic L2N 6072.
This marvelous collection of 36 tunes covers all of the bases in the five year period mentioned in the title. The arrangement is in chronological order (a volume two to cover 1935 to 1940 was planned but never issued). However, not all of the performances here are definitive versions, as Columbia did not have every singer under contract. From 1930, there is Ethel Waters with "I Got Rhythm," Paul Whiteman and Jack Fulton (vocal) for "Body and Soul," Frankie Trumbauer and Harold Arlen (vocal) for "Happy Feet," and Isham Jones's version of "Stardust." And all the other years are just as rich in performances and textures. Artists include Ruth Etting, Louis Armstrong, the Dorsey Brothers, Ted Lewis, Bing Crosby, Kate Smith, Al Jolson, Eddie Duchin, Gene Austin, Lee Wiley, and Mildred Bailey.

Full discographical information is given for each track, as well as cogent notes of about 100 words or so for each item.

P1.5*   **The Fifties Greatest Hits.** two discs. Columbia G 30592.
     This twofer concentrates on the early fifties, when Mitch Miller was in charge of production. It is a reasonable anthology of popular song hits from Rosemary Clooney, Tony Bennett, Guy Mitchell, Percy Faith, Frankie Laine, Johnny Ray, and Mitch Miller, among others. Stress here was on the continuation of tradition of the solo vocalist surrounded by an orchestra, and, of course, all of these songs ("Cry," "Commona My House," "Yellow Rose of Texas") became hits in their own right.

P1.6   **Hawaiian Steel Guitar: 1920s to 1950s.** Folklyric 9009.

P1.6a   **Hula Blues.** Rounder 1012.
     Hawaiian music made a great impact in the United States around the time of the First World War, as almost every restaurant and hotel featured a dance band utilizing this music. Prime responsibility for this lies with the introduction of the steel guitar and the bottleneck style of chording (not just each individual string, as in the blues). It was instrumental in adding more depth and another dimension to blues, country, and old time music; jazz, to some extent; popular music generally; and modern versions of r 'n' b and rock and roll. The Rounder collection is the more "scholarly," with careful annotations by Robert F. Gear about the beginnings of the steel guitar style in Hawaii and its subsequent introduction to the mainland. The sixteen selections come from the 1920s and 1930s. The most prolific musician here was Sol Hoopii (Gear furnishes biographical notes for all the leaders), with "Hula Blues," "Farewell Blues," "Hawaiian March," etc. Other creators include Frank Ferera, the Biltmore Orchestra, Lemuel Turner, and Roy Smeck.
     The Folklyric album does a complementary job, ranging more into the country field (it also supplements Old Timey LP 113: *Steel Guitar Classics*, which was solely old time music). The early recordings show variety, such as twin steel bodied guitars (popular for projection and tone in the days before amplification), collective soloing, bands augmented with percussion and ukuleles, marches (very popular in Hawaii), and vibrato techniques. Side two moves from the 1930s through to the 1950s, with some uptempo jazz from Roy Smeck, some Hawaiian-influenced western swing (plus interactions of two lead steel guitars), right through to Jerry Byrd's intricate riffs on "Hilo March." The sixteen tracks here have good notes by Chris Strachwitz.

P1.7   **Makin' Whoopee: The Music of Walter Donaldson.** World Records
     SH 229 (British issue).
     Composer Donaldson frequently had his lyrics fashioned by Gus Kahn. His exceptionally sharp phrasing fitted in well with the British dance bands to which he had particular appeal. The sixteen tracks here come from 1925-1931 and are arranged in chronological order. The cuts include "My Baby Just Cares for Me"; "A Girl Friend of a Boy Friend of Mine"; the ebullient Jack Hylton showing off with "Yes Sir, That's My Baby," the title track, and "Love Me or Leave Me";

and Bert Firman with "My Blue Heaven." The vocals are handled in distinguished fashion by Hylton himself, Sam Browne, or Maurice Elwin.

P1.8   **1926, 1927, 1928.** three discs. RCA LPV 557, 545, 523.
     These discs reveal some of the flavor from the "jazz age." The hodgepodge of material here includes some jazz, some dance bands, vocalists, comedy and novelty numbers, and other items illustrative of cabarets, Broadway shows, dance halls, radio and vaudeville. Many of the performers included can still be heard today in varying forms or in works from later in their careers. Each disc has sixteen selections, and the performers are (among others): Gene Olsen, Gene Austin, the Revellers, Jesse Crawford, Helen Kane, Leo Reisman, Duke Ellington, Helen Morgan, and Fred Waring's Pennsylvanians.

P1.9*   **Original Sounds of the 20s.** three discs. Columbia C3L 35.
     This is a better set than the RCA "year" packages (see item P1.8) in that it concentrates on the popular items that abounded in the day. The heavy jazz influence is felt through the performances of Paul Whiteman, Big Crosby, Duke Ellington, the Dorsey Brothers, Miff Mole, Joe Venuti, Louis Armstrong, Ted Lewis, Bix Beiderbecke, and Earl Hines. Female vocalists include Blossom Seely, Ruth Etting, Ethel Waters, Helen Morgan, Sophie Tucker, Kate Smith, and Bessie Smith. Other performers that are representative of the period were Rudy Vallee, Buddy Rogers, and Cliff Edwards. The 48 tracks are nicely complemented by a plush booklet that describes the period and each of the songs.

P1.10   **Paper Moon.** [various artists]. Paramount PAS 1012. (Music from the
            original film soundtrack).
     Set in the thirties, the movie *Paper Moon* achieves some of its authenticity (as *Last Picture Show* did) by letting the audience hear original music from the period. That the music always seemed to be coming out of a rough mechanical source is enough justification for letting the original, pinched sound reproduction stand without doctoring it for modern high fidelity. We all know what tiny sounds come from tiny transistors; the same happened in former times with unsophisticated reproduction techniques. Here, then, are fifteen diverse original recordings, including performances by Paul Whiteman ("It's Only a Paper Moon"), Dick Powell ("Flirtation Walk"), Hoagy Carmichael ("Georgia on My Mind"), Bing Crosby ("Just One More Chance"), and Tommy Dorsey. But *Paper Moon* should have presented more country, blues, and jazz as this was the period where radio and records broke down musical regionalism, although there is the marvelous Blue Sky Boys' version of "Banks of the Ohio." As to the music, this disc will remain a wide ranging anthology of popular American music from a bygone era, and the incredible thing is that somehow Paramount got RCA, MCA, and CBS to cooperate on leasing the tracks.

P1.11   **Singing Sweethearts on the Air.** Star Tone ST 204.
     Fifteen examples, from 1930-1940, of acceptable broadcast performances are handled here. Lee Wiley is featured on "You Came to My Rescue" and likewise Connee Boswell for "These Foolish Things Remind Me of You." Other selections include "Young and Healthy" (Frances Langford), the torchy "Please Make Me

Good" (Helen Morgan), plus others by Ruth Etting, Jane Froman, Mildred Bailey, Gertrude Niesen, and Harriet Hilliard (of "Ozzie and . . . " fame). This disc is typical of what the airwaves were like when radio shows were listened to for their vocal content.

P1.12   **The Sound of the 20's.** Pelican LP 116.

This anthology collects various 78 rpm records from the 1920-1930 period and includes Eddie Cantor, Al Jolson, Paul Whiteman, Ruth Etting, Helen Kane, and others. The fourteen tracks comprise "Broadway Melody," "I Can't Give You Anything but Love," "When the Red Red Robin Comes Bob Bob Bobbin' Along," "Makin' Whoopee," "Ain't She Sweet," "Baby Face," and so forth.

P1.13   **Supper Club Singers.** Stanyan SR 10112.

The material here is illustrative of a *style*, as fourteen cabaret singers are represented in this collection from the 1930s down to the present. Most of the tracks are reissues, and some of the singers, of course, are not as well known as others. Highlights come from Carmen McRae, Hildegarde, Greta Keller, Eartha Kitt (not a typed singer; she really ought not be here), Mabel Mercer, Sylvia Sims, and Liesbeth List. All of them concentrate on voice, phrasing, and choosing material relevant to the performance environment.

P1.14*   **Those Wonderful Thirties.** two discs. Decca DEA 7-2.

Yes, the music came from the thirties, but not all of the singers and the performances here are the originals. Of the twenty selections here, originals include Cab Calloway's "Minnie the Moocher," Bill "Bojangles" Robinson tapdancing with "Just a Crazy Song," Jane Froman's "Lost in a Fog," Ethel Waters's "Dinah," Francis Faye's "No Regrets," Libby Holman's "Moanin' Low" (actually from 1929), and Sophie Tucker's 1937 "The Lady Is a Tramp." Others involve re-recordings, such as the items by Mary Martin, Ethel Merman, and Jimmy Durante. Still, this is a worthwhile anthology of material from that period, despite some recordings that were made as late as 1949.

P1.15   **A Tribute to Burt Bacharach: Composer, Arranger, Conductor.** Scepter SPS 5100.

Bacharach has done many things, as indicated in the title to this record. This "tribute" is unique in that Scepter Records made efforts to obtain rights to songs that they didn't have, as, for example, Bobby Vinton's original interpretation of "Blue on Blue" (from Epic) and Gene Pitney's dramatic "The Man Who Shot Liberty Valance" (from Musicor Records). All the fifteen items here are in the pop vein, with B. J. Thomas and "Raindrops Keep Fallin' on My Head," Dionne Warwicke and "Walk on By," the Shirelles and "Baby It's You," and Jerry Butler with "Message to Martha." This is actually a "greatest hits" type disc, but with the composer being the thematic link.

P1.16   **A Tribute to Duke Ellington: "We Love You Madly."** two discs. Verve V6S-8818.

Drawing on a number of albums in the Verve catalog, MGM quickly put together this collation to cash in on the television show of the same name. It is one of the few discs available that acknowledges the compositional skills of any jazzman. All of the tunes were written by Ellington, and although his own band at any particular moment would give the definitive versions, there are other, equally good and cultured, performances here. Ella Fitzgerald swings with "Love You Madly," Count Basie and his band create rhythms in "Perdido," Oscar Peterson reflects in "Sophisticated Lady," Coleman Hawkins performs "In a Mellow Tone," Stan Getz improvises on "It Don't Mean a Thing," there's a slick Wes Montgomery version of "Caravan," and Gene Krupa does "Take the A Train." Other tunes include "Prelude to a Kiss" (Billie Holiday), "Don't Get around Much Anymore" (Louis Armstrong), "Mood Indigo" (Johnny Hodges), and "Cotton Tail" and "Satin Doll." A very good set of records, these explore the extremes of Ellington's music.

P1.17   **Twenty Years of Number One Hits.** two discs. Columbia KG 32007.
Every song in this album hit the number one spot on the best selling record charts during the years 1952 through 1972. These are by the original artists, such as Johnny Ray's "Cry," Janis Joplin's "Me and Bobby McGee," Johnny Cash's "A Boy Named Sue," and Johnny Mathis's "Chances Are." Many of the singers, of course, have dropped out of sight. Who remembers Toni Fisher and "The Big Hurt"? Or even Gogi Grant? Half of this album is in electronically reprocessed stereo; the rest is in modern stereo. Of course, these hits are only representative of one record company's output.

VOCAL STYLISTS

MALE

Innovators

P2.1*   **Gene Austin. This Is Gene Austin.** two discs. RCA VPM 6056.
Austin was one of the first American singers to achieve international success in the 1920s. He was a pioneer in crooning, and as he made hundreds of records that were pushed on his radio shows (he was one of the first radio personalities), he claimed over 86 million in sales. Besides singing, he also composed (such as "When My Sugar Walks down the Street," "How Come You Do Me Like You Do?," and "Lonesome Road"). The twenty tracks here examine his career in terms of his songs, beginning with the 1927 epic—his all-time seller—"My Blue Heaven," plus "My Melancholy Baby," the unique 1928 "Ramona" (supported by a pipe organ), and such others as "St. Louis Blues," "I've Got a Feeling I'm Falling," "After You're Gone," "If I Could Be with You One Hour Tonight," "When Your Lover Has Gone," and "All I Do Is Dream of You."

P2.2*   **Tony Bennett. At Carnegie Hall.** two discs. Columbia C2S 823.

P2.3*   **Tony Bennett. Tony's Greatest Hits, v.1/2.** two discs. Columbia CS 8652 and 9173.
Master of dramatic intensity, Bennett had been the prime singer for whom the "cover" recording was adapted: whenever Columbia found a hit song in the

1950s, they would give Tony first crack at covering it, and it would always sell. Thus, there are the hits from 1951, "Because of You," "Cold, Cold Heart" (borrowed from Hank Williams), and "Blue Velvet"; from 1953, the impressively soaring "Rags to Riches" and the classical "Stranger in Paradise"; from 1956, "Can You Find It in Your Heart?," "Just in Time" and "In the Middle of an Island." When the bottom fell out of this market in the rock and roll days, Bennett took to extensive touring, which helped him more than he realized: it resulted in one of the first one-man concerts at Carnegie Hall, where he received acclaim. (This was also one of the first times that a singer was not restricted to the three-minute time limit of records, especially with popular songs.) And of course, he developed what is now his theme, "I Left My Heart in San Francisco." The original anthologies of his hits are to be preferred to later discs bearing the same name, as these mentioned in the heading are the originals, while the others are more recent re-recordings.

P2.4*   **Al Bowlly.** World Record SH 146 (British issue).
     None of the recordings here were under Bowlly's name, and indeed, many were issued without his name even appearing on the record. Yet, he was one of the largest selling vocalists around the world, singing in a high style reminiscent of Bing Crosby. Whereas Crosby usually had insipid instrumental accompaniment (perhaps the better to set off his voice), Bowlly had the entire resources of the Ray Noble band in its various configurations (New Mayfair Dance Orchestra, New Mayfair Novelty Orchestra, etc.). Noble's was perhaps the finest dance or light-music band ever assembled in the twentieth century. Thus, for the audience, not only was there a top flight vocalist but a top flight band. This is immediately evident from hearing the first track on this 16-item album: "All I Do Is Dream of You," with Bowlly chanting the lyrics over a hard-driving, semi-jazz percussive band lead by Ray Noble, and with all the proper sustaining notes in place. Other big hits from this album include "Guilty" and "Did You Ever See a Dream Walking?" (the latter from the film *Sitting Pretty*), plus the perfectly marvelous "Twentieth Century Blues," from Noel Coward's *Cavalcade*. Of special interest is the romantic ballad "Sweet and Lovely," with the Savoy Hotel Orpheans being led by the American Carroll Gibbons at the piano. See also the annotation for Ray Noble (item P5.102).

P2.5*   **Nat "King" Cole. Story.** three discs. Capitol SWCL 1613.
     Cole was a jazz pianist before he discovered that he had a voice. When he began singing with his trio, he was immediately requested by Capitol to sing pop vocal items. "Sweet Lorraine" launched his vocal career. His experience as a church organist greatly assisted in his knowledge of textures, and for this reason, his singing was gospel-inspired, yet smoothed out for the masses. All of his recording career was for Capitol. This present set, released in 1961, contains 36 songs plus a 24-page booklet. Selected items include "Send for Me," "Looking Back," "Nature Boy" (his first really big hit), "Embraceable You," "Unforgettable," "Ballerina," and "Non Di Mendicar." The only song missing is Cole's 1962 hit version of "Ramblin' Rose." The silky soft sheen of a master craftsman's voice had great influence on many other singers who accordingly tried to modulate their style, especially Johnny Mathis.

P2.6*   **Perry Como. The First Thirty Years.** four discs. RCA LFL 4-7522
          (British issue).

    Perry Como, one of the first Italian-American singers to gain a foothold in
the American and international market, began his career as a vocalist with the Ted
Weems orchestra, remaining six years (1936-1942). These four discs from Britain
capture his career from 1945 to 1975, emphasizing the earlier two decades when
most of his successes were recorded. First up is "Till the End of Time," from 1945,
which he still sings. Throughout, his talent, personality, and charm shine forth.
Not all of the material is good, but Como's stylings and relaxed voice were able
to overcome the triteness of "Delaware," "Glendora," "Hot Diggity," and "Kewpie
Doll." He was better suited to such as "Magic Moments," "I Believe," "Dream
along with Me" (his theme), "Because," "Temptation," and "Prisoner of Love."
Moving with the times into the rock and roll area, he was successful in capturing
the spirit through "Catch a Falling Star," "Don't Let the Stars Get in Your Eyes,"
and "Round and Round." More modern songs from the sixties include "And I
Love You So," "For the Good Times," and "It's Impossible." Some rare items here
include "I Love You and Don't You Forget It" and "Father of Girls." This is a
valuable collection for both its notes and packaging (although the selections are
not in chronological order), as well as for the remarkable consistency of Como's
voice, which showed no noticeable deterioration or loss of quality in the time
covered here.

P2.7   **Bing Crosby. Rare Early Recordings.** Biograph BLP C13.

P2.8*   **Bing Crosby. Story, v.1/2.** four discs. Columbia CE2E 201/2.

P2.9   **Bing Crosby. With Paul Whiteman.** Columbia CL 2830.

P2.10   **Bing Crosby. Wrap Your Troubles in Dreams.** RCA LPV 584.

P2.11*   **Bing Crosby. Musical Autobiography.** five discs. Coral CDM5P 801
          (British issue).

    Crosby was the romantic idol of many people. His relaxed style, the easy-
going nonchalant ease with which he sang, and the occasional whistle or "dooby-
doo" endeared him to most listeners. And, of course, he spawned a whole generation
of imitators, the best-known of whom was Russ Columbo (see item P2.29). Recording for a number of companies (Victor, Columbia, OKeh, and Brunswick) in the
twenties and early thirties, Crosby found his early successes with Paul Whiteman.
Originally, he and his group, the Rhythm Boys, were turned down by Whiteman,
but they made it on the second try.

    The Biograph reissue concentrates on his most "jazzy" efforts, such as "My
Kinda Love," "I've Got the World on a String," and "Let's Do It," with accompaniment by Whiteman, Dorsey Brothers, Victor Young, Bunny Berigan, and Jimmy
Grier (from 1928 through 1933). The Columbia collections cover the same time
period and present the popular Crosby warbling "Mississippi Mud," "Makin' Whoopee," "My Supressed Desire," and even "St. Louis Blues," with Duke Ellington.
Color and shading did not come easy to Crosby: he had to practice over and over,
and his high voice mellowed as the years passed. With much radio work and live

performances, he was singing all the time, and his voice naturally dropped down a few notes into a lower, more relaxed range. The RCA album has five tracks with Whiteman (1927-1928), with two tunes from *Showboat* ("Ol' Man River" and "Make Believe"). The other eleven items are with Gus Arnheim's orchestra, and emphasize the sweet, swinging dance rhythms exemplified in his first really big hit, "I Surrender Dear" (from 1931). "Wrap Your Troubles in Dreams" and "Just a Gigolo" followed. Moving over to Decca in 1934, Crosby produced a string of sentimental ballads, which aided his movie career (and vice versa). Typical successful titles include "Sunday, Monday or Always," "Don't Fence Me In," "Blues in the Night," "Sweet Leilani," "Pennies from Heaven," his theme "When the Blue of the Night Meets the Gold of the Day," "Swinging on a Star," the epic "White Christmas" (still a steady seller), and "Silver Bells." His later songs from the 1950s included "Around the World" and "True Love," the latter with Grace Kelly. Crosby pioneered the art of popular duets, and he made titles with such as Rosemary Clooney, Connee Boswell, Mary Martin, and the Andrews Sisters, all of which were popularly received. Because of his hectic activities, Crosby was one of the first singers to be attracted to the tape medium, and many of his radio shows were pre-recorded. The Coral reissue contains 89 songs.

P2.12*   **Al Jolson. Story.** five discs. Decca DL 8034/8.
Jolson began recording in 1911 for Victor and then moved to Columbia and Brunswick until 1932. He did not record again until the mid-forties, when he did the soundtrack for the two movies loosely based on his life story. He was soon to die, but he had the pleasure beforehand of seeing an immense revival in his music. Thus, the Decca collection was recorded rather late in his life, but all indications show that he had lost none of his endearing charm from earlier days, except that his voice was now lower. The earlier material is available on various anthologies, and it amounts to no more than a half dozen selections. The *Story* contains some seventy tracks, including his best, well-known tunes: "Sonny Boy," "April Showers," "Mammy," "Swanee River," "California Here I Come," "Toot Toot Tootsie," and "Rockabye Your Baby with a Dixie Melody." As a performer who emerged from the stage and vaudeville with a powerful voice in the period before electric amplification and recording, Jolson was extremely influential on up and coming singers. His style was evocative of the then "jazz age," and he was able to translate cantor singing into the even flow of popular music.

P2.13*   **Johnny Mathis. All Time Greatest Hits.** two discs. Columbia KG 31345.
Ex-athlete Mathis was signed to Columbia in 1955 with the express purpose of producing soft ballads. His warble-type voice has succeeded for over twenty years (to produce his sound, his jaw must visibly shake; this is apparent when he tours, which is one reason that he does not tour or appear on television very much). His *Greatest Hits* album (Columbia CS 8634) was important for two good reasons: this was the first "great hits" type album ever, and it stayed on *Billboard's* charts for 400 weeks—eight years!!! The double album contains all those hits ("Chances Are," "The Twelfth of Never," "Wonderful! Wonderful!," "It's Not for Me to Say," and "Wild Is the Wind") plus, of course, what he has scored with since: "Misty," "A Certain Smile," "Teacher, Teacher," "Gina," and "What Will Mary Say?"

P2.14*   **Frank Sinatra. With Tommy Dorsey.** six discs. RCA SD 1000 (British
           issue).

P2.15   **Frank Sinatra. In the Beginning.** two discs. Columbia KG 31358.

P2.16*   **Frank Sinatra. Deluxe Set.** six discs. Capitol STFL 2814.

P2.17*   **Frank Sinatra. A Man and His Music.** two discs. Reprise FS 1016.

P2.18   **Frank Sinatra. Greatest Hits.** Reprise FS 1025.
           The above seventeen discs document the incredible career and influences of
the world's finest male pop singer, Frank Sinatra. He began on the Major Bowes
Talent Show in 1937, singing with the Harry James band for 1939-1940, and then
with Tommy Dorsey for 1940-1942. With Dorsey, Sinatra learned his breathing
techniques, which have produced his perfect singing style and interpretation of
lyrics; he did this by imitating Dorsey's trombone phrasing. The English six-disc
set has *all* the recordings made by Sinatra with Dorsey (over 75 of them), and it
makes a fine introduction to the world of big band music as well. Stateside, there
is RCA LPV 583, a sixteen-track compilation, or a badly-put-together Camden budget reissue. His biggest successes at this time were "I'll Never Smile Again," "Oh
Look at Me Now," "Violets for Your Furs," "This Love of Mine," and "Night and
Day."
           In late 1942, Sinatra left RCA to go out on his own and record under his own
name. He was one of the first vocalists to do this, and in a way, this spelled the
end of the big bands. Instead of the record label reading " [band name] with vocal
accompaniment," it now began to read " [singer] with instrumental accompaniment"; and it was no longer necessary to have a "big" band do the backing, as a
small combo was enough for a singer with a voice that went well with a microphone.
At about this time, "band singing" also developed, which involved the full tune,
with all verses and choruses being taken by the singer. (Previously, the chorus and
maybe the odd solo voice had been sufficient for the big band recording.) Sinatra
re-joined Harry James in 1943 to record the epic "All or Nothing at All," the song
that began the swooning and hysteria of "bobby soxers." The label read "Frank
Sinatra, accompanied by the Harry James Orchestra," quite a turnabout in just a
few years, and the dam was broken for other song stylists to burst forth. Other
early hits from this period include "Sunday, Monday, or Always" from 1943,
"People Will Say We're in Love," "Saturday Night Is the Loneliest Night of the
Week," "Dream" (an equally big hit for the Pied Pipers), and "They Say It's
Wonderful."
           By 1950, Sinatra was not getting the hits anymore, being encapsulated in
a rigid style. Charging career mismanagement at the hands of Mitch Miller, then
his producer at Columbia, Sinatra left for Capitol records. This too was significant,
for Sinatra had always been in the vanguard of influential singers. The former big
band vocalist, now a solo act, thus could also protect his career from over-production
or strait-jacket confinement. He began to have a large say in what he wanted to
record, and how it was recorded—the beginning of artistic integrity in recording.
Capitol had a great stable of arrangers—Nelson Riddle, Gordon Jenkins, Billy May—
and Sinatra utilized them all. The decade of the 1950s was Sinatra's finest overall

period. Each album for Capitol was at least a minor gem, culminating in the exceptional *Come Fly with Me* set arranged by Billy May. Typical hits from this period of abundance included "Young at Heart," "Learning the Blues," "Love and Marriage," "Hey! Jealous Lover," "Witchcraft," "Chicago," "Nice and Easy," "Can I Steal a Little Love?," "High Hopes," and "Talk to Me." At the same time, he was building a parallel career as a serious actor (winning an Oscar for *From Here to Eternity*). No longer was he "just another singer" who could be bought and sold from club to club, recording company to company.

With good business sense, and realizing his capability, in 1960, Sinatra again led the way for other singers and performers by leaving Capitol and establishing his own label, called Reprise (now part of the WEA complex with Warner Brothers, Atlantic and Elektra). He was just as popular as ever, although age was slowing him down somewhat—the hits did not come as fast, times were changing, and band arrangements became slicker. Yet, Sinatra by this point was so influential that anything he recorded could sell well to a predetermined audience that had grown older with him. The Reprise years (a well-named company, when one considers it) included such immense hits as "The Second Time Around," "Call Me Irresponsible," "Strangers in the Night" (his first big "smash" hit for Reprise, in 1966, six years after creating the company), "That's Life," "Softly, As I Leave You," "Something Stupid" (along with daughter Nancy), and the anthem for the period— "Goin' out of My Head." It was also at this time that he developed his current theme song, "My Way," a salute to individualism.

P2.19*   **Mel Tormé. Best.** Verve. V6-8593.

P2.20   **Mel Tormé. Live at the Maisonette.** Atlantic SD18129.

P2.21*   **Mel Tormé. Velvet Fog.** Vocalion 73905.
Tormé could have had varied careers. He is a good pianist and drummer, a superb composer (he wrote "The Christmas Song" for Nat King Cole, as well as material for himself such as "Stranger in Town," "Abie's Irish Rose," and "California Suite"), and, of course, an excellent vocalist. To many, he is witty and brainy, as reflected on the *Velvet Fog* album. To others, he is simply being frank with the audience—and this, too, is where his forte lies, as revealed on the *Maisonette* set. Always the *non pareil* entertainer, Tormé enchants his audiences with what have been categorized as "shimmering renditions," "intimate mannerisms," and "supple delivery." The live set, from September 1974, shows him weaving musical masterpieces into "melodic tapestries." All types of material, from Jule Styne, Rodgers and Hart, through to Stevie Wonder are represented here, highlighted by an eighteen-title Gershwin medley. Often, he accompanies himself on piano.

P2.22*   **Rudy Vallee. Croons the Songs He Made Famous.** RCA International INTS 1343 (British issue).
Despite the scorn and abuse heaped upon him, Vallee was a very popular singer of the twenties and thirties, as well as a movie actor. Later in life, he would always concentrate on self-parody, which gave rise to the haughty image that he was supposed to have had earlier in his life. Certainly, his songs are anything but arrogant. His close identification with a megaphone and college songs led him

to record albums such as *Stein Songs* for MCA. The material here from RCA is
largely in that style, with a touch of New England hauteur plus the identification
of the Heigh-Ho Club in New York: "My Time Is Your Time," "Stein Song,"
"Whiffenpoof Song," "Good Night Sweetheart," "Marie," and "I'm Just a Vagabond Lover."

Standards

P2.23   **Ed Ames. This Is Ed Ames.** two discs. RCA VPS 6023.
    Coming out of the Ames Brothers as a solo act, Ed Ames delivered his no-
nonsense style of cabaret singing for RCA and was a consistent selling performer.
His best period was around 1965, and he was responsible for such sterling songs
as "My Cup Runneth Over," "Try to Remember," and "Who Will Answer?"

P2.24   **Eddy Arnold. Best.** RCA LSP 3565.
    The "Tennessee Plowboy" had never really been considered a true country
singer, since his voice was far too smooth for moaning lyrics and down-home flavor.
He then became the first country star with a pop following, and all kinds of people
were buying his records in every market imaginable (including several black markets).
Since 1945, he has ground out a notable series of hits that includes "Cattle Call,"
"Richest Man," "Gonna Find Me a Bluebird," "Bouquet of Roses," and "Anytime."
Lately, he has struck pay dirt by switching completely to pop music, recording
the syrupy "Make the World Go Away" and "The Tips of My Fingers."

P2.25   **Eddie Cantor. Sings Ida and His Other Hits.** RCA Camden S 870.
    Cantor performed in many vaudeville shows and revues on Broadway. In
addition, he was a successful comedian of the silent film era and was an exceptionally well-liked personally. In the early 1950s, he had an impressive television show.
Throughout the years, he had made an occasional recording, but most of his songs
were associated with his stage work and his films. Some of Cantor's major contributions to popular music were his discoveries of Bobby Breen, Dinah Shore, and
Eddie Fisher. This disc is largely comprised of re-recordings of favorites and requests,
such as "Makin' Whoopee," "Dinah," "Ida," and "My Baby Just Cares for Me."
Older works are represented as well; for instance, "If You Knew Susie," "Ain't
She Sweet," and "Ma, He's Making Eyes at Me."

P2.26*   **Hoagy Carmichael. Stardust.** RCA LSA 3180 (British import).

P2.27   **Hoagy Carmichael. Legend.** Kimberly 2023.
    Greatly influenced by Bix Beiderbecke and the Wolverines ("Skylark" is based
on a Bixian passage), Carmichael organized his own "hot" jazz groups and began
writing melodies. "Stardust" was originally a stomp, but it was slowed down, and
words were added by Mitchell Parrish in 1931. After 1929, music composing occu-
pied most of Carmichael's time, and with the Depression in mind, ballads of a
sentimental mood predominated ("Georgia on My Mind," "Rockin' Chair," "One
Night in Havana," "Lazy River," "Lazy Bones," "Judy," "One Morning in May,"
"Two Sleepy People," and so forth). The RCA disc pulls out his better efforts

from 1927 to 1934; the Kimberly is from the mid-fifties, with a small group to accompany him (Art Pepper and Harry Edison, among others). Carmichael's voice reflects his songs—easy-going, nonchalant, and able to withstand the ravages of time.

P2.28   Don Cherry. Greatest Hits. two discs. Monument KZG 32334.

Balladeer Cherry, with a light but husky voice, is mainly remembered for hits from the early 1950s, such as "Band of Gold," "Wild Cherry," and "Ghost Town." This collation, reaching back to 1953, presents a good package for the mainstream popular music collection.

P2.29*   Russ Columbo. A Legendary Performer. RCA CPL1-1756e.

Columbo was the most successful of the Bing Crosby imitators; an accident in 1934 ended his short life at the age of 26. He made only 27 songs during his recording career (1930-1932), and it would have been nice for RCA to issue all of them on a double set. His major work was in films made between 1929 and 1934. Popular taste at this time, affected by the Depression, favored the romantic and sentimental song as a form of escape from the realities of everyday living. Columbo, along with Crosby, possessed the ability to sing with apparent sincerity; he was a top-flight crooner, often injecting humming into his songs. His firm voice, with good intonation, comes across best on the sweet songs "Sweet and Lovely," "Where the Blue of the Night," "Time on My Hands," and "Auf Wiedersehen, My Dear."

P2.30   Vic Damone. Best. Harmony HS 11128.

A find from the Arthur Godfrey Talent Scouts radio show, Damone had a string of successes in the late forties (such as "You're Breaking My Heart") that are unfortunately not available on long playing records at present. However, during the mid-fifties, he did do some wonderful work for Columbia, mostly reinterpretations of stage and film songs, such as "On the Street Where You Live," "Gigi," "An Affair to Remember," and "Do I Love You?" (the latter from the *Cinderella* television show). He fits solidly into the Italian-American tenor-baritone school, as did Como, Sinatra, Martin.

P2.31   Sammy Davis, Jr. Greatest Hits. Reprise RS 6291.

P2.32   Sammy Davis, Jr. Mr. Entertainment. MCA Decca DL 74153.

Davis has always been thought of as being an "entertainer" in the large sense of the word, complete with stage shows and tours. He has never had great success in terms of record sales, but he has had more than his fair share of airplay. Beginning with his father and uncle in vaudeville, Davis began to record for Decca in 1953, creating stylish interpretations of "Hey There," "Something's Gotta Give," "That Old Black Magic," and "I'll Know." In 1962, he moved to Reprise (Frank Sinatra's label) and continued his string of triumphs with tasteful renditions of "I've Gotta Be Me" (a sort of theme for him now), "The Shelter of Your Arms," and "What Kind of Fool Am I?"

P2.33*   Neil Diamond. His 12 Greatest Hits. MCA 2106.

Since 1969, Diamond has composed and sung his own material, which is largely expressive of exceptionally personal feelings. That he has continued to triumph is no small matter, for many have condemned the sweetness of the offerings. Perhaps his having written the soundtrack for *Jonathan Livingston Seagull* has made others look back and re-evaluate their earlier opinions. Certainly, his music has sold more and gotten more airplay since the film. Material here includes "Sweet Caroline," "Play Me," "Stones," "Brooklyn Roads," "Shilo," and the comic "Brother Love's Traveling Salvation Show." This is good material that falls into the so-called "pop" category.

P2.34*   **Billy Eckstine. Greatest Hits.** MGM 2353 071 (British issue).

P2.35*   **Billy Eckstine. Mr. B. and the Band.** two discs. Savoy SJL 2214.
    "Mr. B."—as he was known—became a band leader after leaving Earl Hines's orchestra. He took with him (or gathered around him) many of the fermenters and creators of bop music: Gillespie, Parker, Navarro, Gene Ammons, Dexter Gordon, Art Blakey, Sonny Stitt, Lucky Thompson, Miles Davis, and others. During the two years that they recorded (1945-1947) for National, they were a hotbed of activity. The Savoy discs collate 32 titles, with effective solo passages by Gordon and Navarro (plus Eckstine's own trombone solos, as on "Blues for Sale") but it was his baritone vocal solos that stood out as a mellowing of the then-current jump singers. In some respects, he could be thought of as a precursor of soul. Eckstine himself has stated that this was his most effective singing period (as on "Jelly Jelly," "Tell Me Pretty Baby," or "Time on My Hands"). As a popularizer of bop elements, he was most effective, and the arrangements by Jerry Valentine were first rate. Unfortunately, lack of money forced the band to shut down in 1947 after two years, and Eckstine either led a small group occasionally or went solo from this period onward. The MGM collection comes from 1947, and from 1950 through 1954, when he was at his heights in pursuing a solo career. Recorded in New York and Hollywood, with accompaniment by such various men as Roy Eldridge, Teddy Wilson, Max Roach, and Lester Young, Eckstine presents such classics as "I Apologize," "Love Me or Leave Me," "Tenderly," "How High the Moon," "No One but You," and "As Long As I Live."

P2.36   Entry deleted.

P2.37   Entry deleted.

P2.38   Entry deleted.

P2.39   **Tommy Edwards. Very Best.** MGM S 4141.
    Tommy Edwards had been a singer for a good many years, until he was persuaded to create nostalgic and overly-sweet items that appealed to just about everybody's sentimentality. "It's All in the Game" was originally written by a former U.S. Vice President (!); "The Morning Side of the Mountain" dwelt on age differences, while "I Really Don't Want to Know" is pure selfishness (but nicely). Other selections from the 1958-1960 period include "Love Is All We Need," and "Please Mr. Sun."

P2.40* José Feliciano. Feliciano! RCA LSP 3957.

Feliciano, like so many other pop and reinterpretive stars, continued to produce a stream of records in the 1960s and 1970s, most of which were low-drawer material. His is also a visual presence, with the flash of his strong fingers on his guitar and his constant rocking back and forth as he sings and plays. This present album was his strongest effort, and it was also the one that sold the most and climbed highest on the charts, after which he coasted for about four years. It was laden with Beatles' material ("In My Life," "And I Love Her," "Here, There and Everywhere"); Hebb's "Sunny" (written after JFK's assassination); the Doors' "Light My Fire," the one tune that kicked along the album and eventually would sell more copies than the original; the Mamas and Papas' "California Dreamin' "; folky material from Fred Neil and Tom Paxton; and, just to make it more eclectic (Feliciano can really sing anything), Gerry Marsden's "Don't Let the Sun Catch You Crying" (from the Pacemakers), and Burt Bacharach's "There's Always Something There to Remind Me." This is a good, sensitive, and strong album.

P2.41 **Eddie Fisher. Greatest Hits.** RCA ANL 1-1138

Fisher was one of the very few to break into what has been called the Italian-American "mafia" of singing, yet he is Jewish. In style and presentation, he exhibited the same soloistic qualities as the Italian tenors and baritones. This twofer collation presents his better work through a long association with RCA, beginning in 1950 with "Thinking of You," continuing with 1951's "Anytime" and "Lady of Spain" in 1952, and on to the 1953 big year of "Oh, My Papa" (his best work ever) and "I'm Walking behind You." In addition, the twelve tracks also contain "Dungaree Doll," "On the Street Where You Live," "Ko Ko Mo," and his one attempt at folk music, "Cindy, Oh, Cindy."

P2.42 **George Formby. Souvenir.** London Ace of Clubs ACL 7906.

Formby was an excellent banjo and ukulele player, but his work was often overshadowed by the terrible songs that he sang. His outstanding achievement was the contribution that he made to the British war effort through his tours and films; and many Americans still recall the nonsensical effect that this buck-toothed performer had on their funnybone. Titles on this collection are derived mostly from his film work, such as "When I'm Cleaning Windows," "Fanlight Fanny," "Leaning on a Lamp Post" and "Why Don't Women Like Me?" The trite lyrics are charming in retrospect, but the highlight of each selection is undoubtedly the banjo breaks.

P2.43 **Bobby Goldsboro. Greatest Hits.** United Artists UAS 5502.

Goldsboro was originally involved with Roy Orbison as his guitarist. Possessing a reasonably good voice that could be manipulated by producers, and with sharp material, he began to record as a solo act in 1964. The collation here includes such small gems as "Honey," "Little Things," "Autumn of My Life," and the very important "See the Funny Little Clown."

P2.44 **Robert Goulet. Greatest Hits.** Columbia CS 9815.

Working with the Canadian Broadcasting Corporation in the 1950s in Canada had its rewards for Goulet, especially a tryout for *Camelot*'s Sir Lancelot. He won, and settled down for the supper club crowd in the United States. A deep baritone, his voice came through while many listeners were preoccupied with tenors and rock music. Typical creations that he has made his own by his style include "What Kind of Fool Am I?," "My Love Forgive Me," and "Summer Sounds."

P2.45*   **Dick Haymes. Best.** MCA MCFM 2720 (British issue).
Haymes developed in the big band period, succeeding Frank Sinatra in the bands of both Harry James and Tommy Dorsey. He exhibited good pitch and tone, which perhaps made him a favorite with the jazz crowd. His entire career in the 1940s is spanned here, beginning with some 1943 tracks supported by the Song Spinners' vocal harmonies (the AFM had a recording ban on instrumentalists at the time). "You'll Never Know," his first million seller, comes from this period. In addition to two Gershwin numbers with Judy Garland (from films Haymes starred in with her), there are also his standards, "How Blue the Night" and "It Might As Well Be Spring," and the lovely "Stella by Starlight." Most of the arrangements for the twenty selections have been done by Victor Young or Gordon Jenkins (and both studio bands accompanied Haymes as well). The excellent notes are by Alan Dell.

P2.45a   **Don Ho. Greatest Hits.** Reprise RS 6357.
Apart from host Webley Edwards and diverse instrumental albums, Don Ho is the only performer who is still working the Hawaiian music circuit that was so popular about seventy years ago. But many of his minor successes, such as "Tiny Bubbles," really have little to do with this music from the Islands. The main strength here lies in the accompanying musical background.

P2.46   **Engelbert Humperdinck. His Greatest Hits.** Parrot XPAS 71067.
As the result of a lot of hype to find (or create) a second "Tom Jones," Humperdinck (born Arnold George Dorsey) was groomed in the fashion of the cabaret singer. His voice, bland as it may seem to many people, is carefully contrasted with mechanical, technical expertise in the production and selection of material. Thus, he has truly been shaped by the a and r men for the English Decca company. Nonetheless, his music is certainly enjoyable (whether the source is known or not), and his first major success was the old country music hit "Release Me" in 1967. This was followed by "Les Bicyclettes de Belsize," "Am I That Easy to Forget?," "A Man without Love," and "There Goes My Everything."

P2.47   **Burl Ives. Best, v.2.** two discs. MCA 2-4089.
MCA did a nifty job in separating popular folk material from simply popular material in the preparation of these sets. (For a further note on Ives, see the *Grass Roots* volume in this set.) The enjoyable pop material is found on volume two (folk music on volume 1), a selection of twenty tracks that includes such chart successes as "A Little Bitty Tear," "Call Me Mr. In-Between," "The Long Black Veil," "Green, Green Grass of Home," "Funny Way of Laughin'," and "Mary Ann Regrets." Much of this material is simply watered-down country music, but Ives does have a familiar voice (he sang for many children) with a distinct accent, and the sparse accompaniment is devoid of such over-production techniques as strings.

P2.48*   **Jack Jones. Greatest Hits.** Kapp 3559.

Jack Jones is a truly talented singer who appears to have found more success in England (where they appreciate such things) than in his native United States. His night club work is impeccable; he began in 1962, and his family's musical background helped him immensely. Titles include "Lollipops and Roses" (his first hit), "Wives and Lovers," "Dear Heart," "She Loves Me," and "Our Song."

P2.49*   **Tom Jones. This Is Tom Jones.** Parrot XPAS 71028.

One of the first pop singers to directly emulate Elvis Presley in the 1960s, Tom Jones extended all of the familiar mannerisms. His voice became more blues-inflected (indeed, it is difficult at times to say whether he sings "black" or "white"). His stage presentation became more exhibitionistic, perhaps what the middle-aged ladies demanded: to be reminded of Elvis (Presley never toured Britain; Jones has the entire market). He has sold almost as well in North America, with such typical tracks as "What's New Pussy Cat?," "It's Not Unusual" (his first success), "Green, Green Grass of Home," "Delilah," and "She's a Lady."

P2.50*   **Frankie Laine. Golden Hits.** Mercury 60587.

P2.51   **Frankie Laine. Greatest Hits.** Columbia CS 8036.

Laine was discovered by Hoagy Carmichael; he was one of the few remaining singers who never needed a microphone (except for recording), because his powerful voice could carry to the back of any hall or auditorium. His ten year career of important material in the history of popular music began in 1946, for Mercury, and continued through 1950. He sang a mixture of jazz and country items with strong backing and, of course, his strong strident voice (which many people mistook for "black")—as on "The Cry of the Wild Goose," "That's My Desire" (from 1947), "Shine," "Mule Train," and "That Lucky Old Sun." In 1951, he signed with Columbia and began a second career that embraced "Jezebel," "Jalousie," "High Noon," "Hey Joe," "Someday," the classic "I Believe," "Tell Me a Story" (with Jimmy Boyd), and perhaps his last great success, "Moonlight Gambler," which harkened back to "The Cry of the Wild Goose."

P2.52   **Rod McKuen. Back to Carnegie Hall.** two discs. Warner Brothers 2WS 2731.

McKuen is an author and poet who has turned some of his work into over 1,500 song compositions (appearing on over 100 albums in eight languages). He has written for Eddy Arnold, the Kingston Trio, Limeliters, Jimmy Rogers, and even Jacques Brel. Many, though, are not enamoured of his gravelly voice. On this occasion, he is in Carnegie Hall for his fortieth birthday and promotes himself as a chansonier and communicator. This album comes with textual lyrics, which stand up rather well as poetry on their own. The many songs here include "Jean" (written as the theme for the movie, *The Prime of Miss Jean Brodie*), "The Far Side of the Hill," "The Sky's So Wide" (from *Lee's Song*), "If," "Sunday," "Happy Is a Boy Named Me," "Blessing of the Day," and "To You." These are impressionistic pictures of the romantic life.

P2.53   **Gordon MacRae. New Moon.** Capitol SM 219.
MacRae's pre-eminence came as a result of light, frothy musicals, perhaps culminating with *Carousel*, which fitted him perfectly. On the side, he had been recording for Capitol in the late 1940s and early 1950s, which resulted in his famil-iar stylizations of "Hair of Gold, Eyes of Blue" and "Rambling Rose" (both 1948), "So in Love" (from 1949), plus some materials from his films (*Tea for Two, Moonlight Bay, Sail Along Silvery Moon*).

P2.54*   **Dean Martin. Best.** Capitol DT 2601.

P2.55   **Dean Martin. Greatest Hits, v.1/2.** two discs. Reprise RS6301, 6330.
Martin was never given much of a chance for singing success. He began his career with vocal imitations before moving up to being straight man for Jerry Lewis. But after their split, his career fell under the influence of Frank Sinatra and the Italian-American school of singing, with modifications by way of Perry Como. Martin's first big success was "Memories Are Made of This" from 1955, although "That's Amore" sold more copies (three million). Other selections from his Capitol period (1955-1959) included "Volare," "Angel Baby," and "Return to Me." When Sinatra formed Reprise records, Martin moved along with him, and thereby got his second "number one hit," the engrossing "Everybody Loves Somebody (Some-times)," which was later to be the theme on his television show. Other items, with uptempo beats to stay in tune with the times, included "Houston," "Send Me the Pillow That You Dream On," and "I Will."

P2.56   **Tony Martin.** Decca DL 8366.

P2.57   **Tony Martin.** RCA Camden 412.
Martin's career started as a saxophonist on the Lucky Strike Hour in 1932. By 1936, he had become a matinee idol and a dance band vocalist. He had appeared in such films as *Follow the Fleet, Till the Clouds Roll By, Easy to Love,* and so forth. Thus, throughout a twenty-year recording career, with most items taken from the cinema, Martin laid down his famous baritone renditions of "Begin the Beguine," "September Song," "Day In–Day Out," "The Donkey Serenade," "Tonight We Love," "To Each His Own," "Walk Hand in Hand," and the dramatic "La Vie en Rose."

P2.58*   **Al Martino. Best.** Capitol SKAO 2946.
Al Martino was a discovery of Mario Lanza; indeed, he may just have been the last of the Italian-American school of popular music, for his languid stylings are in the same mood as those of Como, Martin, or Sinatra. In 1952, he had a hit with "Here in My Heart"; but nothing else was successful until he signed his Capitol recording contract in 1961, whereupon he re-recorded "Here in My Heart," and it was a commercial success all over again. Other typical tunes that made people sigh included "I Love You Because," "I Love You More and More Each Day," "Spanish Eyes," and "Living a Lie."

P2.59*   **Vaughan Monroe. Best.** RCA ANL1-1140.
     Monroe started his band in 1940, and it was a pleasant conglomeration; but
the economics of scale wages and war-time conscription depleted his resources,
despite the success of his first 1940 effort, "There I Go." Later, he would perform
as a soloist, beginning with the 1947 "Ballerina" through to the ridiculous "Black
Denim Trousers" from 1955 (no one can figure out if this latter song was recorded
as a joke or whether Monroe was serious in recording it; certainly, it was one of
the very first of the rock 'n' roll songs). His deep, throaty baritone impressed many
people, and of course, he was the subject of many imitations. Other songs include
his most famous, and theme, song, "Racing with the Moon," plus "Cool Water,"
"Ghost Riders in the Sky," the 1949 "Mule Train," and the 1949 "Red Roses
for a Blue Lady." In summation, much of his material involved popular song renditions of country and western materials. The twelve tracks here even include "Let
It Snow! Let It Snow! Let It Snow!"

P2.59a   **Wayne Newton. Best.** Capitol ST 2797.
     Newton got his break on the Jackie Gleason show on television. His prime
years were mainly 1963-1968, and his cherubic appearance meant a large audience
whenever he played Las Vegas. His appeal is slight on records, as he is mainly a
nightclub performer, preferring show material and light entertainment to highlight
his high, pinched, boyish voice. Titles here include his first success "Danke Schoen"
(from 1963), "Red Roses for a Blue Lady," "Remember When," and "Apple
Blossom Time." In style, he lies halfway between Bobby Vinton and Don Cherry.

P2.60   **Gene Pitney. Big 16.** Musicor 3008.
     Pitney grew up through the rock and roll era, with a high voice evocative
of the many stylings around during that time period. He was also a proficient composer (e.g., "Hello Mary Lou," which he fashioned for Rick Nelson). Some of his
singing and writing was for movies, such as the themes for "Town without Pity"
and "The Man Who Shot Liberty Valence." Other selections from this sixteen-track
compilation include "Only Love Can Break a Heart," "Mecca," and "It Hurts to
Be in Love."

P2.61   **Lou Rawls. Best.** Capitol SKAO 2948.
     Rawls straddles, a little unevenly, the worlds of soul and pop music. Audience
appeal is thus very wide, and in retrospect, he can be treated as a popular singer
employing the phrasing of gospel singers and a growl on occasion (he, like so many
other soul singers, came out of the gospel groups of the fifties). He had moderate
successes in the singles market, but his strength lay in the shows he did at posh
supper clubs and his innumerable appearances on television. His is the definitive
version of "Yesterdays." Other material here includes "Love Is a Hurtin' Thing,"
"Your Good Thing (Is about to End)," "Showbusiness," and the important "Dead
End Street."

P2.62   **B. J. Thomas. Greatest Hits, v.1/2.** two discs. Sceptre 578, 597.
     A pop singer of immense vocal range (but merely a recreator, if one is called
upon to characterize his singing), Thomas is known for "Raindrops Keep Falling
on My Head," perhaps the best song to come from a non-musical movie in the

1960s. Other pop items include "I'm So Lonesome I Could Cry" and "Hooked on a Feeling."

P2.63   **Dick Todd. Blue Orchids.** two discs. RCA AXM2-5509.

"I wonder where Dick Todd is tonight?" was one of the more successful gag lines from the days of 1930s radio, for Todd sounded exactly like Bing Crosby through no fault of his own (i.e., he was born that way). The idea was that if Crosby acted up on Tommy Dorsey's radio program, Dorsey would replace him with Todd. To our ears, he certainly could, for the 32 tracks here are all Crosby-type ballad material, from 1938's "Deep Purple" to 1942's "Someday Sweetheart." Todd recorded over 200 titles for RCA, and he was known as the "Canadian Crosby" (because of his having grown up near Calgary and Montreal).

P2.64   **Jerry Vale. Greatest Hits.** Columbia CS 9459.

Incredibly enough, Guy Mitchell discovered Vale and put him in touch with Mitch Miller at Columbia records. Singing in the Italian-American relaxed ballad school, Vale has come through with such older ballads as "You Don't Know Me" and "Have You Looked into Your Heart?" His first big success was in 1956 with "Innamorata."

P2.65*   **Fats Waller. Ain't Misbehavin'.** RCA LPM 1246.

Many of the details on Waller's life and style may be found in the *Jazz* book in this set, but the material on the disc here contains twelve very choice examples of the popular side of Waller's stride piano. Along with lyrics by such composers as Andy Razaf and others, he was able to contribute to the corpus of popular music. Each of the selections here is a gem, with Waller's own vocal on "Ain't Misbehavin'," "Honeysuckle Rose," "I Can't Give You Anything but Love," "Two Sleepy People," "I'm Gonna Sit Right down and Write Myself a Letter," "Tea for Two," and "It's a Sin to Tell a Lie."

P2.66   **Andy Williams. Greatest Hits.** Columbia KCS 9979.

P2.67*   **Andy Williams. Million Seller Songs.** Cadence 3061.

With Archie Bleyer's Cadence label, Andy Williams was a very commercial rock and roll singer of the ballad school. His efforts fashioned such greats as "Canadian Sunset," "Lonely Street," "I Like Your Kind of Love," "Butterfly," "Walk Hand in Hand," "Hawaiian Wedding Song," and "Village of Ste. Bernadette." All were done by double-tracking his voice in harmony, a device borrowed from Les Paul and Patti Page. It was effective for a few years, but in 1961, the big money called from Columbia to turn him into another Tony Bennett in the cabaret style. Thus, Williams's soft relaxed voice (again, in the Italian-American ballad style) in one tracking only, produced such heart-rending ballads as "Dear Heart," "Moon River," "Days of Wine and Roses," "Can't Get Used to Losing You," "A Fool Never Leaves," and "Hopeless." Beginning with a church choir, Williams retained his angelic look and posture throughout three years of singing on the *Tonight Show.*

FEMALE

Innovators

P2.68*   **Ella Fitzgerald. Best.** two discs. Decca MCA2-4047
Her recording career with Decca has spanned the time from the Chick Webb orchestra (1938) into the late fifties—almost twenty years. Her first official recording is here—the perennial "A-Tisket A-Tasket," a fairly good self-penned novelty tune that has been identified with her since 1938. At age eighteen, she was a scat singer with Webb, and she later assumed control of his orchestra (after he died in 1939). Fitzgerald has perhaps been the most influential of all the early jazz singers, although her later career has downplayed the more buoyant aspects of her earlier music. Her ear is exact, her phrasing is perfect, and she has immense clarity of tone. Many female singers have modeled themselves on her. The 23 items here include "Undecided," "Stairway to the Stars," "Into Each Life Some Rain Must Fall" (with the Ink Spots), "Flying Home," and "How High the Moon." In the mid-1950s, she produced a superb series of *Songbooks* celebrating the compositional skills of several writers for the theater (see items P6.111, 114, 119, 126).

P2.68a*   **Connie Boswell. Sand in My Shoes.** MCA MCFM 2739 (British issue).
Later known as Connee, Boswell was hailed by Irving Berlin as the finest ballad singer in the business. Her New Orleans upbringing seems to give her and the Boswell Sisters a jazz feeling, for many of their songs had "hot" choruses, and accompaniment was usually the full Dixieland sound of Bob Crosby or the Dorsey Brothers. Some six of the twenty titles here definitely point out the jazz nature of their modern, close harmony vocals—Berlin's own "Top Hat, White Tie and Tails," "Let Yourself Go," "I'm Putting All My Eggs in One Basket," "Cheek to Cheek," "I'm Gonna Sit Right down and Write Myself a Letter," and "The Music Goes 'Round and Around." These were the last six sides made by the group, over the cusp of 1935-1936. Connie then began a solo career, but already her breath control (learned from Caruso records) and her arranging abilities were an influence on the young Ella Fitzgerald. The fourteen other tracks here cover 1936-1941, with an assortment of studio bands led by John Scott Trotter, Ben Pollack, Bob Crosby, and others. Her warm and melodic phrasing fit perfectly with Bing Crosby's on "Yes Indeed," while her lyric interpretation of Ellington's "I Let a Song Go out of My Heart" provided that correctly intimate but swinging sensuality.

P2.69*   **Judy Garland. At Carnegie Hall.** two discs. Capitol SWBO 1569.

P1.70*   **Judy Garland. Deluxe Set.** three discs. Capitol STCL 2988.
These five discs nicely capture the dynamic style exhibited by latter-day July Garland when her movie successes were over (see also items P6.144-46 in the **Stage and Film** section). The April 23, 1961, set is considered a major record because of audience empathy, good voice, and the general run of electricity. Having risen through the ranks of vaudeville to the MGM studios and Andy Hardy movie fame, Garland went on to *The Wizard of Oz, Meet Me in St. Louis,* and *Till the*

Clouds Roll By, among others. Her stage presence was strong, her voice clear, and her vocals clearly enunciated in a soaring style. Her recreations here include "That's Entertainment," "I Can't Give You Anything but Love," "Come Rain or Come Shine," "Swanee," "The Man That Got Away," and "Chicago."

P2.71*   **Lena Horne. Collection.** two discs. United Artists UAD 60091/2 (British issue).

P2.72*   **Lena Horne. Lovely and Alive.** RCA LSP 2587.
    Horne started her career as a Cotton Club chorus girl, and then progressed through the bands of Noble Sissle and Charlie Barnet. One of her earlier successes was the title "Stormy Weather," with which she has always been identified. A husky voice greatly complemented her physical features as she became a very popular cabaret singer. Although she is associated with very few tunes, she does have much strength in the interpretive fields, such as the careful craftsmanship on "Boy from Ipanema," "Unchained Melody," "Fine Romance," "On Green Dolphin Street," "Willow Weep for Me," "Moon River," and "Somewhere."

P2.73*   **Cleo Laine. I Am a Song.** RCA LPL1-5000 (British issue).

P2.74*   **Cleo Laine. Live!! At Carnegie Hall.** CPL1-5015.
    Cleo Laine has been recording for almost twenty years in her native Britain; *I Am a Song* collates the better themes from the past. Her orchestrations are almost always handled by Johnny Dankworth, a reedman-jazzman who is also her husband. The quality of Laine's singing is about as dramatic as anyone could hope for. Her fans and admirers include millions in England, as well as some of the "select" in the United States. Laine projects class in everything that she does: choice of material (little known but highly melodic compositions); tasteful arrangements (in consultation with Dankworth); a sincerity that gives a fresh interpretation to virtually every overworked, standard ballad; a range of three octaves; and mannered breathiness that immediately converts a popular song into an art song, such as Sondheim's "Send in the Clowns" or Kern's "Bill" (she sang in *Showboat* in the British revival). "Music" by Carole King provides another good occasion for showing off her vocal capabilities. Smart and domineering in her handling of the lyrics, Laine brassily attempts the familiar; "Big Best Shoes" (from an earlier musical by Sandy Wilson, in which she had appeared), and "Stop and Smell the Roses" (with strong arrangements by Dankworth) are but two examples.

P2.75*   **Peggy Lee. Greatest.** three discs. Capitol DKAO 377.
    Lee's most successful recordings have been for the Capitol label, although she has done good work for Columbia, MCA, A & M, Atlantic, and others. She began with Benny Goodman in 1941, but it was not until 1948 that her husky, strident voice finally captured a wide audience with "Mañana," a number one-charted song from that year. Unfortunately (for those of wide popular tastes), Lee never had another hit recording until the 1958 "Fever" (a rhythm 'n' blues hit for Little Willie John), quickly followed by "Is That All There Is?" from 1959. However, it is not a continual string of pop music for the masses that creates a singer; Lee has a very dynamic stage presence, which puts her in the same class

as Cleo Laine and Shirley Bassey. She has complete control over her material, and always emphasizes the necessity of a cabaret rapport with the audience. Thus, she has fans who continually buy her records.

P2.76*   Vera Lynn. When the Lights Go on Again. Stanyan SR 10032.
From the girl next door—the sweetheart of the Armed Forces—comes this lovely collection of EMI recordings that chronicles the songs of the war years in Britain. Lynn, after singing with numerous dance bands, toured widely in the African campaign, where she became wildly accepted by the boys. Shortly afterwards, she recorded "Auf Wiedersehen," which sold a remarkable 2.5 million copies in the U.S. and helped to launch her *Sincerely Yours* radio request show. Here are such sterling, nostalgia-evoking songs as "This Is the Army," "Lili Marlene," "A Nightingale Sang in Berkeley Square," and "Bless Them All." Her superb intonation, with dark coloring on the descending notes, perfect diction and pronunciation, is utterly right on "We'll Meet Again," and it is no wonder that it was used in *Dr. Strangelove*. And, of course, she practically owns "The White Cliffs of Dover." She is not quite as successful on the bouncy, fast tempo numbers such as "Don't Fence Me In," but this is just a minor flaw in an all-around superb album.

P2.77*   Carmen McRae. The Great American Songbook. two discs. Atlantic SD2-904.
Carmen McRae had a good nightclub record (on Mainstream MRL 309) a decade ago, and this present disc is an extension of it, being recorded at Dante's in L.A. with Jimmy Rowles (piano) and Chick Fiores (drums). The relaxed mood and excellent sound lend a beautiful presence; you feel as if you are really where she is. Material includes eighteen selections by Ellington, Porter, Mal Weston, Mancini, Mercer, the Bacharach-David team, and even Leon Russell. "What Are You Doing the Rest of Your Life?" (which is, by now, on everybody's "super-mood" album) features a superb vocal-guitar duet with Joe Pass. McRae has established excellent rapport with the musicians. On the obligatory love medley ("Easy Living/Days of Wine and Roses/It's Impossible"), one notices the slide from one song to another, one chorus to a verse (and vice versa) heralded by the musicians.

P2.78*   Mabel Mercer. A Tribute to Mabel Mercer on the Occasion of Her 75th Birthday. four discs. Atlantic MM4-100.
Mercer is one of the definitive singers in popular music. Her approach to music involves intelligence, imagination, formal phrasing and diction, and personal taste. She can interpret lyrics in every possible way, and for this, she is adulated by other singers and lyricists (she has over 1,000 songs in her repertoire). This Atlantic set brings together four previously issued albums, containing 55 selections: *Mabel Mercer Sings Cole Porter, Midnight at Mabel Mercer's, Merely Marvelous,* and *Once in a Blue Moon.* All of the tunes are sophisticated (and if they were not meant to be, then Mercer invests them with that quality), such as rare Porter ("Experiment," "Looking at You," "I'm Ashamed That Women Are So Simple") or Wilder ("Is It Always Like This?"), Bernstein ("Some Other Time"), Kern ("All in Fun"), Rodgers and Hart ("You're Nearer"), Coward ("Sail Away"), plus Coleman, Cory, Gershwin, etc. Quite often, Mercer is able to make her voice blend in with the instruments so as to seem actually to be one of them.

P2.79*   **Jo Stafford. Greatest Hits.** Columbia CL 1228.

P2.80*   **Jo Stafford. Sweet Singer of Songs.** Vocalion VL 73866.

Jo Stafford is one of the greatest popular singers of all time. Her low, husky voice and perfect phrasing are instantly recognizable. Unfortunately, she is badly represented in the in-print catalog. Arising from a folk music background, she began in 1935 with the Stafford Sisters Trio on radio. She later recorded with Tommy Dorsey and was a member of the important Pied Pipers group. In 1955, she had her own radio show. With Columbia in the 1950s, she had a string of popular successes, such as "Shrimp Boats," "You Belong to Me," "Make Love to Me," "Teach Me Tonight," "Rag Mop," and even some Hank Williams pieces, such as "Jambalaya" and "Hey, Good Lookin'." For Decca (ten tracks on this Vocalion budget reissue), she made "September in the Rain," "I Cover the Waterfront," "Love for Sale," "Night and Day," and "Blues in the Night" (among others).

P2.81   **Maxine Sullivan and Bob Wilber. Close as Pages in a Book.** Monmouth-Evergreen MES 6919.

P2.82*   **Maxine Sullivan and Bob Wilber. The Music of Hoagy Carmichael.** Monmouth-Evergreen MES 6917.

These two records demonstrate the effectiveness of Maxine Sullivan as both a jazz singer and chanteuse. Characterized for many years as the girl who sang "Loch Lomond" with a swing beat from the Onyx Club in New York City (it reappears here on MES 6919), Sullivan had appeared with Claude Thornhill's orchestra and then at many supper clubs and dining lounges. She came out of retirement a few years back and won instant success with this pair of records. She appears on five of the fourteen songs devoted to Carmichael; the others are handled by most of the World's Greatest Jazz Band (for which Wilber is soprano saxophonist and clarinetist). Hoagy's work is wide open to jazz interpretations, and the selections recorded here give it credibility ("Georgia on My Mind," "Skylark," "Stardust," "In the Cool, Cool, Cool of the Evening," "Rockin' Chair," "Lazy River," etc.). Most of the twelve tunes on the *Close* album have been associated in some way with Sullivan, such as her first recorded song, "Gone with the Wind," as well as "Darn That Dream," "Harlem Butterfly," and "Jeepers Creepers." The backing here is with a piano trio. Good songs, good sound, and good settings.

P2.83*   **Sarah Vaughan. Golden Hits.** Mercury 60645.

P2.84*   **Sarah Vaughan. 1955.** Trip TLP 5501.

"The Divine Sarah" has been characterized as being a musician's singer. From singing in church choir, she won a talent show at the Apollo Theater, where first prize was a singing date with Earl Hines. Along with Billy Eckstine, she was hired as one of the band's vocalists. When Eckstine left, so did she—to pursue a solo nightclub career. Over the years, her material has been diversified— some might say "commercialized"—and the Mercury disc collates some of her popular chart successes, with a largely indifferent series of backings. Here are

"Broken Hearted Melody" (her biggest hit), "Smooth Operator," "Whatever Lola Wants," "Fabulous Character," "Mr. Wonderful," and "C'est La Vie." More interesting, in a jazz context, are the classic performances reissued from the Emarcy catalog on Trip; actually, the date here should be 1954. She has good material for her voice, and superb and sympathetic accompaniment from Clifford Brown (trumpet) and Paul Quinchette (tenor sax). Of note is the muted chorus taken by Brown with Vaughan on "April in Paris." Other songs: "Lullaby of Birdland" (a good swinging number), "He's My Guy," and "You're Not the Kind." Nothing she has done since these nine selections surpasses this classic set.

P2.85*   **Ethel Waters. 1938/1939.** RCA Black and White 741.007 (French issue).

P2.86*   **Ethel Waters. Greatest Years.** two discs. Columbia KG31571.
   Ethel Waters has had three distinct recording modes: blues singer, stage and screen singer, and jazz singer. (See item P6.170 and her annotations in the *Jazz* volume in this set.) Her light, lilting voice ably contrasted with those of many other blues singers, and she was able to cash in on the fringe market of white buyers who liked their blues delivered in a sophisticated, or urbane, manner. The first disc of the Columbia set, from 1925 to 1928, documents this period. When Columbia realized that they had a star on their hands, they quickly shifted Waters to popular material, as on the second disc of the Columbia set. With session musicians such as the Dorsey Brothers, Benny Goodman, Mannie Klein, Joe Venuti, Eddie Lang, and Adrian Rollini, she recorded "When Your Lover Has Gone," "Please Don't Talk about Me When I'm Gone," "Love Is the Thing," "Don't Blame Me," and "Come up and See Me Sometime." Much of the material here is by Dorothy Fields and Jimmy McHugh. Waters had a brief reprise for sixteen recordings with RCA a few years later and was accompanied by Eddie Mallory in renditions of "Frankie and Johnnie," "They Say," "If You Ever Change Your Mind," and "Georgia on My Mind," with such superb performers as Tyree Glenn, Benny Carter, Shirley Clay, and Milt Hinton.

Standards

P2.87*   **Mildred Bailey. Her Greatest Performances, 1929-1946.** three discs. Columbia C3L 22.
   Mildred Bailey was originally a song plugger who sang songs being considered for publication by Tin Pan Alley. She signed on with Paul Whiteman for 1931-1933, and her success came easy. After this period, she sang with Red Norvo (from 1936 to 1939) and was married to him. Between 1933 and 1942, she sang many times with Dorsey, Goodman, Wilson, and others. She became known as a jazzman's singer, and in fact, she was more popular with jazz performers than she was with the public. Her bouncy, cheery personality easily shone through a very pudgy body, and although she was troubled most of her life, her songs were gay and fresh. She was influential in getting jobs for many people, including the early Bing Crosby (who was a friend of her brother, Al Rinker). Her sweet lilting voice wafted over many a hot jazz accompaniment, and undeniably, she was the best of the white jazz singers (followed closely by Lee Wiley).

The 48 recordings here attest to that. Unfortunately, this set is not in strict chronological order, but her development can easily be heard through distinct time periods. Items include "When Day Is Done," "Give Me Liberty or Give Me Love," "Someday Sweetheart," "Honeysuckle Rose," her theme "Rockin' Chair," "Thanks for the Memory," "Don't Be That Way," "Prisoner of Love," "There'll Be Some Changes Made," and "Lover Come Back to Me." There are also a number of novelty items here. Personnel varied from time to time among the accompanists, but included members from the Basie band, Roy Eldridge, John Kirby's orchestra, and Mary Lou Williams.

P2.88   **Pearl Bailey. Echoes of an Era.** two discs. Roulette RE-101.
     Pearl Bailey is a true entertainer and showperson. She has recorded for diverse companies over the years, and some of her best work was done for Roulette, as the twenty selections here testify (from 1957 to 1963). Along with her are husband (and drummer) Louis Bellson and arranger-conductor Don Redman, who was so influential with McKinney's Cotton Pickers. "Pearlie Mae" (as she was affectionately known) climbed up the hard way through the latter days of vaude-ville and the black bands of Noble Sissle, Cab Calloway, and Cootie Williams as their girl vocalist. Many of the items here are show or Broadway tunes, such as "Two Ladies in the Shade of de Banana Tree" (from *House of Flowers*), "Let's Do It," "I Want a Man," "Legalize My Name," and "Summertime."

P2.89   **Shirley Bassey. Live at Carnegie Hall.** two discs. United Artists LA 111-H.

P2.90*   **Shirley Bassey. Very Best.** Columbia SCX 6529 (British issue).
     Like Cleo Laine, Shirley Bassey was very popular in England for years before crossing the Atlantic to the United States market. The Columbia discs collate some of her bigger successes there, from 1959 through 1968, including her first American hit, "Goldfinger," the emotional "The Party's Over," the dramatic "I (Who Have Nothing)," and "If You Love Me." The intensity and diversity of Bassey's vocal-izings fit in nicely with Cole Porter material (as on both discs above), and she handles quite well "I've Got You under My Skin," "Just One of Those Things," "Easy to Love," and her best effort, "I Get a Kick out of You." The Columbia disc has twenty tracks. The United Artists twofer comes from her most resound-ingly successful concert in the United States, and it features reinterpretations of her older works (e.g., "Big Spender") and, of course, her marvelous rapport with an audience.

P2.91   **Teresa Brewer. Music, Music, Music.** Coral 57027.
     A short girl with a big voice that ultimately grates on the ears, particularly in her enunciation, Teresa Brewer was still the largest selling female singer of the early 1950s. She began recording in 1949, churning out cover hit after cover hit, making them more palatable to the masses (who were ignoring the r 'n' b music of the time). Thus, she made million sellers out of such country items as "Richochet" (1953), "Empty Arms" (1957) and "Let Me Go Lover" (1954); or such r 'n' b tunes as "Pledging My Love" (1955) or "Boll Weevil." The height of novelty was reached with "Rickey Tick Song," and maudlin inspiration and sentimentality

came from "A Tear Fell" and "A Sweet Old Fashioned Girl." Without Brewer and similar cover singers, though, there would be no popular music history.

P2.92   Anita Bryant. Carlton 1172.
A former beauty queen, Anita Bryant assumed the vacant mantle of Teresa Brewer in 1959. She continued the fashion of covering songs in a "Sweetheart" way, and was one of the first to employ the sweetening production techniques of excessive instrumentation (mainly strings). This disc nicely cumulates such hits as "Do-Re-Me," "Paper Roses," "In My Little Corner of the World," and "Till There Was You."

P2.93*   Vicki Carr. The Golden Songbook. two discs. United Artists UA LA 089-F2.

P2.94   Vicki Carr. Live at the Greek Theatre. two discs. Columbia KG 32656.
As a song stylist, the multi-lingual Carr has her devoted cult following. The United Artist set collates twenty tracks for which she often gets requests, such as easy listening renditions of "By the Time I Get to Phoenix," "It's Not Unusual," "Nowhere Man," "Them There Eyes." Other materials draw from the mainstream of popular music ("Bye Bye Blackbird," "My Melancholy Baby," "Baby Face," and "Time after Time") or from the stage ("I've Grown Accustomed to His Face" and "The Surrey with the Fringe on Top"). The live twofer album concentrates on foreign material and shows her great rapport with the audience.

P2.95*   Petula Clark. Greatest Hits. Warner Brothers WS 1765.
Immensely popular and successful in Britain and France (where she had sung in both French and English since 1949), Clark at last burst upon the American scene in 1964 with the dynamic "Downtown," which became an anthem for the decaying city core; it was covered by a number of country and western singers as "Uptown." In the role of chanteuse (reflecting the French background), Clark did provide certain good examples of popular theater songs (before virtually disappearing in 1967), such as "This Is My Song" and "Don't Sleep in the Subway." Other notable efforts included "I Know a Place" (in a debt of gratitude to the Beatles), "My Love," and "I Couldn't Live without Your Love."

P2.96*   Rosemary Clooney. Rosie's Greatest Hits. Columbia CL 1230.
Beginning as part of the Clooney Sisters with the Tony Pastor orchestra in the 1940s, Rosemary Clooney went on to establish herself as a solo artist after 1949. At first, she concentrated on acceptable standard songs, such as the 1952 "Tenderly" or "Memories of You," but her natural inclinations were towards semi-novelties, sung sometimes with a dialect accent reminiscent of Italy ("Mambo Italiano" from 1954, or even William Sarayon's "Commona My House" from 1951—written when he was a mere lad of fifteen—and 1952's "Botch-a-Me"). She was also covering country music, such as "This Ole House" (from 1954) or the earlier Hank Williams item, "Half as Much." She was close to stage songs as well, scoring her biggest success with "Hey There" (1954) and "I've Grown Accustomed to Your Face" (1956). All in all, Rosie was very personable and well-liked, a perfect foil to Bing Crosby on his radio program.

P2.97   **Doris Day. Greatest Hits.** Columbia CS 8635.

P2.98   **Doris Day. With the Les Brown Band, 1940-1945.** Joyce 1020.

Although Doris Day might be remembered best as the feckless consort of
a host of bumbling husbands and suitors in 1960s movies, her career did begin as
a singer with Les Brown's band. For five years, she was the band's female vocalist,
and participated in "Sentimental Journey" (as found on Joyce). However, with
the hit song "Love Somebody" (1948) and a beginning movie career that featured
her singing, her primary work began to be in movie musicals, such as *Moonlight
Bay* (with Gordon MacCrae) and *Calamity Jane* (with Howard Keel). She was able
to combine a girl-next-door look with cloying, teasing vocals to produce such numbers as "Que Sera, Sera," "Secret Love," "Teacher's Pet," "Everybody Loves a
Lover," "Tunnel of Love," and "Anyway the Wind Blows." The Joyce reissue
also presents "There I Go," "Saturday Night," "Dream," and "Don't You Know
I Care?"

P2.99   **Ruth Etting.** Biograph BLP C3.

A popular singer from 1926 through 1932 (represented here on this disc),
Ruth Etting was renowned for the politeness in her voice. She was associated with
the Ziegfeld *Follies* and *Whoopee*, and her musical arrangements were tasteful,
with emphasis on the better-known ballads being given their definitive readings.
Selections here include "Deed I Do" and "Body and Soul"; in fact, this is a better
selection than the long-deleted Columbia ML 5050 disc.

P2.100   **Georgia Gibbs. Song Favorites.** Mercury 20114.

Her Nibs, Miss Gibbs will long be remembered as the number one song stylist
covering other people's recordings, mostly from the r 'n' b field. She usually did
a fair job, and can be classed as a singer in her own right. Surely, she did draw
attention to some of these original songs, even if they had to be cleaned up. For
instance, Hank Ballard's great sexual r 'n' b classic, "Work with Me, Annie" became
"Dance with Me, Henry" in its transformation under Mercury's a and r men. Her
first hit was in 1952, "Kiss of Fire." Then came "Dance with Me, Henry," "I Want
You to Be My Baby," "Goodby to Rome," and a cleaned-up "Tweedle Dee"
borrowed from the great LaVern Baker.

P2.101   **Eydie Gormé. Greatest Hits.** Columbia CS 9564.

Gormé sang with the Tex Beneke orchestra before landing a job on the early
version of the *Tonight* show. While with Columbia records, she set impeccable
styles and, later, married Steve Lawrence. Some of her efforts are really quite good,
such as the semi-novelty "Blame It on the Bossa Nova," or "Don't Try to Fight
It, Baby." Other material is acceptable as well, such as "I Want You to Meet My
Baby."

P2.102   **Juanita Hall.** Monmouth-Evergreen MES 7020.

It is almost inconceivable to picture anyone else but Juanita Hall as the
brassy Bloody Mary in *South Pacific*, as she brought to life one of Broadway's
most memorable characters. This record gives us her two songs from that show:
the simple folk wisdom of "Happy Talk" and the alluring "Bali Ha'i." But she

also liked to sing blues and pops, and it is a joy to hear some never-before-released examples of her enthusiastic and energetic style. Among the ten selections, all with big band backing, are "Way Down Yonder in New Orleans," "Basin Street Blues," "Solitude," "More Than You Know," and "After You've Gone."

P2.103   **Annette Hanshaw, v.1.** Fountain FV 201 (British issue).

P2.104*   **Annette Hanshaw. Sweetheart of the Thirties.** Halcyon HAL 5 (British
            issue).
    Annette Hanshaw was dubbed the "Personality Girl," but she so disliked show business that she retired in 1934. The Fountain disc is the first of a series documenting her complete output, beginning with the Pathé recordings of 1926. Throughout the 1920s and early 1930s, Hanshaw certainly was a prolific recording artist, well known for such early works as "Black Bottom," "Six Feet of Papa," "If You See Sally," "Song of the Wanderer," and the ever-lovely "It Was Only a Sunshower."

P2.105*   **Helen Humes.** RCA FPM1-7018 (French issue).
    Humes was a light singer with the Basie organization (see full Basie annotations in the *Jazz* volume). She originally recorded eight blues titles in 1927, at a young age, with James P. Johnson. By 1937, she appeared with Al Sears before replacing Billie Holiday with Basie. Her style is both limpid and fresh, with some evidence of presence, and as these same characteristics are noticeable in Holiday's work, then it is easy to see why Basie picked her as a replacement. With the band, Humes did the pop and ballad material while Jimmy Rushing did mostly blues. The ten tracks here come from a 1958 Los Angeles session with sympathetic musicians led by Red Norvo—Willie Smith, Jimmy Rowles, Mel Lewis, Bud Shank, and Eddie Miller. The sterling arrangements were crafted by Shorty Rogers. Two of the selections were by Humes/Norvo ("I Sing the Blues" and "Shed No Tears"), while all of the others were standards (e.g., "They Can't Take That Away from Me").

P2.106   **Joni James. Award Winning Album.** MGM 3346.
    James began her recording career in 1952, and her distinctive nasal sound soon caught on in middle America, as it was a sort of compromise between the then-current country music and the dictates of the pop market. Thus, there are such items as "Your Cheatin' Heart" (from Hank Williams), the sacred "Give Us This Day," "Little Things Mean a Lot," plus "Why Don't You Believe Me?," and "You Are My Love." In 1954, she became the first pop singer ever to appear with the Cleveland Symphony Orchestra.

P2.107   **Greta Keller. Great Songs of the Thirties.** Stanyan SR 10042.
    Keller was a marvelous Viennese singer and dancer who once wanted to perform in opera. She had a superb microphone voice and knew how to handle one (this was in the same era as Bing Crosby, who simultaneously developed his microphone voice as well). Later, she was featured on radio and became known for her good war work. Typical successes included "What a Life!," "Auf Wiedersehen,

My Dear," "With All My Love and Kisses," "Dis-Moi 'Je t'aime'," "Don't Let It Happen Again," and "Trust in Me Once in a While."

P2.108   **Eartha Kitt. Revisited.** Coral CP 102 (British issue).

P2.109*   **Eartha Kitt. That Bad Eartha.** RCA LPM 1183.
        Kitt, a dancer-turned-singer, was one of the stars who developed from the New Faces series on Broadway (where she introduced "Santa Baby" in 1953). Many of her songs were performed in a purring, naughty style that had much humor in its day; but they also have stood the passage of time quite nicely, as a listen to these two records will attest. Her most seductive song was undoubtedly "C'Est Si Bon," but others included "Somebody Stole de Wedding Bell," the long "If I Love Ya Then I Need Ya, If I Need Ya I Wantcha Around," "Let's Do It," "Après Moi," "Angelitos Negros," and "Uska Dara."

P2.110   **Jane Morgan. Greatest Hits.** Kapp 3329.
        Morgan was a popular artist from the 1940s, but she reached acclaim in the late 1950s at a period too late for anything but torch songs, such as "Two Different Worlds" and "Fascination." Roger Williams produced her work, which included "With Open Arms," "Happy Anniversary," and the very startling "The Day That the Rains Came."

P2.111   **Patti Page. Golden Hits, v.1/2.** two discs. Mercury 60495, 60794.
        Page developed as a band singer, with the then-current sounds of country and western music strongly influencing her sweet delivery. The most active time in her career was from 1948-1962, beginning with her first record "Confess" (in 1948), where she began the innovative technique of singing harmony with herself by means of overdubbing with the then-new device of taping. Her first real big hit was "Tennessee Waltz," and over three million copies were sold. Other tunes that have stood well the passage of time include "Allegheny Moon," "Mockingbird Hill," "Changing Partners," "Left Right out of Your Heart," and "Cross over the Bridge"—all with that same country flavor. If anyone promoted the cross-over of musical styles in the 1950s, then it was surely Patti Page, who assisted in the transition from country to popular music. Other tunes here include "Old Cape Cod," the ungrammatical (and hence funny) "(Throw) Mama from the Train," and the worst song ever recorded—at least according to every single critic of note—in terms of its effect, circumstances, taste, and changing markets: "(How Much Is That) Doggie in the Window?"

P2.112*   **Les Paul and Mary Ford. The World Is Still Waiting for the Sunrise.**
        Capitol ST 11308.
        Les Paul mastered the art of overdubbing with tapes plus other special recorded effects that highlighted guitar playing. In fact, he now has a guitar model named after him, and many rock guitarists today acknowledge his influence. With multiple tracks available on tape, he played all the guitars and re-recorded his wife's voice so that she could harmonize with herself. The airy lightness of the music (and what then seemed to be pyrotechnics of a high level with both voice and guitar) succeeded in selling well and in having a goodly influence on other performers and

imitators. As with any innovative technique, many others began experimenting with tape; Sam Phillips (of Sun records) developed the tape delay that was to create his "Sun sound" or rockabilly music. In 1951, "How High the Moon" became the number one song in America. This was followed by "I'm Sittin' on Top of the World" in 1953. Other big numbers here include "Vaya Con Dios," "The World Is Waiting for the Sunrise," their first recording of "Lover," and the novelty "The Carioca."

P2.113*   **Edith Piaf. Deluxe Set.** three discs. DTCL 2953.

P2.114   **Edith Piaf. Pleins Feux Sur Edith Piaf.** two discs. Philips 6641.134 (French issue).

P2.115*   **Edith Piaf. Recital, 1962.** Pathe SPAM 67.092 (French issue).
Edith Piaf had seen much tragedy throughout her life; consequently, all her music was extremely personal, and her unhappiness was clearly reflected in her singing. She began as a waif who sang for her supper in Paris music halls and on the streets of Montmartre. Later she became a star in French movies, and although she seemed to have financial security, her emotional needs were not being satisfied, except through song. She believed that she belonged to the French people, and her poignant voice with its penetrating, dark quality was always directed to the audience. The 66 songs on the three sets listed present most of her greatest numbers, which include "Vallee," "La Vie En Rose," "La Foule," "L'Accordeoniste," "T'Es Beau, Tu Sais," "Je Ne Regrette Rien," and the song that later became associated with her the most in North America: "Milord." Her phenomenal stage performances are revealed on the 1962 concert disc; her empathy with audiences has never been surpassed by anyone.

P2.116   **Helen Reddy. Greatest Hits.** Capitol ST 11467.
Australian-born Reddy has been the source of much independence for women in the music business, most likely through "I Am Woman." This is remarkable in itself, since, if singers are supposed to lead the life that they sing about (many do), she obviously did a complete reversal away from her first hit song, "I Don't Know How to Love Him" (from *Jesus Christ Superstar*). In many songs, her accent comes through, such as in "Ain't No Way to Treat a Lady." Other treats here are "Angie Baby," "Emotion," and "Delta Dawn."

P2.117   **Della Reese. Classic Della.** RCA LSP 2419.
Reese was a gospel singer who once was associated with Mahalia Jackson, the Clara Ward Singers, and the Erskine Hawkins orchestra. Branching out on her own, she took the gospel style with her, fashioning such early successes on the Jubilee label as "In the Still of the Night" and "Time after Time." Later, with RCA, she did "Don't You Know," "Not One Minute More," "Someday," and "Bill Bailey." At the time of 1959-1963, it was fashionable and better (in a commercial sense) to stay in the pop world, rather than to work with the then-emerging soul music (Nancy Wilson and Dionne Warwicke were in this position as well).

P2.118   **Dinah Shore. Best.** RCA ANL 1-1159.

P2.119   **Dinah Shore. Lavendar Blue.** Harmony 7239.

P2.120   **Dinah Shore. With Xavier Cugat, 1933-1940.** Sunbeam SB 305.
          Dinah Shore has had a remarkable career. Her velvet tones have been captured
with Xavier Cugat and Eddie Cantor, and her own radio and television shows.
Her durability is astonishing, considering that she began to record with Cugat in
a Spanish or Latin framework as early as 1937. The Sunbeam disc includes sixteen
tracks, not all with Shore, but featuring "My Shawl," "Isle of Capri," "La Paloma,"
"Jalousy," and the "Breeze and I." Sterling hits from the RCA 1940-1945 period
included "Yes, My Darling Daughter," "I Hear a Rhapsody," "One Dozen Roses,"
and the charming "I'll Walk Alone." The Columbia Harmony set comes from
1946-1949, with "Doin' What Comes Naturally," "I Love You for Sentimental
Reasons," "Bibbidi-Bobbidi-Boo," "Lavender Blue," "Buttons and Bows," and
"Baby, It's Cold Outside."

P2.121   **Kate Smith. Best.** RCA LSP 3970.

P2.122   **Kate Smith. Miss Kate Smith, 1926-1931.** Music for Collectors MFC
          107.
          Kate Smith is probably best known for at least two songs: "God Bless Amer-
ica" and "When the Moon Comes over the Mountain." The RCA disc is a series
of recreations of her earlier successes. The reissued MFC disc collates interesting
material from a five year period when she began singing with the Charleston Chasers
("One Sweet Letter from You" and "I'm Gonna Meet My Sweetie Now"). Indeed,
she was one of the red hot mamas in the Sophie Tucker mold. In addition to the
"Moon" song, she also recorded "Sharing," "Grievin'," "Wabash Moon," "Good
Night Sweetheart," "I Got Rhythm," and "Shine on, Harvest Moon"—and these
are among the sixteen tracks.

P2.123   **Dusty Springfield.** Philips 600.220.
          Dusty Springfield has been more of a British success than a North American
one. She broke into music through the folk revival, and in 1964, recorded such
material as "Silver Threads and Gold Needles" and other country-folk items.
Over the years, though, she has found a growing audience in America that has
been taken by her vocal stylings on such items as "I Only Want to Be with You,"
"Wishin' and Hopin'," "You Don't Have to Say You Love Me," "All I See Is You,"
and "Son of a Preacher Man."

P2.124   **Kay Starr. All Starr Hits.** Capitol SM 11323.
          Kay Starr has gone full circle. She began her career in 1940 as a country
singer of hillbilly tunes, switching later to the jazz mode as a vocalist with Charlie
Barnet (1943-1945), after stints with Joe Venuti, Bob Crosby, and Glenn Miller.
A throat infection made her voice lower and huskier—so much so that she had to
stop "trilling" (which she could no longer do anyway) with the band and begin as
a solo act. In 1946, she achieved this and began a string of successes that emphasized her unique vocal skills (which were coupled with a hard edge, as if she really

meant what she said in a bitchy sense): "I'm the Lonesomest Girl in Town," "Wheel of Fortune," "Changing Partners," "Angry," and, of course, "Bonaparte's Retreat." In the 1970s, still singing, Starr went back to her country roots to take advantage of the upsurge in interest in country music throughout the United States.

P2.125   Gale Storm. Hits. Dot 15070.

For a two year period (1955-1957) Gale Storm had a remarkable stroke of luck with her covers of important rhythm 'n' blues songs. Not especially good as a singer (she was better known as an actress and television personality, as on *My Little Margie*), through over-production, echoes, and tape dubbing, she achieved great success for the Little Richard song, "I Hear You Knocking," the ubiquitous "Memories Are Made of This," the insincere "Teen Age Prayer," plus the fashionable symbolism of "Ivory Tower" and "Dark Moon." The techniques used to enhance her voice soon spread to other studios and other singers.

P2.126*   Barbra Streisand. The Barbra Streisand Album. Columbia CS 8807.

P2.127   Barbra Streisand. Greatest Hits. Columbia KCS 9968.

Streisand's high, nasal voice plus the impeccable production stylings behind her won immense popularity within a matter of weeks of release. Her first album is her brightest, a solo album that contained blues, rhythm 'n' blues, and ballads—including "People" from her 1964 *Funny Girl* success. This was quickly followed by two others in the same vein; later, a "greatest hits" compilation was issued to take care of the oft-requested items. Unfortunately, during the past ten years, in combination with her acting and musical roles on television, stage, and films, Streisand appears at times to have turned to self-parody.

P2.128   Sophie Tucker. The Great. Coral CP 100 (British issue).

P2.129   Sophie Tucker. Greatest Hits. Decca DL 74942.

P2.130*   Sophie Tucker. Last of the Red Hot Mamas. Columbia CL 2604.

Coming up through vaudeville, cabarets, and black-face minstrel acts, Sophie Tucker had a long and rewarding career. Her first records were actually cylinders (1910 through 1912). The original and biggest hits, actually being white covers of black music (thirty years before the practice became widespread in the fifties), began in 1923 with "Aggravatin' Papa"; then came "Come on Home," "Red Hot Mama" (1924), "After You've Gone" (with Miff Mole in 1927), plus "There'll Be Some Changes Made" and "One Sweet Letter from You." The Coral album continues the progression from 1928, when Sophie's best days were over, but there is a certain loveliness from such minor gems as "Some of These Days," "Who Wants Them Tall, Dark, and Handsome?," "You Can't Sew a Button on a Heart," and, of course, the endearing "My Yiddishe Momme."

P2.131   **Caterina Valente. Golden Favorites.** Decca DL 74504.

P2.132   **Caterina Valente. Greatest Hits.** London PS 441.
     This French-born singer, largely European-based and singing in many lan-
guages (as Nana Mouskouri would), has fashioned many elpees for her many fans.
These two compilations—from different record companies—will give as good an
overview as any others, particularly since one of them (the Decca) contains her
greatest, and most requested song, "Malagueña," originally recorded in 1955
(a Cuban song, but with a German vocal!).

P2.133   **Dionne Warwicke. Golden Hits, v.1/2.** two discs. Sceptre 565, 577.
     Warwicke (the "e" was added later) comes from a solid church background.
She was discovered by Burt Bacharach while she was singing demonstration records,
and, beginning in 1962, he used her as a sort of funnel for the recording of his
and Hal David's songs. She was immensely successful, mainly because she had
virtually exclusive rights for a time to many of Bacharach's tunes (and both he and
David were surely the best popular songwriting team since 1950). Thus, this set
is almost all Bacharach (he did some of the arranging and production work as
well): "This Girl's in Love with You," "Walk on By," "Anyone Who Had a Heart,"
"Reach out for Me," "Message to Michael," "Alfie," "I Say a Little Prayer,"
"I'll Never Fall in Love Again," "Valley of the Dolls," her first hit "Don't Make
Me Over," and "Do You Know the Way to San Jose?" This same package was also
put out as *Decade of Gold* (two discs, Sceptre S 596).

P2.134   **Nancy Wilson. Best.** Capitol SKAO 2947.
     Discovered by Cannonball Adderley, Wilson set the standards for an entire
school of imitators. Her forte was sophisticated love songs, such as "Face It Girl,
It's Over" and "The Right to Love." With George Shearing and Cannonball, she
recorded many Broadway and Hollywood-type albums. But her pure voice for pop
soul was ideal for the supper club circuit, not for musicals (nor as an interpreter
of musical ideas). Her sweet and mellow voice comes through on "Uptight,"
"(You Don't Know) How Glad I Am," and "Peace of Mind."

GROUPS

Innovators

P2.135*   **Boswell Sisters. 1932-1934.** Biograph BLP C-3.

P2.136*   **Boswell Sisters.** five discs. Jazum 21, 30, 31, 43, and 44.
     The Boswell Sisters have been ill-served by reissues, as they have appeared
on a mere half-dozen tracks for various anthologies. Considering their type of
singing and influence, much more of their material should have appeared by now.
Produced under license with Columbia, the Biograph set embraces their more
jazz-y work with such performers as Bunny Berigan, Mannie Klein, Tommy and
Jimmy Dorsey, Joe Venuti, and Eddie Lang. The singing trio from New Orleans
also played diverse instruments (such as the piano, cello, saxophone, and violin)

and often accompanied themselves. They recorded a few average sides in 1925, disappeared from the studios until 1930, and then made solid contributions until disbanding in 1936, when Connee Boswell continued as a solo act.

The trio revolutionized close-harmony singing, borrowing aspects from barbershop groups and old time music. For the first time, they employed the human voice as a section of the orchestra. Every song they recorded was changed in some way from the original writing (key changes, slowing down, speeding up, etc.). With the great Berigan punching out what could be called "trumpet obbligatos," the Boswells created minor classics in "There'll Be Some Changes Made," "Hand Me down My Walkin' Cane," "Mood Indigo," and "Sophisticated Lady." The Jazum set features more of Connee's solo outings, away from the trio; some items of note include "I Found a Million Dollar Baby," "Time on My Hands," "Down on the Delta," "Stardust," and "It's the Talk of the Town."

P2.137*   **The Fifth Dimension. Greatest Hits on Earth.** Bell 1106.
This quintet of three guys and two girls stormed the pop market with their versions of Jimmy Webb's "Up, Up and Away" and Galt MacDermot's "Aquarius/ Let the Sunshine In." Because of their style and instrumentation, they became identified with the softer elements of r 'n' b. There is no funk here, just extremely satisfying vocals. But as with most groups of the soul type, their act was a visual one, which succeeded in compounding their effect on the musical tastes of America. Through numerous appearances in clubs, shows, and on television, the Fifth Dimension carved out a respectable market for their styles.

P2.138*   **Mitch Miller. Mitch's Greatest Hits.** Columbia CS 8638.

P2.139*   **Mitch Miller. Sing along with Mitch.** Columbia CS 8004.
Originally a classically-trained oboist (and performer with the CBS Symphony), Miller rose to prominence at Columbia as an artist and repertoire man; he was directly responsible for covering many of Hank Williams's hits (and other titles from the area of country music) for the Columbia stable. His other accomplishments include turning down an offer to buy the contract of Elvis Presley from Sun Records, and a general distrust of rock and roll. Columbia was firmly in the pop and country bag, which is why for many years they had no real rock and roll (and later, rock) music, except where it crossed with country, as in rockabilly (e.g., Marty Robbins, Johnny Cash). Miller arranged for Guy Mitchell ("My Heart Cries for You"), Doris Day ("Que Sera, Sera") and Johnny Mathis ("Chances Are"), but of course, he also led his own house group on television from 1958 through 1960, thus being in part responsible for the folk revival. His method was simply to form a "singalong" with words that could be read on the TV screen at home. To that end, he resurrected "Yellow Rose of Texas" and "March from the River Kwai (Colonel Bogey)" for his biggest successes, as well as "Autumn Leaves," "Lisbon Antigua," "Children's Marching Song," "Do-Re-Mi," and "Song for a Summer Night."

P2.140*   **The Mills Brothers. Best.** two discs. MCA2-4039.
From their earliest start in radio, the Mills Brothers developed a unique imitation of a whole range of instruments, doing this through vocalizing

self-provided musical backgrounds with but a simple rhythm guitar added. They began recording in 1934 for Decca (when it was founded) with such as "My Gal Sal," "Sweet Georgia Brown," and "Miss Otis Regrets." Their biggest outright success was probably "Paper Doll," from 1942. Others of their hits from the forties on this twofer include "Till Then" and "You Always Hurt the One You Love" (from 1944), "Someday (You'll Want Me to Want You)" (1949), "Glow Worm" (1952), "Suddenly There's a Valley" (1955), and "Yellow Bird" (1959). Other successes have included "Lulu's Back in Town," "Rocking Chair Swing," "Naughty Lady of Shady Lane," and "You Tell Me Your Dream, I'll Tell You Mine."

P2.141*   **Fred Waring. Best.** two discs. MCA2-4008.

P2.142   **Fred Waring. Broadway Cavalcade.** two discs. Capitol ST 1389/90.

P2.143*   **Fred Waring. Waring's Pennsylvanians.** RCA LPV 554.

The oft-recorded Waring has been active for about fifty years in organizing singing and performing groups. He was once a choral singing master, having founded the Fred Waring Glee Club; subsequently, he became a radio favorite. Perhaps his most outstanding alumnus was Robert Shaw. One device that Waring used was to mix up the vocal ranges within his group, so that all the contraltos, tenors, etc., would be separated and people would not know where the music levels were coming from. In the RCA set, which contains some of his earliest recordings, he is concerned with low-keyed voices, hot trumpet solos, and banjos in the background. The other four discs are from a wider-ranging period of time, and while none were ever commercially successful, the singing was first rate, and they will always remain a source of inspiration to choirmasters everywhere (such as the early Ray Conniff). The material includes Broadway, show tunes, popular standards, and ballads of the day.

Standards

P2.144   **Ames Brothers. Concert.** Coral 57031.

P2.144a   **Ames Brothers. Best.** RCA ANL 1-1095.

One of the best of the innumerable quartets that lured enchanting melodies into four part harmonies, the Ames's early career is covered for Decca (1949 through 1952) with "Wang Wang Blues," "Music! Music! Music!," "Rag Mop," and "Sentimental Me." Moving over to RCA, they had better success in the 1953-1957 period (before rock and roll eliminated them) with "My Bonnie Lassie," "It Only Hurts for a Little While," "If You Want to See Mamie Tonight" (from *The Revolt of Mamie Stover*), "Melodie D'Amour," "You, You, You," "Tammy," and "The Naughty Lady of Shady Lane." In fact, they were all over the charts. The tradition is now carried on by Ed Ames, the lead singer who sent solo, thereby breaking the act.

P2.145*   **Andrews Sisters.** Ace of Hearts AH 21 (British issue).

The Andrews Sisters borrowed many pages from the Boswell Sisters' book, and they went on to even greater fame. They were at their peak during World War II, having grown up during the vaudeville period and through radio shows. Between 1937 and 1957, they claim to have sold over fifty million records. Their first big success was "Bei Mir Bist Du Schon," in 1937, followed by such efforts as the 1938 "Hold Tight, Hold Tight," the 1939 "Beer Barrel Polka," "Oh, Johnny! Oh, Johnny! Oh!," and "Beat Me Daddy, Eight to the Bar," plus tunes from 1940 ("I'll Be with You in Apple Blossom Time"), 1941 ("Yes, My Darling Daughter") and 1942 ("Pennsylvania Polka"). War-time successes included Latin influences, such as "Rum and Coca Cola," "South American Way," and "Rhumboogie." Their last pop hit was "I Wanna Be Loved," from 1950. Many of their tunes were successfully covered by the Glenn Miller Orchestra, and the Andrews Sisters did some fine ground-breaking work with Bing Crosby. Unfortunately, reissued material available on Paramount, Decca, Dot, and Capitol in North America is all remakes of earlier successes. If the originals are required, then the Ace of Hearts from Britain must do.

P2.146   **The Carpenters. Singles, 1969-1973.** A & M SP 3601.

The syrupy-sweet slickness of the Carpenter brother-sister team has helped out more than just a few depressed people. Their gaiety, freshness—and most important of all—their conveyance of spontaneity and honesty—all produced a lilting pick-up to most people. "Top Forty" radio always finds a place for such a group, with their services always in demand. This collection of their best single 45 rpm efforts includes such masterful (in terms of the audience to which they are directed) reinterpretations as "Ticket to Ride," "Top of the World," "Superstar," plus the monster Paul Williams epic "Rainy Days and Mondays." Other material includes "We've Only Just Begun" and "Close to You." The act has, naturally enough, spawned more than a dozen fairly successful imitators.

P2.147   **The Chordettes.** Cadence 1007.

Mainly active from 1954 through 1958, when they fell victim to the rock and roll music that had no place for singing trios and quartets, the Chordettes produced soft, swinging, even rolling, records, some of them cover for the advanced r 'n' b music of the day, such as "Eddie My Love" or "Lollipop." Other successes for this harmonic group included "Born to Be with You," "Teenage Goodnight," and the effervescent "Mr. Sandman."

P2.148   **Ray Conniff. Greatest Hits.** Columbia CS 9839.

Conniff began as an arranger for the Bunny Berigan band before moving on to Bob Crosby, Artie Shaw, and Harry James. For Columbia, he arranged for Johnny Ray's "Walkin' in the Rain" and Guy Mitchell's "Singin' the Blues," plus material for Johnny Mathis. With a group of four female voices (plus overdubbing), he struck on the idea of doubling them with trumpets and clarinets, and, for four male voices, with trombones and saxes. This had a well-blended effect of voices plus instruments, yet only eight singers were used in all. His biggest success was undoubtedly "'S Wonderful," followed by "Say It with Music" and "Somewhere My Love" (from *Doctor Zhivago*). But other melodies have included

"So Much in Love," "Midnight Lace," and "Memories Are Made of This." A few times a year, Conniff releases some very pleasant re-interpretations of modern popular hits that are always enjoyable to listen to.

P2.149* Four Aces. Best. two discs. MCA 2-4033.
This was one of the premier vocal quartets that developed along the lines of the Mills Brothers and extended well into the 1950s and early 1960s. It is now largely a lost art form, but close harmonies with a high lead predominated in such groups. Recording since 1951, the Four Aces were very popular in their day, beginning right off the bat with "Tell Me Why" and leading through definitive versions of "Three Coins in the Fountain," "Stranger in Paradise," "A Woman in Love," and "Love Is a Many Splendored Thing" (from the film of the same name; they sang the soundtrack's opening titles).

P2.150 Four Lads. Moments to Remember. Harmony HS 11369.
During 1955 to 1957, the high, tight harmonies of the Four Lads were all the rage, and many imitators were spawned. Their biggest hit was undoubtedly the college-inspired title track, with a vocal that shot clear through falsetto with enough volume and impact to shatter glass (figuratively). Coming down to earth, this quartet also recorded "No Not Much," "Who Needs You?," and "Standing on the Corner," all major hits.

P2.151* McGuire Sisters. Best. two discs. Coral CXB 6.
From the Arthur Godfrey Talent Scouts of 1954 through to the return of "good" music, the McGuire Sisters were one of the most successful of the singing sister trios. Their brash styles were firmly based on the close harmonies they employed, along with the solo at the verse. Their earlier years saw such commercial victories as "Goodnight, Sweetheart, Goodnight," "Sincerely" (their biggest seller, and copied from an r 'n' b group), "Muskrat Ramble," "He," "Picnic," "Something's Gotta Give," and "May You Always."

P2.152 Sergio Mendes. Greatest Hits. A & M 4252.
The Latin beat of Mendes, coupled with "Brazil 66" (now "Brazil 77" or even "Brazil 88"), recreated and reinterpreted standards of the day into easy listening. The two-girl chorus ("Brazil 66") usually sang along with Mendes's piano stylings, as on "The Look of Him," "The Fool on the Hill," and "Scarborough Fair."

P2.153* New Vaudeville Band. Fontana 27560.
With a beat and rhythm section like a wind-up soldier, the New Vaudeville Band brought both humor and high camp into popular music. The lead singer sounded as if he was using a megaphone, and his "oohs," "aahs," and sighs harkened back to Rudy Vallee's style. It was exceptionally good fun, with such tunes as the original "Winchester Cathedral," recreations of "Lili Marlene," "Whispering," and "A Nightingale Sang in Berkeley Square." They were the first pop group to investigate nostalgia and to be an influence on now-current trends (a decade later after their success) toward reviving pre-World War II materials (such as now done by the Manhattan Transfer and diverse other groups). Their album was a one shot

effort, and they quietly disappeared. But others now working in the genre listened carefully and remembered. . . .

P2.154   **Tony Orlando and Dawn. Greatest Hits.** Arista AL 4045.
          Recreating soft nostalgic pieces, Orlando and his two-girl back-up chorus harken back to another time. Some of their material is gaily syncopated to fit into a mild ragtime construction and hence, it reflects the dances and marches of that period. None of this material is "pap" or wishful thinking; all of it is sincere, but in a commercial sense. Titles include "Tie a Yellow Ribbon 'round the Ole Oak Tree" (written by a prisoner), "Say, Has Anybody Seen My Sweet Gypsy Rose?," "Candida," "You're a Lady," "You Say the Sweetest Things," and "Who's in the Strawberry Patch with Sally?," among the twelve total selections.

P2.155   **Louis Prima and Keely Smith. Hits of Louis and Keely.** Capitol T 1531.
          Prima was a long-time jazz trumpeter and singer from the late thirties and early forties; Keely Smith was his wife at the time of this set, in the mid-fifties. Singing a few classics with a scat style, the duo produced such interesting items as "Black Magic" and other recreations of jazz and pop ballads. This interesting performance was closely reminiscent of those by Jackie and Roy Kral, except that Prima stuck to successful material while the Krals engaged in theater songs.

P2.156   **Sandpipers. Greatest Hits.** A & M SP 4246.
          This anonymous group was perhaps the leader in slickly urbane folk, country, and rock reinterpretations for the mass popular market. Tempos were slowed, the music was modified to suggest soft caresses, and many singles were released for the "Top 40" market. Renditions here include "Guantanamera" and "Louie, Louie." This is awfully nice listening; and we find it difficult to say anything against this music.

P2.157   **The Seekers. Georgy Girl.** Capitol T2431.
          The Seekers (or the New Seekers, as their reincarnation was known until they split up in 1973) could be likened as the British equivalent to Peter, Paul and Mary (if one thinks in terms of commercial folk music). Their reinterpretive style produced slick sounds with no personality beyond the vocals; however, they sold well and were nicely received wherever they went. Developing in a vacuum in Australia, they shortly moved to the United Kingdom and began to cover, in soft-folk terms, some of the current hits of the day. This disc contains their better efforts, and it could stand as a "Greatest Hits" set because some tracks here were previously released on other albums. Their one big hit—exclusively theirs—was the title track "Georgy Girl" from the film of the same name, which smashed all sales records for discs of this type. Other tunes here include the Beatles' "Yesterday," the Mamas and Papas' "California Dreamin'," Dusty Springfield's "Island of Dreams," plus folk material from Pete Seeger ("Turn, Turn, Turn"), Bob Gibson ("Well, Well, Well"), Tom Paxton ("The Last Thing on My Mind"), and Doug Kershaw ("Louisiana Man").

P2.158   The Smoothies. Easy Does It. two discs. RCA Bluebird AXM2-5524.

This vocal trio, as indicated by their name, had a very smooth sounding harmonic structure to their singing. Over the years (the material here is from the late thirties and early forties), the female singers changed many times, but the two men were constants. Easy-going, soporific, pleasant songs and melodies include "If I Had My Way," "Three Little Fishes," "Breezin' along with the Breeze," "Love Grows on the White Oak Tree," "Ciri-Biri-Bin," "I Love to Watch the Moonlight" among the 32 selections. The notes are good on the singing trios of this period.

P2.159   Sonny and Cher. The Beat Goes On. Atco SD11000.

Early in the beginnings of rock music and flower children, Sonny and Cher Bono were regarded as the epitome of the rebels, largely a result of their stage act and countless appearances on late night talk shows. This visual style concentrated on throwing flowers and wearing outrageous costumes, plus the seductive outfits worn by Cher. Their biggest efforts were "I Got You Babe," an early song of undying love, and a revival of the epic "The Beat Goes On." Other song tracks here include "Gypsies, Tramps, and Thieves," "Baby Don't Go," "Little Man," and "Do Right Woman, Do Right Man."

P2.160   Swingle Singers. Bach's Greatest Hits. Philips 600.097.

Bach has been the subject of many jazz interpretations over the years, but it took Ward Swingle to assemble a group of eight French singers and vocalize the various fugues and preludes. Taking a page from the book of jazz singing, Swingle introduced the scat elements of bop music (Ella Fitzgerald, Bing Crosby, and Lambert, Hendricks and Ross). Nothing is lost in the translation, and, indeed, it is possible to follow the various contrapuntal lines by listening for the separate vocal lines. None of the music here comes from any cantata; all are from the *Well-Tempered Clavier* or diverse suites and partitas. Some keys were changed to accommodate the human voice, and the element of swing was introduced by using syncopation.

INSTRUMENTAL ENSEMBLES

[Note: While these works are issued under both group and individual names, they all have in common the sweetening (violins, etc.) that makes them tend to sound very similar. Even some of the organ and "solo" piano pieces have this added touch, which is why they are listed here.]

P3.1*   Herb Alpert. Greatest Hits. A & M SP 4245.

Alpert was originally a session man in the late fifties. By the sixties, he had founded his own record company (A & M) and began employing the style of Mexican and Spanish marching bands. As a trumpet player, Albert capitalized on the hard sound of trumpet and Latin percussions. He had many imitators, but none were as successful as he was. The period here is 1962-1966, after which much of this kind of music peaked in popularity. Yet it still sounds as fresh today as it did over a decade ago. Material includes "The Lonely Bull," the epic "Taste of Honey" (a re-make of the Beatles' hit), "Whipped Cream," and the double-barrelled hit that helped to win an Oscar for a cartoon—"Spanish Flea" and "Tijuana Taxi."

P3.2   **Leroy Anderson. Anderson Orchestra.** Decca DL 74335.
Anderson took several unusual themes and commercialized them. Thus, he was able to produce such novel items as "The Syncopated Clock," "Sleigh Ride," the grandiose "Blue Tango" (a million seller in 1952), "Promenade," and even "Fiddle-Faddle." The tune he is best remembered for is probably "The Typewriter."

P3.3   **Floyd Cramer. Best.** RCA LSP 2886.
Cramer, as employed by Chet Atkins, was responsible for creating the piano aspect of the "Nashville Sound": a light tinkling with a smooth bass roll and the occasional blue note, quite often sounding like a honky-tonk piano played at slow or half-speed. Coupled with Atkins-style guitar and strings, and perhaps a female chorus or two, Cramer's piano sound pervaded the Nashville scene of the late 1950s and 1960s in an effort to create markets for sales. Cramer, who has done work for Jim Reeves and Jim Brown, spun off his stylings into instrumentals that fell relatively flat in the country world but were good potential cross-overs to the popular market. With such items as "Last Date," and with no twangy steel guitar, Cramer's was the epitome of light cocktail music.

P3.4   **Jesse Crawford. Best.** two discs. MCA2-4051.

P3.5   **Lenny Dee. Best.** two discs. MCA2-4042.

P3.6   **Ken Griffin. Best.** two discs. Columbia G 30552.
Of all the solo instruments, the organ is perhaps the one that carries the most weight in establishing a mood or theme for easy listening. The reason is not hard to find: most other instruments can be simulated on even the cheapest organs. The home popularity of organs has reinforced purchase of organ music, and to accommodate this, Schwann's catalog even has a separate section entitled "Organ." To these ears, the music is very pleasant in its place, but we find most organists sounding alike. Material is mostly pop and standards, pretty safe for home listening, but with perhaps an emphasis on bouncing music, wedding music, waltzes, Hawaiian, and so forth. The three organists above have been prolific in the past, and these six discs cumulate perhaps the best of their works. Mood items include "I've Told Ev'ry Little Star," "Softly, As in a Morning Sunrise," "Hello, Young Lovers," from Crawford's set; while Dee tackles a few more contemporary items such as "Gentle on My Mind," "Cabaret," and "A Taste of Honey." Griffin tends to be more relaxing, and of the group, is really our favorite for late night enjoyment, especially with "Ebb Tide" and other nature themes.

P3.6a   **Eddie "Lockjaw" Davis. The Cookbook.** two discs. Prestige P 24039.
Although primarily known as a jazz saxophonist, Davis had contributed to modern popular music through his "Chicken Shack" style, the sound that started it all, in 1958. Davis teamed with organist Shirley Scott plus a rhythm trio to

create a tenor-plus-organ ensemble to run through simple phrasing and ballad material. The formula was a success, and this twofer includes their original versions of such uptempo numbers as "In the Kitchen," "Have Horn Will Blow," "Skillet," "The Broiler," and "The Rev." During the 1960s, there was a great profusion of such groups.

P3.7   **Erroll Garner. Concert by the Sea.** Columbia CS 9821.

P3.8*   **Erroll Garner. Play It Again, Erroll.** two discs. CBS 88129 (French issue).

If there is a place in jazz for romanticism coupled with jazz stylings, then the obvious master (and perhaps the only one) is Erroll Garner. His stride style embraced the strength of his left hand to play pseudo-guitar chords, while the right hand emphasized the time-delay beat. On slower items, he was lushly romantic. The double CBS set comes from the early fifties and features "Lover," "Poor Butterfly," "Love for Sale," "St. Louis Blues," "Honeysuckle Rose," and "The Man I Love" among its 21 tracks. The well-known *Concert* album reflects his personal style, capturing the full flavor of his romantic tempos, especially in "It's All Right with Me," "Where or When?," and "Autumn Leaves." It should be noted also that Garner was the composer of "Misty."

P3.9*   **Stan Getz. Greatest Hits.** Polydor 2304.074 (British issue).

P3.10   **Stan Getz. Plays.** Music for Pleasure MFP 5226 (British issue).

Tenorist Getz is probably the best known jazz soloist in the popular, relaxing music field. He established his reputation with Woody Herman's band, and then went on to meld the Lester Young-Coleman Hawkins styles in a series of small group recordings. Interestingly enough, these series seem to come at ten-year intervals. The first, 1952, was for Verve and featured standard ballads with Duke Jordan (piano) and Jimmy Raney (guitar), who were perfect foils for the lyrical, warm tones of Getz. "Time on My Hands," "The Way You Look Tonight," "Lover Come Back to Me," "Body and Soul," and "These Foolish Things" are included in a very successful set in which Getz's technical proficiency allowed for *no* clichés. His elegance makes it all seem easy, and he never sounds hurried, or at a loss for ideas, as the solos are preconceived unities. Certainly this record is not dated.

The next highlight was in 1962, with the *bossa nova* craze. Getz was directly responsible for that from his *Jazz Samba* album. The Polydor reissue here nicely covers the 1962-1964 period, during which he made "Desafinado" (with Charlie Byrd), "The Girl from Ipanema" (with Astrid Gilberto's little girl vocal), and the enchanting "Corcovado." Other Brazilian musicians included Antonio Carlos Jobim, Luis Bonfa, and Joao Gilberto. And another upswing in Latin rhythm was created by Getz's merging jazz with the samba. Other popular material in this set (from 1967) includes "Early Autumn." In 1972, Getz again made several popular recordings in diverse forms (these can be found in the *Jazz* volume in this set).

P3.11   **Earl Grant. Greatest Hits.** MCA 246.

Earl Grant was a classically trained singer and organist who often played in many supper clubs. He personally created the organ sound stylings that were so often imitated but never duplicated. His own emotional renditions were a god-send to young lovers and to sentimentalists of the 1950s and 1960s. Typical selections include "Ebb Tide" (which I think he *owned* until he died), "Swingin' Gently," "The End," plus his own versions of popular songs of the time such as "Evening Rain," "House of Bamboo," "Fly Me to the Moon," and a really splendid recreation of "Fever."

P3.12   **Los Indios Tabajaras. Maria Elena.** RCA ANL1-1179.
These two instrumentalists and vocalists combined South American Indian tunes and rhythms, plus Spanish motifs, with English popular songs. Always a safe mood group for that after dinner rest, their album contains twelve tracks featuring the title selection, "Moonlight Serenade," "Star Dust," "Ay Maria," "Ternura," and "Baion Bon," the latter being an infectious little melody from Brazil.

P3.13   **Shelly Manne. And His Friends.** Contemporary C 3527.
Manne became known as a leader of the West Coast school of "cool" jazz (see the *Jazz* volume for further details on that mode). Earlier, he had played with Stan Kenton and Woody Herman as a powerhouse drummer; subsequently, he has performed on many recordings. His major technique is simply accenting and giving room to the soloist. This disc comes from 1956, and it was the largest selling jazz album in its day. All the songs are from *My Fair Lady*, and this disc was instrumental in starting a trend of jazz discs devoted to show scores. On piano was André Previn, and the bassist was Leroy Vinnegar. The most spectacular item here is "Wouldn't It Be Loverly?"

P3.14*   **Modern Jazz Quartet. Blues on Bach.** Atlantic SD1652.

P3.15*   **Modern Jazz Quartet. Collaboration.** Atlantic SD1429.

P3.16   **Modern Jazz Quartet. European Concert.** two discs. Atlantic SD2-603.

P3.17   **Modern Jazz Quartet. Porgy and Bess.** Atlantic 1440.
Pianist John Lewis has been completely influenced by the European classical tradition of music culture and scholarship, much more so than any other jazz musician. He put together a quartet that included Milt Jackson on vibraharp, Percy Heath on bass, and Connie Kay on drums (initially, the drummer was Kenny Clarke), and contemplated playing highly structured "classical jazz," with heavily-scored performances done while wearing tuxedos. To some extent, and for 25 years, the MJQ succeeded in carving out a niche for itself in the jazz world, largely influencing no one, but playing sincerely. Its greatest successes came early on, such as the Stockholm concert in the European twofer cited above. Here may be found their basic repertoire, perhaps played in a little looser manner than in the studios. The Bach album, recorded in 1974, collects together fresh interpretations of diverse chorales, preludes, and fugues. The MJQ is most successful at transposing lyrical classical music, and it continued in this vein with the earlier *Collaboration* offering, with Laurindo Almeida, which has proved very popular with the cocktail set. Spanish-type music included "One Note Samba" and the splendid twelve-minute

adagio from Rodrigo's *Concerto de Aranjuez*. This dream music was relatively
faithful to the original, with contrasts provided by Almeida's guitar and Jackson's
vibraharp.

Of all the versions of Gershwin's *Porgy and Bess*, the MJQ's remains the best
for soft listening. It lacks the flash of Miles Davis's and Gil Evans's Columbia
interpretations, and it lacks the individual power that other jazz performers put
into just one version of one tune. But for cohesiveness and the proper evocation
of Gershwin's intents, this album must be given a high rating. Here are "Summertime," "Bess, You Is My Woman," "My Man's Gone Now," "I Love You, Porgy,"
"It Ain't Necessarily So," "Oh Bess, O Where's My Bess?," and "There's a Boat
Dat's Leaving Soon for New York." Pastoral sounds, Heath's walking bass, Jackson's
romantic vibes—all are fused together in a near-perfect portrait.

P3.18*   **George Shearing. Lullaby of Birdland.** two discs. Verve 2683 029
          (British issue).

P3.19   **George Shearing. Special Magic.** Verve 2353 107 (British issue).
          Shearing, a British-born blind pianist, moved to the United States in 1947.
Previously, he had done some jazz arranging and work for the BBC, but he felt
that he could widen his scope in the New Land. In doing so, he has become an
enigma, creating the first cocktail jazz. Essentially, he took the ideas of bop—as
a flavor—and applied them to lightly swinging standards, such as "September in
the Rain." By this action, he popularized certain aspects of bop, and he was accepted
by both the commercial and the jazz worlds. In 1949, he picked up a contract
with MGM, and by 1952, he had fashioned the lovely title, "Lullaby of Birdland"
(so-named after the club where he got his American start). The recordings here
cover his best period, 1949-1954, and were laid down in both New York and
Los Angeles. The style of his then-quintet was a simple unison of piano, vibes,
and guitar, with drums and bass providing rock-steady rhythm. Most tunes were
uptempo, to reflect his configuration of instruments: "I'll Be Around," "Body
and Soul," "Spring Is Here," "My Silent Love," "The Continental," and such
adventurous items as "Point and Counterpoint," "Good to the Last Bop," and
"How's Trix?"

P3.20   **Jimmy Smith. Best.** Verve V6-8721.
          Smith is a funk organist who has taken the Davis "Chicken Shack" technique
one step further, with newer sounds and rhythm accompaniment. Here he has
recorded the theme from *Walk on the Wild Side*, such Chicago blues as "Got My
Mojo Working" and "I'm Your Hoochie Coochie Man," and such rhythm and blues
items as "Respect," "What'd I Say?," "One Mint Julep," and "Chain of Fools."
Most of the material comes from his best reinterpretive period, 1962-1967.

P3.21*   **Ben Webster. Ballads.** two discs. Verve 2683.049 (British issue).
          Webster was a superb craftsman, projecting a mighty breathy tone through
his tenor saxophone. He simply paraphrased the melody with little exploration
of harmonies. This realignment and alteration affected the range of the saxophone
tone as on "That's All" and "Don't Get around Much Anymore." Throughout
his career, he was Ellington-inspired, having spent most of his time with that band.

These 25 tracks are lifted from the 1953-1959 period, with the so-called "house" bands of Verve: Oscar Peterson, Benny Carter, Harry Edison, and Teddy Wilson. They are all quartets, trios, or small groups, augmented by discreet strings arranged by Ralph Burns and Billy Strayhorn. Some typical easy listening tracks that presaged much of the Muzak in mood music of the 1970s include "When I Fall in Love" (where Webster takes a quiet beginning to a gradual crescendo and vibrato), "Time after Time," "Chelsea Bridge," "Blue Moon," and "Willow Weep for Me."

P3.22   **Ruth Welcome. Third Man Theme.** Capitol SM 942.
     The zither is a multi-stringed instrument from the Middle East and certain other Islamic cultures. It was employed with great success in the instrumental version of the theme music from the movie *The Third Man*. Additionally, Ruth Welcome, who played the zither for the movie, spun off several other popular tunes and some folk-ethnic items as well in a stunning display of her virtuosity. This album remains a curio today; there was really no zither explosion.

P3.23   **Roger Williams. Best.** two discs. MCA 2-4106.
     Williams has a doctorate in musical theory; he is also the son of a music teacher, as well as the master of many musical instruments. He certainly knew techniques, and through clever arranging patterns, he was able to develop just the right amount of production for tender non-vocal ballads. These he played on the piano, after winning Arthur Godfrey's *Talent Scouts* show, and they included: "Wanting You," "Near You," "Hi Lili, Hi Lo," "Till," "Yellow Bird," and "Born Free."

NOVELTY AND HUMOR

ANTHOLOGIES

P4.1   **Goofy Greats.** two discs. K-Tel Anthology NC 437.
     For this citation, we have to rely on the mass-merchandising of K-Tel television records. It may be unlikely that this record will still be available, but it does a great job of illustrating a particular form of rock 'n' roll record that has not yet been commercially assimilated: the novelty-parody. Certain of these tracks can be found on other anthologies, but not as in this thematic work. There are 28 tracks here, and the proliferation of this type of tune is one reason that rock 'n' roll declined. Anything with the ability to parody itself cannot take itself seriously, and eventually the whole thing becomes a joke. Tunes here include such important items as "Purple People Eater," "Itsy Bitsy Teeny Weeny Yellow Polka Dot Bikini" (by Brian Hyland), the sickening "Yummy, Yummy, Yummy, I've Got Love in My Tummy," "Snoopy and the Red Baron," "Ahab the Arab," and "Alley Oop." The only things lacking are Stan Freberg's caustic records and the "talking" series with snippets of a number of recordings re-arranged (often in a question-"answer" format).

P4.2 **Musical Madness.** Bandstand Records 7118.

P4.3* **Screwballs of Swingtime.** Bandstand Records 7106.
    These 32 tracks cover thirty years or so in the jazz world, and include many diverse parodies of styles—even beyond the jazz world. What can one make of Oscar Peterson and Clark Terry spoofing the blues on "Incoherent Blues"? And then country music going down the drain, led by Jo Stafford, the Pied Pipers, and Tommy Dorsey in "Friendship" and "Them Durn Fool Things [These Foolish Things]" and "Serutan Yob [Nature Boy]"? Dance spoofs include Charlies Barnet's "The Wrong Idea" and his "Darktown Strutters Ball" and even Tommy Dorsey's "Am I Dreaming (or Are All My Favorite Bands Playing)?" The most marvelous cuts come from the vitriolic pen of Bud Freeman, probably jazz's best joker: "For Musicians Only" and "Private Jives [Private Lives]." About the only tune here that non-musical or non-jazz fans will find puzzling is "Moldy Fig Stomp," which is a Dixieland selection played by be-boppers and swingmen such as Charlie Shavers, J. J. Johnson, Coleman Hawkins, and others.

P4.4* **Reefer Songs.** Stash 100.
    The theme of this album makes for a hilarious collection of jive lyrics, and it is all backed with jazz in the same spirit; consequently, there is some all-round excellent listening. Many are classics of the genre, such as Barney Bigard's 1945 "Sweet Marijuana Brown," Stuff Smith's 1936 "Here Comes the Man with the Jive," and Trixie Smith's 1938 "Jack, I'm Mellow." One of the funniest, certainly, is Harry "The Hipster" Gibson, who (in 1944) recorded "Who Put the Benzedrine in Mrs. Murphy's Ovaltine?" Ella Fitzgerald takes the vocal on the 1938 "Wackey Dust." By now, the reader should know that we are talking about a sixteen-track collation of humorous songs detailing the jazz and bluesman's involvement with marijuana and cocaine (heroin was not very funny to these people), and these cover the period 1932-1945.

P4.4a **Jonathan and Darlene Edwards. In Paris.** Corinthian Cor 103.

P4.4b **Jonathan and Darlene Edwards. The Original Piano Artistry.** Corinthian Cor 104.
    Through the mid- and late-fifties, Paul Weston and his wife Jo Stafford used to entertain their friends with off-key performances. When committed to disc, under the names "Jonathan and Darlene Edwards," the songs became underground favorites (winning 48 stars in a Leonard Feather review in *Downbeat*). Edward's pyrotechnics on the keyboard were nothing less than astounding, especially when all dizzy fingers turned to thumbs. His entrances were carefully crafted and set off against the rhythm of bells, tympani, and cymbals—all of which went off at the most inappropriate moments. Darlene's voice wavers at the precise moment of slow pitching, and her off-key phrasing and breathing (she has vocals on about half of the 24 tracks) are neatly revealed as they create embarrassing points in songs such as "I Love Paris," "Paris in the Spring," "Autumn in New York," "It's Magic." Jonathan's tour de force is "The Poor People of Paris." There is good instructional value here as everything about what *not* to do is prominently displayed. This is too rich a feast to hear all at once, though, and there is

something different to hear each time a familiar tune is replayed. In the previous two decades, all that modern technology could come up with to improve on the performances was to render the reissue into out-of-phase electronic stereo.

STANDARDS

P4.5   **Stan Freberg.** Capitol SM 2020.
Freberg was the master of sarcastic parody and satire. His creative genius soon led him into advertising, but before then, he spent a decade recording his own versions of popular tunes and songs, such as "St. George and the Dragonet," modeled on the television show and concerning the activities of a knight with the affectations of a cop. "Day-O" was the "Banana Boat" song in Belafonte style, complete with ringing bongo drums played by a beatnik who couldn't stand the music. "Heartbreak Hotel" shows the problems of recording studios, as does "The Great Pretender." "Try" was his first takeoff, this time on the Johnny Ray title "Cry." Other songs here include the stunning "John and Marsha" and "The Yellow Rose of Texas."

P4.6   **Homer and Jethro. Country Comedy.** two discs. RCA Camden
CXS-9012.
Of all the country singers who give an image of cornseed falling out of their hair, Homer and Jethro lead the pack. Yet this belies their effectiveness in song parody, as they were leaders in the field. The twenty selections here cover all kinds of pop songs, country songs, and rock and roll items. "Let Me Go, Blubber" comes from "Let Me Go, Lover," while "Oh, My Pappy" is derived from Eddie Fisher's "O My Papa." "Your Clobbered Heart" is "Your Cheatin' Heart." "The Battle of Kookamonga" came from Johnny Horton's "Battle of New Orleans." Other tunes retained their same title, such as "Gone," "Cold, Cold Heart," "Mister Sandman," "Too Young," and "Sixteen Tons." They were exceptionally fluid and proficient in their duet singing style, and many of their parodies showed ingenuity.

P4.7*   **Spike Jones. Best.** RCA ANL 1-1035.

P4.8*   **Spike Jones. Spike Jones Is Murdering the Classics.** RCA LSC 3235.
Combine sound effects with a working band, add some parody, and even some fresh material, and one has Spike Jones, surely the maddest, most insane man to ever tackle take-offs of popular material. He used revolvers, garbage cans, cuckoo clocks, and so forth to graphically illustrate the foibles and overworked motifs of many of Tin Pan Alley's successes. He was clever and original in arranging all of these noises into a systematic order and pitch so that they do indeed blend in with what there was of the original music. Stand-outs from the first collation include Carl Grayson's voice on "Cocktails for Two" and "You Always Hurt the One You Love"; Doodles Weaver commenting on the marvelous "William Tell Overture" and "Dance of the Hours"; and the various motifs developed in "Chloe" and "My Old Flame." The "classics" album shows another side, taking popular or catchy tunes from serious compositions and reconverting them to parodies. This was a little more difficult, as there were no lyrics to murder. Note "Rhapsody from

Hunger(y)" or "Pal-Yat-Chee" or even "The Blue Danube." The highlight here
is the long (thirteen-minute) selection based on Bizet's "Carmen." Bravo!

P4.9   **National Lampoon. Goodbye Pop, 1952-1976.** Epic PE 33956.
        The Lampoon gave us *Lemmings*, which was about the 1969 Woodstock
Festival of the Arts. On that disc, they parodied all of the current popular singers
in their own styles. This satirical disc carries on, but mainly concentrates on the
1970s and on styles (or genres) rather than individual singers. Thus, there is "Kung
Fu Christmas" (about soul music and politics), "Art Rock Suite" (concerning
the art song in rock music with nonsense lyrics), "Down to Jamaica" (with reggae
rhythms and again nonsense lyrics: "filé gumbo, natty lox, guava jelly"), the
"B Side of Love" (a whining country and western song about venereal disease),
and "I'm a Woman" (which concerns women's liberation). A fun album.

P4.10*   **Tom Lehrer. An Evening Wasted With . . .** Reprise 6199.

P4.11*   **Tom Lehrer. Songs.** Reprise 6216.

P4.12   **Tom Lehrer. That Was the Year That Was.** Reprise 6179.
        Tom Lehrer was a brilliant mathematician who turned his attention to songs
that were actually singable by many campus habitués through the 1950s and early
1960s. Some are topical (mostly on the third record above, such as "Smut,"
"Whatever Became of Hubert?," "The Vatican Rag," and "George Murphy") and
thus fail to carry forth to a new generation. But his earlier work was all-encompas-
sing: nothing was spared his vitriolic pen. The marvelous "Poisoning Pigeons in
the Park" is only matched by the intricate rhyming of "The Elements." His piano
style is light and airy; his voice is weak. However, his satiric material is first-rate.

BIG BANDS

INTRODUCTION

        "Popular music" changed drastically in the 1920s. Dancing styles shifted
away from the waltz and other nineteenth century styles to the foxtrot and other
variations that arose during World War I. Dance music moved with it, and the
saxophone replaced the violin in the European-type string ensemble. Black rhythms
developed with the newer jazz forms: ragtime, Charleston, black bottom (which
later became the twist), etc. Radio and records created an additional market for
the dance band, so for an orchestra to be successful during this period, its music
had to be both listenable and danceable, satisfying both the surge of people who
attended hotels, dance halls, and clubs and those at home with radios and records.
As a result, dance bands traveled, playing concerts and broadcasting *nightly* from
major American cities.

Development

As more work developed, the dance band became a professional unit with all members fully employed (previously, dance bands were assembled for one social function only). Special materials needed to be composed, and arrangements had to be written so that audiences could identify one band from another by each one's particular "sound." Paul Whiteman's band was the first to succeed in all three areas: dancing, recording, and broadcasting. Others followed: Lopez, Selvin, Gray, Goldhette, the Dorseys, the various black bands of Henderson, McKinney, Basie, Ellington, Kirk, Lunceford, etc. Previously, though, many dance bands had success in live performance, but these were not available on disc prior to 1922: Art Hickman (1913), Ted Lewis (1916), Paul Specht (1916), Meyer Davis (1916), Isham Jones (1916), George Olsen (1917), Vincent Lopez (1917), Jan Garber (1918), and Paul Whiteman (1918).

The differing "sounds" of each band depended on different instrumentation and soloists. Material comprised novelty tunes, dance tunes, show tunes from diverse "Scandals" or "Follies," and semi-classical selections. These items were carefully considered for appropriateness to records, live performances, and broadcasts—depending on the occasion. Each band also specialized in theme music. Whiteman and other dance bands liked the popular song (as projected by such performers as Crosby or the Rhythm Boys); Ellington preferred the blues or whatever showed off his leading soloists; Wayne King used waltzes, Lopez used Latin rhythm dances; Lunceford preferred a brassy sheen with noise. Whiteman's major contribution to the big band's development, though, was to take a good melody and arrange counter-melodies as variations instead of simply repeating the melody. By 1921, all dance orchestras had modeled their arrangements on Whiteman's. The next major advance (Henderson and Redman) was the sectional arrangement in swing, where the reeds battled the brasses in a tension punctuated by driving drums. Thus was born the swing era, and the decline of dance music. Rhythms were so intense that they were fatiguing to dance to all night long, and fans would just listen. It was then, not so much a hop from the ragtime and military bands of pre-World War I to the swing age.

A parallel development in Britain was primarily sparked by the European tours of the post-war military entertainment bands (notably that of James Reece Europe). But when Americans shifted over to swing music in the 1930s because of black influences, the British dance band—with no such black character available—retained its 1920s style through to the end of World War II, polishing and advancing dance rhythms to perfection through the bands of Roy Fox, Ambrose, Lew Stone, Jack Hylton, and Ray Noble. Broadcasts continued, as did recording activities. But the record industry tapered off in the United States during the Depression, thus reducing the number of discs exported to Britain. There was little first-hand knowledge of the changes in America, but there was knowledge of Latin rhythms, which intruded in the form of tangos, rhumbas, mambos, congos, sambas (later, the bossa nova), cha chas, etc. Indeed, this was so much the case that the British developed a real feel for this music; by 1950, the best in Latin music—popularized style—was coming from England.

In addition to dance bands and jazz bands, there was a third (but later) popular orchestral development: the "semi-classical" arrangement that led directly into mood music. The term did not exist until the late 1950s, and even then, it only was a category for record stores to display their wares. "Semi-classical" is essentially a full orchestra following a single melodic line; orchestration is heavy on strings, and may feature a rhythm section and/or solo instrument: trumpet (such as Bobby Hackett on the Jackie Gleason albums), accordion (Al Caiola), guitar, harmonica, etc. Patterns also emerge, such as strings accompanying a rhythmic lead for a change, but all is still in the basic unified manner and *sweetly* played. All of this can be traced to Mantovani's addition of sweet strings in 1951 to the older waltz "Charmaine." Its impact (tender lushness from a dreamy world) had influence on Chet Atkins for the Nashville sound of the late 1950s and of course, created the need for added instruments in a newly developing "stereo console" world. Moods are programmed for listening—people rarely dance to semi-classical music: they just cuddle in protective sounds awash with romantic colors. It is the ultimate background music, even with the volume turned up all the way; but unlike Muzak, it is music to be listened to as well as heard. Mood pieces are processed from country music, classical melodies, jazz, opera, and especially the musical stage (themes, incidental music, film scores). The leading orchestras in the United States that perform this music are those of Andre Kostelanetz and the late Percy Faith; Mantovani is the British exponent.

Big bands are far from dead to the specialist, as they exist on records of all kinds. Sources include air checks, original but unreissued 78 rpm records, bootleg tape concerts, film sound tracks, etc. Companies releasing this material include Bandstand, Sounds of Swing, Jazz Archives, Big Band Archives, Swing Era, Hep, Joyce, Bygone, First Heard, Sunbeam, and Extreme Rarities. And besides those of the bands annotated in the following sections, these companies have immense materials devoted to Will Bradley, Bob Chester, Larry Clinton, Jimmy Grier, Phil Harris, Horace Heidt, Hudson-deLange Orchestra, Jack Jenny, Elliot Lawrence, Hal McIntyre, Tony Pastor, Teddy Powell, Boyd Raeburn, Bobby Sherwood, Freddy Slack, Charlie Spivak, and Jerry Wald. Big bands and dance bands of the 1960s and 1970s incorporated many musical changes that had evolved since 1945: new instrumental groupings, complex Latin rhythms that had proved exciting, and added sweetening (strings).

Literature

The dance bands have often been passed by in favor of the jazz swing bands in critical appreciation. But of late there has been much reinterpretation. The two biggest, most successful bands were Benny Goodman's, as chronicled by Connor (18a) and Glenn Miller's, as documented by Flower (38) and Simon (116). Both were innovative, and these books also feature details of the spin-off bands. Four general surveys have been published since 1971. Simon (116) comments on the big bands and the big names, arranged by leader; McCarthy (75) concentrates on dancing, with a chronological approach. The latter is evenly divided between British and American bands. Rust (107) is mainly British in scope, from 1919-1944.

Simon (117) has a collection of reviews and critical pieces originally published in *Metronome* (1935-1955).

For the past ten years, British companies have reissued the best of British dance bands. RCA Bluebird just started in 1975, but it—and other companies— might be given impetus by Rust's (105) discography of American dance bands, a large work which covers 2,373 white bands (black bands are already listed by Rust in 107a).

The same comments expressed on periodical articles in the "Mainstream Popular Music" section also apply here.

ANTHOLOGIES

P5.1   [Readers' Digest Anthologies.]
The single best series of anthologies that we have seen in the Mainstream Popular category have been put together by *Readers' Digest*. Their offerings are blockbuster in size and efforts, despite some electronic stereo effects. The "big band" collections include *The Incomparable Tommy Dorsey* (RDA 92-A, four discs), *The Unforgettable Glenn Miller* (RDA 64—A, six discs), and *Swing with Artie Shaw* (RDA 89-A, four discs). Several other anthologies reveal the breadth and scope of the swing period, and these include *The Great Band Era* (RDA 25-A, ten discs), the *Kings of Swing in the Groove* (RDA 45-A, six discs), *Swing Hits* (RDA 76-A, six discs), and *Swing Years* (RDA 21-A, six discs). All of these showcase an incredible variety of bands. The vocalists are ably represented on *Hear Them Again* (RDA 49-A, ten discs), featuring the likes of Crosby, Sinatra, Como, Belafonte, Lena Horne, Helen Morgan, Sophie Tucker, Fanny Brice, and the great Caruso. All of the above material comes from original masters held by larger commercial firms, such as RCA and Decca. *Readers' Digest* does have other collections, but those are re-interpretations by various house bands.

P5.2*   **Big Bands Greatest Hits, v.1/2.** four discs. Columbia G 30009 and KG 31213.

P5.3*   **Themes of the Big Bands.** Swing Era LP 1001.

P5.4*   **This Is the Big Band Era.** two discs. RCA VPM 6043.
These seven discs very adequately present the most popular renditions of the big band items from the 1930s and 1940s. The vast majority of them are simply each band's theme pieces, which usually developed from one of their earlier hits and were constantly sent out over the airwaves. The Columbia sets give forty items (a little short on the number of titles that could have been accommodated, and in electronically reprocessed stereo). Included are the bands of Lionel Hampton, Charlie Spivak, Duke Ellington, Claude Thornhill, Kay Kyser, Tony Pastor, Ray Noble, Glen Gray, Woody Herman, and Guy Lombardo, along with the appro- priate vocalist of the time singing a few choruses. These bands were, of course, under contract to Columbia and its subsidiaries at the time.

The RCA compilation was intended to be a sampler to a later-aborted series. It is arranged in rough chronological order, beginning with Bennie Moten's "South," an early impressive popular theme from 1928, through to Larry Clinton in the early 1950s. Included along the way are definitive performances by Bunny Berigan's band, the bands of Ziggy Elman, Lionel Hampton, Earl Hines, Duke Ellington, Count Basie, Tommy Dorsey, Benny Goodman, Artie Shaw, Charlie Barnet, Erskine Hawkins, and, of course, Glenn Miller. It is unfortunate that MCA (formerly Decca) could not produce a similar distillation, as RCA, Decca, and Columbia were the "big three" of recordings in 1930-1950. But the Swing Era issue takes up the slack somewhat by presenting some well-known and some not so well-known items, such as the bands of Van Alexander, Raymond Scott, Ziggy Elman, Art Mooney, Vincent Lopez, Artie Shaw, Mal Hallett, Tony Pastor, and Jan Savitt.

INNOVATORS

P5.5*   **Bunny Berigan. The Great Dance Bands of the '30s and '40s.** RCA LPM 2078.

P5.6   **Bunny Berigan. The Great Soloists.** Biograph BLP C 10.

P5.7*   **Bunny Berigan. His Trumpet and His Orchestra, v.1.** RCA LPV 581.
       Berigan put in much hard work with innumerable dance bands during the 1930s although occasionally, he made sessions with small groups under his own name, as accompanist to the Boswell Sisters. For a period, he was in the Mound City Blue Blowers. These studio jazz sessions can be found on the Biograph reissue set of Vocalion, Brunswick, Columbia, and ARC recordings. In 1935 he joined Benny Goodman, and his most famous solo from that association was in "King Porter Stomp." Most of his style was derived from Armstrong, with added lyricism, and there are some Beiderbecke influences, particularly exemplified by his 1938 recordings of "Davenport Blues," "In a Mist," "Flashes," "Candlelights," "In the Dark," and "Walking the Dog." His other big solo was from Tommy Dorsey's recording of "Marie." He created a big band, which was often said to be "rough," but it was one of the best dance-jazz units around. In 1936, he recorded his theme, "I Can't Get Started" (on the Biograph disc), and then found success with a large band version one year later (on the LPM 2078). The *Dance* music was straight-forward, while the more jazz-y items are to be found on the LPV 581 album (along with the Beiderbecke items). Berigan was a "romantic" character because of his extremely good looks and his alcoholism (which killed him in 1942).

P5.8*   **Tommy Dorsey. Complete, v.1+ (1935-1950).** [in progress; probably twelve discs.] RCA AXM2-5521/+ [v.1 only].

P5.9*   **Tommy Dorsey. This Is Tommy Dorsey and His Clambake Seven.** two discs. RCA VPM 6087.
       Dorsey is most remembered for his sweet trombone and his theme, "I'm Gettin' Sentimental over You." His was the most commercial of the big swing bands, and its longevity can be attributed both to his sound and to the fact that

he had little competition from other trombone leaders (most bands were led by clarinet players, trumpeters, or pianists). The 200 or so tracks to be included eventually were originally recorded between 1935 and 1950. The big band outings have vocals by Edythe Wright, Frank Sinatra, Jack Leonard, Jo Stafford, and Stuart Foster (among others). Most of the arrangements were by Sy Oliver, and the tunes were medium-paced standards (such as "Blue Skies," "Night and Day," "Smoke Gets in Your Eyes," "Tea for Two," "Star Dust," and "On the Sunny Side of the Street"), watered-down jazz tunes (such as "That's A-Plenty," "Beale Street Blues," and "After You've Gone") or originals to fit the band's styles (such as his theme, "Song of India," and "Who?," "Boogie Woogie," and "Opus One"). The Clambake Seven was Dorsey's group within a band (Shaw had the Gramercy Five; Goodman, his quartets and trios), and quite often they let loose with some real scorching jazz. The twenty items that RCA has chosen to reissue here are largely from their popular repertoire, and they include "The Music Goes 'Round and 'Round," the top novelty song of the 1930s—"Rhythm Saved the World," "You Must Have Been a Beautiful Baby," and "The Milkman's Matinee." Most of the vocals here were handled by Edythe Wright.

P5.10*   **Duke Ellington. Presents Ivie Anderson.** two discs. Columbia KG 32064.
        This is an excellent set, produced by Frank Driggs with interesting notes by Helen Dance. The 32 tracks cover 1932-1940 in chronological order, with most of the selections from 1935-1939. Full discographical data is presented, including the order on the instrumental solo breaks. All of the material has been released before on 78 rpm, and most has been reissued on elpees (such as the Columbia C3L 27 and 39 sets of the sixties). Yet, this is a brilliant concept album, pulling out those tunes that featured vocals by one of the very few "popular" black singers. Anderson's even vibrato and supreme breath control were probably the result of her incurable asthma, which eventually caused her death in 1949. She was one of the few black singers that did not have a rough growl and blues-based voice, and this gave her an appeal to wider audiences.
        Less than half of the material here was composed by Ellington. One of the best of Anderson's songs was "Stormy Weather," although the version here is from 1940. Other important renditions were made of "A Lonely Co-Ed," "I'm Satis-fied," "Isn't Love the Strangest Thing?," and, of course, "Mood Indigo." She also sang naughty songs with double entendres, such as the flagwaver "I'm Checkin' Out, Goombye" or "I've Got to Be a Rug Cutter." Most of the amusing songs were written for the Cotton Club crowd, then subsequently recorded. The excep-tionally stable band over this period presents their usual top drawer performances, with stunning work from Johnny Hodges, Rex Stewart, Ben Webster, and Cootie Williams.

P5.11*   **Benny Goodman. Helen Forrest: The Original Recordings of the 1940s.**
        two discs. Columbia KG 32822.
        This set of twenty tunes illustrates an excellent idea: theme material associated with one vocalist. This mood type of music does not conflict at all with Goodman's jazz elements in the small group or his swing elements in the big band format. The period here is about eighteen months (1939 to 1941), and in addition to good music, this short span reveals steady progress and direction, especially valuable

in any study of Helen Forrest. Some of the sides are rare, and the musicians come and go, as Goodman's band is in the transitional stage away from swing; among them were Charlie Christian, Ziggy Elman, Cootie Williams, Johnny Guarnieri, Lou McGarity, and Mel Powell to name but a few.

P5.12*   Isham Jones. RCA LPV 504.
Jones's band was a well-trained, well-disciplined unit that produced stock arrangements for current tunes. The sixteen tracks here, all recorded between 1932 and 1934, show some of the touches of Gordon Jenkins's early arrangements. Jones had been recording since 1922 (a fairly successful dance band), and the mood was continued here with such tunes as "Sentimental Gentleman from Georgia," "Music, Music, Everywhere," "China Boy," "Dallas Blues," and "Blue Room." He always made a conscientious effort to incorporate jazz themes into his dance music (as one can see from the tracks listed above), and when he died, the band became a nucleus for the First Herd, led by Woody Herman, who was an active member at that time. The slow blues music of Jones was livened up until the Herman band became known as the "Band that Swings the Blues."

P5.13*   Ted Lewis, v.1/2, 1926/1933. two discs. Biograph BLP C7/8/ .
Here are 32 tracks of hokum (light, humorous music), featuring Muggsy Spanier, Benny Goodman, Fats Waller (with four charming vocals), Jimmy Dorsey, and George Brunies (among others). The other vocals are by Ted Lewis—"Mr. Happiness" himself. Some of these tracks have been reissued before by Columbia Special Products, but these are not generally available in record shops. No matter, for it is all lovable music—kitsch and nostalgia—e.g., "Just a Gigolo," "When My Baby Smiles at Me," "Egyptian Ella," and "Dip Your Brush in the Sunshine," the latter with a blistering clarinet solo by Goodman, who is himself urged on to greater heights by Lewis. These are basically vaudeville-type "happy promises" tunes with a jazz arrangement that partially nullifies their Tin Pan Alley origins. They were very successful, as 26 of the selections were recorded after the Depression set in.

P5.14*   Glenn Miller. Best. RCA LSP 3377.

P5.15*   Glenn Miller. Plays Selections from "The Glenn Miller Story." RCA LPE 1192.

P5.16   Glenn Miller. On the Air, v.1/3. three discs. RCA LPE 2767/69.
These five discs will provide the essentials to form the base of a collection of the more popular Miller tunes. The first two, with only two duplications between them, give about 24 of the Miller band's biggest hits and sellers. The material includes "In the Mood," "Chattanooga Choo Choo," "Tuxedo Junction," "Juke Box Saturday Night," "Kalamazoo," "St. Louis Blues," "String of Pearls," and "Little Brown Jug" (among others). However, the sound is somewhat hollow because of the electronic gimmickry.
The three-volume set of air shots lets us listen to Miller as he actually sounded outside of the recording studio. The tracks are all mixed up, coming from different time periods and different places, but in sum, they range from 1938 to 1941 and

include such locations as the Cafe Rouge, Paradise Restaurant, Glen Island Casino, and Meadowbrook. Of particular interest may be "Song of the Bayou," a composition never recorded unless truncated because it was considered too long; however, on the radio, though, Miller played it out to its 4:40 timing. Many of the items on this set comprise novelty tunes or covers of existing hits (e.g., "Yes, My Darling Daughter," "I Don't Want to Set the World on Fire," and "A Nightingale Sang in Berkeley Square"). George T. Simon, noted biographer of Miller, contributes notes. Overall, there appear to be few differences in how the tunes were played (either in the studio or "live"), but there is a distinct vibrancy on the live reissues. No doubt this was because of the highly arranged and stylized performances by the band for recordings.

P5.17*   **Leo Reisman, v.1. RCA LPV 565.**

There is wide variety scattered among these sixteen tracks (and RCA has not yet come up with volume two). Reisman's was a society band, and he put several of them out on the road—playing his arrangements, but not comprising all of his men. At one time, he had twenty such bands, but stayed in Boston as much as he could. The music here comes from 1929 to 1940, and Reisman's (for the most part) plays only as an orchestra that backed vocalists. Thus, the collection includes a Lewis Conrad vocal, "What Is This Thing Called Love?" (with Eddy Duchin on piano), a Lee Wiley vocal on "Time on My Hands," Fred Astaire singing "Night and Day," Harold Arlen performing "Stormy Weather," and others, such as Gertrude Niesen, Clifton Webb, Adele Astaire, and Lee Sullivan (Reisman takes the vocal refrain on "Without That Gal!"). He was one of RCA's best selling artists: his music was danceable; the songs, popular; and the vocalists and sidemen, outstanding. Reisman's group had many firsts: first to use blacks, creating integrated bands; first to make a long-playing record—in 1931 ("The Bandwagon"); first to appear on radio—in 1921; and first to record binaural records (they were never released). He was always smooth and romantic, limiting his jazz to trumpeter Bubber Miley's solos. He introduced Latin rhythms but was generally not an innovator; however, he did capitalize on trends and fashions.

P5.18*   **Paul Whiteman, v.1/2.** two discs. RCA LPV 555 and 570.

P5.19*   **Paul Whiteman.** Columbia CL 2830.

Whiteman was one of the most influential musicians and conductors of the 1920s. At a trying time, he nurtured successful jazz units within his orchestra. Although his musicians played superb stock arrangements superbly scored, they were free to record on their own (provided that they used other members of the band), with the security of a regular paycheck from Whiteman every week. (This was often around 300 dollars, a fairly hefty sum in those days.) Thus, musicians such as Bix Beiderbecke, the Dorsey Brothers, Red Nichols, Joe Venuti, Eddie Lang, Jack Teagarden, and vocalists such as Bing Crosby, Mildred Bailey, and Dinah Shore, got their start in both the big band world and in independent recordings. In fact, many jazz collectors only consider Whiteman worthwhile because of Beiderbecke's performances.

Whiteman made music and recording history in a number of ways. In addition to promoting a watered-down version of jazz (but "jazz," nevertheless) by calling himself "the King of Jazz," he also commissioned many songs and tunes. For RCA, he created "symphonic jazz," such as on "Meditation," based on themes from the opera *Thaïs*; or he commissioned works such as Grofé's *Grand Canyon Suite* or Gershwin's *Rhapsody in Blue* (both from 1924). That same year saw no less than 52 of his bands playing his arrangements around the world at the same time. As orchestral leader, he played for both *George White's Scandals* and *Ziegfeld's Follies*. In 1927, he took over Jean Goldkette's jazz-oriented band (including Beiderbecke and Trumbaner). The RCA material is derived from 1920-1928 and 1930-1937 sessions; CBS had him under contract from 1928-1930. After 1938, he began to record for Decca, but with jazz firmly established, the Depression still raging, and better dance bands, Whiteman's activities declined. Typical tracks on volume one include "Whispering" and "Japanese Sandman." Volume two has Crosby and Beiderbecke for "Dardanella," "Mississippi Mud," "Side by Side," and "Rocking Chair."

AMERICAN DANCE BANDS

Pre-War

P5.20   **Gus Arnheim. 1932.** Sunbeam HB 304.
      Arnheim was leader of one of the finest hotel bands in the United States and also did extensive recording with Bing Crosby. The material here all comes from one year, and includes soft but danceable interpretations of such items as "It's the Girl," "Love for Sale," "Red, Red Roses," and "Stardust," from among the fifteen tracks on the set.

P5.21*   **Charlie Barnet, v.1/2.** two discs. RCA LPV 551, 567.

P5.22   **Charlie Barnet. Best.** two discs. MCA2-4069.
      The 51 items here give incontestable evidence that Barnet's band was the best of the white swing dance groups, bar none. The 1939-1942 period was a climax in their performing career, which becomes quite evident by re-listening to the music and discovering how fresh it still seems. Barnet was the epitome of swing: he had impeccable musical tastes; he had a relaxed personality (and was easy to get along with); his band did not latch onto a particular sound and stay with it; the band was reasonably stable; and they emphasized "head arrangements," as Basie did, where nothing was written down except for a few guides. His band was the first white band to play the Apollo Theater (in 1933), and he returned many times. Although "Cherokee" was written by Ray Noble, it became Barnet's theme: Billy May did the "head" on strips of paper, and Barnet improvised the tenor solo (which has since been copied many times, note for note). Many of the tunes here are originals, plus some others like "Night and Day" and "Lament for a Lost Love." The MCA effort comes from Decca recordings of 1942-1945. It is a more commercial sounding album, most of the twenty tracks being with vocals by Kay Starr, Art Robey, and Fran Warren. Tunes include "Skyliner," "Drop Me Off in Harlem," "Smiles," and the epic "The Moose," with a sterling piano solo by the underrated Dodo Marmarosa. The Decca material was certainly challenging, as

these were war years and big band personnel were constantly changing because of the draft.

P5.23*   **Cab Calloway. Hi De Ho Man.** two discs. Columbia G 32593.
    Calloway's CBS material previously had long been out-of-print on this side of the Atlantic, and it certainly is great to welcome him back. Covered here is his 1935-1947 period, with such titles as "Nagasaki," "Jumpin' Jive," "A Chicken Ain't Nothing but a Bird," "Minnie the Moocher," and the title track. This is a good representative selection, and should prove worthwhile to those who "rediscovered" Cab through his performances in *Hello, Dolly!* Although he seemed to be nonchalant and relaxed on stage while performing, and this extended to his band as well, Calloway ran a tight ship and fired anyone who failed to play music his way. In jazz importance, his band was mainly a training ground for future musicians. His style of scat singing—"hi-de-hi, ho-de-ho"—gave him great stage presence, and this was later recognized by his being given roles in movies (*Stormy Weather*) and on stage (*Porgy and Bess*, as Sportin' Life, and in *Hello, Dolly!*).

P5.24   **Coon-Sanders Nighthawks. Radio's Aces.** RCA LPV 511.
    Once known as the Kansas City Nighthawks, this group of dance jazzmen was the first jazz group to broadcast live over the airwaves (on KDKA, Pittsburgh). That distinction apart, they were well known as the house band at Muehlebach Hotel in Kansas City, and formed part of the hotel dance band tradition. There are sixteen tracks on this album, and there are good notes on the hotel band phenomenon. Vocals were by either pianist Joe Sanders or drummer Carlton Coop. Both sing on "Wabash Blues" and "I Ain't Got Nobody."

P5.25   **Jimmy Dorsey.** Dot 25437.

P5.26*   **Jimmy Dorsey. Best.** two discs. MCA2-4073.
    When the Dorsey Brothers split up, they abandoned their Dixieland roots as well. For the balance of the 1930s, the New Orleans influence declined steadily, until by 1940, there was no trace in either of the brothers' work. Tommy became more successful than Jimmy, probably because Jimmy left to form his own group from scratch, while Tommy retained the 1935 band. Tommy, though, had stronger arrangers in Sy Oliver, and stronger singers in Frank Sinatra and the Pied Pipers, Jack Leonard, etc. Jimmy had Bob Eberly and a few hits, such as "Maria Elena," "Amapola," "I Hear a Rhapsody," and "Tangerine." The Dot collection was the last thing that he did; it stems from his success in being reunited with Tommy for the Jackie Gleason summer replacement television series "The Stage Show." Some interesting remakes with a hot clarinet, uptempo passages, and heavy percussion can be found in "So Rare" and "June Night."

P5.27*   **Eddy Duchin. Original Recordings.** Columbia CS 9420.
    Duchin led a very successful recording and dance band throughout the 1930s and 1940s, characterizing much popular music in his velvet smooth pianistic stylings. He recorded in 1932-1933 for Brunswick (now Columbia) and, together with vocalist Lew Sherwood, created "Speak to Me of Love" and "Try a Little Tenderness." From this same period came a glossy instrumental treatment of "Night and Day."

From 1938 until the recording ban of the 1940s, he was back with Brunswick (after spending five years with Victor), this time with a female vocal lead (Patricia Norman) for "Ol' Man Mose" and an instrumental "Stormy Weather." Duchin was one of the earliest matinee idols, as thousands swooned over his good looks.

P5.28*   **Jean Goldkette. 1926-1929.** RCA FXM 1-7136 (French issue).
Goldkette's band was one of many that performed hot dance music. But his band, located in New York, also had many jazz musicians beginning to come into good performances in their own right, such as Joe Venuti (violin), Eddie Lang (guitar), and Jimmy Dorsey (clarinet and alto sax). Bix Beiderbecke played for a time as fourth trumpet! These were the cream of white New York professional jazz musicians, moonlighting after hours and creating early jazz classics (some of which were recorded; see *Jazz* in this set). Of the sixteen tracks here, four especially stand out: "Take a Good Look," "Just Imagine," "Just One More Kiss," and "So Tired," with Hoagy Carmichael.

P5.29   **Benny Goodman. Accompanies the Girls.** Sunbeam SB 111.

P5.30   **Benny Goodman. The Great Vocalists.** RCA International INT 1021 (British issue).
The second album is a very polite spinoff of various songs associated with Benny Goodman, and it is especially appropriate for this volume as it has many of the "swing" elements necessary for middle-of-the-road or mainstream popular music. There are only ten tracks, but each is a minor gem. The period is 1935-1939, and the singers are Ella Fitzgerald from 1936 ("Goodnight My Love" and "Did You Mean It?"), Johnny Mercer from 1939, Jimmy Rushing with "He Ain't Got Rhythm," and two of Goodman's regulars, Martha Tilton ("Thanks for the Memory" and "The Lady's in Love with You") and Helen Ward ("Between the Devil and the Deep Blue Sea" and "There's a Small Hotel"). "Sing" was beginning to replace "swing" as the vocalists stepped out of the big bands to go on their own (Sinatra, Stafford, Forrest, Como, Peggy Lee, and others). This record is a reminder of the type of work the big band vocalists did in the swing era, and it is a valid historical document for illustrating both the trend and the transition period. The first album is more a nostalgia piece, but it is equally valid. The period is 1931-1933, when Goodman was a session musician. The sixteen tracks here include such singers as Annette Hanshaw, Ethel Waters, Lee Morse, and the Boswell Sisters. Hanshaw had a cute, perky voice and was very popular; Lee Morse was country-inspired, and occasionally yodeled on her records.

P5.31   **Benny Goodman. Radio Broadcasts from the Congress Hotel, 1935/36.** five discs. Sunbeam SB 128/132.
On November 6, 1935, after initial success at the Palomar in Los Angeles, Goodman opened for a month at Chicago's Congress Hotel. Attendance rose, and he was offered a new contract from month to month, until radio commitments forced him to New York after May 1936. This seven-month engagement was the longest continuous spot in one location that Goodman was ever to play; overall success, awards, radio and films were still two years ahead for him. Chicago was his home town, and here he also presented "jazz concerts" (no dancing allowed)

with integrated bands including Fletcher Henderson and Teddy Wilson. (The
start of the Goodman trio was here.) NBC broadcast the Congress engagement each
Monday night, and this incredible five-disc set presents the programs for December 23,
1935, and January 6 through February 17, 1936—almost two months. While the
sound is variable and a little scratchy at times (these come from Robert F. Thompson,
who had 17 twelve-inch all-aluminum 78 rpm discs to work from), the music comes
through crystal clear. The 66 tunes include repetitions of "Let's Dance" and
"Goodbye" (his themes). Some of the band members at the time were Art Rollini,
Jess Stacy and Gene Krupa; Helen Ward handled the vocals (some songs are here
that she never recorded).

These broadcasts are continuous, just as they were performed; and as air
checks go, they are superior to others (hear "Limehouse Blues"). In the history
of popular music, transcriptions such as these are of great importance. For instance,
there are a number of firsts and stylistic examples here. These are the initial recordings of much Goodman material (e.g., "Someday, Sweetheart"); the only recordings
of "Where Am I?" are here, as well as "I've Got a Feelin' You Are Foolin'," "Lost,"
et al. At this time Goodman had a dance orchestra—it swang, but it was not hot.
Thus, this pre-Hampton, James, Elman, Wilson period featured *polished* "pop"
tunes, with excellent arrangements (some staff, some Henderson). Just previous
to the Congress Hotel engagement, Goodman had picked up over 100 stock arrangements, many of which got their first airing on these broadcasts. Of all the musicians
here, perhaps Joe Harris (the trombonist) was the outstanding soloist, next to
Goodman. Good notes (especially those by Russ Connor, co-author of *BG: On
the Record* [18a]) and good jacket design round out this item, which is absolutely
essential for the Goodman collector and for all large phonodisc libraries.

P5.32*   **Glen Gray and the Casa Loma Orchestra. Best.** two discs. MCA2-4076.

P5.33   **Glen Gray and the Casa Loma Orchestra. Great Recordings.** Harmony
         HL 7045.

Gray's band, one of the premier dance bands in America, got its name after
a one-night stand at Casa Loma in Toronto. On balance, this is all good music that
never quite swings in the same manner as the British dance bands of Hylton, Noble,
Ambrose, et al. However, there is much gold here. The Harmony reissue begins
with 1929, and features white mood versions of "Royal Garden Blues," "Put on
Your Old Grey Bonnet," and "Blue Jazz." Pee Wee Hunt (who was to go on with
big bands of his own) is heard on vocal and trombone, as well as early Ray Eberle,
who sings and plays alto. The MCA collection of twenty items covers 1934-1942,
and will certainly appeal to the nostalgia buff—particularly Kenny Sargent's vocal
on "Don't Do It Darling" from 1942. In many respects, Glen Gray paved the way
for swing music by featuring the arrangements of guitarist Gene Gifford.

P5.34   **George Hall. His Taft Hotel Orchestra, 1933-1937.** two discs. RCA
         Bluebird AXM2-5504.

P5.35   **Richard Himber. His Ritz Carlton Hotel Orchestra, 1934-1935.**
         two discs. RCA Bluebird AXM2-5520.
         During the 1930s, over 100 hotels at one time in New York City offered
live entertainment. Most of these were devoted to dance bands, and RCA has
restored to the catalog two of the greatest working groups of that period. Hall's
group featured Dolly Dawn and her Dawn Patrol (Loretta Lee and Sonny Schuler)
as vocalists. The 32 selections include some inspired versions of "There's a Cabin
in the Pines," "Infatuation," "Blue in Love," "Shine," "No Strings," and "It's
a Sin to Tell a Lie." Himber's group had Joey Nash's vocals, and the 32 tracks
here are centered on tunes from reviews, stage shows, and motion pictures (including *We're Not Dressing* and *Melody in Spring*): "It's Psychological," "Lullaby
of Broadway," "Autumn in New York," "Tea for Two," and "What a Difference
a Day Made."

P5.36*   **Gene Krupa. His Orchestra and Anita O'Day, Featuring Roy Eldridge.**
         two discs. Columbia KG 32663.
         This is a straightforward reissued set. It encompasses the more danceable
(and hence less jazzy) tunes from Columbia C2L 29 (*That Drummin' Man*) plus
many others not available for some time. The period for these items is 1941-1942,
plus some from 1945. Eldridge only appears on fewer than a quarter of the selections. Anita O'Day comes through with a superb vocal on "Boogie Blues," and
there is a stunning duet between Eldridge and her on "Let Me off Uptown." This
is not a definitive set, as "Lover," "Disc Jockey Jump," and other tunes are not
here. But it fills the gap, and leaves the listener with some comparative material
to rank against that of Helen O'Connell, Helen Forrest, Ivie Anderson, et al. It
will also furnish evidence of trends and development among what were known as
"big band thrushes" in an earlier era.

P5.36a   **Kay Kyser. World of Kay Kyser.** two discs. Columbia CG 33572.
         Kyser's band originated in Chicago, and it was deeply in the Guy Lombardo
"soft" approach (cascading notes and sugary melodies). As the 1930s progressed,
Kyser turned more and more to "professional novelties" (that is, reasonably good
songs with twists that were competently performed), such as "Horses Don't Bet
on People" or "Love on a Greyhound Bus." By the mid-forties, he was even experimenting with jazz effects as heard on "Jingle, Jangle, Jingle," and "Ole Buttermilk
Sky." Kyser's early success was actually based on his network radio show, in which
he played games based on the titles of songs. Known as the "College of Musical
Knowledge," it provided much fun through the dreary days of the Depression.
         A wide variety of tunes and styles can be found on this Columbia reissue,
which comes with a good set of liner notes and virtually complete discographic
data. Naturally, his theme—"Thinking of You"—is here, as well as his biggest
success, Frank Loesser's "Praise the Lord and Pass the Ammunition" (which,
incidentally, was arranged over the telephone, and recorded the next day). Novelties
include the performance of trumpeter Merwyn Bogue (under his stage name,
Ishkabibble), the "Woody Woodpecker Song," "Three Little Fishes," and "Strip

Polka." Kyser's sound developed through consistency, as his personnel seldom changed over sixteen years. His male vocalist was usually Harry Babbitt, and he ran through a succession of female singers (including Jane Russell, heard on "As Long As I Live"). After Babbitt's tenure, other personable crooners such as Mike Douglas ("The Old Lamplighter") appeared. Kyser was the first to introduce the vocalist over the opening bars of the music, and this effect created an image of the singer, and even enhanced his/her ability to step out in front of the band as a distinct personality. Despite being firmly in the second rank of big band orchestras, Kyser's group brought a great deal of contemporary feeling to the music of the day, some of which does not wear too well today.

P5.37*   **Guy Lombardo and His Royal Canadians. Sweetest Music This Side of Heaven.** two discs. Decca MCA2-4041.
     This set captures the essence of the originator of the "soft" danceable music that crass commercializers have turned into modern day Muzak. The 48 tunes here are reflective of the over 100,000,000 records sold by Lombardo. Beginning with nine members in 1921 in London, Canada, the group crossed to the United States and got their first break with a radio broadcast that began in 1927 and continued for many years. In 1929, they began a 33-year "winter" stay at New York's Roosevelt Grill. They were very popular on radio, being selected for over a dozen years as the "number one" orchestra by radio people. During World War II, Lombardo introduced many popular songs (albeit because of a dearth that resulted from conscription; Lombardo's orchestra members were too old to be drafted!). Because of their unique sound (involving saxophones and clarinets) and permanence (quite a few of the band members are Lombardo relatives or in-laws), the band was able to capture any song and render it in their style over and over—they never changed throughout the years. Songs here (with vocals by Carmen Lombardo, Jimmie Brown, Don Rodney, Kenny Gardner, and various trio ensembles) include such originals as "Coquette," "Sweethearts on Parade," "Boo-Hoo," and "Seems Like Old Times." Novelties included "I'm My Own Grandpaw," "Enjoy Yourself," and "Swingin' in a Hammock." Classical music inspired "Humoresque" and "Tales of the Vienna Woods," and there are other selections as well from the world of jazz. The late Lombardo's band was great for New Year's Eve celebrations and he thus became an American tradition.

P5.38   **Vincent Lopez. The Swingin' Sweet Bands, v.1.** Swing Era LP 1007.
     Lopez, who died near the end of 1975, led his first band in 1916. His radio show was widely known throughout the 1920s and early 1930s. As did Paul Whiteman, Lopez always encouraged his sidemen to better themselves (which they did; and eventually, many left to form their own bands). These included Glenn Miller, Charlie Spivak, and Artie Shaw. Betty Hutton sings with this version of the Lopez band, and the tracks here include "Dark Eyes," "Blue Moon," and "Blowing Bubbles."

P5.39*   **Glenn Miller. Complete, v.1,2,3,+ (1938-1942).** [in progress, probably twenty discs.] RCA Bluebird AXM2-5512, 5514 (v.1 and 2); AXM2-5534 (v.3).

Glenn Miller means many different things to many people. To some jazz fans, he was one of the leaders of the big band swing movements. To musicians, he was an ideal leader who had captured a unique sound by means of his sterling arrangements. To most people, his orchestra was one of the best dance bands in the nation. To all of them, though, there is the experience of incredibility felt when one considers his very brief career and of nostalgia felt in many attempts to recapture that brief past. The immediate pre-war period in American history is firmly fixed in most minds as the time that the Depression was licked, "swing" was king, and the last time in American history that a carefree nonchalant air pervaded the United States. The impact of the Miller band was comparable to the impact of Basie's and Ellington's, except this wouldn't last since Miller had only five years before he died. However, three of those years (1940-1942) saw him on top and in 1940, one out of every three jukebox plays was a Glenn Miller song.

The above compilation is the best and most ambitious of the Miller anthologies. For too long, RCA has been putting out his material in North America in jumbled fashion, and often with electronic or false stereo. This RCA Bluebird effort will eventually finish at around twenty records, and it will contain all of the Miller band's RCA studio recordings—in chronological order and in monophonic sound. Its acquisition, though, need only be made by avid fans and the larger music libraries, for there are many "great hits" issues of Miller band material available.

Miller's ascendancy was keyed into his arranging ability. For years, he was a session musician like the Dorseys, Mannie Klein, Teagarden, and Goodman. By experimenting with reed sounds, and replacing the lead trumpet with a clarinet (a novel idea then), Miller achieved his lush, full sound. Borrowing a leaf from the black swing bands, Miller also imployed the riff. He had excellent service and continuity from saxist Tex Beneke, who also sang on the novelty selections; Marion Hutton and Ray Eberle, the band vocalists; and, of course, the Modernaires (singing group). Each of these sets has 32 tracks beginning with such early material as "My Reverie" and "And the Angels Sing"; carrying on through his first big hit, "Little Brown Jug," to "Moonlight Serenade," "Sunrise Serenade," and "Tuxedo Junction"; and going to later items, such as "Handful of Stars." Good notes, good sound, and (in the case of the early years) good jazz—all are here.

P5.40   **Glenn Miller. Remember Glenn.** two discs. 20th Century Records T-904.

Most of the material here has been issued before in either the original or later versions. There are twenty cuts, originally Movietone S 72018 and MTM 1003. But there is a difference here. All of the Miller items come to us from film soundtracks and, hence, are very superior in sound quality to other reissues from RCA. And, of course, we get the original of "Sun Valley Jump" and "It Happened in Sun Valley."

P5.41   **Glenn Miller. Sunrise Serenade.** two discs. RCA Camden CXS-9004(e).
     This is a superb collection of Miller material from 1938-1942; the eighteen selections are mostly pop hits and dance ballads. In the beginning, Miller covered hits originated by other bands. A good example here is Ray Eberle's vocal version of "And the Angels Sing," originally a hit for both Ziggy Elman and Benny Goodman around 1939. But Miller's unorthodox arranging approach—which focused on the reed section (high clarinet over the top of the saxophones, letting it play lead with the tenor sax)—had a romantic effect on both listeners and dancers alike. To know that some of these tunes are potent, one need go no further than 1939's "Sunrise Serenade," "Moon Love," and "To You." The singing of the Modernaires (Miller's back-up chorus) was so enthusiastic that it kicked along the main vocalists, notably Tex Beneke, the saxist who could also sing. (He's heard here on the definitive versions of "Juke Box Saturday Night" and "Three Little Fishes," along with Marion Hutton.) Wartime successes noted here include "The White Cliffs of Dover" and "A Nightingale Sang in Berkeley Square," both renditions being ably performed by Ray Eberle, who had one of the "sweetest" voices of the male big band vocalists. The tunes on this album are especially reflective of the fact that Glenn Miller's band was first a popular dance band that concentrated on pop hits.

P5.42   **Ozzie Nelson. 1936-1941.** Bandstand BS 7119.
     Nelson was a successful bandleader before he turned to radio and humor. Harriet Hilliard (of ". . . and Harriet" fame) was the band's featured vocalist, singing in a lilting style with a somewhat husky voice. Titles here include "Swamp Fire," "Streamline Strut," "I'm Looking for a Guy," "Josephine," "Soliloquy," and "The Man Who Comes Around."

P5.43   **George Oleson and His Music.** RCA LPV 549.
     Oleson material covers such a wide range that it is very indicative of the jazz age: dance halls, ballrooms, radio, and Ziegfeld show recreations. Of special interest here are tracks with Fred MacMurray in his early vocal years (before becoming an actor), especially on "After a Million Dreams."

P5.44*   **Jan Savitt. The Top Hatters, 1939-1941.** Decca DL 79243.
     Savitt's ensemble was typical of the many swinging big bands that developed on the scene after Benny Goodman's group had opened many doors. These fourteen selections are some of the more popular items that the band recorded. Some leading jazz performers were with Savitt, including Cutty Cutshall on trumpet. But it is all mannered music that is reflective of its time, such as "720 in the Books," "It's a Wonderful World," "Rose of the Rio Grande," and "Green Goon Jive." This is one of the better of the big bands that compromised between dance and swing music.

P5.45*   **Artie Shaw. The Complete, v.1+ (1938-1947).** [in progress, probably sixteen discs.] RCA Bluebird AXM2-5517+ (v.1+).

P5.46   Artie Shaw. Free for All. Epic EE 22023.

Artie Shaw's has always been regarded as second only to Benny Goodman's when it came to considering clarinet led swing bands. While Goodman may have had the fluency of the clarinet and better arrangements, Shaw had a more modern sound and was closely listened to by the first of the be-boppers. His arrangers were more interested in *shading* than in building to the riff climaxes found in swing. He experimented a great deal, particularly for his Victor recordings (employing Latin rhythms and strings, for instance). His early recordings for Brunswick are on the Epic release above, which presents a mixture of one of his staples—show tunes ("All Alone," "Night and Day," "Blue Skies," et al.)—and originals ("The Chant," "Nightmare," "Freewheeling," "Non-Stop Flight," and the title selection). At this time, all arrangements were by Shaw himself.

With show tunes came an encouragement to lyricism, and his music was further characterized by a firm beat, relaxed solos, and regimentation in the ensemble passages. The RCA sets document the popular flavor, with vocals by Tony Pastor, Billie Holiday, Helen Forrest, and Lena Horne. Big production numbers include "Begin the Beguine," "Indian Love Call," "Frenesi," "Star Dust," "Temptation," "Carioca" and " 'S Wonderful" ("Nightmare" will be found on the Epic set). During many "retirement-vacations" from recording and performing, Shaw came up with new devices, which included "Concerto for Clarinet," a nine-and-a-half minute attempt to embrace classical influences.

P5.46a*   Ted Weems. 1928-1930. The Old Master TOM 23.

Weems was probably the best of the American dance band leaders in the period immediately before and during the first years of the Depression. Of the many records he made, his best come from Victor between 1923 and 1933. Unfortunately, he was just ahead of his time and ahead of the swing bands. Masterful selections here include "Talk of the Town," "What a Day!," "The Glory of Spring" (with Frank Munn, vocal), and the sweet voice of Parker Gibbs on "Who Wouldn't Be Blue?," and "You're the Cream in My Coffee."

Post-War

P5.47   Les Brown and His Band of Renown. Sentimental Journey. Columbia CL 649.

P5.48   Les Brown and His Band of Renown. Best. two discs. MCA2-4070.

P5.49   Martin Denny. Exotica, v.1-3. three discs. Liberty 7006, 7034, 7116.

P5.50   Webley Edwards. Best of Hawaii Calls. Capitol SM 141.

P5.51   Webley Edwards. Hawaii Calls' Greatest Hits. Capitol ST 1339.

P5.52   Les Elgart. Greatest Dance Band in the Land. CBS Encore 13168.

P5.53   Ferrante and Teicher. Our Golden Favorites. United Artists UAS 6556.

P5.54   Jackie Gleason. **Close Up**. two discs. Capitol 255.

P5.55   Morton Gould. **Jungle Drums**. RCA LSC 1994.

P5.56   Ted Heath. **21st Anniversary Album**. London PS 535.

P5.57   Eddie Heywood. **Canadian Sunset**. RCA LSP 1529.

P5.58   Gordon Jenkins. **Best**. two discs. MCA2-4078.

P5.59   Sammy Kaye. **Best**. two discs. MCA2-4027.

P5.60   Sammy Kaye. **Best**. two discs. RCA VPM 6070.

P5.61   Hal Kemp. **Great Dance Bands**. RCA LPM 2041.

P5.62   Entry deleted.

P5.63   Wayne King. **Best**. two discs. MCA2-4022.

P5.64   Wayne King. **Best**. RCA LSP 3742.

P5.65   Andre Kostelanetz. **Broadway's Greatest**. Columbia CS 8627.

P5.66   Andre Kostelanetz. **Wonderland of Hits**. Columbia CS 8839.

P5.67   Enoch Light and the Light Brigade. **12 Smash Hits**. Project 3 S 5021.

P5.68   Paul Mauriat. **Blooming Hits**. Philips 600.248.

P5.69   Billy May. **Sorta-May**. Capitol M562.

P5.70   Russ Morgan. **Best**. two discs. MCA2-4036.

P5.71   Frank Pourcel. **Only You**. Capitol M578.

P5.72   Nelson Riddle. **Greatest Hits**. Capitol SM622.

P5.73   David Rose. **Holiday for Strings**. MGM S 3215.

P5.74   David Rose. **The Stripper**. MGM S 4062.

P5.75   Lawrence Welk. **Best**. two discs. Coral 757455/6.

P5.76   Hugo Winterhalter. **Best**. RCA ANL1-2483.

The above records have in common the fact that the conductors are actually also the arrangers and strive for a full, lush sound. Consequently, this combined annotation deals with various styles of arranging popular songs, but all have the lush sound as a base. Les Brown's has one of the better track records of the groups whose annotations are combined into this one large annotation, despite his having had only one major hit: "Sentimental Journey." The twenty tunes on the MCA compilation also include "From This Moment On," "Mexican Hat Dance," and "Dream." Martin Denny began as a member of a jazz quartet in Hawaii, but since then, he broadened his approach to perform a unique blending of Hawaiian and Oriental sounds, including bird calls, the pounding of surf, tinkling noises (from glasses and bamboo sticks), and other devices.

On a larger scale, Webley Edwards is perhaps better known through his having had a radio program "Hawaii Calls." In fact, his records and program may have been the only exposure to lush romantic Hawaiian music that many listeners ever experienced ("Blue Hawaii," "Hawaiian Wedding Song," "My Isle of Golden Dreams").

Trumpeter Les Elgart led his 1950s band (as recorded here) through a light and airy period while fulfilling the demands for dances on the college circuit. The bland, watered-down arrangements (originally conceived by Bill Finegan and Nelson Riddle) were exceptionally popular. Brother Larry led the saxes.

Ferrante and Teicher, although a piano duo, qualify here by virtue of the big band setting that they employ. Their biggest successes lay in movie themes ("Exodus" and "The Apartment"), and they also covered other themes sung by vocalists, such as "Tonight" and "Midnight Cowboy." Jackie Gleason was primarily an arranger and conductor. His material was noted for mood settings and the brilliant horn of trumpeter Bobby Hackett.

Morton Gould, long known as a classical composer, also composed, arranged and conducted light music that was once known as "the Gould touch." Ted Heath's unit developed from the dance bands of England to become the leading band in post-war United Kingdom, emphasizing swing music, Latin rhythms, strings, and brass effects.

Eddie Heywood was with Benny Carter in 1939 and accompanied Billie Holiday later. His highly structured jazz led naturally to arranged pop music, and he was responsible for a number of hits, including "Soft Summer Breeze," "Begin the Beguine," and "The Man I Love." Gordon Jenkins was a studio arranger and conductor for MCA, largely responsible for the Weavers' first "pop" successes. He can be heard accompanying many of MCA's top singers through the late forties and early fifties, as well as giving his own interpretations of "P.S., I Love You," "Secret Love," "My Funny Valentine," "Dark Eyes," and "Linda."

Sammy Kaye was noted for his "swing and sway" music, and over a long period of time with both RCA and MCA, he recorded such danceable music as "To Each His Own," "Oh, Johnny, Oh, Johnny, Oh!," the hit "I'm Looking over a Four Leaf Clover," "I Understand," "It Isn't Fair," "Daddy," and "Everywhere You Go." Hal Kemp's organization from the 1930s and 1940s (this RCA material is from 1937-1940) was one of the few imitators that successfully crossed the bridge from swing to dance music ("A Foggy Day in London Town," "The Breeze and I," "S'posin' ").

Wayne King was noted for his waltzes. By 1936, his immensely popular radio show had the entire nation dancing in their living rooms to such epics as "The Waltz You Saved for Me" (his theme), "Blue Hours," "Cornsilk," "Melody of Love," "Josephine," and "So Close to Me."

Andre Kostelanetz was a classically trained conductor, arranger, and composer for CBS. He has an enviable record of having sold over thirty million discs since beginning recording in 1940. His light classical, or pop, music beginning with his 1931 radio show, emphasized echo chamber effects and the use of massed strings.

Enoch Light presented tasteful dance music, and his Light Brigade was well-disciplined in the European dance tradition. The band was immensely popular as a New York City operation on a par with the many hotel bands.

Paul Mauriat performs in the tradition of a pianist-led group, emphasizing pleasing melodies around some easy harmonic structure, such as "Love Is Blue" and "Love in Every Room." Billy May started off with jazz, but later he became a superb arranger and conductor for Capitol records. He was directly responsible for some of Frank Sinatra's greatest successes, such as the *Come Dance with Me* album. Of note is his success with the theme from "Man with the Golden Arm," a movie that starred Sinatra.

Russ Morgan became popular as a re-interpreter of such tunes as the 1955 "Dogface Soldier" and the 1956 "Poor People of Paris," as well as "Does Your Heart Beat for Me?" and "The Trail of the Lonesome Pine." Frank Pourcel, another Capitol arranger, emphasized the usual lush strings, and produced the 1959 hit "Only You" (instrumental version).

Nelson Riddle arranged for Frank Sinatra, and when the latter formed Reprise, he took Riddle with him. He, too, concentrated on themes, most notably from "The Proud Ones" and "Route 66." In the 1950s, he was responsible for "Lisbon Antigua" and the follow-up "Port Au Prince." David Rose has done many scores for movies (mostly MGM films) and has acted as musical arranger since the mid-fifties for MGM records. His brazen 1962 rendition of "The Stripper" led to a revival of his music, leading to "Swingin' Shepherd Blues," "Calypso Melody," "Love Is a Many Splendored Thing," "Our Waltz," and "Big Ben."

Lawrence Welk has had amazing success with his television show, which acts as reinforcement on his record sales. Previous to that, he had led the way at the Aragon Ballroom in Santa Monica for eleven years. His "champagne sound"—a smooth yet bubbling quality—was primarily responsible for his appeal to the older people, and he incorporated many accordion melodies into his performances, especially on the 1960 "Calcutta," the 1956 "Moritat," "Last Date," "Beer Barrel Polka," "Bubbles in the Wine," "Anniversary Waltz," and "Riders in the Sky." Hugo Winterhalter was a staff arranger for RCA. A former teacher and violinist (plus reeds), he joined Larry Clinton's outfit in 1938. He arranged for Billy Eckstine, Claude Thornhill, Vaughan Monroe, and Kate Smith. His major prominence came in the 1950s with a string of major successes in "Canadian Sunset," "Memories of You," the 1950 "Count Every Star," "Blue Tango" and, of course, "The Little Shoemaker."

P5.77*   **Ray Anthony. Hits.** Capitol T 1477.

Anthony was a trumpet player who has been in charge of the house band at Capitol Records since 1950. He did much arranging and producing for the company, and while he never had a real hit, his material was worthy for the unified "sound" projected by a trumpet-led orchestra. Many couples danced to such tunes as "Sentimental Me," "Count Every Star," "Tenderly," and "Harbor Lights." He provided interesting covers for the tune "Harlem Nocturne" and two television show themes, "Dragnet" (1953) and "Peter Gunn" (1959).

P5.78*   **Les Baxter. Baxter's Best.** Capitol ST 1388.

Baxter is an individualist among staff conductors. He is employed by Capitol to do composing, conducting, arranging, and so forth; but he also plays the piano and he sings a little. He produced both Nat King Cole and Yma Sumac for Capitol, thus betraying his widely scattered tastes. Overall, he does tend to lean toward Latin music, but his style varies tremendously, which gives him some originality and respite from staleness. Widely diverse material here includes "Unchained Melody" (1955), "High and Mighty" (1954), and "Poor People of Paris" (1956)— all big selling records at a time before rock and roll. His first success was the 1951 instrumental version of Tony Bennett's "Because of You." Others here include "Wake the Town and Tell the People" (1955) and the 1952 "Blue Tango."

P5.79*   **Percy Faith. All Time Greatest Hits.** two discs. Columbia KG 31588.

Canadian-born Faith began as a CBC staff conductor before moving to CBS in 1940, where he became a staff arranger and conductor, backing such singers as Tony Bennett on "Cold Cold Heart" and "Rags to Riches." On his own, his first instrumental hit was "Delicado" in 1952. Typical music here employs a strong bass, lush strings, and some pronounced rhythm. Occasionally, Faith produced some relatively strong theme music, and these are all collected on the twofer cited above: "I Crossed My Fingers," "Till," "With a Little Bit of Luck," "Valley Valparaiso," and theme from "A Summer Place" and "Moulin Rouge."

P5.80   **Arthur Fiedler and the Boston Pops. Best.** RCA LSC 2810.

P5.81*   **Arthur Fiedler and the Boston Pops. Greatest Hits of the '20s, '30s, '40s, '50s, '60s, and '70s.** six discs. RCA ARL1-0035, ARL1-0041-5.

Of all people in the music industry, Arthur Fiedler is perhaps most responsible for the intrusion of popular music into the concert hall, the concert presentation of popular classic works over the radio, and the production of both on disc. (His British counterpart had been Sir Thomas Beecham, through the British "lollipops" concert series that really only concentrated on popular versions of the classics.) Fiedler gave dignity to a variety of popular tunes by scoring them for symphonic orchestra, then using them for encores or for a whole program devoted to Gershwin, Bacharach, etc. At the same time (like Beecham) he took classical motifs and popularized their more melodic aspects, such as tracing the roots of popular music derived from classical themes (and vice versa, when the classical theme is based on folk music). In the six-disc survey, Fiedler has done the immense job of selecting some 65 or so melodies and freshly recording them as decade surveys, beginning with the 1920s and concluding with a premature album on the 1970s (recorded in 1972-1973, this disc can hardly be representative, as there is no Carole King, Gordon Lightfoot, or even John Denver). Some of his selections might be questionable, such as "Amazing Grace," "Lost Horizon," or "The First Time Ever I Saw Your Face," but all arrangements are performed with élan by the Pops. Fiedler has recorded everything from Bach through the Beatles (more individual pieces than anyone else) and has sold fifty million records.

P5.82　　**Harry James. Greatest Hits.** Columbia CS 943.

P5.83*　　**Harry James. Songs That Sold a Million.** Harmony HL 7191.
　　James has not been treated too well in the reissue business. Some of his early jazz is available, particularly that done with Ben Pollack and Benny Goodman; but his band (created in 1937) had an uneasy balance between showmanship, jazz, and dance music. It seems a characteristic of American big band music that a hot trumpeter failed as a band leader, perhaps because the horn is too shrill or too much a virtuoso instrument to blend in with the rest of the group. Certainly the reedists and trombone players had an easier time of it. With a lack of top-notch sidemen, James's records must be noted only for their brilliance in trumpet playing and the vocals, without the overall mesh of a complete orchestra. These selections, though, all did well for the James outfit: "One O'Clock Jump," "Two O'Clock Jump," "Music Makers," "September in the Rain," the difficult "Flight of the Bumble Bee" (which perhaps sums up all that was right and all that was wrong with the James band), and, of course, "Ciribiribin."

P5.84　　**Harry James. Rhythm Session.** Columbia CL 6088.
　　Trumpeter James was strongly influenced by Louis Armstrong. His brassy style is highly decorative, and this is one reason that he was so successful in 1939, when he stopped playing jazz and embraced commercial music. Prior to that, he had worked with Benny Goodman since 1936, and he is also heard on the 1938-1939 Carnegie Hall sets (e.g., "Sing, Sing Sing"). This present disc is one of his most successful albums, with such nifty tracks as "Record Session," "Crazy Rhythm," and "Jeffries Blues."

P5.85*　　**Bert Kaempfert. Best.** two discs. MCA2-4043.
　　Orchestral arrangements have made or broken many bands, and it is the lush, lively sound of Kaempfert that has kept this German an active seller (millions of records in the U.S. alone) for over a decade. Good sound recording, effective use of echo, a stunning vocal chorus for punctuation, and the various trumpet solos by Fred Moch or Charles Tabor—all of these combined to give Kaempfert's orchestra a "sound" that set it off from the rest of instrumental music. He penned many of his hits himself, and thus they were not the tried and true standards that are usually guarantees of success. His efforts included "Afrikaan Beat," "Spanish Eyes," "L-O-V-E," "Danke Schoen," "Stranger in the Night," and "A Swingin' Safari." Other tunes that helped his success were "Wonderland by Night" (the first hit for the band), "Red Roses for a Blue Lady," and "That Happy Feeling." His German outfit was recorded in Germany (where so much good dance music comes from), and this ensured the highest possible technical perfection in reproduction.

P5.86*　　**James Last. This Is James Last.** Polydor 104.678.
　　Master of the non-stop dancing syndrome (which he invented), James Last and his German (and German-recorded, for that highly perfected sound reproduction) band have produced about three or four records a year for over a decade (and have sold millions in the U.S.). Each disc has been full of re-interpretations of current popular successes, plus a few of his own. This collection has lifted a few

of the better, more successful efforts that had been released as singles and thus benefitted from airplay on the radio. (The Non-Stop Dancing series, with 25 minutes of dance music per side, wasn't played over the air but was intended for use in the home.) His more popular tunes include versions of "Greensleeves," "Yesterday," "Sail along Silv'ry Moon," "April in Portugal," and "American Patrol."

P5.87   **Freddy Martin. Hits.** Capitol ST 1582.

P5.88   **Freddy Martin. Best.** two discs. MCA2-4080.
    Martin was a saxophonist who led a good dance band. His main and most important contribution to popular music was in fashioning unique numbers by borrowing heavily from classical themes, such as on "Tonight We Love" (based on Tchaikovsky's Piano Concerto No. 1), "Warsaw Concerto," "Flight of the Bumble Bee" (from Rimsky-Korsakov), "Grieg Piano Concerto in A Minor," plus others. As if to make up for this, he also captured some of the novelty market with "The Hut Sut Song," "Why Don't We Do This More Often?," and "I've Got a Lovely Bunch of Coconuts."

P5.89*   **Claude Thornhill. At Glen Island Casino, 1941.** Monmouth-Evergreen MES 7024.

P5.90*   **Claude Thornhill. On Stage, 1946/47.** Monmouth-Evergreen MES 7025.
    Pianist and arranger Claude Thornhill got his first break by playing at the Casino, which quite rightly was called the "cradle of name bands," for Ozzie Nelson, Glen Gray, the Dorsey Brothers, Larry Clinton, Glenn Miller, and Charlie Spivak got their starts or played extensive engagements there. Material on MES 7024 comes from OKeh and Columbia discs of the time, but it was not similar to what then was played at the Casino, for there was an ASCAP recording ban at the time. Thus, early BMI, traditional, or public domain (P.D.) classics were recorded (e.g., "Humoresque," "Hungarian Dance, No. 5," "Stack of Barley," "Le Papillon," and "O Sole Mio"). The only good that came out of the ban was the flowering of semi-classics as mood and dance music. Personnel at this time included Rusty Derick and Irving Fazola, with Dick Harding handling the vocals. Also here is the early version of his theme, "Snowfall."
    After fighting in the War, he reorganized, but it was difficult, as big bands were going out of fashion, and single vocalists were all the rage. MES 7025 comes from a concert of lush sounds arranged by Gil Evans (e.g., "Early Autumn" and "A Sunday Kind of Love"—both with superb and underrated vocals by Fran Warren). Also, there is some solo jazz writing for Lee Konitz and Red Rodney. Evans looked after "La Paloma," a superb six-minute rendition of the Spanish offering in a unified style that was to crop up again on Evans's own *La Nevada* album for Impulse years later. By 1948, this Thornhill sound was used by Evans for the great nine-member unit lead by Miles Davis. Of the two discs, the first is for big band enthusiasts (the material was a field day for arrangers), while the second, an important document of the era's musical transitions, is of great historical value.

P5.91*   **Billy Vaughan. Golden Hits.** Dot 25201.

P5.92   **Billy Vaughan. Sail along, Silvery Moon.** Dot 25100.
  Vaughan was once a singing member of the Hilltoppers vocal group, but he left in 1955 to become artist and repertoire man for Dot, and then to be their musical arranger. He put together an incredibly successful studio group, largely around saxophones and percussion, and this was one of the first of the studio groups with a distinctive sound. Later would come James Last and Bert Kaempfert (both German). Some of the single hits that Vaughan created here include the title selection of 25100, plus "Blue Hawaii," "Melody of Love," "Shifting, Whispering Sands," the important "Cimarron," the theme from *A Summer Place*, "Wheels," and "La Paloma." This was a great studio band to which to dance.

BRITISH DANCE BANDS

Anthologies

P5.93*   **The Golden Age of British Dance.** two discs. World Record Club
   SH 118/9 (British issue).
  This is a "greatest hits" type of compilation covering the late twenties and early thirties. Most of the tracks are available on other World Record Club sets. The dance band leaders include Roy Fox, Ray Noble, Harry Roy, and Lew Stone.

Standards

P5.94*   **Ambrose and His Orchestra.** two discs. World Record Club SHB 21
   (British issue).
  This EMI material reflects the best of perhaps the best live British upper crust dance band. Ambrose held down the job at London's Mayfair Hotel from 1927-1934, and, being a perfectionist, he disciplined the band itself to perfection as the finest orchestra for dancing to in Europe. He had great help from two Americans he recruited: the trumpeter Sylvester Ahola and the saxophonist Danny Polo. Ted Heath came out of this unit, and Sid Phillips and Lew Stone were among the arrangers. Indicative titles include " 'Leven-Thirty Saturday Night," which was hailed as a masterpiece even by jazz critics; the tender "A Japanese Dream"; the sombre "Moanin' for You"; and, of course, the ultra-sophisticated "Pu-leeze! Mister Hemingway" (the young lady here comments that a chaperone would be in order when dealing with the passionate Hemingway in this item that seems almost like a 1932 *New Yorker* cartoon). The proficient and adept Sam Browne sings most of the vocals (usually just a refrain). Brian Rust contributes good notes.

P5.95   **Bert Firman. 1925-1931.** two discs. World Record Club SHB 30
   (British issue).
  Firman was a pioneer broadcaster who forged the way for the British dance bands through his arrangements. Featuring such performers as Maurice Elwin on

vocals and Ted Heath on trombone, he promoted the idea of hot closing choruses ("Five Foot Two") rather than a simple fade out for the dancers, advanced drumming ("Spanish Shawl"), piano duets (Fletcher Henderson's "Stampede"), and muted trumpets throughout. In a period with few (if any) exclusive contracts, Firman employed many top American musicians and top London talent for his recording ventures, which created a sharp pool of performers for other bands to draw on. The 32 tracks here were recorded under a variety of names, such as Carlton Hotel Dance Orchestra, the Cabaret Novelty Orchestra, the Devonshire Restaurant Dance Band ("Sax Appeal," "Up Jumped the Devil"), the Arcadians Dance Orchestra ("Sentimental Baby," "Ain't Misbehavin' "), and the Rhythmic Eight (for more jazzy numbers such as "Mississippi Mud" and "Diga, Diga Doo"). Throughout, Firman's talented violin alternately played sweet and hot.

P5.96   **Roy Fox. The Bands That Matter.** Eclipse ECM 2045 (British issue).
        Fox was an American by birth, but he had his most successes in England as leader of a very successful dance band orchestra. One of his keys was using "hot" musicians, such as trumpeter Nat Gonella. Songs that became associated with him include "Whispering," "Yes, Yes," "My Sweet Virginia," and "Drowsy Blues."

P5.97   **Carroll Gibbons. 1931-1948.** two discs. World Records SH 167/8
        (British issue).
        Boston-born Gibbons found success equal to that of Fox. His sleepy voice in the vocals on his records made him a British radio star in the 1930s and 1940s. Officially, he was Director of Light Music for the Gramophone Company, and he directed a number of bands that were exclusively for studio sessions and did not perform in public (such as the New Mayfair Dance Orchestra). The selections on this double disc are all derived from his work with the Savoy Hotel Orpheans.

P5.98*   **Jack Hylton and His Orchestra, v.1/2.** two discs. Monmouth/Evergreen
        MES 7033/7055.
        British dance bands in the thirties were definitely better than their American counterparts. The U.S. had "dance bands" and "swing bands" to which the public could dance one way or the other. But the swing units were a late thirties' development and came out of a jazz tradition that was essentially lacking in England. Save for Paul Whiteman's, U.S. white dance bands were pretty thin, while their black counterparts were classed as "jungle music" and were held back in places such as Harlem or the Southwest. English groups assimilated jazz and made it palatable for dancing with a touch of rhythm to it.
        Hylton was a flamboyant showman, the top stage (club) and radio attraction in the British Isles and Europe. Ted Heath came out of his band; and while in the United States, Hylton discovered the Merry Macs and had Fletcher Henderson write arrangements for him. All of the material here comes from HMV, and was recorded mostly from 1928 to 1931, with some from 1935-1936. Of his vast repertoire, these 24 songs accurately reflect the mixture of jazz and dance (he sold 3,180,000 records in 1929 alone!). Characterized by cascading trumpets, effective ensemble passages, and a good use of mutes, Hylton's music swept through the dance floors of the world. He produced such items as the novelty "Kings'

Horses" (veddy British, with fey lyrics), a series of medleys from Charrell's
White Horse Inn (1931), and even jazz like "Tiger Rag" and "Limehouse Blues."

P5.99*   **Mantovani. All Time Greatest.** London XP5 906.

P5.100*   **Mantovani. Golden Hits.** London PS 483.

P5.101*   **Mantovani. 25th Anniversary Album.** London XPS 610.
   [Annunzio Paolo] Mantovani, classically trained as a pianist and violinist,
is *the* most important shaper of modern mood music. At age seventeen, he led
a noted orchestra; within a few years, he was leading his own dance band in Britain.
Employing lush strings and classical motifs, he created a particular "sound" that
was often emulated. Over the past 25 years, his more spectacular successes have
included "Charmaine" (1951), "Theme from Moulin Rouge" (1953), "Around the
World" (1957), and "Exodus" (1961). His heavily stylized treatment—he was largely
responsible for the violin "sweetening" in modern musical arrangements—is clearly
applicable in such items as "Maria," "Moon River," and "They Say It's Wonderful."

P5.102*   **Ray Noble and Al Bowlly, v.1-6.** six discs. Monmouth/Evergreen
           MES 6816, 7021, 7027, 7039, 7040, 7056.
   For Ray Noble, these were the pre-Charlie McCarthy days. Here he led the
HMV house band (known since 1929 as the New Mayfair Orchestra) and recorded
dance music, show music, novelties, and jazz. His was mainly a studio band; it
hardly ever played in public. And he was low in the pecking order at HMV, taking
the next-to-last choice of existing material. His band was composed of largely
unfamiliar performers, perhaps the most notable being trumpeter Nat Gonella.
Other dance bands—led by Roy Fox, Lewis Stone, Ambrose, or Jack Hylton—
had gimmicks and public awareness on their side. Yet, in retrospect, Noble's band
emerges as the best of the British dance bands on record, and these 93 tracks
(1930-1934) plus one 1936 medley are among the best recordings of his career.
   How did all this delayed respect come about? For one thing, Noble was
forced to write his own songs and arrange all of the band's materials. Thus, he
performed some of the most enduring melodies of all time—"Goodnight, Sweetheart," "Love Is the Sweetest Thing," "By the Fireside," "The Very Thought
of You," and "Cherokee" (all are here except the last). For another, his band
was composed of four reeds, four rhythm, three violins, and three to five brass,
which produced *rich*, mellow shadings from a personnel configuration not used
by other dance bands. Third, he used a carbon mike, surrounded by the whole
orchestra in a circle, which gave everyone equal access to a piece of equipment that
topped off the acute highs and smoothed out the bass. Fourth, he always had
superb drumming (especially on "Sailin' on the Robert E. Lee"). Fifth, the arrangements were a smooth blend of sections, with varied ensemble textures that heavily
influenced Glenn Miller. And sixth, but not last, the fourth rhythm player was
a guitarist who could sing—Al Bowlly—and could he sing! This Portuguese-East
African possessed an excellent voice, one superbly set *within* the orchestra. His
intonation and phrasing were dazzling for any song but, of course, he was at his
best on the romantic tunes. Some of the great songs in this collection are Cole
Porter or Noel Coward tunes. Benny Carter's "Blues in My Heart" gets a good

outing, as well as "Maybe It's Because," "Lazy Days," "How Could We Be Wrong?," "Here Lies Love," "Close Your Eyes," and the exceptional "Time on My Hands" (with well-pointed brass and reeds). Much discographic data and many personal reminiscences are to be found throughout the series.

P5.103   **Jack Payne.** World Records SH 143 (British issue).
    Payne led the BBC Dance Orchestra over the airwaves and in the studio as well. He created hundreds of records, on which Ray Noble did most of the arrangements. Payne was noted as a vocalist as well. Items here include "Everybody Dance," "My Dance," "Lazy Rhythm," and "Now's the Time to Fall in Love."

P5.104   **Lew Stone. The Bands That Matter.** Eclipse ECM 2047 (British issue).

P5.105   **Lew Stone. Presenting, 1934/1935.** two discs. World Records SH 177/8
    (British issue).
    Stone has been acknowledged by other musicians as having the best band of all the British dance bands, despite the fact that other bands sold more records. He was primarily an arranger, although he did play piano. Tracks here that have significance include "Tiger Rag," "Milenburg Joys," "Canadian Capers," "As Long As I Live," "Call of the Freaks," "Etude," and "Shades of Hades." As one can see, most are dance band versions of American Dixieland classics; but they work rather well.

LATIN DANCE MUSIC

P5.106   **Stanley Black. The Latin World of Stanley Black.** Decca SPA 265
    (British issue).

P5.106a*   **Carmen Cavallaro. Best.** two discs. MCA2-4056.

P5.107*   **Xavier Cugat. Best.** two discs. MCA2-4072.

P5.108   **Xavier Cugat. Best.** Mercury 60870.

P5.109   **Xavier Cugat. Cugat Cavalcade.** Columbia CS 8055.

P5.110   **Perez Prado. Best.** RCA LSP 3732.

P5.111   **Edmundo Ros. Dancing with Ros.** London PS 205.

P5.112*   **Edmundo Ros. Rhythms of the South.** London PS 114.
    There is no denying that much of the originality of Latin music is lost in its translation into American popular music. The earlier material by any Latin musician who later becomes famous in America is bound to be more "authentic" and reliable than later efforts that have suffered from American production values and over-commercialization. Almost any band that has recorded in Latin America would present a more truthful reflection on that kind of music; however, it is the intent

of this section of the book to relate the impact that such music has had on *American* popular music, and to use the recorded examples cited above as perhaps being the best of the available lot. Modern Latin music has since turned to "salsa," available on such labels as the New York-based Fania, and commented on in *Record World* each week. (This music is a combination of soul, blues, and Latin rhythms; but, obviously, it does not fit into this particular annotation except to mention it in passing.) The ten discs here perhaps accurately show where Latin rhythms have intruded both into big band setups and into the mainstream of American popular music.

Stanley Black probably comes closest to being the best of the British, non-Latin orchestral conductors who were successful in interpreting this style. Carmen Cavallaro had the longest run of successes in America, including, on this 24-track MCA compilation, his version of Chopin's "Polonaise," "Brazil," "Frenesi," "The Lady Is a Tramp," "Dolores My Own," and the ubiquitous but haunting "Padam . . . Padam."

The Cugat material chosen here is a later recording, within the stereo mode. With his nightly radio broadcasts, this rhumba king was responsible for first making Latin American rhythms part of the United States scene: tangos, rhumbas, congas. He recorded for many companies, and his tunes of interest include "Rancho Grande," "Mama Inez," "Babalu," "Oye Negra," "Cu-Cu-Cu-Paloma," "Taboo," "Peanut Vendor," and the "Jewish Wedding Song."

Perez Prado was unique in that he was a big success in his own country many, many years before breaking into the North American market. He was born in Cuba, but called himself the "mambo king" (this dance developed in Mexico but spread around Latin America). On his RCA recordings, he pioneered the sound of soaring trumpets and an organ. On the RCA International series, he began his successes in Latin America in 1947. In the fifties, his material was released in the United States, beginning with "Cherry Pink and Apple Blossom White," a French ballad with Latin rhythms added. This was followed by "Patricia," "Cuban Mambo," "Guaglione" (an Italian melody), and "Que Rico el Mambo."

Edmundo Ros had recorded and played widely in Britain, a country that takes Latin music to its heart on a regular basis and in a steady diet (unlike the peaks and troughs of popularity of the United States).

STAGE AND FILM

INTRODUCTION

Musical comedies are a minority's music—there are no legions of fans. Yet, the musical stage has provided many American standard songs. The capture of musical comedies for the home or for extended listening only came about just before the age of long playing albums. We do not propose to recite here a history of the musical in America, but rather we take note of a number of facts. First, the British recording industry had recorded stage shows as early as 1921, promoting and selling them as packages on several related 78 rpm discs. This did not occur in the United States until Decca (in 1943) recorded and promoted as a special package the first stage show with the original cast—most (not all) of *Oklahoma!* In January

1950, Decca scored another first by releasing the first album of a movie score (*For Whom the Bell Tolls*). In the sections that follow, we have listed the albums by title of show, film, etc., and have deliberately not ranked one against the other; consequently, *shows are not asterisked.*

There is obviously a difference in writing styles between the "popular song" and the "show tune." The latter becomes a "good" song only if it relates to the story by creating the proper mood, by revealing character, or by advancing the action. At all costs, the stage show in its entirety comes first. That it might have potential as a "popular song" is a credit to a song's durability and success, but it should be pointed out that the most successful "show tunes" have been tunes only—the music as an instrumental selection, a dance, or a jazz piece (particularly in the bop and cool periods, where the jazzman could find hidden harmonies). This is because the "show tune" of 32 bars is not fragmented into four 8 bar passages as is the popular song but rather into two 16 bar units that allow for longer melodic lines, more complex chord sequences, and rhythmic patterns. Both this harmonic structure and the specialized content of the lyrics mitigates against public acceptance of the vast majority of "show tunes."

Literature

As opposed to that of most "popular" music, the literature of the music of stage and film is over-abundant. Most, however, are just one step above the fanzine "biopix" level: posh coffee table books with many pictures and illustrations. And most deal with one person or with a lyricist-composer team. There are a good number of survey books that cover both stage and film. Green (48) chronicles 1893-1972, with details of stage performances plus details of film sound tracks in addition to original cast and studio productions. Wilder (136) and Wilk (137), although they present biographical details and critical analysis of songwriters generally, give prominence to the stage and film, for this is from where a goodly number of superb compositions have been derived. Smolian (119) has a listing of all recorded versions of film, theater and television music from 1948-1969. Rust (106) while dealing with "entertainers," gives short biographies and details of which films or stage show a recorded song came from.

For the stage (= Broadway), general surveys were written by Baral (2), Engel (30), Mattfield (78), and Green (48). Ewen (33, 34) also mentions the musical theater in his broader surveys, while Smith (118) is devoted exclusively to musical comedies. There are several good reference materials here. Lewine and Simon (67) have a practical encyclopedia, while Laufe (64) gives facts and figures from 1884-1971 as they relate to productions, plot summaries, costume and set designs. The indefatigable Burton (13) covers 1,500 or so musical productions since 1900, while Lewine (66) lists 12,000 songs from 1900-1971 that originated from the theater. Even reviews of musicals can be traced through Salem (109).

Material on the movie musical is more limited in quality. Burton (14) covers 1927-1952 in much the same way as in his Tin Pan Alley and Broadway musical books. Taylor (126) works his way through 275 major films and 1,443 others (plus 2,750 songs).

Film music has not proved as "popular" as movie musicals. Thomas (127) includes scoring for the silent film in addition to coverage to 1971. Limbacher (69) reprints highly significant articles plus various indexes to film titles, composers, years, and discographical details.

Periodicals—as is common with the dance bands—give broad surveys of a nostalgic nature. They rarely comment on modern stage or movie musicals except to give a long review of the sound track recording. *High Fidelity* (6) and *Stereo Review* (10) are the best for these. Film music is less than adequately covered in the diverse magazines of film criticisms. Other citations can be found through the *Popular Music Periodicals Index* (94) and recordings noted through the *Annual Index to Popular Music Record Reviews* (1).

STAGE

Original Casts

P6.1   [Revues.]

Many cabaret songs and revue materials never get on record; other songs from musical comedies are immediately adaptable to revues. The pioneer in this respect is Ben Bagley, an indefatigable producer who has assembled many fine singing casts and has dug up many rare tunes from great composers. His intent was to display the wares as acceptable material, popular but nonetheless still in the mainstream of the theater. The bulk of his work has been released on the Painted Smiles label. The titles appear to be in a standard form, usually with the name of the composer and "Revisited" after it. Thus, he has put together such marvelous albums as *Vernon Duke Revisited* (Painted Smiles 1342), *Rodgers & Hart Revisited* (Painted Smiles 1341/2, two discs), *Noel Coward Revisited* (Painted Smiles 1355), *De Sylva, Brown and Henderson Revisited* (Painted Smiles PS 1351), *Vincent Youmans Revisited* (Painted Smiles PS 1352), and *Arthur Schwartz Revisited* (Painted Smiles PS 1350). All have been moderately successful in terms of revenue and interest generated.

Perhaps his most efforts have been directed to Cole Porter. He put together *Cole Porter Revisited* (Painted Smiles 1340), the *Unpublished Cole Porter* (Painted Smiles 1358), and a set for Columbia entitled *Ben Bagley's The Decline and Fall of the Entire World As Seen through the Eyes of Cole Porter* (Columbia OS 2810). With Kaye Ballard and Harold Lang, no expense was spared to produce such offbeat Porter items as "Make It Another Old Fashioned, Please" or "Most Gentlemen Don't Love." Other Bagley creations include *Alan Jay Lerner Revisited* (Painted Smiles 1337), *Frank Loesser Revisited* (Painted Smiles 1359), *George Gershwin Revisited* (Painted Smiles 1357), and *Harold Arlen Revisited* (Painted Smiles 1345).

P6.2   **Annie Get Your Gun.** (Berlin). Decca DL 79018.

Ethel Merman, Ray Middleton, Marty May, William O'Neal, and Leon Bibb sing the songs: "Doin' What Comes Naturally," "The Girl That I Marry," "There's No Business Like Showbusiness," "They Say It's Wonderful," among others.

P6.3   **The Bandwagon.** (Dietz and Schwartz). RCA LSA 3082 (British issue).
Fred and Adele Astaire, from 1931, record "Dancing in the Dark," "I Love
Louisa," "Where Can He Be?," and "White Heat."

P6.4   **Bells Are Ringing.** (Styne; Comden and Green). Columbia OS 2006.
Judy Holliday, Sydney Chaplin, Eddie Lawrence, and Jean Stapleton perform
"It's a Perfect Relationship," "Is It a Crime?," "Just in Time," and "The Party's
Over."

P6.5   **Bloomer Girl.** (Arlen; Harburg). Decca DL 79126e.
Celeste Holm, Dooley Wilson, David Brooks, and Joan McCracken sing
"When the Boys Come Home," "The Eagle and Me," "Right As the Rain," and
"I Got a Song." Arlen himself does the song "Man for Sale."

P6.6   **Brigadoon.** (Lerner and Loewe). RCA LSO 1001.
David Brooks, Marion Bell, Pamela Britton, and Lee Sullivan perform on
the title selection, "Almost Like Being in Love," "There but for You Go I,"
"Waitin' for My Dearie," etc.

P6.7   **Bye Bye Birdie.** (Strouse and Adams). Columbia KOS 2025.
Members of the cast included Chita Rivera, Dick Van Dyke, Kay Medford,
Paul Lynde, and others singing "One Last Kiss," "One Boy," "Put on a Happy
Face," "Rosie," and "A Lot of Livin' to Do."

P6.8   **Cabaret.** (Kander and Ebb). Columbia KOS 3040.
Jill Haworth, Jack Gilford, Bert Convy, Lotte Lenya, and Joel Grey sing
the title selection, "Willkommen," "Tomorrow Belongs to Me," "Why Should I
Wake Up?," and "Married."

P6.9   **Camelot.** (Lerner and Loewe). Columbia S 32602.
Richard Burton, Julie Andrews, Robert Goulet, and Roddy McDowall perform
the title selection, "C'est Moi," "If Ever I Would Leave You," "What Do the
Simple Folk Do?," etc.

P6.10   **Carmen Jones.** (Bizet; Hammerstein II). Decca DL 79021.
This features Muriel Smith, Luther Saxon, Carlotta Franzell, June Hawkins,
and Cozy Cole. Cole does a drum solo on "Beat out Dat Rhythm on a Drum."

P6.11   **Carousel.** (Rodgers and Hammerstein II). Decca DL 79020.
John Raitt, Jan Clayton, Jean Darling, Bambi Lynn, and others perform
"Carousel Waltz," "If I Loved You," "June Is Bustin' out All Over," and "You'll
Never Walk Alone."

P6.12   **Cowardly Custard.** (Coward). RCA LSO 6010 (two discs).
The Mermaid Theater cast from London—including John Moffat, Patricia
Routledge, and Tudor Davies—perform in "Someday I'll Find You," "You Were
There," "I'll Follow My Secret Heart," "Mad about the Boy," and "Mad Dogs and
Englishmen."

P6.13   **Damn Yankees.** (Adler and Ross). RCA LSO 1021.
Gwen Verdon, Stephen Douglass, Ray Walston, Jean Stapleton, and the
cast sing "Heart," "A Man Doesn't Know," "Whatever Lola Wants," "Near to
You," and "Two Lost Souls."

P6.14   **Do I Hear a Waltz?** (Rodgers and Sondheim). Columbia KOS 2770.
Elizabeth Allen, Sergio Franchi, Carol Bruce, and Madeleine Sherwood
perform the title selection, "Someone Woke Up," "What Do We Do? We Fly!,"
"Someone Like You," and "Take the Moment."

P6.15   **Don't Bother Me, I Can't Cope.** (Grant). Polydor 6013.
Micki Grant, Alex Bradford, Hope Clarke, Arnold Wilkinson, and Bobby
Hill sing contemporary black themes—the title selection, "I Gotta Keep Movin',"
"You Think I Got Rhythm?," and "So Little Time."

P6.16   **The Fantasticks.** (Jones and Schmidt). MGM SE-3872.
Jerry Orbach, Rita Gardner, Kenneth Nelson, and Richard Stauffer perform
"Try to Remember," "Round and Round," "Soon It's Gonna Rain," and "It
Depends on What You Pay."

P6.17   **Fiddler on the Roof.** (Bock and Harnick). RCA LSO 1093.
Zero Mostel, Maria Karnilova, Beatrice Arthur, Joanna Merlin, and Bert
Convy sing "Tradition," "If I Were a Rich Man," "Sunset," and "Do You Love
Me?"

P6.18   **Finian's Rainbow.** (Lane and Harburg). Columbia OS 2080.
Ella Logan, Albert Sharpe, Donald Richards, and David Wayne perform
"This Time of the Year," "If This Isn't Love," "Old Devil Moon," "Necessity,"
and "When I'm Not Near the Girl I Love," among others.

P6.19   **Funny Girl.** (Styne; Merrill). Capitol STAO 2059.
Barbra Streisand, Sydney Chaplin, Danny Meehan, Kay Medford, and Jean
Stapleton sing "I'm the Greatest Star," "People," "You Are Woman," and "Sadie,
Sadie."

P6.20   **Godspell.** (Schwartz). Bell 1102.
Stephan Nathan, David Haskell, Lamar Alford, and Peggy Gordon perform
"Prepare Ye the Way of the Lord," "Save the People," "Day by Day," and "We
Beseech Thee."

P6.24   **The Golden Apple.** (Moross and Latouche). Electra 5000.
Kaye Ballard, Priscilla Gillette, Jack Whitney, and Portia Nelson perform
in this 1953 intellectual musical that translates the *Odyssey* into a story at the
time of the Spanish-American War. It concentrated on the musical themes of
the period (cakewalks and ragtimes). Ballard renders a good "Lazy Afternoon."

P6.22   **Guys and Dolls.** (Loesser). Decca DL 79023.
Robert Alda, Vivian Blaine, Sam Levene, Stubby Kaye, and cast sing "I'll Know," "A Bushel and a Peck," "If I Were a Bell," "More I Cannot Wish You," "Luck Be a Lady," and so forth.

P6.23   **Gypsy.** (Styne and Sondheim). Columbia S32607.
Ethel Merman, Jack Klugman, Sandra Church, Maria Karnilova, and others perform "Let Me Entertain You," "Small World," "Everything's Coming up Roses," and "You Gotta Have a Gimmick."

P6.24   **Hair.** (MacDermot; Ragni and Rado). RCA LSO 1143.
While the more easily-available original Broadway cast recording (RCA LSO 1150) is also recommended, *Hair* began as an Off-Broadway production. The songs here are "Aquarius," "Hare Krishna," "Good Morning, Starshine."

P6.25   **Hello, Dolly!** (Herman). RCA LSOD 1087.
Carol Channing, David Burns, Eileen Brennan, and Sondra Lee sing "It Takes a Woman," "Ribbons down My Back," "Before the Parade Passes By," and the title selection.

P6.26   **House of Flowers.** (Arlen and Capote). Columbia OS 2320.
Pearl Bailey, Diahann Carroll, Juanita Hall, and Ray Walston perform "A Sleepin' Bee," "I'm Gonna Leave off Wearin' My Shoes," "I Never Has Seen Snow," et al.

P6.27   **Jacques Brel Is Alive and Well and Living in Paris.** (Brel, Schuman, Blau). Columbia D2S 779 (two discs).
With Elly Stone and Mort Schuman in a wide-ranging selection of Jacques Brel's music.

P6.28   **Jesus Christ Superstar.** (Webber and Rice). Decca DXSA 7206 (two discs).
This is the original studio version, made before the Broadway show was mounted. Various rock stars and Yvonne Elliman perform the title selection, "What's the Buzz?," "Poor Jerusalem," "Pilate's Dream," and "King Herod's Song," among others.

P6.29   **The King and I.** (Rodgers and Hammerstein II). Decca DL 79008.
Gertrude Lawrence, Yul Brynner, Dorothy Sarnoff, and others sing "I Whistle a Happy Tune," "Hello, Young Lovers," "Getting to Know You," and "Something Wonderful."

P6.30   **Kismet.** (Borodin; Wright and Forrest). RCA LSO 1112.
Alfred Drake, Lee Venora, and Richard Banke perform such tunes as "Stranger in Paradise."

P6.31   **Kiss Me, Kate.** (Porter). Columbia S 32609.
Alfred Drake, Patricia Morison, Harold Lang, and Lisa Kirk star in "Another Op'nin', Another Show," "Wunderbar," "So in Love," "I've Come to Wive It Wealthily in Padua," "Too Darn Hot," and "Always True to You in My Fashion."

P6.32   **Lady in the Dark.** (Weill and Ira Gershwin). RCA LPV 503.
Gertrude Lawrence, Victor Mature, Macdonald Carey, and Danny Kaye sing "Oh, Fabulous One," "One Life to Live," "My Ship," and "Jenny."

P6.33   **Lew Leslie's Blackbirds of 1928.** (McHugh and Fields). Columbia OL6770.
Adelaide Hall and Bill Robinson perform "Diga Diga Doo," "I Can't Give You Anything but Love," and "I Must Have That Man." This reissue is padded out with differing versions by Ethel Waters, the Mills Brothers, Don Redman, Cab Calloway, and Duke Ellington.

P6.34   **A Little Night Music.** (Sondheim). Columbia KS 32265.
Glynis Johns, Len Cariou, and Hermione Gingold engage in "You Must Meet My Wife," "Liaisons," and "Send in the Clowns." This was based on Ingmar Bergman's film, *Smiles of a Summer Night*.

P6.35   **Man of La Mancha.** (Leigh and Darion). Kapp S-4505.
Richard Kiley, Irving Jacobson, and Joan Diener sing the title selection, "Dulcinea," "Little Bird, Little Bird," and "The Impossible Dream."

P6.36   **Most Happy Fella.** (Loesser). Columbia 3L 240 (three discs).
Robert Weede, Jo Sullivan, Art Lund, and Susan Johnson perform the title selection, "Standing on the Corner," "Happy to Make Your Acquaintance," "Big D," and "Warm All Over."

P6.37   **The Music Man.** (Willson). Capitol SW 990.
Robert Preston, Barbara Cook, David Burns, and Helen Raymond sing "Trouble," "Seventy-six Trombones," "Marian the Librarian," and "Till There Was You."

P6.38   **My Fair Lady.** (Lerner and Loewe). Columbia OS 2015.
Rex Harrison, Julie Andrews, and Stanley Holloway, among others, sing "Why Can't the English?," "Wouldn't It Be Loverly?," "With a Little Bit of Luck," "I Could Have Danced All Night," "On the Street Where You Live," et al.

P6.39   **Oklahoma!** (Rodgers and Hammerstein II). Decca DL 79017.
Betty Garde, Alfred Drake, Joan Roberts and Howard Da Silva perform "Oh, What a Beautiful Mornin'," "The Surrey with the Fringe on Top," "People Will Say We're in Love," and, of course, the title selection.

P6.40　　**On a Clear Day (You Can See Forever).** (Lerner and Lane). RCA
　　　　LSOD 2006.
　　Barbara Harris, John Cullum, Titos Vandis, and William Daniels sing the title
selection, "She Wasn't You," "Melinda," and "Come Back to Me."

P6.41　　**Paint Your Wagon.** (Lerner and Loewe). RCA LSO 1006.
　　James Barton, Olga San Juan, and Tony Bavaar perform such songs as "I
Talk to the Trees," "They Call the Wind Maria," "In Between," and "Another
Autumn."

P6.42　　**Pajama Game.** (Adler and Ross). Columbia S 32606.
　　John Raitt, Janis Paige, Eddie Foy, Jr., and Carol Haney sing such songs as
"I'm Not at All in Love," "Hey, There," "Steam Heat," and "Hernando's Hideaway."

P6.43　　**Porgy and Bess.** (George and Ira Gershwin). Decca DL 79024.
　　Todd Duncan and Anne Brown, the original leads in 1935, present on this
1942 revival disc "Summertime," "I Got Plenty of Nothin'," "Bess, You Is My
Woman Now," "It Ain't Necessarily So," et al.

P6.44　　**Primrose.** (Gershwin and Carter). Monmouth/Evergreen MES 7071.
　　With Percy Heming and Leslie Henson, this production was from the Winter
Garden, London, 1924. It contains, among others, "Boy Wanted" and "Naughty
Baby."

P6.45　　**St. Louis Woman.** (Arlen and Mercer). Capitol DW 2742.
　　Harold Nicholas, Fayard Nicholas, Pearl Bailey, Juanita Hall, and others
sing "Come Rain or Come Shine," "Any Place I Hang My Hat Is Home," and
"Ridin' on the Moon."

P6.46　　**The Sound of Music.** (Rodgers and Hammerstein II). Columbia S 32605.
　　Mary Martin, Theodore Bikel, Marion Marlowe, and Patricia Neway perform
the title selection, "My Favorite Things," "Do-Re-Mi," "Edelweiss," and "Climb
Ev'ry Mountain."

P6.47　　**South Pacific.** (Rodgers and Hammerstein II). Columbia S 32604.
　　Winner of the 1949-1950 Pulitzer Prize for Drama. Ezio Pinza, Mary Martin,
Myron McCormick, Juanita Hall and others sing "Dites-Moi," "Some Enchanted
Evening," "There Is Nothin' Like a Dame," "Bali Ha'i," "Younger Than Spring-
time," et al.

P6.48　　**Sweet Charity.** (Coleman and Fields). Columbia KOS 2900.
　　Gwen Verdon, John McMartin, Helen Gallagher, and Ruth Buzzi perform
"Big Spender," "Too Many Tomorrows," "Baby, Dream Your Dream," and
"Where Am I Going?"

P6.49   **Threepenny Opera.** (Weill; Brecht, Blitzstein). MGM SE-3121.
     Lotte Lenya, Scott Merrill, Leon Lishner, and Beatrice Arthur star in "The Ballad of Mack the Knife," "Pirate Jenny," and "Jealousy Duet." The 1958 complete German version is on Columbia Odyssey Y2 32977 (*Die Dreigroschenoper*).

P6.50   **West Side Story.** (Bernstein and Sondheim). Columbia S 32603.
     Carol Lawrence, Larry Kert, Chita Rivera, and others perform "Maria," "Tonight," "America," "I Feel Pretty," "Somewhere," etc.

Revivals and Studio Versions

P6.51   **Anything Goes.** (Porter). Epic FLS 15100.
     Eileen Rodgers leads the cast on this 1962 stage revival, with such tunes as the title selection, "All Through the Night," "I Get a Kick out of You," "You're the Top," et al.

P6.52   **Babes in Arms.** (Rodgers and Hart). Columbia OS 2570.
     Mary Martin heads the studio cast in a score that probably contains more generally popular hit songs than any other production: "Where or When," "Babes in Arms," "My Funny Valentine," "Johnny One Note," "All at Once," "The Lady Is a Tramp," and "Imagine."

P6.53   **Babes in Toyland.** (Herbert; MacDonough). Decca DL 8458.
     Kenny Baker and Karen Kemple sing the songs here, including "Toyland," "Never Mind, Bo Peep," and "March of the Toys" (six in all). The second side is devoted to Herbert's *Red Mill*, with "The Isle of Our Dreams," "The Streets of New York," and "Because You're You."

P6.54   **Desert Song.** (Romberg; Harbach and Hammerstein). Monmouth-
          Evergreen MES 7054.
     This is the 1927 Drury Lane cast (from London); they perform "The Riff Song," "Romance," "Then You Will Know," "Let Your Love Grow," and "One Alone." (The modern version [studio cast] is on Angel S 35905, with Edmund Hockridge and June Bronhill.)

P6.55   **Funny Face.** (George and Ira Gershwin). Monmouth-Evergreen
          MES 7037.
     Featuring Fred and Adele Astaire, this comes from the 1928 London production. It features a bonus in two of the Astaires' recordings from the London production of *Stop Flirting.*

P6.56   **Girl Crazy.** (George and Ira Gershwin). Columbia OS 2560.
     Mary Martin, Louise Carlyle and Eddie Chappell sing good recorded versions of many hit songs: "Bidin' My Time," "Sam and Delilah," "Embraceable You," "I Got Rhythm," "But Not for Me," etc.

P6.57   **Hit the Deck.** (Youmans; Grey and Robin). World Record Club
SH 176 (British issue).
The original London cast from the twenties performs "Join the Navy,"
"Why, Oh Why?," "Sometimes I'm Happy," "Loo-Loo," etc. (The modern version's
1955 film track on MGM E-3163 is with Tony Martin, Jane Powell, Debbie Reynolds,
and Vic Damone. Seven of the twelve songs here were from the original score.)

P6.58   **Johnny Johnson.** (Weill; Green). Heliodor S 25024.
Burgess Meredith, Lotte Lenya, and Hiram Sherman sing "Johnny's Song,"
"O Heart of Love," "Song of the Goddess," and "On the Rio Grande." This was
Weill's first American score.

P6.59   **Lady, Be Good!** (George and Ira Gershwin). Monmouth-Evergreen
MES 7036.
The 1926 London cast featured Fred and Adele Astaire in their first big
hit production. It ran for nine months.

P6.60   **Naughty Marietta.** (Herbert; Young). Capitol T 551.
This is Herbert's most famous score, with songs like "Tramp! Tramp! Tramp!,"
"Italian Street Song," "I'm Falling in Love with Someone," and "Ah! Sweet
Mystery of Life." They are sung here by Marguerite Piazza and Gordon MacRae.

P6.61   **The New Moon.** (Romberg; Hammerstein). Monmouth-Evergreen
MES 7051.
The 1929 London cast performs "Marianne," "Softly, As in a Morning
Sunrise," "Stouthearted Men," "Lover, Come Back to Me," etc., being led and
conducted by Romberg himself. Evelyn Laye starred. (The modern version's studio
cast can be heard on Capitol SW 1966, with Gordon MacRae.)

P6.62   **No, No, Nanette.** (Youmans; Mandel/Harbach/Caesar). And **Sunny.**
(Kern; Harbach/Hammerstein). Original London casts. Stanyan
SR 10035.
The recent *Nanette* revival on Broadway inspires interest in how it sounded
in its original version in the twenties. American recordings of these original productions (1925 and 1926, respectively) were never available, so these Stanyan reissues
of the London casts are welcome. Considering its vintage, the sound quality is
not bad; in fact, the album boasts of its "glorious, unenhanced monophonic sound"!
Nanette hits included "I Want to Be Happy" and "Tea for Two." *Sunny* has a
less memorable score; its best song was "Who?" Binnie Hale played both Nanette
and Sunny with enthusiasm. Jacket notes are lamentably absent, but there are
reproductions of the original programs.

P6.63   **Oh, Kay!** (George and Ira Gershwin). Columbia OS 2550.
Jack Cassidy and Barbara Ruick are the leads, performing "Dear Little Girl,"
"Clap Yo' Hands," "Do Do Do," "Someone to Watch over Me," "Fidgety Feet,"
etc. The older version, with original cast is on (London recordings) Monmouth-
Evergreen MES 7043, with Gertrude Lawrence.

P6.64   **On the Town.** (Bernstein; Comden and Green). Columbia OS 2028.
This was an expansion of Bernstein's ballet, *Fancy Free*. Nancy Walker,
Betty Comden, Adolph Green, and Cris Alexander perform "New York, New York,"
"Some Other Time," "I Can Cook, Too," and "I Get Carried Away," among others.
Bernstein conducts.

P6.65   **On Your Toes.** (Rodgers and Hart). Columbia OS 2590.
With songs like "There's a Small Hotel," "Quiet Night," and "Slaughter
on Tenth Avenue," ably performed by Jack Cassidy and Portia Nelson, this studio
version easily wins out over the 1954 revival album on Decca DL 9015.

P6.66   **Pal Joey.** (Rodgers and Hart). Columbia OL 4364.
Vivienne Segal and Harold Lang sing "I Could Write a Book," "Bewitched,
Bothered and Bewildered," "Den of Iniquity," and "Take Him." This studio cast
led to the 1952 Broadway revival, which in turn led to the 1957 film with Frank
Sinatra (available on Capitol DW 912).

P6.67   **Red Mill.** (Herbert; Blossom). Decca 8016 *or* Capitol T 551.
See entry No. P6.53.

P6.68   **Roberta.** (Kern; Harbach). Columbia OS 2530.
Jack Cassidy, Joan Roberts and Kaye Ballard are in the cast, performing
"You're Devastating," "Yesterdays," "Smoke Gets in Your Eyes," etc.

P6.69   **Rose-Marie.** (Friml; Harbach, Hammerstein, Stothart). RCA LSO 1001.
This is the only complete version, with Giorgio Tozzi and Julie Andrews.
Includes "Rose-Marie," "The Mounties," "Indian Love Call," "The Door of My
Dreams," and "Pretty Things."

P6.70   **Sally.** (Kern; Grey). Monmouth-Evergreen MES 7053.
From the 1921 London stage production, this starred Dorothy Dickson,
with additional music provided for the ballet sequence by Victor Herbert. Important
songs included "Wild Rose," "The Lorelei," "Look for the Silver Lining," and
"Whip-Poor-Will."

P6.71   **Showboat.** (Kern and Hammerstein II; Wodehouse). Columbia OL 4058.
This 1946 revival disc includes "Ol' Man River," "Can't Help Lovin' Dat
Man," and "Bill." Stanyan SR 10036, a double-disc set with Shirley Bassey and
the London revival cast, is the only complete version available.

P6.72   **The Student Prince (in Heidelberg).** (Romberg; Donnelly). Monmouth-
          Evergreen MES 7054.
This is the 1926 Drury Lane cast, from London, England. Important songs
include: "Golden Days," "Drinking Song," "Deep in My Heart Dear," etc. The
modern version with a studio cast is on Columbia OS 2380, with Jan Peerce,
Giorgio Tozzi, and Roberta Peters. The modern version's film (1954) sound track
is on RCA LSC 2339, with Mario Lanza.

P6.73   **Sunny.** (Kern; Harbach and Hammerstein). Stanyan SR 10035.
See entry No. P6.62.

P6.74   **Tip-Toes.** (George and Ira Gershwin). Monmouth-Evergreen MES 7052.
The original 1926 London cast starred Dorothy Dickson and Allen Kearns, accompanied by twin pianos.

P6.75   **Vagabond King.** (Friml; Hooker and Post). RCA LSC 2509.
Mario Lanza and Judith Raskin tackle the songs "Some Day," "Only a Rose," "Love for Sale," "Nocturne," and "Love Me Tonight."

P6.76   **Wildflowers.** (Youmans; Harback, Hammerstein, and Stothart).
Monmouth-Evergreen MES 7052.
The 1926 London cast, with a large pit band, do interpretations of "Bambalina," "April Blossoms," and "I Love You, I Love You, I Love You."

P6.77   **West Side Story.** (Bernstein; arr. Johnny Richards). Stan Kenton
Orchestra. Creative World ST1007.
Stan Kenton and his arranger, Johnny Richards, found Bernstein's score tailor-made for adaption to jazz as no other Broadway show was. They have used all the resources of a big band to explore all the jazz possibilities of *West Side Story*, and on the whole, they are successful. The best sections are those that build on the tension and climaxes inherent in the story: the taut anticipation of "Something's Coming" and "Cool" and the violent outcome in the confrontation between the two rival gangs. The Latin rhythms of "America" are well handled, and the ballads ("Maria," "Tonight," "Somewhere") are also pleasant listening.

P6.78   **"Themes" Like Old Times, v.1/2.** two discs. Viva V 36018.
Are radio themes "popular music"? They are if they are hummable and retain their patterns in the human memory. Besides the nostalgia value, some were extremely enjoyable, such as Jimmy Durante's "Inka Dinka Doo." There are an unbelievable *180* themes here, about thirty seconds for each, covering all types of programs—science-fiction ("X Minus One"), mysteries ("Sam Spade"), comedies ("Amos 'n' Andy"), popular music shows (Woody Herman), and so forth. Truly an amazing collection.

FILMS

Anthologies

P6.79*   **Fifty Years of Film Music.** three discs. Warner Brothers 3 XX 2736.
These are portions of the original Warner Brothers soundtracks, from 1923 to 1973. Such a wide ranging time span can do no real justice to the music from this studio; however, it can present an overview and can lead on to other materials. (This, of course, is the main justification of anthologies: to present a smattering.) Here are Dick Powell, Ruby Keeler, Joan Blondell, Doris Day, and even Dooley Wilson (performing the gracious "As Time Goes By," from *Casablanca*), singing,

among other items, "42nd Street" and "We're in the Money." Other tracks from
the forties and early fifties include Judy Garland's "The Man That Got Away"
(*A Star Is Born*), Doris Day's "Secret Love" (*Calamity Jane*), and Frank Sinatra's
"Just One of Those Things" (*Jubilee*).

P6.80   **The Golden Age of the Hollywood Musical.** United Artists UA LA
21 5H.

P6.81   **Hooray for Hollywood.** United Artists UA LA 361H.
    With narration by George Raft, the first album contains extracts from the
original scores to certain Busby Berkeley movies, starring Joan Blondell, Ruby
Keeler, Dick Powell, James Cagney, and others. Titles include "Lullaby of Broadway," "I Only Have Eyes for You," and "We're in the Money." Other tracks on
the second, companion volume for Warner Brothers musicals include "Shuffle
off to Buffalo," "The Lady in Red," and "You're Getting to Be a Habit with Me."
Some typical musicals include *42nd Street, Dames, Hollywood Hotel, Wonder Bar,*
and the *Gold Diggers . . .* series.

P6.82   **The Golden Years of Disney: 50th Anniversary, 1923-1973.** Disney-
land WD 50.
    Here is a bonanza for all adults and children: the original sound track versions
of many of Disney's cartoon successes, such as from *Peter Pan* ("When You Wish
Upon a Star"), *The Three Little Pigs* ("Who's Afraid of the Big Bad Wolf?"), from
Snow White ("Whistle While You Work"). Good, clean enjoyable fun, and full of
nostalgia.

P6.83   **The History of MGM Movie Music, v.1.** two discs. MGM 2 SES 15 ST.
    This double album contains various selections from diverse MGM films,
as from original soundtracks. Most of this is film music, and not necessarily from
musical comedies, but it is interesting enough for a starter collection. At the time
of this writing, it has been three years since volume one was released, and there
is no volume two yet.

P6.84   **Stars of the Silver Screen, 1929-1930.** RCA LPV 538.
    These selections come from the first years of the talkies, but they are studio
duplications of soundtrack successes. The sixteen tracks contain such ever-popular
tunes as Maurice Chevalier's "Louise," Delores del Rio's "Ramona" (English version), Jeanette Macdonald's "Dream Lover," plus contributions from Fanny Brice,
Sophie Tucker, George Jessel, Dennis King, and Gloria Swanson.

P6.85*   **That's Entertainment.** two discs. MCA 2-11002.

P6.85a*   **That's Entertainment, Part Two.** MGM 1-5301.
    This is MGM's tribute to itself, an outright nostalgia trip, it is a salute to
such stellar performers as Fred Astaire, Jean Harlow, Joan Crawford, James Stewart,
Judy Garland, and Gene Kelly (among others). At the same time, it restores to
the catalog those songs that had been virtually unobtainable for decades. These

three discs are a good collection for a smattering of film music from musical comedies. Some typical films include *Singin' in the Rain, Showboat, Gigi, An American in Paris, The Wizard of Oz, Hit the Deck, The Bandwagon, Lili, Cabin in the Sky, Easter Parade,* and *Annie Get Your Gun.*

P6.86*   **Those Wonderful Girls of Stage, Screen and Radio.** two discs. Epic B2N 159.

P6.87*   **Those Wonderful Guys of Stage, Screen and Radio.** two discs. Epic B2N 164.

These four discs are similar in concept to the *Encores from the 30s* effort from Epic (see entry No. P1.4). This wide variety of female performances from the thirties includes songs by Marlene Dietrich, Kay Thompson, Lee Wiley, Frances Langford, Mae West, and the Boswell Sisters (among others). The men are ably represented on their set by Dick Powell, Cab Calloway, Harry Richman, Eddie Cantor, Fred Astaire, and others. There are two drawbacks to these compilations: one, most of the tunes have by now been reissued under individual artist collections that have sprung up to cash in on the nostalgia fad; two, the roster is limited to those under contract to Columbia records and its subsidiaries.

Individual Titles

P6.88   **Around the World in Eighty Days.** MCA 2062.

With the title selection, this film soundtrack became the first million seller album for this genre (1958). The theme was recorded by over 85 different song stylists in that first year.

P6.89   **Breakfast at Tiffany's.** (Mancini). RCA LSP 2362.

The composer was Henry Mancini, and this album is his definitive version of the score. "Moon River" was the Academy Award-winning song lifted from the film.

P6.90   **Cinderella.** (Rodgers and Hammerstein). Columbia OS 2005.

This is the television musical comedy, performed only once, and containing one enduring song: "Do I Love You Because You're Beautiful (or Are You Beautiful Because I Love You)?" The cast included Julie Andrews, Jon Cypher, Edie Adams, and Kaye Ballard.

P6.91   **A Clockwork Orange.** Warner Brothers BS 2573.

A catch-all album from the movie score, containing Moog-synthesized versions of classical music by Rossini, Beethoven, and others, some fragments of popular songs (e.g., "Singing in the Rain"), background scorings, and sound effects.

P6.92   **Dr. Zhivago.** MGM 1SE-6ST.

Pushed ahead by "Lara's Theme," the lush and romantic score from this film became the first to sell over *two* million albums (1967).

P6.93   **Exodus.** RCA LSO 1058.
The dramatic theme song from this movie aptly captured the grandeur and religious importance of the movie.

P6.94   **Gigi.** (Lerner and Loewe). MGM S-3641.
One of the very first musical comedies scored for the film on a careful, conscientious basis that reflected the stage production. The cast included Maurice Chevalier, Leslie Caron, Louis Jourdan, and Hermione Gingold. Important songs included the title selection, "I Remember It Well," and "Thank Heavens for Little Girls."

P6.95   **The Graduate.** (Simon and Garfunkel; Grissom). Columbia OS 3180.
The soundtrack was greatly enhanced by the compositions and singing of Simon and Garfunkel, including re-workings of "Sounds of Silence," "Parsley, Sage, Rosemary, and Thyme," and "Scarborough Fair," plus new material such as "Mrs. Robinson."

P6.96   **High Society.** (Porter). Capitol W 750.
With an all-star cast of Bing Crosby, Frank Sinatra, Grace Kelly, Louis Armstrong, and Celeste Holm, the album has its great moments with "True Love," and the title selection.

P6.97   **Love Story.** Paramount 6002.
This is another million seller album, and there were over 280 cover versions of the main theme alone. It has also been the biggest selling taped album, with over 200,000 tapes being sold. If parts of the dialogue are required, both it and the music can be found on Paramount 7000 (two discs).

P6.98   **A Man and a Woman.** United Artists UAS 5147.
With music by Francis Lai, this 1966 Cannes Film Festival winner put the emphasis on rhythm and movement. The samba was written and performed by Baden Powell, the well-known Brazilian guitarist; the heartbeat track ("Stronger Than Us") was beautifully performed, both visually and musically.

P6.99   **Mary Poppins.** (Sherman and Sherman). Buena S-4026.
While this is a children's film, the presence of Julie Andrews and Dick Van Dyke ensured adult attention. Of course, the most famous song from this track is the song with the long name (and it won't be repeated here).

P6.100   **Never on Sunday.** United Artists UAS 5070.
The music was composed by Manos Hadjidakis, and it is entirely representative of most Greek music written for the theater. Utilizing the bouzoukia as the central thematic base, Hadjidakis (a serious music composer) weaves contemporary melodies from folk music.

P6.101   **A Star Is Born.** (Arlen; Ira Gershwin). Harmony HS 11366.
One of the few sound tracks re-issued on a budget label, this stars Judy Garland; and "The Man That Got Away" is the song.

P6.102   **The Sting.** MCA 390.
 Marvin Hamlisch features the music of Scott Joplin and various other ragtime themes (even though he omits the refrain and a third variation from "The Entertainer"). Three of the compositions are his own; the other ragtime items are now in the public domain.

P6.102a   **Stormy Weather.** Soundtrak STK 103.
 Based on the life of Bill "Mr. Bojangles" Robinson, this film had three-fourths of its running time devoted to songs and dances. It was the first major film devoted entirely to black music. Featured on this disc (taken from the optical soundtrack itself) are Lena Horne ("Stormy Weather," "I Can't Give You Anything but Love, Baby," "Diga Diga Do"), Cab Calloway ("Jumpin' Jive," "Lonesome Blues"), Fats Waller ("Ain't Misbehavin' "), Zutty Singleton, and of course, Mr. Bojangles ("Ain't That Something?").

P6.103   **Swingtime.** (Fields and Kern). / **The Gay Divorcee.** (various). EMI
    EMTC 101 (British issue).

P6.104   **Top Hat.** (Berlin). / **Shall We Dance?** (Gershwin and Gershwin). EMI
    EMTC 102 (British issue).
 It comes as a surprise that the soundtracks for these four marvelous Fred Astaire and Ginger Rogers films should be released on a British label. Revivals in that country equal revivals in America, and when EMI acquired the rights to the films, the noted archivist there (Chris Ellis) immediately began to prepare them for soundtrack distribution. Most of the songs are here, and all have been carefully examined to eliminate conversation and multiple choruses (such as in "The Continental"). Thus, while in the film someone may be talking over Astaire's dancing, that is not the case on the disc. From *Swingtime* come "The Way You Look Tonight," "A Fine Romance," and "Pick Yourself Up." From *The Gay Divorcee* come "The Continental" and "Night and Day." From *Top Hat*, there are "No Strings," the title selection, "Cheek to Cheek" and "The Piccolino." This film was probably their finest effort together. From *Shall We Dance?* come "Let's Call the Whole Thing Off" and "They Can't Take That Away from Me." Max Steiner and Nathaniel Shilket split the orchestral duties. Noël Hendrick provides a first rate story synopsis and other notes. Each disc is well illustrated with pictures (including a stiff inserted poster).

P6.105   **Umbrellas of Cherbourg (Les Parapluies de Cherbourg).** two discs.
    Philips PCC 616.
 A stunning score and operatic lyrics make this film track a very rewarding listening experience, entirely separate from the movie.

P.106   **The Wizard of Oz.** (Arlen). MGM S-3996 ST.
 This children's movie gave the world "Somewhere over the Rainbow," the Munchkins, and, of course, Judy Garland.

P.107   **Zorba the Greek.** (Theodorakis). 20th Century TFS 903.
Theodorakis's credits include the films "Electra," "Phaedra," and "The Lovers of Teruel." Greece's premier composer, he has created here a superb score evocative of the Cretan setting, and charming to listen to at home as well.

COMPOSERS

P6.108   **Leroy Anderson.**
Much of Anderson's music is available on his own recordings (Decca 8121 and 74335). Re-interpretations by the Boston Pops (for whom he was an arranger during the late forties) can be found on RCA LSC 2638 (*Music of Leroy Anderson*) with, of course, Arthur Fiedler conducting.

P6.109   **Harold Arlen.**
Fine craftsmanship can be found on Monmouth-Evergreen MES 6918 (*Harold Arlen in Hollywood*), by Rusty Derick and the Winds of Change. These are big band contemporary arrangements of thirteen great Arlen picture tunes. Lee Wiley, with a jazz back-up group, sings eight tunes on Monmouth-Evergreen MES 6807 (*Rodgers & Hart and Harold Arlen*). Tony Bennett sings on Columbia CS 8359 (*String of Arlen*). There was also an Ella Fitzgerald songbook on Verve V6-4057/8, two discs (*Ella Fitzgerald Sings the Harold Arlen Songbook*).

P6.110   **Burt Bacharach.**
In terms of compositional longevity, Bacharach is a relative newcomer. An early success was the soundtrack from *The Blob*, a 1950s horror movie. Dionne Warwicke has probably been the most successful in interpreting his songs, and indeed many were written specifically with Ms. Warwicke in mind. Scepter SPS 5100 is an anthology entitled *A Tribute to Burt Bacharach: Composer, Arranger, Conductor*, as interpreted by Dionne Warwicke, B. J. Thomas, Bobby Vinton, Gene Pitney, the Shirelles, and Jerry Butler, among others. Ronnie Aldritch created an instrumentally sound recording in *The World of Burt Bacharach* (Decca Phase 4 SPA 193, British issue). Arthur Fiedler and the Boston Pops provide lush sounds in the *Burt Bacharach-Hal David Songbook* (Polydor PD 5019).

P6.111   **Irving Berlin.**
Berlin has had much of his music recorded by others, and the list would be too long to cite more than a handful. A premier performance was given by Ella Fitzgerald on Verve V6-4019-2, two discs (*Ella Fitzgerald Sings the Irving Berlin Songbook*). Recreations were made by Monmouth-Evergreen on *Irving Berlin: All by Myself:* volume one (*Everybody Step, 1921-1926*), covering fifteen of the best of Berlin from the Ziegfeld Follies and the Music Box Revues; volume two (*Puttin' on the Ritz, 1926-1930*), with eighteen songs from the later Follies and early motion pictures; and volume three (*Heat Wave, 1930-1933*), incorporating medleys from "Face the Music" and "As Thousands Cheer," as well as his greatest pop successes. These are found on MES 6809/11. There is also one side of Mantovani's *Music of Berlin and Friml* (London 166).

P6.112   **Noël Coward.**
Gertrude Lawrence and Noël Coward perform on the *We Were Dancing*
album from Monmouth-Evergreen (MES 7042), which includes some original scenes.
Bobby Short made yet a third double album set with *Mad about Noel Coward*
(Atlantic SD2-607, two discs). The *Noel Coward Album* (Columbia MG 30086,
two discs) contains diverse material of Coward originals and salutes to his work.
Great Coward Shows (World Record Club SH 179/180, two discs, British issue)
contains original London cast production excerpts from *Bitter Sweet, Cavalcade,
Conversation Piece, Operetta,* and *Ace of Clubs*.

P6.113   **Rudolf Friml.**
Melodies can be found on Westminster 15008 (*Friml Plays Friml*) and Frank
DeVol's good work *Night with Friml* (Columbia CS 8430). There is also one side
of Mantovani's *Music of Berlin and Friml* (London 166).

P6.114   **George Gershwin.**
The jazz-inspired Gershwin has been subject to many improvisations, particularly in the bop period with the changes on "I Got Rhythm." One of the few
jazz records devoted solely to Gershwin was the anthology *The Music of George
Gershwin* (Moodsville MV 33), containing titles by Gene Ammons, Sonny Rollins,
J. J. Johnson, Eddie Davis, Billy Taylor, and the Modern Jazz Quartet. Ella Fitz-
gerald recorded *The George Gerswhin Songbook* in five discs (Verve 29-5), and
for Decca DL 74451 (*Ella Sings Gershwin*). There is a *Gershwin Piano Recital* on
Distinguished 107, the Bobby Short double set *K-Ra-Zy for Gershwin* (Atlantic
SD2-608), and even sister Frances singing *For George and Ira* on Monmouth-
Evergreen MES 7060. Percy Faith made the Columbia *Album of George Gershwin*
(Columbia Special Products CSP EN 2-13719; two discs), and so did Paul Whiteman
as *Great Gershwin* (Coral 57021). Lee Wiley from the 1940s performs on Monmouth-
Evergreen MES 7034, with eight tracks (*George Gershwin and Cole Porter*). The
more modern vocal duo of Ronnie Whyte and Travis Hudson take over on *We Like
a Gershwin Tune* (Monmouth-Evergreen MES 7061). *George Gershwin in London*
(World Record Club SH 185, British issue) contains excerpts from the original
London cast productions of the 1920s.

P6.115   **Victor Herbert.**
Big band music can be found on Columbia O2S-801, by Percy Faith, on
the two discs of the *Album of Victor Herbert*. Andre Kostelanetz puts forward
his versions on Columbia CL 765 (*Music of Victor Herbert*). The Robert Shaw
Chorale sings on *Music of Victor Herbert* (RCA LSC 2515), while Mantovani and
his orchestra perform on London 165 (*Music of Herbert and Romberg*). A similarly
titled album came from Frank Chacksfield, *Best of Herbert and Romberg* (Richmond 30086).

P6.116   **Jerome Kern.**
Jerome Kern: All the Things You Are (Monmouth-Evergreen MES 6808)
covers eighteen great songs, from his last seven years, performed by Reid Shelton,
Susan Watson, and Danny Carroll. Andre Kostelanetz bows in with *Music of Jerome
Kern* (Columbia CL 776), and for the same company, Percy Faith records a

Night with Kern (Columbia CS 8181). Morton Gould arranged *Kern and Porter* for RCA LSC 2559. *Jerome Kern in London* (World Record Club SH 171, British issue) includes excerpts from original London casts performing in the 1920s. A very balanced reissue is from the 1950s by Paul Weston, the *Columbia Album of Jerome Kern, v.1/2* (on Columbia Special Products CSP EN 2-13772; two discs).

P6.117   Alan Jay Lerner and Frederick Loewe.

There is not too much available, probably because the composers are thought of as being "contemporary" without passing into the mainstream. MGM S-3781 is entitled *Lerner and Loewe,* while the double album set on RCA LSP 6005 is simply *An Evening with Lerner and Loewe.*

P6.118   Johnny Mercer.

Much material by Mercer is scattered over several dozen albums. His own singing may be found on *Best* (Capitol T 1858). Tony Mercer sings *Johnny Mercer* on the British Columbia label (SCX 6503) while Frank Sinatra devoted an album to his work, *Sings the Select Mercer* (Capitol DS 1984).

P6.119   Cole Porter.

Cole was another giant when it came to re-interpretation. Recently, there was Bobby Short's double album on Atlantic SD2-606 (*Loves Cole Porter*), Ella Fitzgerald's uptempo versions on *Ella Loves Cole* (Atlantic SD 1631), and Frank Chacksfield's instrumental tunes on *Music of Cole Porter* (London Phase 4 44185). In the 1950s, Ella Fitzgerald recorded the *Cole Porter Songbook* (Verve 2-2511; two discs), Andre Kostelanetz did some instrumentals on *Music of Cole Porter* (Columbia CL 729), and later, Morton Gould delivered a tribute on *Kern and Porter* (RCA LSC 2559). Porter has been the subject of many of Ben Bagley's madcap revivals (on Painted Smiles and Columbia labels: see the reference in the **Revues** annotation at P6.1). Jazz has been kind to Porter as well. Moodsville MV 34 contributes an anthology, *The Music of Cole Porter,* played by the Modern Jazz Quartet, Stan Getz, Gene Ammons, Coleman Hawkins, and Gil Evans, among others. Dave Brubeck made *Anything Goes!* (Columbia CS 9402). With a jazz backing, Lee Wiley made eight records with *George Gershwin and Cole Porter* (Monmouth-Evergreen MES 7034). Thirty-six Porter evergreens are given the medley treatment by Meyer Davis's group on *Plays Cole Porter* (Monmouth-Evergreen MES 6813). Michel Legrand contributes the *Columbia Album of Cole Porter* (Columbia Special Products CSP EN 2-13728; two discs).

P6.120   Richard Rodgers (and Oscar Hammerstein II or Lorenz Hart).

Either alone or with collaborators, Rodgers was a powerhouse in the American musical theater. Melachrino recorded *Music of Rodgers* for RCA (LSP 2513), while Arthur Fiedler and the Boston Pops did *Slaughter on 10th Avenue* (RCA LSC 2294). Cyril Ornadel's orchestra performs admirably on *Rodgers and Hammerstein* (MGM S-3817). Andy Williams sings nicely on *Rodgers and Hammerstein* (Cadence 3005). Frank Sinatra tries hard with *Rodgers and Hart* (Capitol DW 1825), but Ella Fitzgerald is far better with her *Rodgers and Hart Songbook* (Verve V6-4022/3, two discs). There is also an interesting disc on United Artists UAS 6273, *Melodies of Rodgers and Hart.* From the 1940s, there is Lee Wiley's treatment of eight songs on *Rodgers & Hart and Harold Arlen* (Monmouth-Evergreen MES 6807). In a more modern vein, the vocal duo Ronnie Whyte and Travis Hudson made *It's Smooth, It's Smart, It's Rodgers & Hart* (Monmouth-Evergreen MES 7069). The album *Rodgers and Hart in London* (World Record Club SH 183, British issue) features original London casts from the 1920s and includes excerpts from *Lido Lady, Lady Luck, Peggy Ann, Up and Doing, One Damn Thing after Another, Evergreen,* and *On Your Toes.* Andre Kostelanetz made the *Columbia Album of Richard Rodgers* (Columbia Special Products CSP EN 2-13725; two discs).

P6.121   Sigmund Romberg.

Frank Chacksfield's orchestra turns in a good performance on the old Richmond 300 86, *Best of Herbert and Romberg.* Mantovani tries different material on his London 165 effort, *Music of Herbert and Romberg.* Percy Faith produced a *Night with Romberg* (Columbia CS 8108), while Melachrino and his strings produce the *Music of Romberg* (RCA LSP 2106).

P6.122   [Other Composers.]

Beyond those listed above, other songbooks or instrumental versions of the works of individual composers are rare. Joni James created *Songs by Young and Loesser* (MGM 3449), for Frank Loesser and Victor Young. The *Songs of Jimmy McHugh* (Decca 8423) were nicely handled by Russ Morgan. Maxine Sullivan and Bob Wilber ably come to grips with *The Music of Hoagy Carmichael* (Monmouth-Evergreen MES 6917), an album that also features most of the other members of the World's Greatest Jazz Band. Two sets issued in 1964 and 1966 were *Vincent Youmans: Through the Years* (Monmouth-Evergreen MRS 6401/2, two discs), a 36-track compilation of some of his Broadway and Hollywood song hits; and *Dietz & Schwartz: Alone Together* (Monmouth-Evergreen MRS 6604/5, two discs), an album with 32 tunes from 1929-1937, with Nancy Dussault and Karen Morrow, among others. A very good collection of the music of DeSylva, Brown, and Henderson was released by the dance band leader Jack Hylton as *Good News!* (Monmouth-Evergreen MES 7076e). All of the materials here were from their shows, and recorded at the time that the triumvirate was associated with each other (1927-1931).

ARTISTS

P6.123   Fred Astaire. Starring. two discs. Columbia SG 32472.

This is yet another important document in the history of the American theater and film. Between 1935 and 1938, Astaire starred in six movies for RKO Radio—five with Ginger Rogers—and these were acclaimed as the epitome of charm, grace, style, and musical distinction. They *were* the thirties for many people. During this same period, Astaire made thirty recordings for Brunswick, and 29 of them were from these movies. In those days, soundtrack albums were not made, but rather, singers retreated to the studio as modern Broadway stage shows do on Sundays. Astaire was never better than with Rogers, and consequently his voice was never better (there are even a few taps here and there). *Top Hat, Follow the Fleet, Swing Time, Shall We Dance?, A Damsel in Distress, Carefree*—all are here, with the orchestras of Johnny Green, Ray Noble, and Leo Reisman. Only twelve of these selections have been out on elpee before.

P6.124   **Josephine Baker.** Monmouth-Evergreen MES 7023.

Although born in St. Louis, the late Ms. Baker scored her greatest acclaims in Paris, France, where she performed and lived from 1925 until her death in 1975. Her cabaret and revue work was absolutely first-rate, and she was acknowledged as a consummate artist in the field by the time of the 1935 *En Super Folies* in Paris. These sixteen performances in both French and English are from her memorable Parisian revues in the 1930s. Right up until she died she was performing—a striking woman with a striking, youthful figure that approximated that of a woman at the age of 35. One of her last roles was the lead in the French production of *Hello, Dolly!* Titles here include: "Si J'Etais Blanche" (1933), "Confessin' " (1933), "You're Driving Me Crazy" (1933), "Haiti" (1935), "Doudou" (1936), and "Vous Faites Partie De Moi" ["I've Got You under My Skin"] (1937).

P6.125   **Fanny Brice/Helen Morgan.** RCA LPV 561.

Brice was discovered by Flo Ziegfeld for his Follies, and was used in the 1910, 1911, and other versions from 1920 through 1923. She was an excellent stage performer and singer, and of course, her life became the basis for the successful *Funny Girl* show. This early material, eight tracks from 1921 through 1927, covers such revue songs as "Second Hand Rose," "Song of the Sewing Machine," "Cooking Breakfast for the One I Love," and the epic version of "My Man," from the 1927 film of the same name. Helen Morgan was a cabaret entertainer, renowned for sitting on a grand piano while singing. She had two separate careers: her cabaret work and despondent material made her the very first Torch Singer, and she epitomized the genre; her stage and film work (which appears on this album), first in *Showboat* ("Bill," "Can't Help Lovin' Dat Man," both from 1928), and then *Sweet Adeline*, various *Follies*, and films. Some of her best work is here: "More Than You Know," "Don't Ever Leave Me," "Body and Soul," "Frankie and Johnny." She has been widely anthologized.

P6.126   **Frank Chacksfield. Academy Award Songs.** two discs. London CHA S-1.

P6.127   **Dimitri Tiomkin. Movie Themes.** Coral 57006.

These two composer-conductors are well known for their scoring of various films, although Tiomkin has won more awards. (London recordings honored Chacksfield by creating a "Chacksfield" label for him.) A generous selection of material allows us to hear the many mainly instrumental winners, and in fact, "On the Beach" in the Chacksfield version even made it as high as No. 47 on the singles charts in 1960! Tiomkin, the Russian-born arranger, did film scores for *Lost Horizon, Mr. Smith Goes to Washington, Battle of Britain*, etc. For this disc of movie themes, he has reworked such classics as *High Noon* ("Do Not Forsake Me") from 1952, *The High and the Mighty* (1954), *The Old Man and the Sea* (1958), *Giant, Carmen Jones, Guns of Navarone*, and *Friendly Persuasion*.

P6.128   **Maurice Chevalier. This Is Maurice Chevalier.** two discs. RCA VPM 6055.

P6.129   **Maurice Chevalier. The Young Chevalier.** Capitol T 10360.
    Turning from a string of successes in French cabarets and revues such as the *Folies Bergère*, 1909-1913, Chevalier made his mark and gained international fame with American films in the 1930s. The Capitol material comes from Pathé recordings of the 1920s; all are in French. The RCA material comes from his 1929-1935 films, and were recorded in either New York or Hollywood. From *Innocents of Paris* comes his theme "Valentine"; from *The Big Pond* there is "You Brought a New Kind of Love to Me." Other selections include his famous "Louise," "One Hour with You," "My Ideal," and "Mimi." In the late fifties, his career became activated again with *Gigi* (see the citation at entry No. P6.94), and yet again in the early 1970s, when he began a two-year series of farewell concerts around the world.

P6.130   **Noel Coward. Greatest Hits, Volume 1.** Stanyan SR 10025.
    Here are the witty songs of the talented Noël—straight from the horses's mouth. Surely no one could intone the notes with more nuances than Coward himself. His tongue-in-cheek lyrics will tickle your funnybone. Among the twelve gems on this first album are "The Stately Homes of England," "I Wonder What Happened to Him," "Nina" (who refused to begin the beguine in a gentle poke at Cole Porter), "Imagine the Duchess's Feelings" (when her youngest son went Red), and the title song from *Sail Away*. Good sound quality has been preserved in the transfer from the English 78 rpm discs.

P6.131   **Noel Coward and Gertrude Lawrence. We Were Dancing.** Monmouth-Evergreen MES 7042.
    Coward and Lawrence first worked together in 1913 (he was thirteen, she fifteen) playing angels in a morality play in Liverpool. Apart from this, they did three shows together: *London Calling* (1923), *Private Lives* (1930), and *Tonight at 8:30* (1936). Selections from the latter two are on this album; regrettably, this is all they ever recorded. Both were written by Coward specifically for himself and Lawrence. They made a natural pair, stylish and stylized, and the special magic they created comes across beautifully in Coward's songs. To round out the album, there is some dialogue and the theme song from *Moonlight Is Silver*, a 1934 play with Lawrence and Douglas Fairbanks, Jr. It's of interest because the two were having a well-publicized affair at the time, but it's not in the same league as the rest of the record.

P6.132   **Bing Crosby. In Hollywood, 1930-1934.** two discs. Columbia C2L 43.
    The 32 tracks here are studio versions of items from Crosby's films. Eight are derived from *King of Jazz* (1930) with Paul Whiteman ("Happy Feet," "It Happened in Monterey"), three from *The Big Broadcast* (1932; such as "Please"), and others from *College Humor* (1933), *Too Much Harmony* (1933), *Going Hollywood* (1933; including "After Sundown" and "Temptation"), *We're Not Dressing* (1934), and *She Loves Me Not* (1934).

P6.133   **Deanna Durbin.** two discs. MCA DEA 8.
    A child prodigy from Winnipeg, Canada, Durbin created the role of a cultured
girl that many mothers could use as a model for their offspring. Her soprano voice
could cover English, Italian, French, and German. Many of her pictures were loosely
structured to simply take advantage of her voice. She began with *Three Smart
Girls* (1936) and continued until she grew up and outgrew her child roles. Typical
songs from throughout her career include "Someone to Care for Me," "My Own,"
"Because," "One Fine Day," "Loch Lomond," and "It's Raining Sunbeams."

P6.134   **Nelson Eddy and Jeanette Macdonald. Favorites.** RCA ANL 1-1075.

P6.135   **Nelson Eddy and Jeanette Macdonald.** RCA LPV 526.
    Both Eddy and Macdonald were masters of the light operetta. During 1935-
1938, they turned out many, including *Rose Marie*. Typical selections here include
"The Mounties," "Rose Marie," "Indian Love Call," "Ah! Sweet Mystery of Life,"
and "Farewell to Dreams." On her own, Macdonald sang "Italian Street Song,"
"Lover Come Back to Me," and, of course, "San Francisco," from the movie
of the same name with Clark Gable. Pop items from among the twelve tracks on
the first album include "Stout-Hearted Men," "Beyond the Blue Horizon," and
"The Breeze and I."

P6.136   **Alice Faye. In Hollywood, 1934-1937.** Columbia CL 3068.
    These sixteen recordings, some previously unissued, derive from songs
that Faye sang in the movies, such as "George White's Scandals," "Every Night
at Eight," "King of Burlesque," "On the Avenue," and "Wake up and Live,"
among others. All of them were re-recorded in the studio, for in these days there
was no soundtrack recording for discs. Earlier, she had sung with Rudy Vallee's
group. During this time period, she sang in many musicals, and this disc (with
reasonably good sound) serves as a very good memento.

P6.137   **Ella Fitzgerald. The Harold Arlen Songbook.** two discs. Verve V-4046-2.

P6.138   **Ella Fitzgerald. The Irving Berlin Songbook.** two discs. Verve 2683
    027 (British issue).

P6.139   **Ella Fitzgerald. The George Gershwin Songbook, v.1/2.** four discs.
    Verve 2682 004 and 2682 023 (British issue).

P6.140   **Ella Fitzgerald. The Jerome Kern Songbook.** Verve V6-4060.

P6.141   **Ella Fitzgerald. The Cole Porter Songbook.** two discs. Verve 2683 044
    (British issue).

P6.142   **Ella Fitzgerald. The Rodgers and Hart Songbook.** two discs. Verve
    2683 053 (British issue).

P6.143   **Ella Fitzgerald. Sings Broadway.** Verve V6-4059.
Such an immense bundle of goodies! Fitzgerald tore up a storm in the mid-fifties with these songbooks, and rightly so. Her voice is a perfect match to the tunes, and she has also done a creditable job in interpreting some of the more obscure pieces. All of the production was done by the ubiquitous Norman Granz (whose idea it was). Billy May did the arranging for Arlen: "Blues in the Night," "Let's Fall in Love," "Stormy Weather," "Between the Devil and the Deep Blue Sea," etc. Paul Weston gets the kudos for Berlin: "Top Hat, White Tie and Tails," "Puttin' on the Ritz," "How Deep Is the Ocean?," and so forth. The Gershwin set of 53 (!) tracks was arranged by Nelson Riddle, and includes most of his well known tunes. Riddle also arranged the Kern single album. Buddy Bregman arranged the Porter songbook, as well as the Rodgers and Hart set. Here are about 200 titles, some of them the best that the modern world has ever known, sung in impeccable style by Fitzgerald. For a wide-ranging eclectic taste, the Broadway anthology includes material from *Guys and Dolls, Pajama Game, Brigadoon, South Pacific, Me and Juliet, My Fair Lady,* and *Damn Yankees.*

P6.144   **Judy Garland. Best.** two discs. MCA 2-4003.

P6.145   **Judy Garland. Collector's Items, 1936-1945.** two discs. Decca DEA 7-5.

P6.146   **Judy Garland. Forever Judy.** MGM PX 102.
Most of Judy Garland's music from films is available on these five discs. The MCA set includes "(Dear Mr. Gable) You Made Me Love You," from *Broadway Melody of 1938*; "For Me and My Gal" and "When You Wore a Tulip" (both with Gene Kelly); "Meet Me in St. Louis, Louis," "I'm Always Chasing Rainbows," and "Zing! Went the Strings of My Heart." The MGM record was lifted from the actual films; consequently, there is a preponderance of "sobbing violins," tender scoring, and lyrical but light rhythm among the accompaniments. From *Meet Me in St. Louis,* there is "Boy Next Door" and "Trolley Song"; from *Little Nellie Kelly,* "Singing in the Rain"; from *Till the Clouds Roll By,* "Look for the Silver Lining"; from *Babes in Arms,* the wonderful "I Cried for You"; plus, of course, "Over the Rainbow" from *The Wizard of Oz.* The Decca set comprises studio recordings, including some early rare items such as "Stompin' at the Savoy" and "Swing, Mister Charlie," with Bob Crosby's jazz group in 1936. Other tunes include "All God's Children Got Rhythm" from *A Day at the Races*; "Blues in the Night" and "You Can't Have Ev'rything" from films of the same title; various selections from Andy Hardy movies; and the wonderful "This Heart of Mine" from the 1945 revue-type film *The Ziegfeld Follies.* There are superficial notes with these records, but at least there are many photographs.

P6.147   **Al Jolson. The Early Years.** Ember SE 8026 (British issue).

P6.148   **Al Jolson. Sitting on Top of the World.** Vocalion VLP3 (British issue).
Jolson's main impact was over before the 1920s ended. In the pre-World War I years, he starred in a vast number of successful broadway shows and revues, including *La Belle Paree, Vera Violetta, The Whirl of Society, The Honeymoon Express,* and *Dancing Around.* His first recorded songs are on this album, from 1911:

"That Haunting Melody," "Asleep in the Deep," and "Rum-Tum-Tiddle." Although the material was trite, even for its time, the Jolson voice came through loud and clear in spite of the primitive acoustic material. All of this is mostly Victor material (1911 through 1914) and includes such novelties as "Sister Susie's Sewing Shirts for Soldiers" and the epic "Snap Your Fingers and Away You Go." His film roles stressed non-singing, and his career declined in later life until his efforts for the Second World War cause excited interest that led to two biographical films with Larry Parks (and Jolson's singing) and a revitalized singing career (see item P2.12).

The 1920s are represented by the MCA Vocalion reissue. The sixteen tracks cover 1924-1930 and include various studio recreations, such as the title selection from *The Singing Fool* (1928), which also featured "Sonny Boy," "There's a Rainbow 'round My Shoulder," and "Golden Gate." *Big Boy* (1925) had "Miami" and "California, Here I Come." Other film or stage successes represented here include: *Mammy* (1930; "Looking at You"), *Show Girl* (1929; "Liza"), *The Jazz Singer* (1928), *Say It with Songs* (1929), and *Bombo* (1924).

P6.149   Mario Lanza. Greatest Hits. three discs. RCA VCS 6192.

Lanza was greatly responsible for many people appreciating the classical singers through his role in *The Great Caruso*. As a strictly operatic singer, he had a tenor voice that appeared to be no better and no worse than others at the Met. However, he was a native American; and he was handsome, both commodities being precious in the 1940s when it came to tenors. In 1942, Koussevitzky persuaded him to turn professional, and he began his recording career in 1945. His operatic debut was *Madama Butterfly* in New Orleans, but he quickly shifted to films the next year with *That Midnight Kiss*. In 1951, he capped his career playing Caruso. Tracks here include "Be My Love" from *The Toast of New Orleans*, "Because," "Arrivederci Roma" (a perennial favorite), "Vesti La Giubba," "The Loveliest Night of the Year," and "Because You're Mine."

P6.150   Gertrude Lawrence. Monmouth-Evergreen MES 7043.

P6.151   Gertrude Lawrence. Music for Pleasure MFP 1245 (British issue).

P6.152   Gertrude Lawrence. Star. Audio Fidelity 709.

Associated with the Gershwins, Noël Coward, and *The King and I*, Lawrence had a career that spanned over thirty years. Most of her theatrical successes can be found listed under the various show names. The Monmouth-Evergreen set shows her stage presence with "At Your Command," "You're My Decline and Fall," "Impossible You," "Limehouse Blues" and "Nothing but a Lie." Material from the 1927 *Oh Kay!* (which Gershwin wrote for her) includes "Someone to Watch over Me" and "Maybe." Other works here include the 1931 *Nymph Errant* (with Ray Noble's band), *Family Album*, and "You Were Meant for Me," a Blake-Sissle number originally a Coward-Lawrence dance routine staged by Fred Astaire.

P6.153   Beatrice Lillie. Parlophone PMC 7135 (British issue).

Lillie was a marvelous comic performer who developed out of vaudeville and the London stage and revues. She made her New York debut in 1924 and then progressed to movies. This disc collates her early stage work, although, of course, they are studio versions. Included are "Julia" and "Shoot the Rabbit" from 1915, the 1919 "Rolled into One," and the 1934 "A Baby's Best Friend."

P6.154   **Henry Mancini. This Is Henry Mancini.** two discs. RCA VPS 6029.
Mancini is perhaps the most creative composer of theme music alive. Again, like so many others, he had been classically trained and began work in a dance band (in this case, with Tex Beneke). Through his composition work for television shows, and films (such as *Breakfast at Tiffany's*) he has won more Oscars and Grammies than any other artist. No other comment is necessary beyond listing the enjoyable music here: "Peter Gunn," "Mr. Lucky," "Moon River" (Oscar), "Days of Wine and Roses" (Oscar), "Charade," "Pink Panther," "Dear Heart," and themes from "Love Story" and "Romeo and Juliet."

P6.155   **Jessie Mathews.** Music for Pleasure. MFP 1127 (British issue).
A stage star in London and New York for six years, she was once an understudy to Gertrude Lawrence. Between 1930 and 1936, she made numerous films (all of the material here is from those films); much later, she made a good series of albums for children. From 1932, there is "I'll Stay with You," "One Little Kiss," and "Three Wishes." One of her best films was the 1934 *Evergreen*, and of the four tracks here from that movie, "Just by Your Example" and "Dancing on the Ceiling" stand out.

P6.156   **Ethel Merman. A Musical Autobiography.** two discs. Decca DX 153.

P6.157   **Ethel Merman.** Columbia CL 2751.
Merman is a mistress of vibrant movements, a stage presence, and a song belter by virtue of her throaty voice. Since 1928, she has consistently starred in both stage and film with never a letup. She began her career by being employed by Jimmy Durante, and the two of them together must have been a marvelous sight. Her first success was in *Girl Crazy* (with "I Got Rhythm"), and then followed a variety of Berlin and Porter shows (*Annie Get Your Gun, Anything Goes*, etc.). The Columbia material comes from 1932-1935, and features "Eadie Was a Lady," "An Earful of Music," "You're the Top," "I Get a Kick out of You," and so forth. The Decca album takes over from 1940, as with "My Mother Would Love You" (from *Panama Hattie*). Other Merman items may be found under the names of the relevant shows.

P6.158   **Carmen Miranda. The Brazilian Bombshell.** EMI CRLM 1060 (British issue).
Miranda was a very popular cabaret entertainer in Brazil before going to Hollywood for movies, such as the 1939 *Down Argentine Way*. She must be given credit for bringing Brazil into the popular music scene. Her main impact was visual, through her movies, especially when sighted with a pile of fresh fruit on her head. She was an exceptionally enthusiastic and capable singer, which was ideally conveyed by her constant accompanying group, the Bando da Lua. They all helped spread the samba dances around the world. Most of the twelve items here were recorded in the 1939-1942 period, and include "South American Way," "I, Yi, Yi, Yi, Yi,"

"Chica Chica Boom Chic" (which has since lent itself to describing a particular beat promoted by an electric machine for lounge pianists), "A Weekend in Havana," and, of course, "Tico Tico."

P6.159 **Cole Porter. Cole.** Columbia KS 31456.
This is a great historical record. Side one features private recordings that Porter made of himself singing and playing the piano for titles from the 1935 *Jubilee*. The nine short selections include "Sunday Morning Breakfast Time," "When Love Comes Your Way," and the ever-popular "The Kling-Kling Bird on Top of the Divi-Divi Tree." Side two is equally valuable, as it is a selection of performers associated with Porter and singing his songs. Included are Mary Martin's 1938 original recordings of "My Heart Belongs to Daddy" and "Most Gentlemen Don't Like Love," with Eddy Duchin's orchestra; Danny Kaye's "Let's Not Talk about Love" and "Farming," from the 1941 *Let's Face It*; and the marvelous Ethel Merman belting out "You're the Top" and "I Get a Kick out of You," 1934 recordings from the production *Anything Goes*. Every item on this record can be considered important, most especially the debut of the seductive Martin in "Daddy."

P6.160 **Dick Powell.** Decca DL 8837.

P6.161 **Dick Powell. In Hollywood.** two discs. Columbia C2L 44.
Powell began as a band vocalist, recording his first song in 1927. By 1932, he was starring in pictures, and the Columbia set takes him through to 1935. His fairly average tenor voice was reinforced by his good looks and reasonable movie parts. The image is only somewhat conveyed on records. From *The Gold-diggers of 1933* comes "Pettin' in the Park," "Shadow Waltz," and "I've Got to Sing a Torch Song." From *Broadway Gondolier*, there is "Lulu's Back in Town"; there are five selections from *Footlight Parade*, including the epic "By a Waterfall" that was definitely enhanced by the Busby Berkeley theatrics. Other films from which there are selections include *42nd Street, Wonderbar, Happiness Ahead, Twenty Million Sweethearts,* and *Flirtation Walk.* For Decca, his career continued with the 1935 "Thanks a Million" and "Did I Remember?," plus three selections from *On the Avenue* and others from *The Singing Marine, Cowboy from Brooklyn,* and *Varsity Show.* His characterization of Phillip Marlowe effectively halted his romantic tenor leads, but it led on to dramatic success in films.

P6.162 **Bobby Short. Celebrates Rodgers & Hart.** two discs. Atlantic SD2-610.

P6.163 **Bobby Short. Is K-Ra-Zy for Gershwin.** two discs. Atlantic SD 2-608.

P6.164 **Bobby Short. Is Mad about Noel Coward.** two discs. Atlantic SD 2-607.

P6.165 **Bobby Short. Loves Cole Porter.** Atlantic SD 2-606.
Once a year since 1971, Bobby Short has recorded double albums centering on some well-known composer. Not since the Ella Fitzgerald songbooks of the 1950s has there been such a tremendous onslaught on the works of theatrical composers. The Cole Porter work was the first, and it exhibits the characteristics

of the rest of the series: a piano trio, with Short on piano and vocals; a lightly trilling voice, often evocative of how the music was performed in the 1930s; a close, good miking that reflects the intimate nature of the "lounge piano trio." From Porter comes a wide variety of the known and the not-too-well known tunes, with the stress perhaps on the latter—"Katie Went to Haiti," "Hot House Rose"—and some *unpublished* items: "By Candlelight," "Once upon a Time," and "Why Don't We Try Staying Home?" The Coward set contains an unusual "Let's Fly Away," which appeared on the Porter set with words and lyrics by Porter. With Coward, Short uses Porter's music and Coward's lyrics. Coward's music, of course, is particularly suited to the lounge piano. Most of the lyrics for the Gershwin set come from brother Ira, and the album maintains balance between the popular tunes and the today, largely unheard melodies. The Rodgers and Hart tribute includes "On Your Toes," "Where or When," "Johnny One Note," and "With a Song In My Heart," plus some rare items from among the total of 26 tracks (plus medleys).

P6.166   **Noble Sissle and Eubie Blake. Early Rare Recordings, v.1 /2.** two discs. EBM 4 and 7.

    This duo had been a vaudeville act since 1919. Their first break came with their original 1921 musical *Shuffle Along*, a nicely held together series of vaudeville, operetta, and comic sketches, augmented by superb dance arrangements. From there, they took off to compose and produce many other Broadway musicals and touring shows, including the much-vaunted Blackbirds of 1930. These discs are reissues of their best collaborations from 1920-1927. Included here from *Shuffle Along* are "Baltimore Buzz" (the orchestral finale), plus "Oriental Blues" and "I'm Craving for That Kind of Love." Side one of EBM 4 also has "Bandana Days," featuring Sissle's jive talk to Eubie's rag piano, and "Pickaninny Shoes," a weird title from their vaudeville act. The remaining eight tracks feature songs that the team was asked to record for commercial release. These popular tunes were not necessarily their best, but they cannot be dismissed as hack pieces because of this duo's infusion of artistry into them, as was the case with many of Fats Waller's releases. To cash in on sales, most of these tracks had the word "blues" in their titles, but in the main, they were fox trots. These albums were released in conjunction with Robert Kimball and William Bolcom's *Reminiscing with Sissle and Blake* (Viking, 1973).

P6.167   **Shirley Temple. Remember Shirley.** two discs. 20th Century T-406.

    All of these tracks are mostly from the mid-thirties, and they are lifted right off of the optical soundtracks. These are *not* studio recreations. The thirty songs include all of her famous renditions—such as "Baby Take a Bow"—from a wide range of movies that featured Jack Haley, Alice Faye, George Murphy, James Dunn, and Guy Kibbee.

P6.168   **Lee Wiley. Sings Rodgers and Hart/Harold Arlen.** Monmouth-Evergreen MES 6807.

P6.169   **Lee Wiley. Sings George Gershwin/Cole Porter.** Monmouth-Evergreen MES 7034.

Around thirty years ago, in order to create business, New York music stores (never called "record shops," as records were a sideline of the electrical furniture industry and were meant to sell the phonograph, not vice versa) arranged for artists to autograph their records and sheet music, and even to sing. The ultimate accolade was to record these artists for an "exclusive" album of songs. If these artists were from the stage, then this was especially valuable for theater buffs, as they had no other real source of musical theater performances. (The day of the "sound track" album was far off.) Lee Wiley was one of those performers who was so recorded. As a night club and radio singer, she had developed a style of sophisticated singing, emphasizing the melodic and rhythmic subtleties of each phrase, and ultimately sang to each individual listener. This identified her with particular songs that were hers alone. She has been called a musician's singer, for she phrases like a musician and was quite successful recording with small jazz combos. Indeed, she was one of the few outstanding female vocalists of the thirties, with a repertoire heavy on musical comedy items. Perhaps because of the intrinsic worth of the jazz, coupled with the craze for nostalgia, she is enjoying a comeback.

The eight Gershwin items were recorded in 1939 for the Liberty Music Shop, with Max Kaminsky's group of Russell, Freeman, Condon, and sometimes Waller, among others. Gershwin apparently once said that Wiley was his best vocalist. Included songs are: "Someone to Watch over Me," "How Long Has This Been Going On?," "Sweet and Low Down," and "But Not for Me." The Porter selections come from 1940 for Liberty, and feature a smooth Paul Weston orchestra on four tracks and a hot Bunny Berigan group on the other four, with the leader blowing obbligatos behind Wiley. These are "Let's Do It," "Easy to Love," and "Why Shouldn't I?," among others.

For Rabson's shop in 1940, Wiley recorded a Rodgers and Hart album. As with the Gershwin offering, the group is led by Kaminsky and contains "Here in My Arms," "A Ship without a Sail," and "You Took Advantage of Me," among others. Arlen's album was done for Schirmer's in 1945, with various configurations of the Eddie Condon mob, featuring Hackett, Caceres, Butterfield, and Haggart. This was to be the last of the music shop involvements in album production as a sales gimmick. Straight jazz and blues would continue on independent labels even through today, but the emphasis would be on the music, not on promotion. Typical Arlen fare here includes "Let's Fall in Love," "Stormy Weather," and "I've Got the World on a String." The jazz background really swings (Condon was enjoying a comeback via radio at the Town Hall), and perhaps this is the best set done by Wiley with inspiration from "the boys." Certainly these "songbooks" are better than Verve's Fitzgerald-Granz-Riddle epics.

P6.170   **Ethel Waters. On Stage and Screen, 1925-1940.** Columbia CL 2792.

The sixteen selections here are another good example of Columbia's abstracting show pieces from their vast catalog. Waters has had a successful stage and screen career, despite her early upbringing and the blues songs from the early twenties that she later disowned. Her accompaniment here is a mixed bag of string orchestras and jazz session men. Shows include *The Plantation Revue* ("Dinah"), *Africana* ("I'm Coming Virginia"), *On with the Show* ("Am I Blue?" and "Birmingham Bertha"), Lew Leslie's *Blackbirds of 1930* ("You're Lucky to Me" and "Memories of You"), and *As Thousands Cheer* ("Heat Wave" and "Harlem on

My Mind"), plus "Stormy Weather" from 1933. Columbia also acquired six recordings made for the Liberty Music Shop, with selections from *Cabin in the Sky* and *At Home Abroad*.

Rock Music

ROCK MUSIC:
INTRODUCTION

"I'll take a lick from here and there, smooth
them together and put them against our background. I took a chord progression from Dave
Mason's 'Baby Please,' which is the same
progression on Electric Light Orchestra's
'Evil Woman,' and 'How Long' by the Aces.
That song will probably be on our next album.

"If you steal from one guy, you're a thief. If
you steal several ideas from several people, they
call you prolific. There are few masters, so
copying from your idols is what it's all about.
You remold your favorite things to your own
character. Now, people are copying us—it's flattering."
—Randy Bachman of Bachman-Turner Overdrive,
quoted in *Rolling Stone*, April 8, 1976

Rock music *began* in Britain with the English "beat" and "blues" groups.
These bands exported to America the styles and songs originally created by black
American musicians, primarily the gospel-infused rhythm 'n' blues. But rock has
other roots, too. It borrowed its form and feeling from the blues, call and response
riffs plus driving repetitive rhythms from r 'n' b, improvisation from jazz, melismatic singing from gospel, and social consciousness from folk music. By so doing, rock
music became almost parasitic, absorbing and transmuting all aspects of popular
music as well as the main influences in these other forms of music. This synthesis
is augmented by its pragmatic but diverse nature, for rock music tends to re-empha-
size styles of music by reinforcing patterns. Whatever works is usually good, and
stylists tended to stay in one mode of performing, with little variation or exploration. The audience works in a similar but fickle fashion, and there is a common
expression, "you're as big as your last record." For this reason, many performers
do not switch styles.

TECHNIQUES

Rock music is essentially studio-oriented. The recording studio and electronics
are its primary instruments, unlike the vocals in the blues, the instruments of jazz,
or the microphones of the pop singer. Songs were created and written with the
studio in mind, if not always in it; there, they are also mixed and edited from
32 tracks down to two or four, and the music was electronically altered for dynamics, textures, volume, echo, and so forth. Technology gave rock musicians new
instruments such as the electric piano and the electronic synthesizer, as well as
the devices of fuzz tone, reverberation, and wah-wah. The amplifier gave the speaker

systems (and hence the musician) raw, swinging power. Tapes and albums gave the musician time to lay out ideas, that is, enough room for suites, operas, extended songs, variations, experimentation with unstructured music, etc.

Rock music also advanced 1950s rock and roll. During that decade, smart operators uncovered post-war black music and recast the mold to fit young, urbane white singers. The beat was still there, but the voice was now silky instead of rough, accompanying rhythms were simple instead of complex, and lyrics were changed to prevent misunderstandings of words out of context. But the British blues bands, by side-stepping rock and roll and emulating the source of rock and roll, dramatically reversed the sequence. And as was common in every popular music field, once traditional elements or borrowed songs have been exhausted, then performers have to create their own materials. Given the existing technology and format, several streams opened up. The established 32 bar song with a bridge was the first to give way to such innovations borrowed from jazz as changing time signatures and shifting meters; from r 'n' b came blunt lyrics and screaming vocals. In time, this led to the performer's creating all of his own material. This was a true singer-performer-songwriter, for groups now play their own instruments and sing their own songs. Many of the finer soloists and groups even had complete control over their product, down through to the editing, album design, and liner notes. Their instrumental prowess expanded so that both guitar licks (configurations within a chord) and guitar runs (configurations bridging notes between chords in a progression), borrowed from jazz and country music, could easily be performed. They borrowed the mobile electric bass from soul music to pin down the rhythm, thus freeing the drummer from merely keeping the beat. While the 1950s rock and roll scene projected an alienation against parental control of teenagers and defined the society of the rock and roll admirer, it took 1960s rock music to crystallize this feeling of frustration into an ideology and a youth culture idealizing peer control. This, of course, relates to the post-World War II baby boom, for in the era of rock and roll, the large young audience was growing up from ten to fifteen years of age; with rock in 1963, they were at least eight years older (18-23) and now in a position to solidify any alienation.

ROCKABILLY

INTRODUCTION

Rockabilly is the merger of jump blues with rural country music. Despite its racially-mixed origins, rockabilly proved to be a perfect fusion, as both blues and country are musically subdominant oriented and thus easier to merge. In performance style, rockabilly continues the tradition established for country music as being white and southern (through such singers as Webb Pierce or Buddy Holly), but also now added blues rhythms as suggested by Elvis Presley and Sun Records. Indeed, many believe that rockabilly refers only to Sun Records and to its stable of singers.

Techniques

Musically, the emphasis in rockabilly is the beat of four to the bar, characterized by a triplet beat in this 4/4 time; this is modified by an accented off-beat, a contrived echo, a bass that is slapped rather than plucked, and a guitar that plays eight or sixteen to the bar, with the bass note of a chord being slid up an octave, and then down again. The black influence in vocals is the double glottis movement of Buddy Holly, in which he emulates the cry of the blues by singing with a hiccough and stretching his vowels over many notes.

The sound developed accidentally through Sun Records, as Sam Phillips (its owner) was looking for a sound to project that lay midway between country and blues music, two big selling musical genres. If such a bridge could be made, then the resultant style, he believed, would make millions of dollars. And he was right. He found Elvis Presley, a young white singer who sounded black, and recorded two types of material—the white version of a blues ("That's All Right, Mama"— originally credited to Arthur Crudup), and an uptempo blues version of a white bluegrass standard ("Blue Moon of Kentucky"). Both songs sounded remarkably alike in feel, style, and texture, and to all purposes, both were similar songs in the same genre. Yet one was a black blues, while the other was a white country song; and Phillips preferred to release single discs that way, with one example each of the two kinds on the one disc. Thus, both titles would sell to two markets, and Presley would have double appeal. Unfortunately, it did not work out that way, for few blacks bought Presley; but then again, more than twice as many in the white audience *did* buy him. The net cash result was the same, but Phillips had failed in his attempts to merge the two audiences, while being successful in merging the two musical styles, for popular tastes. (It should be noted that bluegrass music had merged pop and blues a decade before, but it was then a minority music.)

In instrumentation, rockabilly features snare drums (with rim shots); the upright bass, which is usually slapped for the heavier textural sound; a rhythm guitar that strums predictable chord sequences; and a lead guitar with a thin sound, emphasizing the higher strings. Most studios used a tape echo, after Sun Records used the device, to slur or add body to the music. All singers used vocals with the double glottis and what was known as "controlled urgency" to project tension. Instrumentally, the sound and the beat were the most important considerations, and they determined the pattern of instrumental solos. Rhythm was supplied by a string bass, acoustic guitar, and drums. The lead instrument was the electric guitar, the piano, or the saxophone; and all accented the second and fourth beats. The range and pattern of the music sprawled. Early efforts in 1954 were still part of country music; hence, groups then used violins and steel guitars. Later, after the black pattern had been comfortably established, further added instrumentation included the r 'n' b saxophone and the piano. Some of this was rockabilly, some of it was not. (This is one of the dangers of classifying anything, but the situation and music must be accepted as such.) If rockabilly, with its electric lead guitar, can be centrally positioned in a spectrum, then immediately on the white side is "country boogie," which features piano as the lead instrument (1940s honky-tonk music), while immediately on the black side are the saxophone and vocal chorus, as featured in "rock and roll."

The lyrical patterns of rockabilly are of secondary importance. They deal with honky-tonk, love, boogie, and fast living, and they employ many common blues terms. Mostly, the lyrics celebrated *both* these facets of life and the music itself (or at least the "sound")–such as dance tunes about the Ubangi Stomp, the later Twist, the even later Locomotion, etc.

The golden years of rockabilly were 1955-1957, an incredibly short time for a new musical genre to take over popular music; it was an important influence in the creation of rock and roll, and later, of rock music. Its success meant that country music of the time almost folded, but when the artists left rock and roll (as it itself declined in 1959), they invariably moved to country music and took their uptempo techniques with them, reinvigorating country music by this conquest. Indeed, many critics have speculated that had rockabilly not happened, country music would have died a natural death.

Literature

There are no books devoted solely to rockabilly music. Bits and pieces can be pulled out of Brown (11), Nite (88, 89), Shaw (115), and Wood (141)–all of whom cover the rock and roll era. General rock surveys mention the rockabilly period in a few pages: Belz (5), Gillett (43), Hopkins (53), Laing (61), and Shaw (114). Specialized monographs include Passman (91), who studied the disc jockeys, and Escott and Hawkins (31), who present a history of Sun Records, the prime movers in the rockabilly period. Propes (95) gives some discographic details but mainly for collecting singles. Both Gillett and Nugent (44) and Whitburn (133) indicate the chart actions since 1955, the former also including England.

Periodicals give some coverage to the era. The British *Country Music People* (2a) and *Country Music Review* (2b) have articles and record reviews concerning rockabilly. *Popular Music and Society* (8) will profile the industry or audience acceptance in sociological terms. *Creem* (3), *Melody Maker* (7), and *Rolling Stone* (9) will occasionally present "nostalgia" articles. Record review citations can be located through *Annual Index to Popular Music Record Reviews* (1) and articles and books through *Popular Music Periodicals Index* (94), under artist or under **Rock 'n' Roll** or **Rockabilly** as headings.

ANTHOLOGIES

R1.1   **The Golden Age of Skiffle.** Marble Arch MALS 1287.
Skiffle was the English equivalent of rock and roll for its time (mid-fifties). Skiffle music was based on old time American music, with broad overtones of blues, country, traditional jazz, and hokum. As a musical genre, it seems to be complete in itself. That it would owe its success to a washboard is all the more incredible. No one could have predicted that by the mid-fifties it would be sweeping England. In combination with old vaudeville tunes, such as Lonnie Donegan's "Will Your Chewing Gum Lose Its Flavour on the Bed Post over Night?" or his "My Old Man's a Dustman," the sweep invaded the United States to re-invest the borrowed musical influences: old time American pieces plus jazz to England;

reinterpreted in terms of British music hall songs and feelings; crossing over to American shores again; and the American reaction (more tunes of a similar nature), which once again traversed the Atlantic for more input into British music. When examining skiffle music, one can see the influences affecting each other, until in combination with American r 'n' b, urban blues, and British heritage, the British blues rock music hit the United States in 1964. With instrumentation on this disc comprising guitar, harmonica, bass, drums, and mandolin, this fun-filled set covers the 1955-1956 period (immediately before Lonnie Donegan's arrival in the United States). Tunes include "Midnight Special," "Railroad Bill," "Stackalee," and "When the Sun Goes Down"; other performers include Chris Barber and Johnny Duncan.

R1.2   **Mercury Rockabillies.** Mercury 6336.257 (British issue).

R1.3   **Rare Rockabilly, v.1/2.** MCA MCFM 2697, 2789 (British issues).
      These discs uniquely illustrate the difficulties that the major recording companies had in finding ways to cash in on the newly developing rock and roll music when it was in the rockabilly stage. Both MCA and Mercury used their country and western roster to promote this music because they felt that rockabilly was, in reality, merely uptempo country and western music (such as Webb Pierce recorded in the genre for Decca). The forty tracks here (a generous sampling) include such typical efforts as the four from Johnny Carroll, a raw singer from Texas ("Rock 'n' Roll Baby," "Hot Rock," "Wild Wild Women," and "Tryin' to Get to You"), the tracks from Don Woody, based in Nashville (which included the original "Bird Dog" motif), the Virginia-born Roy Hall, who did country boogie music while at Nashville ("Three Alley Cats," "Diggin' the Boogie," "Offbeat Boogie," the latter illustrating the mode of rockabilly performance in back of the beat), plus others from Alabama, Louisiana, and Los Angeles. It appears that the scattergun approach was used, but the music does prove quite substantial with whistles, stomps, echoes, hard-edged ringing guitars, and punchy drumming. The second volume of *Rare* includes Justin Tubb, Bobby Helms, Al Cokes, and Johnny Carroll.

R1.4*   **Original Memphis Rock & Roll.** Sun 106.
      This contains some of the best rockabilly and rock and roll music ever made between 1955 and 1960 for the Sun label, a record company that does *not* contribute to anthology reissues. Rock and roll for this company is somewhat arbitrary, as "Rock 'n' Ruby" by Warren Smith is also on a companion issue, *Memphis Country* (Phonogram 6467 013; British issue), which delves into the outright country music in the Sun catalog. Yet many singers are on *both* albums, thus emphasizing their versatility and the problems of marketing these records to the right buyer. Carl Perkins is aboard here with "Honey, Don't"; Bill Justis's "Raunchy" was a great instrumental hit at parties; Carl McVoy's "You Are My Sunshine" is perhaps the greatest of the updated versions of this tune (Gene Autry-inspired?). At the end of the record, though, we get the big hits of Carl Perkins ("Blue Suede

Shoes"), Roy Orbison ("Ooby Dooby"), Charlie Rich ("Lonely Weekends"), and Jerry Lee Lewis ("Great Balls of Fire").

R1.5*   **Sun Rockabillies, v.1/3.** three discs. Phonogram 6467 025/7 (British issue).

Colin Escott and Martin Hawkins have written the definitive history of Sam Phillips and Sun Records. As accompaniment, they have compiled a number of albums to illustrate (musically) the development of the Sun sound and the rockabilly feel. The 48 tracks on this set nicely show how pervasive the Sun influence was. Although some items here have never been issued before, their impact can be calculated on the basis of the material covered and the lyrics espoused at a time when rock and roll was beginning, as compared with when it succumbed to commercial influences. For instance, there is a very good and unreleased "Put Your Cat Clothes On," a screaming wailer by Carl Perkins. Jerry Lee Lewis's unreleased "Milkshake Mademoiselle" exhibits all of the characteristics of the Lewis style plus relevance to a real situation. Similarly, other titles indicate current r 'n' b thinking: "Come on Little Mama," "Ubangi Stomp," "Ten Cats Down," "We Wanna Boogie," "Gonna Romp and Stomp," "Red Cadillac and a Black Moustache," "Where'd You Stay Last Night?," "Tootsie," and "Itchy." The music is programmed in roughly chronological order; so that by volume three, 1960 had been reached and the Sun rockabillys themselves were being drowned in commercial music, with a fuller sound, chickie choruses, strings, and so forth, as opposed to early primitive sounds relying only on a riffing guitar, slight drumming, and strong vocals. Rockabilly music was a direct antecedent to country rock; you can hear the influences in the music of Commander Cody and the "Nashville outlaws."

R1.6*   **The Sun Story, 1952-1968.** two discs. Phonogram 6641 180 (British issue).

This double disc set is meant to accompany the book *Sun Records* (London, England: Hanover, 1974), by Martin Hawkins and Colin Escott. The four sides are thematically divided. "Feelin' Good" (1952-1962), the first, is concerned with Sun's great blues catalog. Here are an early Rufus Thomas, before his shift to r 'n' b; Big Walter Horton; Junior Parker; Joe Hill Louis; and Frank Frost. Side two is "Hillbilly Fever" (1956-1962) with illustrative examples provided by Carl Perkins and Warren Smith (no duplications here with *Sun Rockabillies, v.1/3*, described in item no. R1.5). Side three emphasizes "The Memphis Beat" (1957-1960), showing through Warren Smith, Charlie Rich, and Roy Orbison, the beginnings of commercialization and the inroads of softness into the formerly primitive sound. The fourth side, "Sun in the Sixties" (1958-1966) contains no memorable tunes or selections, but the items are needed to complete the story. Sun Records, begun by Sam Phillips, a disc jockey in Memphis, originally recorded masters for other labels such as Modern (Los Angeles) and Chess (Chicago). Seeing success, Phillips branched out on his own. He discovered Elvis Presley (no examples here, as Phillips sold the masters to RCA as part of the deal in trading), Johnny Cash, Jerry Lee Lewis, Carl Perkins, Charlie Rich—an impressive roster indeed. This set reflects all styles—rockabilly, blues, r 'n' b, soul, and western. Good historical notes are, of course, by Hawkins and Escott.

INNOVATORS

R1.7*   **Bill Haley and His Comets. Best.** two discs. MCA 2-4010.

Haley began recording for Essex records with "Crazy Man, Crazy" in 1953, the first rock 'n' roll song to make the best selling charts in *Billboard*. He soon signed with Decca, and recorded "Shake, Rattle and Roll" and "Rock around the Clock." The former item had been a hit for Joe Turner; the latter was an original. Neither moved anywhere until "Rock around the Clock" was adopted as the opening number in the movie *Blackboard Jungle*. Then it smashed all records and rose to the top of the charts. It also gave adults and parents the impression that rock and roll was associated with hoodlums and delinquents, an impression that was to remain for the rest of the decade. Haley, then, is important for just the above facts. In addition, it is necessary to comment on the music. Haley is essentially a country singer, with western swing background plus a rhythm 'n' blues saxophone. The visual antics of Haley's climbing the double bass, wailing the saxophone from the floor while lying on his back, and picking the guitar with his teeth contributed in no small measure to the group's success with the kids, and its "outlawing" by parents who saw bad habits and country hokum and foolishness in the acts. His music is purely a fusion of the elements described above. Other hits here include "See You Later, Alligator," "Birth of the Boogie," and "Mambo Rock." As other, better singers and performers invaded the genre, Haley's Comets, revealing a lack of sustained drive and good material, quickly burned out.

R1.8*   **Buddy Holly. Best.** two discs. MCA 2-4009.

Much of Holly has been reissued many times in different forms and packages. This double set finally standardizes the work of one of the greatest rock and roll singers ever known. His lasting popularity on records and the accord given him after his tragic 1959 airplane crash are due in no small measure to his accomplishments as a composer and performer. He had relied on his Texas roots to assimilate "Tex-Mex" (Texas-Mexican origin) music and certain aspects of western swing, also including his glottis movement as a replacement for the western yodel. This stringing out of the vocal line ("uh-uh-uh-uh" for the simple "oh") was to have great impact on the development of British singers in the sixties, and it became known as the "Buddy Holly sound." Included among his back-up group, the Crickets, was a bassist named Waylon Jennings, who has since carried on the Texas tradition of independence through his "Nashville outlaw" mode of performance and singing.

Holly's best efforts are on this double set, such as "Peggy Sue" and "That'll Be the Day," and both of these items incorporate the ingenuity of lead guitarists, which in the middle fifties was practically non-existent elsewhere. Today, of course, the main rock instrument is the lead guitar. Many tunes have since passed into the folklore and vocabulary of rock, such as "Not Fade Away," "Maybe Baby," "Rave On," and Paul Anka's "It Doesn't Matter Anymore." For the complete Holly, check Coral 7100-H1-9, a nine-album set from Germany that contains a book, a poster, 100 plus songs, interviews, and several tribute songs.

R1.9*   **Jerry Lee Lewis. Original Golden Hits, v.1/3.** three discs. Sun 102, 103, 128.

R1.10   **Jerry Lee Lewis. Rockin' Rhythm & Blues.** Sun 107.
When Sam Phillips, founder and owner of Sun Records, developed the delayed tape for making echo effects, he immediately applied it to a new singer for the label: Jerry Lee Lewis. Along with Lewis's original boogie piano style (pounding and arpeggios), that later became known as the Jerry Lee Lewis "Pumping Piano," that echo became responsible for a string of hits never since duplicated in sheer buoyancy and energy. The first three records cited represent most of Lewis's Sun material through 1961, and include the flash hits of "Crazy Arms," "Great Balls of Fire," "Whole Lotta Shakin' Going On," "Breathless," "Money," and "High School Confidential." He also had great success with re-interpreting Chuck Berry's material, and that should prove no surprise, as Berry and Lewis came from the same roots. Most of the Berry items are found on the fourth disc (Sun 107), which is an interesting compilation (with minimal duplication) of some of his faster numbers, such as "Good Golly, Miss Molly," "Big Legged Woman," "Hang up My Rock and Roll Shoes," "Sweet Little Sixteen," and "What'd I Say?" This is good party music, and it was very influential on the merger of rock and roll with country, as pointed out by such songs as Hank Williams's "You Win Again," "I'll Sail My Ship Alone," and Charlie Rich's "Break-Up" and "I'll Make It All up to You."

R1.11*   **Elvis Presley. The Sun Sessions.** RCA KPM1-0153.

R1.11a   **Elvis Presley. World Wide 50 Gold Award Hits, v.1.** four discs. RCA LPM 6401.
Presley, the leader of the pack, was the singer from Sun Records who broke through to a wide audience with rockabilly tunes. He and Phillips took older blues and r 'n' b material and gave the items a country feel. Presley took over with an urgent voice—an exceptionally troubled voice that deteriorated with the slower numbers (most notably on "Love Me Tender," his first real love ballad). At the same time, Presley continued to record country items. (Sun Records, as noted in the introduction to this section, issued a rockabilly tune on side A of the single, and a country tune on side B.) The sixteen tracks (and more are inexplicably lost) on the single RCA album present the Sun items and include "That's All Right," "Milk Cow Boogie," "Good Rockin' Tonight," and "You're a Heartbreaker." Country items here include "Blue Moon of Kentucky," "Mystery Train" and the blues "Baby, Let's Play House." These tracks are the ones that collectors keep and play over and over. Presley was the undisputed leader of the rockabillies. His downfall came at the hands of RCA, and this is ably documented with the four-volume set (volume 2, also four discs, is largely pop material from 1967 onwards). Commercial pop items at times became million sellers solely on Presley's name. His major importance was in the fact that white girls could identify him as a singer and lover in their dreams, something that parental guidance would not condone for black singers in the mid-fifties. This breakthrough, which drew in hundreds of other singers, cannot be taken lightly. RCA material included "Hound Dog," "Heartbreak Hotel," "Don't Be Cruel," "Too Much," Blue Suede Shoes," "Jailhouse Rock," etc., among the fifty tracks.

STANDARDS

R1.12   Johnny Burnette. Rock 'n' Roll Trio. Coral CP 61 (British issue).
Like many other British albums, this set was never issued in the United
States. The insatiable demand for rockabilly music in England has determined
the market for these reissues, and they go over quite well. More than half of the
total pressings are exported, mainly to the United States. These twelve tracks come
from 1956 and present the infinitely raunchier, rawer vocalizings of Burnette,
before his later sweet hits of "Dreamin' " and "You're Sixteen" (with violins).
The trio had Johnny on rhythm guitar, his brother Dorsey on slap bass, and Paul
Burlison on lead guitar. These are all dynamite tracks for very aggressive people,
and, of course, they were in advance of their time. Actually, these tunes sold more
to the black market than to the white market, despite the fact that Burnette was
white. Burlison's claim to being a boss at guitar comes out in "Honey Hush" and
"Lonesome Train." The vigorous vocals by Burnette remind one of Buddy Holly,
especially the glottis movement.

R1.13*   Johnny Cash. Original Golden Hits, v.1/2. two discs. Sun 100/1.
Cash certainly had more hits than are displayed on these two discs; however,
the packaging policy of the new owners of Sun Records appears to be to repeat
a few of the big hits with some minor ones. The 22 tracks here are the best that
could be found from Sun and put on two discs.
Cash is mainly a country singer who was turned into the rockabilly mold
by Sam Phillips of Sun Records. Cash was well-equipped for the role, as he recorded
some excellent material by Jack Clement and Charlie Rich. His accompanying
group was the Tennessee Two, with Luther Perkins's superb boogie guitar (straight
from the 1940s honky-tonk styles) plus echo; and the rhythm that they laid down
with plucked, short notes nicely complemented Cash's deep voice. Some good
material here includes "Folsom Prison Blues," "Hey, Porter," "There You Go,"
"Next in Line," "I Walk the Line" (his greatest and most enduring hit, over two
years on the popular music charts), "Home of the Blues," "Big River," and the
poignant "Give My Love to Rose." In conception, this is all country music. Cash
acknowledges his influences as being Hank Williams and Ernest Tubb, and this
is their style of music. But with the marketing of Sun Records, Cash easily crossed
over to the rockabilly and popular music fields bringing with him songs of broken-
hearted love and of the railroad, which added more "guts" to the basic music.

R1.14*   Charlie Feathers/Mac Curtis. Rockabilly Kings. Polydor 2310 293
                (British issue).
Sun did not have a hammerlock on the rockabilly mode of rock and roll.
Charlie Feathers's material for Sun is largely missing (and presumed destroyed),
but the Feathers items here come from Sun's most successful competitor in this
genre: King Records, of Cincinnati, Ohio. The eight tracks are all minor gems
with the fusion of r 'n' b and country, and they span only a one-year period.
"One Hand Loose," "Bottle to the Baby," and "Can't Hardly Stand It"—all reflect
his innate ability to whip up emotions through very serious and realistic lyrics.
His glottis style seems to be derived from Buddy Holly, but it is an early form of
the Holly style.

Mac Curtis's tunes were recorded in Dallas or Fort Worth, Texas, and once again reveal the impact that Texas music has had on the development of just about every major musical genre and style. Curtis was more of a rocker than a hillbilly, with vast shades of existing r 'n' b rhythms. His best works here include "Grandaddy's Rockin'," "Goose Bumps," and "If I Had Me a Woman." Although he played a guitar, he seemed to have a curious similarity to Jerry Lee Lewis; and indeed, with the decline of rock and roll, he transferred to country material, just as Lewis did.

R1.15   Carl Perkins. Blue Suede Shoes. Sun 112.
Perkins is another rockabilly who writes his own material. He flashed on the rock scene in the mid-fifties with his biggest hit "Blue Suede Shoes," an item that he wrote himself. It sold more copies than the Elvis Presley version. This song, more than any other, characterized the attitude of the rockabillies: hard living, hard loving, and hard drinking, with a no-nonsense attitude. Its most current revival is with the "Nashville outlaws" of Waylon Jennings, Willie Nelson, Tompall Glaser, et al. Strangely enough, Perkins has appeared to mellow, refusing to go along with this group and staying with his comfortable present job as lead guitarist for Johnny Cash. Items of importance here, all from the late fifties, include "Turn Around," "You Can't Make Love to Somebody," and "Let the Juke Box Keep on Playing."

R1.16   Charlie Rich. Lonely Weekends. Sun 110.
Of all the Sun Rockabillies, Charlie Rich was perhaps the most country flavored, and after a short excursion with Elvis Presley imitations, he returned to the country fold with Mercury, Smash, RCA, and Epic records. The eleven tracks here are from his Presley days. He was quite credible as a rockabilly, but it was often suspected that he did not have his heart in the action. His biggest hit, perhaps of all time if one counts his re-recordings of it, was the title selection. He wrote this song himself, along with others heard on this set: "Stay," "That's How Much I Love You," "Sittin' and Thinkin'," "Who Will the Next Fool Be?," etc. In this, he was unique, for it was virtually unheard of in those days for a singer in the rock and roll field to be writing his own material.

R1.17*   Marty Robbins. Greatest Hits. Columbia CS 8639.
Although primarily a country singer, Robbins burst onto the rockabilly scene to produce "story songs." His successes were "Big Iron," "Ballad of the Alamo," "Hangin' Tree," and "El Paso." His rockabilly items included "White Sport Coat and a Pink Carnation," "Singing the Blues" (covered effectively by his Columbia stablemate, Guy Mitchell), and the rocker "Just Married." Like so many other singers in this field (such as Carl Perkins and Jerry Lee Lewis), Robbins returned to the country fold.

R1.18*   Gene Vincent. The Bop That Just Won't Stop (1956). Capitol ST 11287.
Vincent was the first of the rock and roll performers to follow along in the wake of Elvis Presley imitators. His initial hit—"Be-Bop-A-Lula"—came out in early 1956 and sold over three million copies. (Many people thought that it was Presley with a new hit.) Vincent personified the tough rock 'n' roller, with the cap, the

motorcycle jacket, the slurred intonation (which got him in trouble when "Huggin' " seemed to be pronounced as "fuggin' "). He was also the first flash-in-the-pan for rock music. All of the tunes on this set of twelve were recorded in 1956 and seem to be in the same groove of music. Some boredom can set in after the first side, but as a document, it is highly significant. It is virtually the only record available that concentrates on just one year of a rock 'n' roll vocalist and has complete discographical information. Such treatment is almost always reserved for a blues or jazz star. This "one year" (actually May to October, 1956) gives the listener an opportunity to hear *original* music as it developed over a short period of time. Vincent wrote most of his own material, and it can soon be heard that much of it was indeed original, not based on black music or other white music before it (e.g., folk, country, pop, etc.). Indeed, Vincent can be characterized as a seminal influence on the early rockers, with unique material that was his alone. He owed nothing to any man.

ROCK 'N' ROLL

> "They sing about us; therefore we exist."
> —after Frank Zappa

INTRODUCTION

This music is a softer-edged variant of rockabilly. It also is a merger of two basic but regional streams of music. Rock and roll took the Southeast's rural country music and blended it with the black r 'n' b of the urban Northeast. Essentially, then, rock and roll was an urban phenomenon of the East Coast, while rockabilly was southern music. Rock and roll took a medium-tempo country song and merged it with a medium-tempo r 'n' b song; rockabilly combined the fast honky-tonk of country with the raw primitiveness of uptempo black jump blues. The obvious results were that rockabilly was more spirited than rock and roll. And Elvis Presley again led the way when he recorded for RCA after establishing a rockabilly image with Sun Records. At RCA, he handled pop ballads and other mid-tempo r 'n' b ballads to define the basic rock and roll pattern.

Throughout all this, rock and roll (but not rockabilly) was encouraged by the performing rights society, BMI. The more singers it enrolled and the more versions of songs that it helped to record, the more money would be returned to its members (and commissions to BMI). Thus began what was known as the "cover" records (i.e., a song that has already been recorded by someone else), in which a white singer would adopt the same song as another country or r 'n' b artist, but sing it in his own pop style for the national market. BMI usually collected all of the rights to country and r 'n' b songs, while ASCAP disclaimed such popular variants at the time); thus, the more that BMI could sell, the better off it would be in its continuing battle with ASCAP. In a study of the seventeen biggest 1954-1956 r 'n' b hits, the white cover version outsold the black original in the white market (except for two titles that had no covers). These white versions sounded different, of course, because they were meant for the white market, and each was originally treated as a novelty-white pop music augmented by a twist or gimmick.

An example of this is the song "Hearts of Stone" recorded by Otis Williams and the Charms. This group supposedly came off the street from a baseball game into a studio and the members were asked if they wanted to make a record. The producer apparently had what he considered to be a hit song but no group to record the vocal; there were also no arrangements for the studio band, because there was at the time no group to be arranged. With minimum rehearsal, Williams's tenor took off with the vocal line. The rest of the group went into a "doo wop" phrase and chanted behind Williams's vocals, which were then in conflict with the melody (rhythm instruments kept the time). He fell behind a few beats, caught up, played with the rhythm, used melisma at the end of a line, and generally sang with the saxophones, which had been employing *rubato* (free style). The result: a danceable, swinging record that is irresistible and difficult to stop playing. The Fontane Sisters did a cover version of "Hearts of Stone," employing white techniques—group vocals (unison or part harmony), even tempos and 4/4 stress, even and short pronunciation of a background chorus, a transcribed saxophone passage, and a prominent rhythm section. The result: a hard, brittle song with a definite enunciation of voices, instruments, and beats (i.e., no blending or bending of notes) into a distinct jerk common to popular dance bands.

Characteristics

Charlie Gillett postulates that five basic forms of rock and roll developed around the country, although some are distinctly r 'n' b patterns. *First,* there was the northern sound of Bill Haley, which was essentially a slick version of western swing music. *Secondly,* there was the Memphis country rock, or rockabilly, contributed by Sun Records and Elvis Presley (the most exciting of all white rock music). *Third,* there was the New Orleans dance blues style of Fats Domino and then Little Richard, both of whom worked in the r 'n' b field but also became popular with the white market. *Fourth,* there was the Chicago rhythm 'n' blues style, personified largely in Chuck Berry, who was inspired by country boogies and thus formed his own distinctive rockabilly style. It is interesting to note that Berry was the only r 'n' b artist in the Chicago mold to catch on; it wasn't until the Beatles' or the Rolling Stones' recreations of the music that other r 'n' b performers would be noted. And *fifth,* there were the vocal group harmonies of rock and roll, beginning with the white-market-oriented Platters, who adapted the best of the r 'n' b doo wop styles. Whether it came from rockabilly, country rock, western swing rock, doo wop, or another variant, the basic form of rock and roll was that of the blues mode, i.e., three basic chords, in this case, the first (tonic or C chord), fourth (subdominant or F chord), and fifth (dominant or G chord) notes of the scale. Changes of key resulted from chromatic leaps rather than from slow modulation.

Vocally, the double glottis was dropped, for it was too rough for a national homogenized (and largely unseen) young audience. The emphasis was on uptempo ballads, and the material largely dealt with first love or puppy love, and—significantly—life styles. The music was associated with the singer, not, as with popular music, directed at the listener. The songs were of the autobiographical type: parental dismay at teenagers; sneaking off for some "lovin' "; the joys of various forms of clothes (songs *about* clothes spread those very styles to the audience and reacted with other topics as well to communicate to the audience new developments in teenage life); dances; and so forth. The influence of the singers was thus more non-musical than musical, and the cults built around their lifestyles developed into a "star" system that previously had been accorded only movie stars. Beset by television, movies were in decline, and a new star system arose for public adoration— this time in rock and roll music. Coming to grips with divisive forces amongst purists in rock music is very difficult, particularly concerning music that developed during the 1954-1959 period (with 1955-1957 being its heyday) in the age of singles rather than of whole albums. Any attempt to further classify rockabilly and other forms of rock and roll music must be done on a single-song basis, which completely obviates anthologies and solo artist collations that may espouse several styles, especially when managers and producers were experimenting for a saleable sound.

Suffice it to say that *all* of rock and roll (and its permutations) had flexibility, but when broken down into regional styles of performing, this flexibility becomes lost. But then the music remains a historical antecedent that returns to haunt groups, such as the resurfacing of rockabilly through the Beatles or that of r 'n' b through the Rolling Stones.

The racial interrelationships of the types of music is murky. Specific examples abound, as noted above, but there was also continuous crossing between the styles of blues, r 'n' b, country, and popular music until the distinctive stylings of rock and soul music emerged after 1963. Between 1959 and 1963, the music of rock and roll was contained within the popular mainstream fold: soft ballads with a beat background, harmony singing, gentle rhythms, and so forth. To many alert rock and rollers, the change in the music became boring and mordant. Thus the initial impact of the Beatles and the Rolling Stones was perhaps greater than was actually musically warranted at the time. It was simply a matter of their filling a vacuum.

Literature

As with rockabilly, rock 'n' roll music is not too well detailed in writing except when treated as "nostalgia." General rock surveys do document this period: Belz (5), Gillett (43), Hopkins (53), Jahn (57), Laing (60), and Shaw (114). More specific items can be found through Brown's (11) encyclopedia, Nite's (90) encyclopedias, Shaw's (115) survey, and Wood's (141) biographical book that also covers some British artists. Passman (91) studied the disc jockey and noted his impact, and Propes (95) gives some discographic details, but mainly for collecting singles. Both Gillett and Nugent (44) and Whitburn (133) indicate the chart actions since 1955, the former also including England.

Periodicals give mainly "nostalgic coverage" to the era: *Creem* (3), *Melody Maker* (7), and *Rolling Stone* (9). *Popular Music and Society* (8) will investigate the sociological impact of rock 'n' roll. Record review citations can be located through *Annual Index to Popular Music Record Reviews* (1) and articles and books through *Popular Music Periodicals Index* (94) under artist or **Rock 'n' Roll** as a heading.

ANTHOLOGIES

R2.1*   **American Graffiti.** two discs. MCA 2-8001.

The 41 items here are the basic, germinal recordings of the 1955-1962 period. If only *one* album from the fifties rock and roll-rhythm and blues music scene is desired, then this set has to be the one. For the first time, all of the major record companies cooperated in putting together an album, for it is essentially a "sound-track" effort to accompany the film *American Graffiti*. (At $1,000 a track for the leasing rights, each recording company had a stake in it.) Other compilations are basically from the vaults of individual companies, with perhaps a few extras thrown in by means of cheap leases from small independent companies that needed the money. What can one say about the first important rock and roll record from Bill Haley and the Comets, "Rock around the Clock"; the first use of the pipe organ in rock and roll, on Del Shannon's "Runaway"; the harp on Buster Brown's "Fanny Mae"; the incessant guitar riff on Booker T's "Green Onion" (the one that would spawn so many pale imitations in soul music and funk); or even the boogie beat on Buddy Holly's "That'll Be the Day"? Even the chatter (edited down from the movie's) provided by Wolfman Jack has its merits. Most of this music is dance music, with "Johnny B. Goode," "Get a Job," "Do You Wanna Dance?" (Bobby Freeman's all time great hit; actually, his only one), "Party Doll," and one of the greatest r 'n' b sock'em tunes and vocals by the Regents: "Barbara Ann." Volumes two and three (MCA2-8004 and 8008) are also available, with material of slightly lesser quality.

R2.2*   **Big 'uns from the 50's and 60's.** EMI One Up OU 2046 (British issue).

This anthology is important for a variety of reasons, not the least of which is that it is a perfect illustration of the attempts made by major companies to successfully cover the hits of smaller, black labels. It was this crossing the line from r 'n' b into rock and roll that broke down barriers of performance and musical styles in the late 1950s. For instance, of the twenty tracks here, "Ain't That a Shame?" (by Pat Boone) came from Fats Domino, and "I Hear You Knocking," (recorded here by Gale Storm) came from Little Richard. Other influences were from country music, such as "The Auctioneer" (covered by Leroy Van Dyke); "Young Love" (by a sickly Tab Hunter) came from Sonny James in the country field, as did "Deck of Cards" (by Wink Martindale) from the late, great Tex Ritter. There is also Pat Boone's "Love Letters in the Sand." Three other notable musical examples here include the inter-racial Dell-Vikings' "Come and Go with Me," which pulled out all the stops on doo-wop groups; Jim Lowe's "The Green Door," the only genuine pre-rock-and-roll rockin' hit here; and the mysterious Nervous Norvus's "Transfusion," which was the first and most influential of the humor records (coming as it did in 1957).

R2.3*   **Cadence Classics, v.1/2.** two discs. Barnaby RB 4000/1.

Cadence was Archie Bleyer's label when Bleyer was musical director for the Arthur Godfrey show. It developed uptempo performances of mainly middle-of-the-road early rock and roll music that proved popular with Mom, Dad, and the kids of the Midwest. Most of the Everly Brothers' hits were recorded for Cadence ("Bye Bye Love," "Wake up Little Suzie," "Problems," etc.), and six of them are here among the 22 tracks. Since the Everlys have their own "hits" album and annotation, the others here are of more importance at this moment. The soft singing of the Chordettes trio includes the theme from the TV show "Zorro," as well as "Lollipop" and "Mr. Sandman." Johnny Tillotson's epic "Poetry in Motion" and "Dreamy Eyes" are here, as well as Eddie Hodges's funfilled "Girls, Girls, Girls Were Made to Love." There is even an early Charlie McCoy ("Cherry Berry Wine"). Of particular note, though, are the very last tracks of both albums: two superb uptempo rock and roll tunes ("Rumble" and "The Swag") from the lead guitar of Link Wray, the person who revolutionized the guitar's role in rock and roll and, later, rock music.

R2.4*   **Cruisin'. 1955-1967.** thirteen discs. Increase 2000/2012. [Cartridge: 8100-2000/2012; Cassette: 5100-2000/2012.]

Each disc has twelve tracks, totaling 156 big hits covering thirteen years (one disc to a year). The gimmick in this package is that actual disc jockeys recreate the mood of the times with station calls, advertising, news items, and the weather. These little details add a wealth of social commentary, although some people become annoyed by the intrusion of the dee jay. On the other hand, many people have bought the cartridge version for playing in their cars, or at the beach, and so forth, in attempts to relive the past by forsaking the present and its multitude of nameless disc jockeys. (True recreation of the past in such cases also includes the words and noises *between* records on a radio station.) Each set has superb notes by Jerry Hopkins (Presley's biographer) that place the songs in context with the events of the year and describe how they all interacted with one another. Of good value are his statements on cover versions, especially since these appeared at about two-year intervals after the original. Record companies involved in this project did not include RCA, but they do have ABC Paramount, Arvee, Calico, Checker, Chess, Co-Ed, Fury, Mercury, Roulette, and so forth. Of course, the first half of the entire set contains more musical gems than the last half (from 1961 on); but it is a record of what we listened to (and yesterday's teenagers are today's adults). Rare items here are mostly from the early period, such as Ray Charles's first version of "I Got a Woman," Hank Ballard's "Annie Had a Baby," the Royal Teens' "Short Shorts," and Duane Eddy's "Rebel Rouser."

R2.5   **Echoes of a Rock Era; The Early Years.** two discs. Roulette RE-111.

R2.6   **Echoes of a Rock Era; The Middle Years.** two discs. Roulette RE-112.

R2.7   **Echoes of a Rock Era; The Later Years.** two discs. Roulette RE-113.

These six discs have reasonably good liner notes by the late, great disc jockey, George "Hound Dog" Lorenz. The sixty items here are mainly in the mainstream of rock and roll *and* rhythm and blues music. Sterling examples of musical innovators from this period include Bo Diddley's "Bo Diddley" (based on an old English ballad, tempered by Creole rhythms); Faye Adams's original "Shake a Hand"; several folk-type numbers by Jimmy Rodgers (who was slightly ahead of his time with "Honeycomb," "Kisses Sweeter Than Wine," and "Secretly"); Buddy Knox's important rocker, "Party Doll"; Dee Clark's screaming "Hey, Little Girl"; Joe Jones's funny "You Talk Too Much"; Little Eva's repetitious but

rhythmically acceptable "The Locomotion" (created by Carole King); and Mary
Wells's first version (the first) of "My Guy."

R2.8*   **The Many Sides of Rock 'n' Roll, v.1/3.** six discs. United Artists UAD
           60025/6, 60035/6, and 60093/4 (British issues).
       United Artists chose to release these important sets only in England (UA
has the rights to many small labels from the fifties, including Liberty, Herald,
Ember, Demon, Modern, Gregmark, Nasco, Chancellor, Imperial, Aladdin, Warwick,
and so forth). The coverage here is of the decade 1955-1965, with most of the 85
tracks being recorded between 1956 and 1959. As is common with most British
reissues, there are competent, readable, historical notes and very intelligent programming. Side one opens with "Rock and Roll Stars," highlighting boogie and boogaloo
artists such as Amos Milburn ("Chicken Shack Boogie"), Thurstan Harris ("Over
and Over"), and Larry Williams ("Bony Maronie"). The first side of the second set
is similar, called "The Original Versions," with Smiley Lewis's "One Night," the
Fleetwoods' "Come Softly to Me," and Bobby Freeman's epic "Do You Wanna
Dance?" The other sides (reflecting the title of this mini-series) include the great
instrumentals of Johnny and the Hurricanes ("Beatnik Fly"), the Ventures ("Walk–
Don't Run"), and Sandy Nelson ("Let There Be Drums"). The section "Groups
of the Fifties" includes early Phil Spector groups such as the Teddy Bears ("To
Know Him Is to Love Him"), the Penguins' eternal "Earth Angel," and the Silhouettes'very relevant "Get a Job" (from whence came the nonsense words "sha
na na," later to be the name of the rock 'n' roll revival group). "Teen Boys of the
Sixties" pays tribute to early innovators Bobby Vee ("Rubber Ball"), Buddy Knox,
Del Shannon, and others. The side devoted to "Groups" includes items by far-
reaching groups such as the Rivingtons (their nonsensical "Papa-Oom-Mow-Mow"),
the Five Satins, the Olympics ("Western Movies"), and the Cadets ("Stranded
in the Jungle"). Not to be forgotten are the "Teen Ballads" of lost love, broken
hearts, and assorted other tragedies. These include Frankie Avalon worshipping
"Venus," Reparata and the Delrons singing "Whenever a Teenager Cries," and the
Crescendos moaning "Oh, Julie." These sets have lots of photographs, reproductions
of posters and hit charts, plus radio playlists. Because of the unique programming
and the notes that trace items from their roots, these albums are highly significant
reissues of the mainstream of rock 'n' roll and r 'n' b music.

R2.9   **Original Early Top 40 Hits.** two discs. Paramount PAS 1013.
       This collection is mainly from the Dot catalog of the middle 1950s. There
is nothing spectacular here in the way of heavy rock 'n' roll; indeed, there are many
covers, such as Pat Boone's "Tutti Frutti" (borrowed from Little Richard), "Ain't
That a Shame" (from Fats Domino), Tab Hunter's "Young Love" (borrowed from
country's Sonny James). *But,* this collection does have several unique hits from the
early days, such as Jim Lowe's "Green Door," an honest rock and roll song from the
time when there was no general rock and roll. Groups include the Hilltoppers
("Trying," "P.S., I Love You"), Billy Vaughan's instrumentals ("Melody of Love,"
"Sail Along Silv'ry Moon"), Lonnie Donegan's epic "Does Your Chewing Gum
Lose Its Flavour on the Bedpost Overnight?," Nervous Norvus's grisly "Transfusion," and so forth. Thirty tracks of good summer music are here.

R2.10*   **Original Hits—Golden Instrumentals.** Dot 25820.

Dot was originally a country music independent label. When it began to record Pat Boone in 1955, the company soon discovered the rich pop market waiting for it (Boone was recorded for the country side of the population on his first records). Accordingly, Dot shifted gears and began to look around for material. Every rock and roll label had some instrumentals for party music, and in 1964, Dot released this set, a compilation of twelve pounding blues rockers, fast ravers, and music characterized by tough saxophone and driving guitar breaks. It has since been reissued a few times, and it actually sold better in England than in the United States. This instrumental music developed from the black influences on white popular music of the forties. First came Louis Jordan, followed by Earl Bostic, Bill Doggett ("Honky Tonk"), and a host of others (including Bill Black, Presley's bassist). Duane Eddy legitimized it, and the Ventures incorporated it. Most of the hits here were one-shot efforts; the performers did a fast fade after the "sequel" failed to rise on the charts. Thus, Santo and Johnny's "Sleepwalk" (utilizing a vocal-steel guitar), Lonnie Mack's "Memphis," the Champs' "Tequila" (featuring a young Seals and Crofts), and the Surfaris' "Wipeout" were solo efforts. Sandy Nelson ("Teen Beat"), Dave "Baby" Cortez ("Happy Organ") and Johnny and the Hurricanes ("Red River Rock") all survived. This is a good party disc.

R2.11   **Phil Spector's Christmas Album.** Warner Brothers SP 9103.

This is one of the better sets of what are now called "novelty" records. In 1963, Phil Spector conceived the idea of a Christmas album utilizing his groups and discoveries plus the unique big band and string lush ensemble sounds called "wall of sound." Thus, the Crystals, the Ronettes, Darlene Love, and Bob B. Soxx and the Blue Jeans made versions of "White Christmas," "Frosty the Snowman," "Bells of St. Mary," "Santa Claus Is Coming to Town," "Here Comes Santa Claus," and others. Similar attempts a decade before were successful for the Drifters (with "White Christmas" and "Bells of St. Mary"). Overall reaction initially was one of "bad taste"; but the album became an underground success and was reissued by Apple Records, through Spector's association with the Beatles.

R2.11a*   **Phil Spector's Greatest Hits.** two discs. Warner Brothers 2SP 9104.

Spector aided the demise of the "classic" rock and roll period by creating a lush, full production for all of the music fashioned for his stable of artists. This meant heavy use of tympani, strings, echos, choirs, and much money. In doing so, he assisted in the birth of the Philadelphia sound; while the music was interesting to listen to, it was not very danceable except with a listless body movement or, at best, some sort of fox trot. Overall, there appeared to be a certain sameness to the music that would have been more varied if most of it had been originally recorded in stereo. Alas, it was not to be, and monophonic controls made the music a "wall-of-sound," producing an acoustic environment along the lines of McLuhanism. These 24 tracks are his best efforts, and include the Crystals ("Da Doo Ron Ron," "He's a Rebel"), the Righteous Brothers ("You've Lost That Lovin' Feelin'," "Unchained Melody," "Ebb Tide"), the Ronettes ("Walking in the Rain," "Be My Baby"), the Teddy Bears (in which Spector did male harmony on "To Know Him Is to Love Him"), Ben E. King ("Spanish Harlem"), Ike and Tina Turner

("River Deep—Mountain High"), plus Bob B. Soxx and the Blue Jeans, the Paris Sisters, Darlene Love, and Gene Pitney.

R2.12*   **Rock 'n' Soul; The History of Rock in the Pre-Beatles Decade of Rock, 1953-1963.** nine discs. ABC Records ABCX-1955/1963.

Although of all the sets of re-issued "goldies" or "goodies" in the rock and roll or r 'n' b scene, this one probably has the most duplication with existing albums. The ABC people, by acquiring a large number of small labels that owned the rights to a wide variety of white and black musical efforts in the fifties, have been able to reissued some valuable items that have lain fallow in the vaults of Duke, Peacock, and other southern labels. For instance, 1953-1955 saw the almighty important and influential Johnny Ace record "The Clock," "My Song," and "Pledgin' My Love." Soon he was to die of Russian roulette, and a whole cult sprang up around his memory. Other early originals here are "When You Dance" (The Turbans), "Speedoo" (The Cadillacs), "Crying in the Chapel" (The Orioles), and "Hound Dog" (the original version by Willie Mae Thornton!). Also, for laughs, there is a weak cover version of "Shake a Hand" by Faye Adams. Throughout the rest of the series—108 tracks in all (twelve to an album)—are select tracks not found elsewhere, such as "Let the Good Times Roll" (Shirley and Lee, 1956), "Next Time You See Me" (Junior Parker, 1957), "Hey, Little Girl" (Dee Clark, 1959). But by the time of "Those Oldies but Goodies" (Little Caesar and the Romans, 1961) and Gene Chandler's 1962 repetitious hit "Duke of Earl" [Dook, Dook, Dook], rock and roll was stagnant, and rhythm and blues was becoming soul. The last three albums here nicely illustrate that fact.

R2.13   **Roots of British Rock.** two discs. Sire SASH 3711.

Most of these single tunes are virtually unknown in the United States, although some made their way into Canada and to other places in the British Commonwealth. This is music of the 1950s from the United Kingdom. At the same time that skiffle and r 'n' b music were finding cults in Britain, the English had their own versions of uptempo, rocking music to emulate the style and speed of American rock and roll music. While these might be "roots" for today's British rock bands, they most certainly did not influence the British blues scene, which relied on Little Richard, Chuck Berry, etc. They did, however, provide gainful employment and experience in playing. Groups include the Tornadoes and the Shadows; soloists include Adam Faith, Cliff Richard, and Lonnie Donegan. Some of the tracks that made it to North America include Donegan's skiffle beat on "Rock Island Line" and novelty songs, and Cliff Richard's "Living Doll."

R2.14   **Scrapbook of Golden Hits; The Platters, the Crewcuts, the Diamonds, the Gaylords.** Mercury Wing SRW 16371.

This interesting disc reflects the adaptation of doo-wop black styles to white vocal stylings. The Platters, a black group, were almost never associated with "black sounds." Their early songs ("The Great Pretender," "The Magic Touch," "Only You") were urbane copies of the melismatic style of cascading notes. The Diamonds, in Maurice Williams's "Little Darlin'," presented a novel style by directly imitating black group singing—so much so that it sold well in the black markets to purchasers who were unaware that the Diamonds were a white group. To one market segment, "Little Darlin' " was a novelty; to another, it was the real thing. The fact that it was a travesty never came to light. "Why Do Fools Fall in Love?" was covered from the Frankie Lymon hit and was almost equally acceptable. The Gaylords, in "From the Vine Came the Grape" and "The Little Shoemaker," were merely extending Italian influences already felt through Perry Como, Tony Bennett, Vic Damone, et al. The Crewcuts, employing falsetto in "Sh-Boom," successfully covered the black r 'n' b hit by the Chords. If anything, this present set emphasizes the influence of rhythm and blues on rock and roll and on the popular music of the middle fifties in general.

INNOVATORS

R2.15*   **Paul Anka. ABC S-371.**
Anka was an early musical genius in the recording business who turned out hit after hit—all written, produced, and arranged by himself. He was the first recording artist to maintain "artistic integrity" and assume full control of studio techniques. This began with "Diana," back in 1957—a song in tribute to his baby-sitter! That he paved the way for future artistic control by other singers is undeniable, and his influence was extended to many vocalists, as he was called upon to write songs for them (e.g., Frank Sinatra). He was in the mainstream of rock and roll with songs about unrequited love, people, and teenage ballads. Never a hard rocker, he did lack a certain punch in his melodic creations, and his voice did tend to degenerate into a whine, particularly with "Put Your Head on My Shoulder" and "Puppy Love." His only driving piece was "Midnight," with the repetition of the last syllable "-night." Other big hits here include "It's Time to Cry," "Lonely Boy," and "You Are My Destiny" (the last a greatly underrated song).

R2.16*   **Chubby Checker. The Twist. Cameo P 7001.**
This is a simply superb party-dance album, being twelve variations on a single theme. Of course, it is up to the dancers whether they want to "twist the night away." These tracks come from 1960 and 1961, when Checker's big smash hit "The Twist" (developed from a Hank Ballard tune of a few years earlier) made a dance craze. Included are such originally titled pieces as "Peppermint Twist," "Pony Time," and "Let's Twist Again."

R2.17*   **Duane Eddy. 16 Greatest Hits. Jamie S-3026.**
The "twangy" guitar of Eddy, often heard among many groups in outright imitation, was perhaps the most successful of the instrumental sounds from the fifties. During 1958 to 1960, Eddy ground out one hit after another, all emphasizing a rather limited guitar style (being played on what sounded like two strings). Yet they were immensely danceable, and included such rocking hits as "Rebel Rouser," "Ramrod," "Cannonball," "Because They're Young" (a theme soundtrack with, unfortunately, far too many strings in the accompaniment), and the jolly "Forty Miles of Bad Road."

R2.18*   **The Everly Brothers. Greatest Hits.** two discs. Barnaby 6006.

R2.19   **The Everly Brothers. Very Best.** Warner Brothers WS 1554.
        Don and Phil Everly were born into a country music family from Kentucky. In addition, they were heavily influenced by sacred music, and this method of raw singing led them to completely expressionable tender love ballads, which seemed to have some meaning. From May 1957, their first effort, "Bye Bye Love," sung in the long country tradition of brother duos (e.g., Monroe Brothers, Morris Brothers, Blue Sky Boys, Louvin Brothers, etc.), remained at the top for half a year. This success was repeated with "Wake up, Little Susie," one of the first of the white "situation" stories. Other hits here among this twenty item compilation include "This Little Girl of Mine," "Claudette," "I Wonder if I Care as Much," "(Till) I Kissed You," the exceptionally romantic "All I Have to Do Is Dream" (later the anthem of the psychedelic movement), and the enigmatic "Problems" (an expression of worries and difficulties in growing up). In 1960, they re-recorded Gene Vincent's "Be Bop a Lula," one of the first instances of such revival. It is generally acknowledged that the Beatles emulated the harmony of the Everly Brothers. The direct country influence was also carried on by the fact that the Everly Brothers were one of the first groups to record "popular" material in Nashville, and under the production of Chet Atkins, a master of country music arrangement and recording. The Warner Brothers record merely shows them later in their career, with no major shift in the musical emphasis. These 1960-1961 efforts included "Cathy's Clown," "Ebony Eyes," "Lucille," and "So Sad."

R2.20*   **Wanda Jackson. Pioneers of Rock, v.2.** EMI Starline SRS 5120 (British issue).
        Jackson was an important country singer who flirted with rock and roll in the 1958-1963 period before returning to country music (and later, to sacred music). The fourteen tracks here are really hard rockers in the rockabilly mold. Material came from Little Richard ("Long Tall Sally"), Carl Perkins ("Honey, Don't"), Don Covay ("Tongue Tied" and "There's a Party Goin' On"), etc. With her rough, raw and emotional voice, she stood out as the sole female rock and roll performer in the rockabilly mold. Her tough-as-nails vocals are as incredible now as they were when first done. Other successful titles here include "Let's Have a Party" and "Money Honey."

R2.21*   **Roy Orbison. Very Best.** Monument 18045.
        Orbison was another of the Sun rockabillies whom Phillips tried to develop. But except for "Ooby Dooby," he never had a Sun hit. During this time, he penned "Claudette," which was turned into a monster hit by the Everly Brothers. During this fertile period, and before he shifted over to country music, Orbison came up with hit after hit. The 1960-1964 age was good to him, with successes for "Only the Lonely," "Candy Man," "Crying," "Pretty Woman," and "Mean Woman Blues." His high, and penetrating voice seemed to go with his image, and the vocals slashed right across the heavy—and sometimes murky—instrumentation.

R2.22*   **Johnny Ray. Best.** Harmony H 30609.

Ray has to be the first white singer given a push into the realms of rhythm
'n' blues. That his first big smash hit—"Cry"—was released on the Columbia OKeh
label (a series of black records) only points out the markets that the recording
companies were aiming for. Vocal assistance on this disc came from the Four
Lads, a few years before they were to have a series of successes themselves. Ray
opened new frontiers for white singers with his epochal stage presence: whining,
sobbing, with handkerchief open, and body twisting. If this book were to be
illustrated, one of the highest priorities for pictures would have to be those of
Ray on stage with facial grimaces. (He had to be seen to be believed.) "The Little
White Cloud" was penned by him, but it was a decidedly weaker effort. Minor
successes followed, although it must be stated that Ray was perhaps the first
of the "one hit" phenomena of the fifties. He resurged briefly a few years later
with "Walkin' in the Rain," a cover of a Sun record originally done by the Prisonaires
(four inmates at a federal penitentiary).

STANDARDS

R2.23   **Frankie Avalon. 16 Greatest Hits.** ABC 805.

During the 1958-1960 period (in fact, right in the middle of the collapse
of rock and roll as a vital, creative musical style), Frankie Avalon burst on the
scene to record a string of hits for Chancellor Records. He was successful because
he found the formula for produced and contrived musical efforts. While he was
not a "genius" at the musical business, his tiny voice (perfectly suitable for early
teenyboppers) was not uninfluential at the time, with the usual number of imitators
catching onto his coattails. Master of the suspenseful draw in music, Avalon stamped
his personality on such hits as "Venus," "Why?," "Gingerbread," and "De De
Dinah."

R2.24   **Bill Black's Combo. Greatest Hits.** Hi 32012.

From the late fifties on through to the early sixties, bassist Bill Black and
his small group had a popular outfit that gave superb re-interpretations of current
hits in a unique pre-funk style suitable for dancing. His only two real hits on his
own were "White Silver Sands" and "Smokie [pts. 1 and 2]." The swing and verve
that he put into the organ parts on "Don't Be Cruel," "Hearts of Stone," "Raunchy,"
and "Cherry Pink" were masterful in interpretive style. He kept variations on a
theme to a minimum, as on the nice "Twist-Her."

R2.25   **Gary U. S. Bonds. Dance Till "Quarter to Three."** Legrand Records
              3001.

As the classic period of rock and roll faltered, some tempos were picked
up and unleashed on an unsuspecting public. These included the high vocals and
wail of Bonds, and the songs "School Is Out," "Quarter to Three," and "New
Orleans"—all good dance music.

R2.26*   Pat Boone. Pat's Greatest Hits. Dot 25071.
   Boone has strong country roots; he married Red Foley's daughter; he was deeply religious; and he was an all-round nice guy. The image of cardigan, slacks, regular short hair cut, and, of course, white bucks meant parental approval. It also spawned a whole generation of Joe College types. Boone's material for Dot was essentially a mixture of watered-down country classics, such as "There's a Gold Mine in the Sky"; popular mood items as "Friendly Persuasion," "Love Letters in the Sand," and Johnny Mercer's "Bernardine"; and the rhythm and blues classics of the day, such as covers of Fats Domino's "Ain't That a Shame," Ivory Joe Hunter's "I Almost Lost My Mind," and Ertegun's "Chains of Love." With a smooth, blasé voice with little strength or intonation—the question remains: how did he do it? In retrospect and by listening to this record, one can tell from the superior arrangements by Billy Vaughan, the high quality of the material, and the vacuum that existed between black singers and the popular market. It is significant to note that Boone's popularity declined at the same time that black performers were finally crashing through to the lucrative white sectors of the market.

R2.27   Freddy Cannon. Swan 721.
   Cannon, following in the footsteps of Elvis Presley, was an ex-truck driver when he began to record over the 1959-1962 period. While his career was short, his use of whoops, hollers, and his odd falsetto on very romping records helped to point the way to Florida as a center of musical dialogue. His five biggest successes were "Okefenokee," "Tallahassee Lassie," "Way down Yonder in New Orleans," "Chattanooga Shoe Shine Boy," and "Palisades Park."

R2.28   Eddie Cochran. Legendary Masters Series. two discs. UAS 9952.
   This double-disc set presents to the public virtually everything that rocker Cochran put out. There is an essay stressing his importance and influence, but unfortunately, it contains few discographical details. His biggest smash was "Summertime Blues," but the other 24 items here are equally interesting. They are all from the 1957-1959 period (Cochran died a tragic death) and include such titles as "Let's Get Together," "Pink Pegged Slacks," "Somethin' Else," "C'mon Everybody" and "Hallelujah, I Love Her So."

R2.29   Entry deleted.

R2.30   Bobby Darin. Story. Atco S-131.
   Darin began his career as a hard rocker in an r 'n' b mode for what was essentially a black label: Atlantic Records. The material here comes from 1958-1962 and includes his well-known efforts such as "Dream Lover" (with a fine pizzicato string arrangement), the first hit "Splish Splash," "Mack the Knife" (the song that turned him into a pop or moodish singer on the cabaret circuit), "You Must Have Been a Beautiful Baby," "Beyond the Sea," and "Things."

R2.31*   Dell-Vikings. Come and Go with Me. Contour 2870 388 (British issue).
   This group was notable for its being one of the very first inter-racial singing quintets (three black, two white). Their biggest hits were the title selection and "Whispering Bells." The intricate harmony took all it could from the doo wop

vocal styles of black groups, and they interjected much verve and many swoops into their presentation. Being active vocally meant actual participation in all of the songs, not just humming backgrounds. These recordings were made in the mid-fifties for Fee-Bee records and set the tone for the many integrated groups to follow.

R2.32   Dion and the Belmonts. Greatest Hits. Laurie 2013.
Dion DiMucci was a happy-go-lucky Italian singer in the Fabian and Avalon mood that superseded the croonings of Como, Damone, Bennett, and Martino. Unfortunately, his happy voice did not often suit the material he performed, e.g., such tragic songs as "Runaround Sue," "Ruby Baby," or even "The Wanderer." The background vocals by the Belmonts were satisfying in a light sort of way, and the overall effort reminds the listener of the r 'n' b streetcorner singer groups in New York City. Dion worked in this mode for about a decade (also getting in over his head with drugs), but he eventually produced one of the better interpretations of "Abraham, Martin and John." Quite a switch was made from the screaming whine to the evocative folk stream.

R2.33   Bill Doggett. King 531.
Instrumental rock and roll or rhythm and blues was often regarded as a novelty, and one of the better performers in this style was the group of Bill Doggett. He was largely a studio man for King Records, but on his own, when studio time was available, he produced important danceable tunes such as "Honky Tonk [pts. one and two]," the inimitable "Slow Walk," and the murky "Slow." This disc cumulates his singles from the 1956 to 1960 period.

R2.34   Fabian. 16 Greatest Hits. ABCX 806.
This record is a concrete example of how much hype was given out during the rock and roll period. The necessity for artistic creation had gone by the boards, so long as the performer could emote—even in a monotone, as resulted here with yet another Italian "discovery." Fabian had good looks (even if he was a trifle paunchy), and this was the selling point. The material he sang was reasonable: nobody cares what *writers* look like or how they sing. He borrowed "I'm a Man" from Bo Diddley, and tried sexual innuendos with "Come on and Get Me," "Turn Me Loose," and "Tiger." As his expression was a perpetual sneer, the resulting music was always thought of as a challenge. Despite his nice-guy clean-boy looks, Fabian soon became the number one vocalist appreciated by motorcycle gangs.

R2.35   Connie Francis. Rock 'n' Roll Million Sellers. MGM S-3794.
The much-maligned Francis had a continual stream of successes from 1958 to 1962, with emphasis on updating such older standards as "Who's Sorry Now?" Her popularity was based on a crying voice, and to some extent on her Italian phrasing (as on "Mama"). Material here includes "My Happiness," "My Heart Has a Mind of Its Own," "Everybody's Somebody's Fool," and "Among My Souvenirs."

R2.36   Bobby Helms. My Special Angel. Vocalion 73874.
Every Christmas, along with Bing Crosby's "White Christmas" and Gene Autry's "Rudolph the Red Nosed Reindeer," there appears a third perennial,

originally recorded in 1957. This is Bobby Helms's "Jingle Bell Rock." Helms was groomed to be a major recording company's answer to the rockabillies. In later life, he went back to pure country music (as did Jerry Lee Lewis), but he scored at this time with "Fraulein," the title selection, and "Jacqueline."

R2.37   **Bill Justis. Raunchy. Sun 109.**
Justis was yet another important session man for a recording studio. When Presley signed with RCA, he also took along Bill Black and Scotty Moore, which depleted the session stable available as back-up for Sun artists. Justis took over with his saxophone and gave the Sun sound a more pronounced feeling for rhythm 'n' blues (a trend that owner Sam Phillips tried to buck, desiring white interpretations of black music). Justis, when not otherwise busy, put together a band to record instrumentals. "Raunchy" and "College Man" were his biggest efforts. The eleven tracks here are derived from 1957-1958.

R2.38   **Brenda Lee. Best. two discs. MCA 2-4012.**
Lee was, with Wanda Jackson, one of the first of the female rockabillies. That they were so unique is quite puzzling. Women have always had a hand in the affairs of popular music, but they certainly dragged their feet with rockabilly music. Lee's career (which is now devoted solely to country music), as detailed on this set, has been one of one long hit after another. This album reveals an abundance of hard rockin' numbers, such as "Sweet Nothings," "I'm Sorry," "Break It to Me Gently," "Dum Dum," "All Alone Am I," and "Emotions." Her later efforts did seem to be more in the country direction, with such hits as "Fool No. 1," "I Want to Be Wanted," and "You Can Depend on Me."

R2.39   **Guy Mitchell. Guy's Greatest Hits. Columbia CL 1226.**
Guy Mitchell, under the tutelage of Mitch Miller, sang Columbia's brand of rockabilly music. In 1950, he signed with Columbia and was completely managed by Miller. His first effort was the smoothed-down version of a country tune, "My Heart Cries for You." Later, during the beginnings of rock and roll, the Miller fusion of rock tempos and country sounds would come out as "Singing the Blues," "Heartaches by the Number," and "Knee Deep in the Blues."

R2.40   **Rick Nelson. Legendary Masters Series. two discs. United Artists UAS 9960.**
Nelson was the most successful of the second generation that followed in the footsteps of their fathers' careers. But then, he had been doing this since the 1940s, when he first appeared on his parents' radio show; and his being on television also gave his career a shot in the arm. Most of what he sang was covered material, or golden oldie hits from years gone by. Lately, he has been developing into a folk-rock artist along the same lines as Dion DiMucci and other retreads. His successes: "Poor Little Fool," "Hello, Mary Lou," "Be Bop Baby," "Stand Up," "Travelin' Man," and "Teenage Romance." As with other sets in this United Artists series, there are good discographical arrangements, good notes, and some pictures.

R2.41   **Bobby Rydell. All the Hits.** Cameo S 1040.

From 1959 to 1963, during the decline of rock and roll music, Bobby Rydell (yet another Philadelphia discovery) put out relatively happy music. Included here are "We Got Love," "Wild One," "Kissin' Time," and "Volare" (a cover of an Italian smash hit).

R2.42*   **Neil Sedaka. His Greatest Hits.** RCA APL 1-0928.

With a tiny voice reminiscent of many growing teenagers, Sedaka cashed in on the love beat of the late fifties (and in no small measure assisted in the decay of rock and roll as a vibrant musical force). Sappy ballads such as "Oh, Carol," (yet another "girl name" song), "Breaking up Is Hard to Do," and "Calendar Girl" led to a successful career that he is still plying. Perhaps the most representative songs in his style were the sugary "Happy Birthday, Sweet Sixteen" or "You Mean Everything to Me."

R2.43   **Shirelles. Greatest Hits.** Scepter S-507.

One of the dominent female groups of the 1959-1963 period, the Shirelles later teamed up with Burt Bacharach for soft-pop material. (Remember Bacharach? He wrote the sleeper hit of the fifties—"The Blob"). Their little girlish voices come through crystal clear on their hits "Will You Still Love Me Tomorrow?," "Soldier Boy," and "Dedicated to the One I Love"—all about unrequited love. The set is rounded out by "Tonight's the Night" and "Foolish Little Girl."

R2.44   **Conway Twitty. Hits.** MGM S-3849.

His name seems to be impossibly conceived, and even contrived (he is really just Harry Jenkins). Yet his major impact was the important song "It's Only Make Believe," which he wrote and arranged himself. The year was 1959, and this was the first song to begin the long decay of rock and roll. His other efforts were not as good as follow-ups. They include "Lonely Blue Boy," "Danny Boy," and "What Am I Living For?" Like many other southerners, he has now returned to his "roots" and records country music for MCA.

R2.45   **Bobby Vee. Golden Greats.** Liberty 7245.

Vee rose to fame when he was asked to step in for a performance shortly after the death of Buddy Holly. Although his material at that time was Holly-type, he later became his own man, singing in the mainstream of pop. His first hit was a cover of the Clovers' "Devil or Angel." Then he adapted the Carole King number "Take Good Care of My Baby," his only number one national hit. Other tunes here, all of them successes of some kind, include "Rubber Ball," "Run to Him," and the interesting "The Night Has a Thousand Eyes."

R2.46   **The Ventures. 10th Anniversary Album.** two discs. Liberty 35000.

The Ventures have recorded over fifty albums together, scoring their most important popularity in Japan, of all places. They are strictly an instrumental group, and their importance is now seen as minimal. But they did start off with the extremely satisfying epic "Walk, Don't Run." With three guitars and a drum, there was no need for overdubbing. All of this is excellent dance music. Along with the hit "Perfidia," they have tended to concentrate on significant popular tunes and various theme songs from television, such as "Hawaii Five-O."

R2.47   **Bobby Vinton. Greatest Hits.** Epic BN 26098.
     Possessed of an incredibly soft and sweet voice, sometimes reaching into the high ranges, Vinton was never accused of being a syrupy singer, nor of being a whiner. Coming as he did at the low point of the rock and roll decay in late 1962, he perhaps best epitomizes the status of the balladeer at this troubled time. He scored four number one hits in a row, including "Roses Are Red," "Blue Velvet," "Mr. Lonely," and "There, I Said It Again." Other hits included "Long, Lonely Nights" and "Blue on Blue."

REVIVAL

R2.48   **Dr. John. Gumbo.** Atco SD 7006.
     This is Dr. John's "roots" album. Previous to this effort, he was into a voodoo or Creole bag, with various song and dance shows and mysterious incantations and effects. With this album, he renounced all that. By exploring his roots in the New Orleans scene (as a session pianist and guitarist, plus some writing and arranging chores), he presents to the listener a microcosm of the Crescent City's role in shaping r 'n' b and early rock and roll. Dr. John's real name is Mac Rebennack, and he began with studios in the early fifties, playing with Shirley and Lee, Fats Domino, Little Richard, Professor Longhair, and Huey Smith. The "gris gris" music is gone here, and funk is in. He called it good time New Orleans blues and stomp music with a little Dixieland jazz and some Spanish rhumbas: a basic 2/4 beat with compounded rhythms and added syncopation. Important recreations here include "Iko Iko" by Sugar Boy; some Huey Smith piano on "Blow Wind Blow"; an updated version of "Let the Good Times Roll"; and some Professor Longhair, such as "Tipitina."

R2.49*   **Jerry Lee Lewis. The Session.** two discs. Mercury SRM2-803.
     Beyond a shadow of a doubt, this is the greatest album to come out of the rock and roll revival period. Lewis, an acknowledged master of the rockabilly mode who shifted into pure country during the 1960s, was persuaded to get together with a bunch of English rockers who had been influenced by his work from the mid-1950s. He was right at home with the English boys, who derived their musical understanding from r 'n' b rather than blues music. Accompanying musicians include Andy Bown, B. J. Cole, Peter Frampton, Rory Gallagher, Alvin Lee, Brian Parrish, Klaus Voormann, and Gary Wright. This is indeed a "roots" album, right from the first cut: "Drinking Wine Spo-Dee O-Dee," originally recorded for Atlantic in 1949 by Sticks McGhee and covered later by Lewis. This leads on to Jimmy Reed's "Baby, What You Want Me to Do" and "Big Boss Man"; Charlie Rich's "No Headstone on My Grave"; Johnny Ace's "Pledging My Love"; Chuck Berry's "Memphis" and "Johnny B. Goode"; a Little Richard medley; Ray Charles's "What'd I Say?"; and others like "Sixty Minute Man" and "High School Confidential." A dynamic album in every respect, all numbers on this are uptempo and feature Lewis's famous "pumping piano."

R2.50   Mothers of Invention. Cruisin' with Reuben and the Jets. Verve 6-5055X.

The Mothers of Invention, led by Frank Zappa, are known as the best of the avant garde rock groups, along with the Fugs. By coupling jazz and classical influences with humor, Zappa's group was able to capture a large segment of the intellectual market in rock. This album was, as Zappa explained, their attempt to break into AM radio. Underground FM does not sell records; Top Forty AM does. Zappa retitled his group "Reuben and the Jets" and wrote all new material based on the style of the rock and roll fifties. All of the selections here, including the marvelous and nonsensical "Desiree," were potential hits—back in the fifties. While the album failed to go anywhere, it developed (as other Mothers albums did) a vast underground following. And in fact, it was directly instrumental in the creation of Sha Na Na and the subsequent whole rock and roll revival of the early seventies (see R2.51). The disc itself has since been reissued many times. Once again, Zappa and his boys were in advance of their time and unable to reap the financial rewards.

R2.51*   Sha Na Na. Rock & Roll Is Here to Stay! Kama Sutra KSBS 2010.

Sha Na Na, named after the nonsensical lyrics in "Get a Job" (as sung by the Silhouettes), was a group of students at Columbia University. They performed for fun, and were immediately spotted as talent for a record company. They specialize in revival music of the fifties, although of late they have been adding their own modern material. Sha Na Na spawned whole groups of singers who cashed in on the nostalgia revival for rock and roll (as a movement away from the complexities of hard rock). But no group has been able to come close to Sha Na Na in the evocation of feeling for the period of the "greasers." And, as with many such imitative groups concentrating on just one musical genre, theirs is a highly visual act, complete with outrageous costumes from the period (T-shirts, gold lamé outfits, straight leg jeans, sunglasses, motorcycle jackets, duck tail haircuts, etc.). On this album, their first and best, they give exact interpretations of older rock and roll hits. The lyrics are given, as well as the original artist, writer, and year of release. Besides the title track, the fourteen selections include the Del Vikings' "Come Go with Me," the Monotones' "Book of Love," Mark Dinning's "Teen Angel" (their most dramatic stage offering), Presley's "Heartbreak Hotel," and the Big Bopper's "Chantilly Lace." On record, they sound just as good as the originals—but when the originals are still in print, why bother? This set is justified for inclusion here mainly because of its importance in the revival movement.

MODERN ROCK 'N' ROLL

THE SIXTIES AND SEVENTIES

Modern rock and roll has its antecedents in the derivative 1959-1963 period, when rockabilly and covers of r 'n' b songs had played out. The music at this time was in the mainstream of the popular song: love ballads, reasonably proficient lyrics, little depth, and paeans to dances and the "good white life." After the arrival of the harder, more brittle rock music, existing rock and roll transformed itself into what was known as "soft rock." The first evidence of this was the late arrival of the Beach Boys in 1962. They emphasized, at the beginning, hot rod music (fast living and fast dying), but the topic was so restrictive that they branched out to what became known as "surfing music" (a distinct emphasis on sunshine, beaches, parties, and good times) in conjunction with their California base and their name. In technique, they stressed vocal harmonies that later became so dominant in California music (later known also as "California rock") that it was also applied to country harmonies and sweet songs sung by urbanites. California rock can be thought of as either a reaction to the East Coast dominance of brittle music or as a form of music reflecting the simple, easy lifestyle of warmer climates. At any rate, the Beach Boys and their imitators were the first to "cover" honest rock and roll songs rather than r 'n' b materials. Thus they developed a toned-down version of music that was itself a toned -down version of r 'n' b, and was more akin to white music (country and popular songs) than any other variant of rock and roll before it. California music took the boogie bass, the twelve bar blues, and the after-beat to create a watered-down country blues that was speeded up, imitating such innovators as Chuck Berry. In the fifteen years since the Beach Boys first recorded, this type of music has gradually softened until today it finds acceptability with a mellowed rock and roll audience and those adults who just prefer the popular song.

Some exponents of modern rock and roll include the Mamas and Papas, Lovin' Spoonful, Bread, America, and the duos of Brewer and Shipley, Gallagher and Lyle, Loggins and Messina, and Seals and Crofts. At the same time, the boogie beat was maintained by such early rock and roll stars as Jerry Lee Lewis and Carole King. Others worked in louder versions, such as Creedence Clearwater Revival.

ANTHOLOGIES

R3.1   **Bang and Shout Super Hits.** Bang 220.

This is a motley collection of material from the 1960s, largely in the pop rock and roll vein. Of note is the McCoys' original version of "Hang on Sloopy," a crowd pleaser and rallying point (Rory Gallagher was with the group then). Neil Diamond material plus Van Morrison's "Brown Eyed Girl" (his first big success in both an artistic and a commercial sense) complete the picture. From the ladies, there is Erma Franklin's "Piece of My Heart," a real tearjerker.

STANDARDS

R3.2   **Association. Greatest Hits.** Warner Brothers WS-1767.

One of the best examples of soft rock of the sixties was the Los Angeles-based Association. Their high, tight multi-part vocals on "Cherish," "Windy," "Never My Love," and "Along Comes Mary" were clean and wholesome. Along with the Mamas and the Papas and the Lovin' Spoonful, the Association made some excellent lightweight music. Their influence on later groups like Bread is obvious, and while they can be safely put away as "Top 40," they were symbolic of the age of innocence of rock. They were one of the first of the pop groups to write their own material (they also scored the film *Goodbye, Columbus*).

R3.3*   **Beach Boys. Spirit of America.** two discs. Capitol SVBB 11384.

During 1962-1966, the Beach Boys, led by Brian Wilson, created a whole new genre of rock and roll: surfing music. This ultimately led to the so-called "California Sound," or "L.A. Sound," of high harmonies later perfected by Crosby, Stills, Nash, and Young. If the Beach Boys were not singing about the pleasures of surfing, then it was about motor cars and races. Their variations on a theme included "Surfin' Safari," "Little Deuce Coupe," "Surfer Girl," "Surfin' U.S.A. " (from Chuck Berry),"I Get Around," "409," "Fun, Fun, Fun," "Dance, Dance, Dance," and the ultimate "Help Me, Rhonda." They assimilated all of the current interests and themes of the "youth culture" plus various musical styles, to embrace racing, surfing, beer drinking, folk music, Dylan, r 'n' b, and so forth. Their high harmonies and instrumentation put them on a par with the early Beatles (another non-original group at the outset), and the two groups became the leaders in rock and roll music at this stage in rock's development. The Boys' last songs in this genre include "Barbara Ann," which harkened back to the Regents 1950s version, and the prophetic "Good Vibrations," which looked ahead. Despite being the sentimental favorites of American rock critics and audiences, they ceased to be an influence. In 1967, they were working on a concept album similar in intent to the Beatles' and the Rolling Stones' epics, but it was killed by Capitol. Had it appeared, there could have been some influential changes in rock music at an earlier date (particularly in country rock).

R3.4*   **The Beatles. Rock 'n' Roll Music.** two discs. Capitol SKBO 11537.

Disgust with the Bay City Rollers in 1975 led many aging rock fans to create a Beatles revival. Earlier, Capitol had reissued four discs of material from 1964-1970, all penned by the Beatles. This present double-set only has half original items; the others are from the r 'n' b-rockabilly roots of the Beatles' first recording years. These are the records that, when released as singles in 1976, made many youngsters rediscover the Beatles. At one time (May 1976), they had all 23 of their singles listed in the Top 100 in England. What ahppened? Simply good, efficient rock and roll with a heavier beat. The 28 tracks here include their covers of the Isleys' "Twist and Shout," Little Richard's "Long Tall Sally," Chuck Berry's "Rock 'n' Roll Music" and "Roll over Beethoven," Carl Perkins's "Everybody's Trying to Be My Baby" and "Matchbox," plus three golden efforts from Larry Williams ("Dizzy Miss Lissie," "Slow Down" and "Bad Boy"). Their originals are the more spirited offerings, such as "I Saw Her Standing There," "I Wanna Hold Your Hand," "Revolution," "Get Back," "Back in the U.S.S.R.," etc. Also, there is only one duplication with the four records issued as a retrospective.

The Beatles are different, though, from functional rock and roll. For one thing, they used r 'n' b songs with loud drumming. Beyond that, their vocal harmony and phrase building led to high tension; they used a piano and harmonica far before these instruments became common in rock; they were fresh out of the stable at the time (1964) that rock and roll was stale in the United States but *not* stale in Britain; and, in their own material, they used unique and demanding chord changes—they were one of the few rock and roll groups who not only could play their own instruments, but could play them well. (It should be noted also that the British "invasion" of the U.S. market was possible because, in addition to the Beatles and the Stones, Britain always had scores of groups doing their own louder versions of good rocking music. Thus, the groups were there when the market became ready for them.)

R3.5   **Bread. Best.** Elektra EKS 75056.
     Bread was a latter day development of the Lovin' Spoonful's school of soft rock. Led by guitarist-vocalist David Gates, they had originally started as a studio band concentrating on singles rather than on albums. Their existence covered 1970-1973, and they were very prolific during that time, with harmonies on "Make It with You," "Baby I'm-a Wanta You," the epic "Sweet Surrender," "Let Your Love Go," "Diary," and "It Don't Matter to Me." Larry Knechtel joined the group in 1971 and furnished his sweetly romantic piano, later heard on Simon and Garfunkel albums (such as the fantastically lush introduction to "Bridge over Troubled Water").

R3.6*   **Creedence Clearwater Revival. Chronicle.** two discs. Fantasy CCR-2.
     CCR—as the group was known—was originally a boogie band that concentrated on burning riffs provided by John Fogerty. It had been called an updated rock 'n' roll band primarily because of its success with Dale Hawkins's "Suzy Q," an early rock and roll hit from the fifties. The music was quite simple: recurring riffs on a funky guitar, four-on-four drumming, and blurred, raw vocals. CCR had its greatest success with shorter numbers. This two-volume set of their "hits" (unlike their first set, which concentrated on the longer numbers) presents twenty miniatures such as "Proud Mary," "Bad Moon Rising," "Down on the Corner," mostly written by Fogerty. Other items here included another Hawkins track ("I Put a Spell on You") and Otis Blackwell material like "Good Golly, Miss Molly." This record is a good example of later rock and roll material.

R3.7   **Four Seasons. Edizione D'Oro.** two discs. Philips 6501.
     For some time now, this group has been known as Frankie Valli and the Four Seasons, as Valli did most of the work in establishing the group's style. He had a piercing soprano range in his vocal, almost to the point of being a whining castrato. In public performance today, he does the same styling but with much effort. The wails on this set are largely from the 1964 to 1969 period, with "Sherry," "Big Girls Don't Cry," "Dawn," "Ronnie," "Rag Doll," "Walk Like a Man," and "Can't Take My Eyes off You."

R3.8   **Bobby Goldsboro. Greatest Hits.** United Artists UA 5502.
     As a pop singer, Goldsboro leaves a lot to be desired, particularly in his mannerisms. A rocker he is not, but he appears to be most representative of the sixties penchant for a particular style of Top 40 AM music. The efforts here are derived from the 1964-1968 period, and they include his largely successful songs such as "Honey," "See the Funny Little Clown," "Little Things," and "Autumn of My Life."

R3.9   **Lesley Gore. Golden Hits.** Mercury 61024.
     Gore replaced Connie Francis in the wailing and whining form of material. Thus, her 1963-1965 period supersedes Francis's influences. "It's My Party" (where she can cry if she wants to, and indeed she did) was a logical progression

from Connie Francis. And then to follow up the hit, Gore produced her thematic sequel, which was something that others usually did: "Judy's Turn to Cry." With other moderate successes such as "You Don't Own Me" and "She's a Fool," Gore continued on her merry way. But one redeeming song has stayed around, the one that she is remembered for in a happy light, the nifty "Sunshine, Lollipops, and Rainbows," a veritable haven of happiness.

R3.10*   **Guess Who. Best. RCA LSPX 1004.**
This Winnipeg-born quartet emphasized riffs and catchy tunes. All of their instrumental tracks revolve around the melody, with no surplus notes. Thus, strong melodic constructions and easy-to-hear vocals have made this the premier group in the modern rock and roll period. Randy Bachman (later to go into heavy metal music) left in 1970, after the bulk of these tunes were recorded. His guitar influences at this period came from Chet Atkins's lyricism. Burton Cummings furnished the sparse piano and the vocals. Really top-notch successes include the bitter "American Woman" (a satire on the United States by a Canadian group), "These Eyes," "Shakin' All Over," "No Sugar Tonight," and "Laughing."

R3.11   **The Hollies. Greatest Hits. Epic KE 32061.**
The British "invasion" of the United States during the early Beatles era counted among its numbers the distinctive sounds of the Hollies. Although they never were of major stature like their close relations, the Kinks, they left a mark on modern rock. Their tight, complex harmony and unusual arrangements were listened to in California and can be easily heard on the early albums of the Mamas and the Papas and of Buffalo Springfield. Later, in 1969, Graham Nash would leave this group and lend his talents to Crosby, Stills, Nash and Young—to create one more Hollies-like singing group. The Hollies may have failed due to the poverty of the material they had to work with. Who can ever forget "He Ain't Heavy, He's My Brother," "Bus Stop," "Tell Me to My Face," or "Stop, Stop, Stop"? The Hollies, like the Zombies, struggled onward with changed personnel, but they have not recaptured their earlier success.

R3.12   **Tommy James. Best. Roulette 42040.**
A consistent pop singer, James turns in his work on a systematic basis. His best work appears to be from 1966-1970 with his back-up group the Shondells, and the tunes were "Crimson and Clover," "Crystal Blue Persuasion," and "I Think We're Alone Now." While these efforts were not of sterling quality, they did reflect his interest in perfecting small gems. His only alternative was to continue with hokum music, which unfortunately brought better financial rewards, selections such as "Hanky Panky" (a new dance style), and "Money, Money."

R3.13   **Jan and Dean. Legendary Masters Series.** two discs. United Artists UAS 9961.
Along with the Beach Boys, Jan and Dean were the prototypes of the surfing music groups. But they were not necessarily in the same singing mode. Their success bore remarkable resemblances to that of the Beach Boys. Surfing music included "Surf City" and "Honolulu Lulu," and racing music included "Dead Man's Curve" and "Little Old Lady from Pasadena." Between 1962 and 1966, Jan and Dean were

a duet, but it was not until after they split that they became cult figures. The melodies and plot lines for all of their songs were far better crafted than the mild tones of the Beach Boys. Jan and Dean actually told a believable story, which gave them sincerity and honesty in what many have called a nasty business.

R3.14   **Jay and the Americans. Greatest Hits.** United Artists UA 6453.
A pseudo-patriotic singing group that never seemed to rock in the traditional sense, Jay and the Americans devoted a lot of time and effort to putting together popular music that would sell to kids. Such items as "Cara, Mia" (a good solid American song, in view of immigration figures) and "This Magic Moment" sold very well indeed. Not far behind in this 1961-1968 period were "She Cried," "Only in America," and "Come a Little Bit Closer."

R3.15*   **Carole King. Tapestry.** Ode SP 77009.
This record is included here for a number of reasons. The most obvious is that it has sold more copies than any other elpee by a single artist (over ten *million* world-wide), which is enough for inclusion. However, it is also very good rock and roll music. Carole King and her ex-husband Gerry Goffin were responsible for a large number of hits around the early sixties, such as Little Eva's epic version of "Locomotion" (Eva was working as a domestic with the Goffins at the time). Other such songs included "Will You Still Love Me Tommorrow?" and "You Make Me Feel Like a Natural Woman." She did especially good work with Phil Spector when he was beginning his "wall of sound" approach. Good selling items here include "I Feel the Earth Move" and "It's Too Late," both of which have been covered successfully by others since the 1971 release of this album. Lyrics and personnel notes are included on the back cover.

R3.16   **Gary Lewis and the Playboys. Golden Greats.** Liberty 7468.
Back in the mid-sixties, it was fashionable for many sons and daughters of recording, television, or film stars to turn up in the studios and perform something. Such things as a name can certainly help a career, but oh, that Gary Lewis would be the son of Jerry Lee, rather than simply of Jerry Lewis. Nevertheless, the aural evidence provides some justification for inclusion here. This disc contains the best of his efforts, as it is concentrated on just the 1965-1966 period. His "hit" material included "This Diamond Ring," "Count Me In," "Save Your Heart for Me" (a direct steal from country music), and "Everybody Loves a Clown."

R3.17   **Johnny Rivers. Golden Hits.** Imperial 12324.
Johnny Rivers is the stereotype of the "cover" man: one who takes other people's songs and translates them into equal or better successes. Some would say that this was good business; others would scream "parasite!" In any event, he did much to popularize musical trends and singers, and to bring the music to a wider audience. His hits, then, include his versions—all equally good rockers when compared with the originals—of "Memphis" and "Maybelline" (both from Chuck Berry), "Seventh Son" (from blues roots by way of Albert King), "Mountain of Love," "Poor Side of Town," and "Secret Agent Man." Of late, he has been working on reggae rhythms (as on the album *L.A. Reggae*), and together with Johnny Nash, has exploited this musical genre in America.

R3.18*   **Lovin' Spoonful. Very Best.** Kama Sutra KSBS 2013.
At a time (1965) in the history of rock when the genre was completely dominated by British bands, the Lovin' Spoonful was an American breakthrough. Combining ragtime and rock rhythms, country "good time" harmonies, and folk lyricism, the Spoonful brought rock home to the streets of New York. They were, for a few brief moments in two years, the answer to the Beatles. Their music was infectious, and one hit was followed by another: "Do You Believe in Magic?," "Day Dream," "Summer in the City," "Nashville Cats," and "Did You Ever Have to Make up Your Mind?" Led by Zal Yanovsky and guitarist John Sebastian, the Spoonful, along with the Mamas and the Papas and the Byrds, created the soft rock boom *and* some very happy sounds.

R3.19*   **Mamas and the Papas. 20 Golden Hits.** ABC/Dunhill DXS-50145.
The California good time sound came along all at one time (1965)—the Byrds, the Beach Boys, and Cass Elliot, guitarist John Phillips, Denny Doherty, and Michelle Phillips. The last four were an important group since, along with their fellow New Yorkers in the Lovin' Spoonful, they reinstated the pride in American rock 'n' roll that had been missing once the Beatles came on the scene. Their tight, four-part bittersweet harmonies were clear and clean, and they personified the beginning of a movement (flower power). "California Dreamin' " would lead many westward to the Valhalla of rock. One hit followed another: "I Saw Her Again," "Monday, Monday," "Creeque Alley," "A Little Dream of Me." The end of the Mamas and the Papas in 1967 marked an end in American popular music— an end to innocence.

R3.20*   **The Monkees. Re-Focus.** Arista Bell B 6081.
The Monkees were a group especially assembled for the television series. Many hundreds of boys were auditioned, mainly for photogenic qualities, while music was secondary. Indeed, the quartet's members never met until they began to film. They were not allowed to play any instruments; consequently, they could not tour before their mass audience (although the show was top rated in watcher appeal) until they insisted. Their tours, then, were not musical highlights, since they could just barely perform. Their singing style was modeled on that of the Beatles, for that was the intent of the show: to present "typical lifestyles" of a successful singing quartet (who else could they be? the Rolling Stones? no American mother would stand for it!). Their RCA recordings were the ones that made the radio air plays and the record sales, but their music for the TV soundtrack had a more pronounced, heavier rhythm, clarity of vocal expression, and immensely better sound and mixing. Hence, our preference for "soundtracks." All of their big hits are here: "Monkee's Theme," "Last Train to Clarkesville," Neil Diamond's song "I'm a Believer" (their greatest selling single), plus others on this eleven-track collation.

R3.21   **Gary Puckett and the Union Gap. Greatest Hits.** Columbia CS 1042.
This quintet presented melodic rock and roll through the Beatles period in contemporary rock music. The typical titles—all of them hits—included "Woman, Woman," "Young Girl," "Lady Willpower," and "Over You," retaining the virtues of love (and lost love) through teenage aches and pains of growing up.

R3.22   **The Righteous Brothers. Greatest Hits.** Verve V6-5020.
This duo were not brothers, but rather Bobby Hatfield and Bill Medley
(who provided the definitive deep bass voice). Both were put together by Phil
Spector to create what was known as "blue-eyed soul": black music sung by white
men. Spector produced them with his "wall of sound" approach that emphasized
echo, strings, tympani bombs, and so forth, so that there was no silence at all.
Their gospel and r 'n' b work even led to their music's being played on unsuspecting black radio stations (which, of course, promptly withdrew the records from
their playlists when the boys were discovered to be white). The importance here,
though, lies in the production values, the good studio work (they could not appear
in concert), the response to Sam and Dave, and the reworkings of popular material
into a contemporary vein: "Great Pretender," "Unchained Melody," "Ebb Tide,"
"You'll Never Walk Alone," "The White Cliffs of Dover" (which seemed to be
done by many black groups), and of course their biggest, most acclaimed hit,
"You've Lost That Lovin' Feelin'."

R3.23   **Carly Simon. Best, v.1.** Elektra 7E 1048.
These ten cuts represent the most popular rocking numbers of Carly Simon,
who, along with her piano playing, strives for a path midway between contemporary pop and rock, which is exactly the position of modern rock and roll. The
engaging "You're So Vain" is supposedly about a rock star, but it has overtones
for every man she has ever met or had an association with. The other tracks here
include all of her melodic works: "Anticipation," "No Secrets," "The Right
Thing to Do," "Mocking Bird," and "Night Owl."

R3.24   **Nancy Sinatra. Greatest Hits.** Reprise RS 6409.
Sinatra's daughter found some success recording for his label, but this added
boost to Nancy's short career opened the way for other female singers in the venue
of rock and roll through the 1960s. All of her album jackets were bold, showing
off boots, leather, and skin; but marketing could not dim the appeal of the uptempo
macho music inside the jacket: "These Boots Are Made for Walkin'," "How Does
That Grab You, Darlin'?," and the marvelous duets with composer-arranger-producer
Lee Hazlewood, such as "Jackson" and "Summer Wine," both songs covered by
the country market (reversing the normal procedure).

R3.25   **B. J. Thomas. Best, v.1/2.** two discs. Scepter S-578/597.
Continuing in the vein of the pop singers from the fifties, Thomas presents
his brand of rock 'n' roll pop. This includes the Academy Award-winning version
of "Raindrops Keep Fallin' on My Head," the catchy "Hooked on a Feeling,"
and the tear-jerker "I'm So Lonesome I Could Cry."

ROCK

INTRODUCTION

Musical analysis of rock can be expressed in terms of form, rhythm, melody,
and harmony. The basic *form* of rock music is the twelve bar blues idiom, but it

is flexible enough so that either the vocal or the instrumental solo can sustain a note or embellish it. And, of course, there are variations in symmetry, such as those created in the innovative Beatles pop songs, "Yesterday," where the opening phrase is seven bars, or their "Michelle," which has a sixteen bar phrase divided into 10 + 6 rather than 8 + 8. But these are rarities, borrowed from the form of the musical stage song. The *rhythm* of rock music has its origins in both r 'n' b and country music, but the basic overall rhythm is the straight eighth note division of the beat, which occurred with the Twist dance style. Here the bass player became more important than the drummer. Additional polyrhythms were created, but these were of the experimental type, such as accents on the off-beats, or bent notes to keep a musical overlay on the straight eighth notes.

As rock is derived from the blues, the *melodic* inflections of the blues line are followed by flatting the third, fifth, and seventh notes. Modes were also used after the Beatles introduced modal melodies and modal harmonic progressions to rock. For instance, "I Want to Hold Your Hand" (their first American hit, recorded in November 1962) used I - V - VI - IV, ending on III rather than the normal I - IV - V. This subdominant orientation came from folk music and jazz improvisations, where modal progressions were extensively used in the late 1950s. Thus, it was relatively easy for folk and jazz artists to shift to rock music, for these would be successful musicians playing early rock and roll patterns and they could only improve rock music. For instance, consider John Phillips of the Mamas and Papas, a leader in modern rock and roll who used modal progressions based on his extensive folk repertoire.

The most common melodic modes used are the Ionian (major scale), the Aeolian (natural minor), the Mixolydian (a major scale with a flatted seventh, as on the Beatles' "Norwegian Wood" or as used by Jim Hendrix), and the Dorian (a harmonic minor scale with a sharp sixth and flatted seventh). The harmonic structure of rock music is largely triadic (no ninths are used). The most common modal progression in rock is from I to a flat VII (C major triad to a B^b major triad). This progression was not used in general American popular music before, except for folk, blues, and country. (There are others, such as the weak I to iii, or ii to IV.) Another characteristic of rock harmonics is the use of one or two chords throughout an entire piece, very similar to Indian raga music. The most common are a II chord as a major triad with chromatic changes *or* I to flat VI (a C triad down to an A^b triad).

Technical Effects

Modern rock music probably could not exist without the advances in electronic technology of recent years. Specific, distorted effects can be used by relatively unskilled musicians to hide any technical musical deficiencies, such as limitations in the rhythmic patterns and chord structures that a guitarist can play. All of these devices (such as the ones that follow) should really be used sparingly, as they are difficult to control and do not really contribute to the music in the way of melody, rhythm, or harmony. Shaw said "sensory overload . . . is a means of liberating the self, expanding consciousness, and rediscovering the world." The effects of these common devices revolve around distortion through electronic manipulations, as:

1) *Fuzz tone*—This distortion device produces a blurred sound, and with the right power and speaker, even a rasping or dirty sound. It was first attempted in a primitive way by Link Wray, who simply punched small holes into his speakers. The fuzz tone device merely lops off the peaks and troughs from the sound waves, thus ensuring no sharp or distinct notes.

2) *Reverberation*—This echo effect is achieved by elongating the duration of sound, or by delaying sound through tape echo, as Sun Records did with its rockabilly records. It can be created either mechanically or electronically, and adds depth by creating the illusion of an echo (other terms here are *vibrato* and *electric reverb*). The advantage of an electrical device is that several echoes can be blended together at once and rapidly repeated.

3) *Feedback*—By feeding the issued notes back through the amplifier, the sound's intensity can be increased. This is only used for certain notes, and unlike other devices, it can rarely be controlled without indepth use and experimentation.

4) *Wah-wah*—This device has been successfully used for many years by *brass* instrument players, simply by placing a hat over a horn's bell and waving it. But of course, this cannot be done with an amplified speaker. Instead, a foot pedal is used to send an electric signal up or down one octave.

5) *Editing*—Mixing down 32 or so tracks into only two or four for stereo or quadrophonic reproduction is a difficult task at best, and the engineer-producer must choose what instruments to emphasize, where on the stereo or quad spread to place them, and the various sound levels. All of this is called the "mix," and developing the proper mix has now become a high art form. Editing also includes speeding up or slowing down a tape (or running it backwards) for special effect, introducing electronic devices or electronic "music," deleting mistakes and adding corrections, etc. In the hands of a sophisticated producer, the eventual music *could* resemble nothing like what actually happened in the studio. And, of course, several different tracks could be recorded at different times and places with different people, and then consolidated. Phil Spector, Lou Adler, and Tom Dowd are most adept at this.

6) *Electronic instrumentation*—A wide variety of both electrified instruments (electric piano, organ, saxophones, flutes, violins, trumpets, etc.) and electronic synthesizers (A.R.P., Moog, Mellotron, Echoplex, etc.) have been developed in order to push out new and mystifying sounds.

Lyrics

Rock music is fragmented when it comes to fans who support the music. Not only are there different formats, but there are also diversified themes that might not appeal to all persons interested in rock music. Some of the handles given to these formats include country rock, jazz rock, blues rock, folk rock (and a sub-genre, good time rock), punk rock (or pop rock), soft rock (usually equated with modern rock and roll), acid rock, and hard rock (better known now as "heavy metal music"). By analyzing their lyrics, these can be grouped together into eight distinct themes (in no particular order):

1) *Summertime paeans*—Odes to the good life of celebration and surfing, these can also be instrumentals. Because of their good-time nature and relation to soft rock (plus the fact that they do not fulfill the musical analysis tests of rock music), they are located with modern rock and roll. Most love ballads fall within this category.

2) *Dance music*—This is happy music, with no social commentary. Throughout the last 25 years, it had limited popularity, but it was unpretentious and honest, stressing dance rhythms. In 1975, it resurged as "disco" music.

3) *Sexual themes*—Either implied or explicit, conventional sexual adventures were also linked at times with sadism, masochism, and perversions. Originally, this was the derivation of the term "rock and roll"—physical emulation of sexual intercourse. Sexualism was the one dominant theme of 1950s' r 'n' b.

4) *Rebellion—Either* non-violent (the self-consciousness of growing up and the loss of innocence, coupled with the need for group or peer unity) *or* violent (protest against the "Establishment"—law, police, complacency, war efforts in Viet Nam). This music was best handled in the form of a satire or of a parable. If a record was too explicit, then, as with early sexual songs, it was banned from the airwaves.

5) *Civil rights*—This social cause was espoused by whites in the 1960s, then by blacks in the 1970s. Strange as it may seem, white rock music in the 1970s has been silent on the matter of civil rights.

6) *Social concerns*—Problems (but few solutions) are discussed in rock music. Material here concerns pride, interracial relationships, slums, ghettos, "messages," "lessons," and "advice."

7) *Drugs*—Either implied or explicit drug use is covered, along with psychedelic trips, acid music, similes, and metaphorical drug use expressions.

8) *Lifestyles*—This usually means the world of the rock super star, which is usually a male macho world, and lyrics concern his musical roots and life on the road.

The genre "rock music" has been divided—for the purposes of this book—into its various formats, beginning with the "Rock" section. This is one of the smallest categories in this book, but then, there was so much trite music produced. And the good music that does exist only has a history of 25 years (unlike all the other categories, which stretch back to before the turn of the century).

Literature

Rock music is just beginning to come into the sphere of the critical writer. There are three types of materials available. The general surveys include Belz (5), Gabree (40), Gillett (41), Hopkins (53), Jahn (57), Laing (61), Rublowsky (104), Shaw (114), and Williams (138). The second type is more polemical, political, and personal, emphasizing that rock music is a way of life. These include collected articles, originally published in the rock press or mass media, by Christgau (17), Goldstein (46), Landau (62), Marcus (76), and Meltzer (81).

General collections of other writers' works were edited by Eisen (28, 29) and Marcus (77). Polemics include those of Redd (99) and Schafer (111). The third type of book comprises biographies. Interviews or sketches of individuals or groups can be found in Guralnick (49), Lydon (72), Rivelli (101), and Somma (120). Gleason (45) examines the San Francisco sound through the Jefferson Airplane and the Grateful Dead. Williams (139) looks at Phil Spector and the Los Angeles pop music scene. Roxon (103) and Stambler (121) present encyclopedic works setting forth biographical details on a large number of rock performers; the two are complementary, as Roxon goes up to 1967 and Stambler continues from then to 1973.

The rock music industry comes under surveillance with Dilello's (25) story of Apple Records, Gillett's (41) study of Atlantic Records, Denisoff's (22) scholarly criticism of the record industry and its markets, and Passman's (91) classic study of the impact of the disc jockey. Lieber (68) and Wise (140) both emphasize aspects of performing, along with group formation, equipment, instrumentation, touring, agents, etc.

Many specific studies are fruitful—and more are needed. Laing (61) discusses how folk rock developed, while Berendt's (6) popular jazz book details jazz rock. Groom (48) summarizes the British blues revival. Other books on British rock and its history include those by Cohn (18), Flattery (37), Gillett (42), and Mabey (73).

No discographies (like those in jazz or blues) can be found, but Gillett and Nugent (44) and Whitburn (131, 132) document the rise and fall of singles and albums on the charts. Propes (96) presents a guide to 1960s record collecting in the singles market. *Rolling Stone* (102) has released two volumes of record reviews, covering the 1968-1973 period.

Nearly every magazine has an article now and then on rock music or a rock personality. General magazines with adequate reviews and occasional articles include *High Fidelity* (6) and *Stereo Review* (10). Specific periodicals geared to the rock fan come and go, depending upon finances. The ones that have remained include *Circus* (1), *Creem* (3), and *Melody Maker* (7). *Crawdaddy* and *Rolling Stone* (9) are less than half music and have been since 1972.

Specific periodicals examine one aspect of rock music. *Contemporary Keyboard* (2) and *Guitar Player* (5) provide guidance and instruction for performing on those instruments, respectively. *Popular Music and Society* (8) will examine rock music's sociological impact, while *Downbeat* (4) will investigate jazz rock. Record reviews can be located through the *Annual Index to Popular Music Record Reviews* (1); periodical articles are located through the *Popular Music Periodicals Index* (94) by name of artist or under the genre heading **Rock Music** and its diverse permutations.

ANTHOLOGIES

R4.1*   **The History of British Rock, v.1/3.** six discs. Sire SAS 3702, 3705, 3712.

Overall, these six discs are perhaps one of the finest compilations of "golden hits," being exceeded by only a few of the r 'n' b or rockabilly sets. In total, there are 84 tracks from some forty artists or groups (some involving the inevitable personnel changes), and all aspects of the rock movement are covered except blues (which appears as a separate compilation on Sire SAS 3701). The range and diversity of the British popular music scene at this time (roughly 1963-1968) were far greater than in the United States. Songs were crisp and tight; all vocals, secure; instrumentation, innovative and impeccable. Female singers were treated as equals (Petula Clark, Dusty Springfield, Dandie Shaw, etc.), and there were quotas to be met for British "needletime" on the radio, plus all the pirate stations (such as Radio Luxembourg). Compare this set with any American pop compilation from the same period, and it will be readily apparent why the British invasion succeeded.

Of the several styles, groups dominate. Included are the early Beatles (with Tony Sheridan) singing "Ain't She Sweet," an innocuous number with a rock and roll beat that even made the American pop charts, and "My Bonnie"; the Hollies' "Bus Stop" and "Look through Any Window"; the Bee Gees' "Jive Talking," "I've Got to Get a Message to You," and "Massachusetts"; plus some harder rocking groups, as with Cream's "Sunshine of Your Love"; the Troggs' "Wild Thing" (later a success at Monterey with Jimi Hendrix); the Swinging Blue Jeans' "Hippy Hippy Shake"; the Dave Clark Five's "Bits and Pieces" and "Glad All Over"; the Kinks' "Long Tall Sally" and "All Day and All of the Night"; Manfred Mann's "The Mighty Quinn" and "Pretty Flamingo"; etc., etc. Male vocalists include Rod Stewart, Elton John ("Rock and Roll Madonna," "Lady Samantha"), Van Morrison ("Brown Eyed Girl"), David Bowie, Donovan, and the duos of Peter and Gordon, and Chad and Jeremy. Big successful heavy metal groups include early outings by the Who and Deep Purple. This excellent cross-section covers all styles of development during the period and comes from a wide variety of British labels: EMI, Phonogram, Pye, Polydor, CBS, Track, MCA, DJM, Immediate, RSO, Apple, Purple, Warner Brothers, Atlantic, Bang, and Ember.

R4.2*   **Woodstock, One and Two.** five discs. Cotillion SD3-500 and SD2-400.

1969 was the Year of the Rock Festival in the United States. The first successful one was in 1967 at Monterey (unfortunately, never issued on album); after Woodstock, the crowds got too large, and many were ill-run or prohibited by local laws hurriedly passed by town councils. Festivals were held on islands, in stadiums, in volcanoes—any place that could handle large crowds. Few were recorded, and

most of those were done poorly. Even the Woodstock sets are rough in spots.
But then, with a half million fans and the constant shuffle of musicians, who would
expect perfection? The festival was an interesting rock phenomenon that soured
at the end of 1969 with the Rolling Stones concert at Altmont, California, where
there were gruesome beatings and a murder, all documented on the screen through
Gimme Shelter. All aspects of American rock, folk, and country music were
presented at Woodstock, and most of it appeared on these five discs (some performers were not granted releases from their contracted recording companies). Offerings
in the folk troubador tradition came from Joan Baez, Country Joe and the Fish,
Arlo Guthrie, Richie Havens, John Sebastian, Melanie, and Crosby, Stills, Nash
and Young (the latter sounding woefully out of tune, as they had barely gotten
together in their group). Hard rock came from Jimi Hendrix (including the stunning
version of "Star Spangled Banner"), Ten Years After, the Who, Joe Cocker, Jefferson Airplane, Santana, and Sly Stone. Blues were derived from the Paul Butterfield Blues Band, Canned Heat, and Mountain. This was—and still is—a very impressive document.

INNOVATORS

R4.3*   **Beatles. 1962-1966.** two discs. Apple SKBO 3403.

R4.4*   **Beatles. 1967-1970.** two discs. Apple SKBO 3404.

R4.5*   **Beatles. Abbey Road.** Apple SO 383.

R4.6*   **Beatles. Revolver.** Capitol ST 2576.

R4.7*   **Beatles. Rubber Soul.** Capitol ST 2422.
      The Beatles were probably the most important group in rock music; certainly
their individual efforts have not even come near the group's successes. It was
through the Beatles that the British invasion into American rock and roll began
and that the concept of modern rock was to begin. The Beatles introduced the album
to rock music. Later in their career, they would also write their own songs. There
were four good reasons for this: Paul McCartney, John Lennon, George Harrison,
and Ringo Starr (to list them in the order of their popularity) were an engaging
quartet of witty individuals with cheeky remarks. They developed their music
from rockabilly roots, *not* from the blues, as other British groups did. Their influences were Bill Haley, Chuck Berry, Duane Eddy, Chet Atkins, and the harmony
of the Everly Brothers. (Berry, although r 'n' b, was in the country mold; he was
almost akin to rockabilly.) Later, when recording, the Beatles would cover Motown
hits of sophisticated r 'n' b or soul music, itself a transmutation of r 'n' b through
popular music "washing."
      In essence, the 1963-1964 success of the Beatles was a repeat of the music
of a decade earlier. The irony here is that this music was sent back to the United
States, even though it was American music to begin with. And it took three years
for the Beatles' efforts to cross the Atlantic (now it is done in days). But nothing
lasts forever; the teenyboppers that created the Beatles went on to the Animals,

Manfred Mann, Gerry and the Pacemakers, the Dave Clark Five, the Who, etc. And today, it is the Bay City Rollers, as each emerging rock group reinvents the wheel, so to speak. Yet the fans created by the Beatles (as with those of any group) stayed loyal even though these fans were displaced to an extent by the continual stream of ten to fourteen-year-old girls who always buy the records of the period. (The girls grow up, but the new members of that age group keep replacing them— and new singers come on the scene as well.) Evidence of this: in the summer of 1976, Capitol reissued 23 Beatles singles, and they all made the Top 100 chart in England through sales to teenyboppers who had never heard of the Beatles before.

The early career is documented in the rock and roll section previous to this one; that is where that material belongs. Their experimental work (such as it is) is in the section that follows. What concerns us here are the self-penned compositions that demonstrate strength and integrity. What set the Beatles apart from the rock and roll mainstream were their vocal harmonies and phrase building, which led to tension; insistent drumming; unique and demanding chord changes; use of harmonica and piano; plus their freshness. They soon became darlings of the press, because they were intelligent when most of the pop artists were simply very inarticulate and they awakened critics to a belief that, yes indeed, there *was* something to write about in the world of rock. Their substantial contributions include the following: new musical areas were created or opened up because of their interest in different musical instruments, such as Harrison's sitar; they introduced new styles, sounds, and forms of music (see the general introduction to rock music for comments on "Michelle" and "Yesterday"), including both low and high humor; they were the first rock act to be secure, even having their own label; their vocal harmonies were borrowed from country music, with vocal trade-offs between harmonized and straight ensemble singing, which opened the door to such groups as Buffalo Springfield and Crosby, Stills, Nash and Young, as well as the field of bluegrass; they spawned many imitators, but mostly in the United States (only Herman's Hermits and the Hollies were their direct imitations in Britain), which had the effect of revitalizing early rock and roll and Top 40 AM pop music; and they helped to reduce Britain's trade deficits by opening the door for other such acts to tour the United States and the rest of the world. Most of the other groups that did cross the Atlantic, though, turned out to be blues-based bands of substance, returning an even earlier music to the United States.

The four discs of collated items (*1962-1966* and *1967-1970*) present a good overview of all the Beatles' successes, either on elpees or as singles. Three albums do stand out for special mention. *Rubber Soul* (from 1965) was the first advanced rock music, with lyrics shaped and influenced by Bob Dylan, no less. It was their first experimentation with electronics, as on "Norwegian Wood" with George Harrison's sitar. "Michelle" is a model of popular song writing, while "In My Life" is pure Dylan, as is "I've Just Seen a Face." Critics have tried to characterize this album as folk rock, head music, and/or country rock but have not succeeded. Whenever a reference is made to it now, it is simply acknowledged by its title, as if we are all supposed to know how to classify it. At any rate, the social commentary here is gutsy. *Revolver* (1966) has been called the first acid album, full of musical digressions, eclecticism, and the broadening of styles through "Eleanor Rigby," "Yellow Submarine," and "Good Day Sunshine." *Abbey Road* (1969) has been called their finest album—certainly it was their last in a cohesive sense—with "Come Together," George Harrison's love song "Something," and the complicated changes on "I Want You (She's So Heavy)."

R4.8*   **Jeff Beck. Blow by Blow.** Epic 33409.

Beck was born into the British blues. After leading several groups, always dissatisfied and full of inner tensions, he managed to assume the leadership of a tight little group, as on this album: just a quartet with no clutter and definite accompaniment to his technical guitar. Often accused of being unemotional, Beck is the guitarist's guitarist, able to work in any genre with a highly pyrotechnical display of flash in jazz and blues. This album is surely the finest rock album of instrumentals to come along in the 1970. Material included his interpretations of the Beatles' "She's a Woman" and two Stevie Wonder items, "Cause We've Ended As Lovers" and "Thelonius." George Martin (of the Beatles' early career) produced this work and kept Beck under his thumbs so that he would not become excessive.

R4.9*   **Blood, Sweat and Tears. Hits.** Columbia KC 31170.

As formed by Al Kooper, BS&T represented a radical departure for rock in 1967. His idea was basically to adopt the jazz strains so evident in modern music to a rock mechanism. By creating an ensemble of eight or nine pieces (a rock quartet plus four or five horns—trumpets, saxes, and trombones), Kooper was able to harken back to the days of big band music. At the same time, his music also was influential in the resurgence of jazz groups. One musical form was feeding the other, and vice versa. The musical interplay is basically the guitar versus the horns versus the vocalist, who takes ultimate command of the presentation. This triangulation works well in arrangements, but it depends on the vocalist to resolve the stress and tensions thereby created. David Clayton-Thomas supremely filled this role, with his moans, growls, and exceptionally fluid voice. But BS&T died and revived several times when Clayton-Thomas left and later rejoined (he initially replaced Kooper). Jazz rock was born with such tunes as "Spinning Wheel," "You've Made Me So Very Happy," "And When I Die," and "Lisa, Listen to Me."

R4.10*   **Elton John. Greatest Hits.** MCA 2128.

Elton John is *the* rock superstar personality, not only of the 1970s, but also of the 1960s, for he has been with us for quite some time. He is known as a synthesizer of pop music. He has collected widely in all forms of rock, rock and roll, r 'n' b, and popular music from the past (at least that recorded since 1939) and has analyzed everything to form a style of his own in his tunes. He spent years putting in service to various rock groups in England, and even his stage name has been synthesized from the names of two of them—Elton Dean and John Baldry. In 1968, he linked with Bernie Taupin's lyrics to create little gems of rock music, and in many respects, Taupin is more important than John. Taupin had long been concerned about urban blight, loneliness, social problems, and so forth, as revealed in the classics "Border Song" and "60 Years On"; occasionally he will be concerned with the mythical American West and South—a past that involves violence, love, and fantasy. John, in complete contrast, goes on his separate performing way, emphasizing simple melodies on a soft, blues piano that can also range to the Jerry Lee Lewis pumping style (one of his early mentors in the synthesis of rock and roll music). He has been called "the master of preciousness," and this perhaps is derived from his style of combining the best aspects of José Feliciano with those of Johnny Mathis. He sings at the top of his range, with little variation; thus he needs superb musical accompaniment, and he usually gets it. Excess—some may say wretched excess—can be found on "Honky Cat," "Rocket Man," "Yellow Brick Road" (all of these are the monster singles that helped to sell the individual albums), "Saturday Night's Alright"—a genuine rocker—and the tender "Your Song."

R4.11*   **The Kinks. Greatest Hits.** Reprise MRS 6217.

R4.12   **The Kinks. Greatest Hits: Celluloid Heroes.** RCA APL1-1743.
     Along with the Rolling Stones and the Hollies, the Kinks are the oldest surviving British group still retaining a reasonable facsimile of their original starting lineup. They've been through a variety of stylistic transitions, but they have always been among the best and most highly regarded groups. Their latest image is as Britain's most effete band; yet the Kinks began their career as one of England's first "punk rock" ensembles. After two false starts in the Mersey-style of ballad singing, the Kinks regrouped drawing upon Chuck Berry's influences. They drew on the Mersey groups' emphasis on rhythm but exaggerated it out of proportion. Dave Davies played a heavily rhythmic lead guitar, seconded by Jimmy Page on the early records. The Kinks' producer, Shel Talmy, later used his experience to craft the Who's early successes. The Kinks' first albums had some of the most raw and crude energy in the rock/r 'n' b side. They were the first British group to write original hard rock music equal to the early 1950s r 'n' b successes, and this was long before the Yardbirds and the Rolling Stones began to write their own material.
     They were influenced by Phil Spector to the extent that they employed a "wall of sound" on their early records, such as on "You Really Got Me"; but under the impact of rave ups—then so common in the clubs—the Kinks played around with mounting volume and consistent textures to replace the r 'n' b horn riffs then so dominant in American soul music. Songs such as "Tired of Waiting for You," "All Day and All of the Night" led to "Who'll Be the Next in Line?," an early model of the Kinks' complex, elaborate harmonies and experimentation with lines of sound. This evolved into the satire of "A Well Respected Man" (about the middle class) and the effeteness of "Dedicated Follower of Fashion," as well as the show *Arthur* (annotated later in the experimental section). The Reprise set covers their years up through 1966. With a new label (RCA), Ray Davies came into his own as a good composer of short stories that were very detailed compressions of the pathos of everyday life. By this time, they had become almost folk-like in their relation to the English music hall style of singing and portrayal. The compilation on RCA lifts some of their finest materials out of the album context. "Muswell Hillbilly" came from the elpee of the same name and relates the country influences of the singers that performed in the Muswell clubs. "Everybody's a Star (Starmaker)" came from their *Soap Opera* album. Other little vignettes are found in "Celluloid Heroes," "Sitting in the Midday Sun," "Sitting in My Hotel," and "Face in the Crowd."

R4.13*   **Rolling Stones. Beggars Banquet.** London PS 539.

R4.14*   **Rolling Stones. Got Live (If You Want It).** London PS 493.

R4.15*   **Rolling Stones. Hot Rocks, 1964-1971, v.1/2.** four discs. London NPS 606/7 and 626/7.

R4.16*   **Rolling Stones. Let It Bleed.** London NPS 4.

The Rolling Stones characterized the hard, tough sounds of the 1960s. Whereas the Beatles derived their influences from Motown and the rock and roll period (especially the Everly Brothers), the Stones were influenced by r 'n' b created from Chuck Berry, Bo Diddley, and Jimmy Reed. In this respect, they were the opposite of the Beatles. Where the Beatles seemed to be positive, the Stones were negative. Their early work as composers, once they got over the r 'n' b covers heard on the *Hot Rocks* sets, expressed tension in their themes of an arrogance and disdain mixed with both ennui and frustration. Both themes were derived from living in desperate times. Prime examples were "Get off of My Cloud" and "I Can't Get No Satisfaction." With sex added, this transmuted to "Let's Spend the Night Together." Their charisma was largely a product of their mean and nasty looks, coupled with the moodiness of vocalist Mick Jagger and the menacing behavior of lead guitarist Keith Richards. The other three were fairly stable: Charlie Watts, drummer; Bill Wyman, bassist; and Brian Jones, rhythm guitar (but later replaced by Mick Taylor, Robbie Lane, and others). All were needed for the chunky rhythms to be laid down.

The Stones through this period were the leaders of what was briefly called "the London sound," a hard black sound that emphasized guitar riffs sustained right across songs from start to finish. Many of their best tunes had this tension of riffs offset by steady drone drumming. To some, it was blunt noise; certainly, there was a lot of activity and few pauses. Throughout their career, the Stones were very negative towards women, which may have added to their appeal to women who liked a trace of sadism. At any rate, the stage movements of Jagger (unfortunately not available on disc) exuded sexuality; to some, he appeared to be "all lips and no hips." On almost all of the titles found on these records, the Rolling Stones reveal themselves to be good musicians: the structures of the tunes are logical, the lyrics are powerful, the textures merge with the melodies, and the guitar playing of Richards is superb and often underrated.

The live album was chosen because it was the best recording ever of a rock concert. All the top hits are here, there is excellent sound and excellent instrumentation, and in stereo, the listener feels as if he is "front row center." This November 1966 album will stand for a long time as the model of concert recording. *Beggars Banquet* was their first really strong album in toto, with the horrifying Satanic "Sympathy for the Devil," "No Expectations," "Street Fighting Man," and "Prodigal Son." *Let It Bleed* was their last successful album, with the imposing "Gimme Shelter" and its guitar riff, "Love in Vain" from bluesman Robert Johnson, Keith Richards's guitar on "Monkey Man," the dramatic production of "You Can't Always Get What You Want" (utilizing a boys' choir), and "Country Honk," a parody of both country music and their earlier hit "Honky Tonk Woman." This last track was the beginning of the end, for most of what they have done on their own label since 1972 has been self-parody. In a sense, then, the Stones have gone commercial.

R4.17*   **The Who. Live at Leeds.** MCA Decca DS 79175.

R4.18*   **The Who. Magic Bus.** two discs. MCA2-4068.

R4.19*   **The Who. A Quick One (Happy Jack).** two discs. MCA2-4067.

Before *Tommy*, the Who were unknown in America beyond an appearance in the film *Monterey Pop*, where they busted all of their instruments. They were *the* mod band of London from 1964 onwards, but they failed to make a significant dent in the American market despite "Pictures of Lily," "Happy Jack," and "I Can See for Miles." All of these songs are powerful rockers bristling with energy, and one can only surmise that their failure was due to lack of promotion: Decca never had a rock group and didn't know what to do with them. Their music then, as now, deals with the forces of change (e.g., "My Generation"), and their stage act was to become the model of musical "destruction theater," with guitar smashings and smoke bombs. Such tunes as "Anyway, Anyhow, Anywhere" present their choreographed chaos in heavy metal; their hard rock sound is best heard on their legendary version of "Summertime Blues" (both titles from the *Leeds* album). Peter Townshend is the lead guitarist, master of feedback, and composer; John Entwhistle is the bassist; the late Keith Moon was the heavy, driving drummer. All three in this trio are countered by Roger Daltry, the vocalist, and part of their tension results from the fact that the group sounds like, and is, one of the first rock power trios with a separate vocalist. This distinctive sound led to experimentation and showmanship (particularly with *Tommy*, annotated in the experimental section at R9.27) utilizing unusual programming and satire. The 47 tracks here are mostly short pop numbers (the Who didn't then go in for long recordings), including "Call Me Lightning," "A Legal Matter," "Boris the Spider," "Whiskey Man," "Cobwebs and Strange," plus the titles mentioned above and the title tracks.

STANDARDS

R4.20*   **Duane Allman. An Anthology, v.1/2.** four discs. Capricorn 2CP 0108
          and 0139.

Allman led a double life. He was the excellent lead/slide guitarist for the Allman Brothers and contributor of original material; he was also a first rate session guitarist. Both facets are explored in these four discs, issued as a tribute after he died. His diverse session works were recorded during 1967-1971, and this four-year span covered the entire field of rock, country, soul, and blues—he was versatile in all genres. His accompaniment here, mainly for Atlantic-Atco records, includes "Hey Jude" with Wilson Pickett, "The Road of Love" with Clarence Carter, "The Weight" with Aretha Franklin, and "Games People Play" with King Curtis for the soul material; accompaniment to John Hammond, Delany and Bonnie, Derek and the Dominoes ("Layla," the live version); "Statesboro Blues," "Standback," and "Dreams" from Allman Brothers performances; plus some unissued or obscure works including a 1968 B. B. King medley, some unissued Eric Clapton-Allman duos ("Mean Old World") and early Hourglass (the first Allman Brothers band). Of note is the thirteen-minute excursion into Fenton Robinson's "Loan Me a Dime," sung by Boz Scaggs. Allman made a significant contribution to American music, taking away some of the fame for guitar prowess from the British, who seemed to be all over the place at the time.

R4.21 **Argent. Anthology of Greatest Hits.** Columbia KE 33955.
The work of Rod Argent continues his influences from the Zombies' period of his life. This is a basic rock group of good technical skills, employing classical devices such as arpeggios and electronic synthesizers in addition to a goodly proportion of jazz themes (rather than improvisation). Russ Ballard handled the vocals and guitar on such items as "Liar," "Hold Your Head Up," and the epic "Thunder and Lightning," all found on this eight-track compilation.

R4.22* **Bee Gees. Best, v.1.** Atco SD 33-292.
The Gibb Brothers have been performing since 1956. Barry (vocals), Maurice, and Robin (quavering vocal) were the first to replace the Beatles' early successes on the British charts. Their tight harmony singing plus good original material made them sound very similar to the Beatles, but they operated more in the pop mode, using lush sweetening. They were one of the first groups to use the complex interweaving of strings and voices. As they developed, they employed newer and unique devices such as religious incantations, a cappella interludes, and even filtered voices. Typical illustrative tracks here include "New York Mining Disaster, 1941," "Close Another Door," "Sir Geoffrey Saved the World," "Singer Sang His Song," and "Holiday."

R4.23 **Bonzo Dog Band. The History of the Bonzos.** two discs. United Artists UALA321-H2.
Originally beginning as the Bonzo Doo Dah Dog Band, this group specialized in the humorous song, as a cross between the British music hall and early Frank Zappa. Thus, it had a chance of succeeding, as it was rhythmically pleasing and lyrically teasing at the same time. Their outrageous stage show was one of the first of the theater "glitter" acts. Vivian Stanshall handled the vocals and the production end, "Legs" Larry Smith was the frenetic drummer, Neil Innes played piano, Rodney Slater did the sax, and Roger Spear worked on reeds. Their freak humor basically involved parodies of standard rock and roll motifs. Their unorthodox procedures came directly from Zappa and the Mothers of Invention. Some of their most appealing work included "Can Blue Men Sing the Whites?," an obvious take off; the weird "I Left My Heart in San Francisco" and "Release Me"; "Canyons of Your Mind," which featured what was then billed as the world's worst guitar solo as a parody on all guitar solos, plus an Elvis-inspired voice. "The Intro and the Outro" introduces the band, which also included the Count Basie organization on triangle ("thank you"). Stanshall and Innes wrote most of the material. They are completely indescribable, except for this effort by Chris Welch: "They have wandered erratically from brilliance to banality. They have made a lot of people laugh. They stalk a strange path between art and rock, success and disaster. Their essence is sustained spontaneity and rebellion." Welcome to the schizoid world. . . .

R4.24   **David Bowie. Images, 1966-1967.** two discs. London BP 628/9.
Bowie has long been the darling of rock critics, especially in his later career
with his stage show. Unfortunately, his records have never sold well (in comparison
to others), and his material is very highly related to his stage show. The tunes and
lyrics simply fall flat when heard as a waver on the stereo. But in the mid-sixties,
he was innovative with his theater songs, with a voice that sounded remarkably
like Anthony Newley's. The cuts here are from the pre-Ziggy Stardust days, when
he was also known as Davy Jones. All of the eccentric items here were also written
by Bowie: "Rubber Band" is a love song with tuba accompaniment; "The Laughing
Gnome" and his brother have moved into Bowie's chimney and write songs for
him; "Mr. Gravedigger" is a morbid song in a cappella style. Good variety on this
double album, with a bouncy "Karma" and an intellectual "Love You till Tuesday."
Since this period, Bowie has switched from theater songs to theatrics.

R4.25   **Chicago. Greatest Hits.** Columbia PC 33900.
Following hard on the heels of Blood, Sweat and Tears, Robert Lamm organized a similar quartet plus three horns and initially called the Chicago Transit
Authority. Although it began operations in the area of jazz rock, it swiftly shifted
gears to a distinct pop orientation. Chicago came up with a notable series of
double albums plus a four-album set from Carnegie Hall (which was essentially
a repeat on the stage of their studio creations). Because of their pop mode, they
have consistently received a poor press coverage. While BS&T introduced serious
jazz themes, Chicago merely borrowed the instrumentation for background sweetening. There was no conflict to resolve amidst the pieces played. Typical items here
include "Just You 'n' Me," "25 or 6 to 4," "Color My World," "Make Me Smile,"
and "Does Anybody Really Know What Time It Is?"

R4.26   **Joe Cocker. With a Little Help from My Friends.** A & M SP 4182.
Joe Cocker emerged from the world of the "working class blues" of skiffle
music and rock 'n' roll. He became, by the time of this recording date in 1969,
a supreme interpreter of material: harsh vocals with a raw screaming voice that
conveyed deep emotion. The title track here is largely incoherent, but this was
the album that set him up as a rock singer. Other tracks here include "Delta Lady"
and "Feeling Alright." Joe Cocker won world renown for his stage antics.

R4.27*   **Judy Collins. Colors of the Day: Best.** Elektra EKS 75035.

R4.28   **Judy Collins. In My Life.** Elektra EKS 74027.

R4.29   **Judy Collins. Wildflowers.** Elektra EKS 74012.
By the late 1960s, Judy Collins made an abrupt shift in her interpretive
style of singing—to become a *chansonniere* with a variety of material both contemporary and old. Thus, with great assistance from arranger-conductor Joshua Rifkin,
she embarked on theater and art songs that displayed the stunning variety of her
voice. From the *Wildflowers* album came the Joni Mitchell hits "Both Sides Now"
and "Michael from Mountains," three Leonard Cohen selections, Jacques Brel's
"The Song of Old Lovers" and a ballad by Landini. *In My Life* ended with the
title track, a Beatles song, two more Cohen works (including "Suzanne"), Dylan's

"Tom Thumb Blues," Donovan's "Sunny Goodge Street," songs by Randy Newman, Brel, and Richard Farina, and a long medley (very dramatic) from *Marat/Sade*. Some of these are on the "best" album, but also there will be found "Poor Immigrant" (her masterful interpretation of the Dylan song), an updated Ian and Sylvia tune ("Someday Soon"), Sandy Denny's "Who Knows Where the Time Goes?," and "Cook with Honey."

R4.30　　**Delaney and Bonnie and Friends with Eric Clapton. On Tour.** Atco S-33-326.

Following his brief fling with the super-group Blind Faith, guitarist supreme Eric Clapton joined Delaney Bramlett's band to create some of the best rocking music of his career. Backing Delaney and Bonnie's vocals—southern deep-fat-fried and twice as powerful—Clapton takes extended but tasteful solos, such as the one on "Things Get Better," that point up his emergence not just as a flash guitarist but a master of its new electronic vocabulary. Delaney's finest work can be heard on his tribute to Robert Johnson, "Poor Elijah." Clapton would later steal Bramlett's rhythm section to create Derek and the Dominos. But in 1970, "Slowhand" got together with country funk and created a beautiful album.

R4.31　　**J. Geils Band.** Atlantic SD 8275.

This Boston-based group performed blues, r 'n' b, and soul ballads. Although it is often typed as a blues band, only four of the eleven tracks here are actually blues. They have been favorably compared to the Rolling Stones and could prove a successor to mainstream rock. Peter Wolf is the lead vocalist, J. Geils is the lead guitarist (with a heavy orientation towards jazz), and Magic Dick makes intelligent use of the harmonica. The neat rhythm section is tight and concise; there are also no horns, as the piano and harmonica can sustain the needed riffs. Thus, this band does not suffer from wretched excess as others do. Typical tracks include the good instrumental "Ice Breaker," Albert Collins's "Sno-Cone," John Lee Hooker's "Serves You Right to Suffer," and Otis Rush's "Homework."

R4.32　　**Jethro Tull. M.U.—The Best of Jethro Tull.** Chrysalis CHR 1078.

This eleven-track survey has been extracted from several Tull albums, such as *Benefit*, *Thick As a Brick*, and *Living in the Past*. Ian Anderson is the mover of the group, as they augment his showpieced flute. Material is eclectic, reflecting all of the forms of music assimilated into the rock world: "Teacher," "Bungle in the Jungle," "Fat Man," "Locomotive Breath," and "Nothing Is Easy."

R4.33　　**Manfred Mann. Best.** Janus JLS 3064.

Manfred Mann and the boys originally considered themselves jazz improvisers, but found that the key to success and money lay with pop. With "Do Wah Diddy Diddy," they became the first British group after the Beatles to get a number one single hit in the United States (1964). A next song was "Sha La La," but then silence reigned on these shores for four years until the rare Dylan song—"The Mighty Quinn"—came back in 1968 with Mann vocals. The group at this time had Mann, Mike Hugg, Michael D'Abo, Tom McGuinness, and Klaus Voorman (Paul Jones was replaced by D'Abo in 1966; Jack Bruce moved to Cream and was replaced by Voorman—and so it goes . . .). Mann played the organ and other keyboards, which tended to predominate on softer ballads such as "Pretty Flamingo," with Paul Jones.

R4.34   **Dave Mason. At His Best.** Blue Thumb ABTD 880.
Mason is one of the creators of the great rock and roll-type love songs. He, along with Stevie Winwood, formed the nucleus of Traffic. Mason left for a solo career, but paid his way by contributing as a session man on diversified records. He recorded three Blue Thumb albums, and this collation picks nine tracks from those sets. Over the years, his output has been small, with him preferring to concentrate on polished writing or re-interpretations of others. Some typical titles here include "Only You Know and I Know," "Look at You Look at Me," "Headkeeper," and "Shouldn't Have Took More Than You Gave."

R4.35*   **Maria Muldaur.** Reprise MS 2148.

R4.36   **Maria Muldaur. Waitress in the Donut Shop.** Reprise MS 2194.
Muldaur had done good work for Jim Kweskin's Jug Band and other assorted good time outfits. Her distinctive style lies firmly in the mainstream popular music world. She is simply superb in her interpretations of songs, flowing in her vocalizings with correct emphasis, inflections, nuances, etc. The 21 tracks here are a collection of blues, folk, popular and country items, such as Jimmie Rodgers's "Any Old Time," Skip James's "If You Haven't Any Hay," Clarence Ashley's "Honey Babe Blues," and Fats Waller's "Squeeze Me." Original material in her style was contributed by Wendy Waldman, David Nichtern, and Anna McGarrigle. Many, many musicians contributed their services including those currently in the fields of bluegrass, contemporary blues, and r 'n' b, plus a soft jazz backing put together by Benny Carter. A very pleasant mixture, the records can be played over and over with no loss of momentum.

R4.37   **Procol Harum. Best.** A & M SP 4401.
Procol Harum says their name is Latin for "beyond these things"; but any metaphysical values in their music disappeared after their blazing first success entitled "A Whiter Shade of Pale." This surrealistic song was based on the Bach cantata *Sleepers, Awake*, with lyrics simulating stream of consciousness thought action. They were one of the first groups to use the piano and organ in combination (Matthew Charles Misher usually played both). The slower tempos were full of dignity, but some critics said that they were plodding. Throughout, however, they showed good lyrics (by Keith Reid, a non-performer) in an age when lyrics meant little, and good guitar from Robin Trower, who later imagined himself as Jimi Hendrix. Other tracks here include "Conquistador" (recorded with the Edmonton Symphony Orchestra in Canada), "Salty Dog," "Shine on Brightly," and "Long Gone Geek."

R4.38   **Bonnie Raitt.** Warner Brothers WS 1953.

R4.39*   **Bonnie Raitt. Give It Up.** Warner Brothers BS 2643.
     Raitt, daughter of theater-musical performer John Raitt, comes to the rock
interpretation scene with a solid background of blues and r 'n' b influences. She
is virtually alone in this field, for few women are attracted to the blues well enough
to record them. Her prime sources have been the late Fred McDowell, from whom
she learned slide guitar, and Sippi Wallace, from whom she learned vocal phrasing.
Blues aside, she does perform in a number of idioms, such as 1920s jazz style,
r 'n' b (as on Barbara George's "I Know"), and such singer-songwriter material
as Jackson Browne's "Under the Falling Sky." In common with Steve Goodman
and Maria Muldaur, she has attracted a wide variety of musicians to work on diverse
pieces. On her first album, which contained the blues "Mighty Tight Woman,"
Tommy Johnson's "Big Road," Robert Johnson's "Walking Blues," and "Women
Be Wise," she has Junior Wells on harp, Wells's saxist A. C. Reed, and Peter Bell
on guitar. Her own slide guitar is quite good for this largely blues album; the second
album has a more jazz feel, assisted by Dave Holland's acoustic bass, Merl Saunders's
piano, and Paul Butterfield's harmonica. Again, there are some Sippi Wallace songs
and a few more originals, including the title track, which details a choice between
a woman and hard living.

R4.40   **The Rascals. Greatest Hits: Time/Peace.** Atlantic SD 8190.
     The Rascals were one of the very first of the blue-eyed soul groups. They
were born in New York City and came from the environment described by Phil
Groia in his remarkable book *They All Sang on the Corner*. This white group
with the hard black sound was led by Felix Cavaliere on organ; they had impeccable
harmonies and tight arrangements. Titles include "Groovin'," "People Got to Be
Free," the wonderful "Good Lovin'," the Wilson Pickett song "In the Midnight
Hour," and "I Ain't Gonna Eat My Heart out Anymore."

R4.41*   **Leon Russell.** Shelter SW 8901.
     With a career that spans back to 1955, Leon Russell has been, among other
things, the most sought-after session man in rock, the leader of the southwestern
U.S. funk movement, a c & w singer, and one of the most influential record producers to be found. His recorded solo albums have been spotty, but this, his first
on his own, is a delightful "jam" featuring Russell on his frenetic piano, George
Harrison, Ringo Starr, Bill Wyman and Charlie Watts (from the Rolling Stones),
Eric Clapton, and Klaus Voorman, among others too numerous to mention. The
dozen good-time cuts include "Prince of Peace," "Can't Be Satisfied," and "Shoot
Out on the Plantation." Russell's influence is tremendous. Few musicians in hard
rock, country rock, or the peculiar brand of laid-back funk that emanates from
Texas-Oklahoma (Doug Sahm, Kinky Friedman, Steve Miller) have not borrowed
a lick or two from him. His work with Joe Cocker and with Delaney and Bonnie
shows in particular his gospel sound and powerful vocal style.

R4.42*   **Santana. Abraxas.** Columbia KC 30130.
     Carlos Santana organized a rock quartet with four percussionists added to
play many different drums and cymbals. He combined jazz rock with a Latin

beat and African rhythms to create a riffing percussion sound, with an abrupt guitar slashing through the counter-rhythms. This album features exceptional melodies; there are few vocals, and those that do exist are merely chanted. Tracks include "Jingo," "Black Magic Woman," and "Oye Como Va." Santana played throughout the Mission District of San Francisco and inspired other bands to create some of the same music, which soon was referred to as "chicano rock."

R4.43   **Bruce Springsteen. Born to Run.** Columbia PC 33795.

Springsteen's harmonies are full of echoes from the past. In him, the listener can identify Sam Cooke, Elvis Presley, Chuck Berry, Roy Orbison, Buddy Holly, Bob Dylan, Van Morrison, and even the Band. Springsteen is a remarkable fusion of Latin, soul, jazz, and rock and roll music. Overall, though, he has been most influenced by British rock music. He writes about social stratification with a subjective view of sewer life that is at once abstract and bizarre. He appears to revel in the dirt and grease of life on the street. Yet the lyrics are believable, as they are created in journalistic style. The only problem is that he has a poor voice.

R4.44*   **Rod Stewart. Best.** two discs. Mercury SRM2-7507.

"Rod the Mod" was into deep r 'n' b in London, England, from 1964 onwards. He played harmonica on Millie Small's reggae hit of that year "My Boy Lollipop," worked with Jimmy Powell and the Fifth Dimension, Long John Baldry, the Hoochie Coochie Men, Steampacket, Julie Driscoll, Brian Auger, etc. To make ends meet, he also did cover versions of current hits for the cheaper budget labels. With the Immediate label, he came to the attention of Jeff Beck, and was hired as lead vocalist. He later went onto the Faces, but sang better without them under his own name. His ballads and blues work have been influenced by Motown, Sam Cooke and Richie Havens. His characteristically hoarse voice on these eighteen tracks from 1972-1974 is more emphatic on his own compositions, such as "Maggie May," "An Old Raincoat Won't Ever Let You Down," "Gasoline Alley," and "Every Picture Tells a Story." Other songs were contributed from the books of Bobby Womack, Elton John, Jimi Hendrix, the Beatles, the Rolling Stones, and the Who.

R4.45   **Ten Years After. Stonedhenge.** Deram DES 18021.

Alvin Lee founded this group in 1965, naming it to celebrate the tenth anniversary of the discovery of Elvis Presley, i.e., Ten Years After "life began" in 1955. But there the resemblance ends, as flash guitarist Lee updated rock and roll through blues and boogie. Lee played exceptionally fast and correct, but still with light textures, possibly a creation of Ric Lee the drummer. It was swift music with roots deep in the rock and roll period. This, their second and best album, featured "Going to Try," "Woman Trouble," "Sad Song," and the epic "Speed Kills."

R4.46   **Three Dog Night. Joy to the World—Their Greatest Hits.** ABC Dunhill DSD 50178.

"Dog" is the most successful rock group operating; they are a business organization in the commercial sense. Beginning in 1968, they sang other people's works so that they wouldn't be bogged down with always having to produce an album of material. They thus gave up royalties for sure-fire hits. There are three distinctive lead singers, backed by a rock quartet playing arranged music. Material is chosen with care, and the results have been solid gold albums and singles—all of them. When they tour, they are always sold out, and they play at stadiums with tens of thousands in attendance. They gross millions each year (over six million dollars in 1970). All of the music is executed in a professional sense, and over the years they have elevated the singer-songwriters to some measure of financial security, such as Hoyt Axton ("Joy to the World," "Never Been to Spain"), Randy Newman ("Mama Told Me Not to Come"), Kenny Loggins ("Pieces of April"), Laura Nyro ("Eli's Coming"), plus others such as the John-Taupin song "Lady Samantha" and "Easy to Be Heard" from *Hair*. Good value here, as there are fourteen selections.

R4.47   **Zombies.** Parrot PAS 71001.
In the wake of the Beatles, the Zombies were one of the first British groups to enchant the American pop-loving public. Led by pianist-composer Rod Argent, they created inventive pop rock full of subtle moods and swirling melodies. Since they were operating in the mid-sixties, at just the dawn of rock, bits and pieces of the sounds of later groups can be heard in Zombie music: the Kinks, Moody Blues, and Procol Harum all were influenced by this under-rated band. Rod Argent would later leave to form a group called, unsurprisingly, Argent, that would attract some attention from 1970 on. Colin Blunstone, vocalist and guitarist, would pursue successful solo work. Typical titles on this disc include "Tell Her No," "She's Not There," "I Don't Want to Know," and "Time of the Season."

BLUES ROCK

INTRODUCTION

Blues rock was a British development. The blues revival in the United States was a culmination of the urban folk music and urban blues craze and the development of British rock music based on black music, accented by the proliferation of skiffle (jug) bands in England. Rock musicians in England further extended the country blues-folk-jug-band idiom into Chicago blues. They tried to approximate the unintentional distortion of electric blues recordings (the Chicago blues men used old equipment that was falling apart and malfunctioning). These blues-rockers experimented with fuzz-tone and sustained notes as well. The British leaders were Jimmy Page, Eric Clapton, and Jeff Beck (all ex-Yardbirds), plus Jimi Hendrix from the United States, who traveled to England for his success and picked up an English bassist and drummer. (He was profoundly influenced by Clapton.) Vocalists, however, simply did not exist. For some reason, no one was ever found that was better than mediocre. The two vocal leaders—Robert Plant (of Led Zeppelin) and Rod Stewart—had to spend a decade in developing. On the other hand, American groups such as Electric Flag, the Paul Butterfield Blues Band, and the Blues Project, had several good vocalists. But their recordings were strictly in the Chicago mold, changing only with added amplification—and cleaning up the distortion. Unfortunately, this interpretation made the blues seem monotonous and lacking in excitement.

Blues rock was most of the British invasion of the mid-sixties, when rock and roll was given a big shot in the arm by amplification. After the Beatles came several similar pop groups, followed by a whole alphabet of British musicians working in the blues mode. American imitators of British imitators of British imitators of Chicago blues quickly followed, and by the end of the 1960s, folk rock, acid rock, and blues rock coexisted in neat categories. But then folk rock transmuted into troubador music, and blues rock adopted some of the technical devices of the fading acid rock. The result of this latter amalgamation was heavy metal (hard rock) music.

ANTHOLOGIES

R5.1   **Anthology of British Blues.** Daffodil SBA 16017 (Canadian issue).

R5.2   **History of British Blues, v.1.** two discs. Sire SAS 3701.

R5.3   **Raw Blues.** London PS 543.

R5.4   **Power Blues.** London PS 579.

R5.5   **World of Blues Power, v.1/3.** three discs. Decca SPA 14, 63, 263 (British issue).
British rock music of the 1960s has usually been divided into two streams. One is the American white imitation fostered by the Beatles, who later wrote their own material with sparse rock accompaniment; the other is the American black imitation fostered by the Rolling Stones from an r 'n' b derivation and by Cream from the Chicago blues. The lovely material on these eight discs covers the latter, and the shift to heavy metal music that followed. The first two sets are performances in the blues styles but only as done by white British performers; the London-Decca reissues are a combination of black and white. The Daffodil concerns the rich Immediate catalog of T. S. McPhee, Jimmy Page (Led Zeppelin), plus some of the Rolling Stones on a few cuts, as well as Clapton and Savoy Brown.

For the Sire set, producer Mike Vernon has packaged 24 tracks from his own Blue Horizon label, fleshed out with material from Declon, EMI, Pye, and Saydisc records. This cohesive whole spans the 1962-1970 period, with most activity occurring from 1962 through 1965. Copious notes place the British blues in context and describe the shifting personnel and influences; plus, there are pictures. The set opens with a strong Cyril Davies R 'n' B All Stars' "Country Line Special," takes in Alexis Korner and John Mayall, Spencer Davis with the Winwood brothers, the Yardbird period of Eric Clapton, the Graham Bond Organization (Bruce, Baker, Heckstall-Smith), and Johnny Almond. There are several terrific cuts, one in particular being "Stone Crazy" with a Rod Stewart vocal and backup from the Anysley Dunbar Retaliation (Peter Green, Jack Bruce). Other performers include Kim Simmonds (Savoy Brown), Ginger Baker, Long John Baldry, and Keith Relf. None of these records ever was the success that typical rock records were; however, they were indicative of the music of the time.

A more successful compilation is the series on British Decca (London Records in the United States). Decca had a policy of recording bluesmen, both black and white, for its pop and jazz catalogs. Normally, these are separate. But somebody got the bright idea of compiling a series of blues albums with stars of the rock world augmenting the bluesmen's performance (or what Decca owned the rights to). Thus, there is the mixture here of separately recorded black and white blues, plus the occasional integrated session. This is good for comparing and contrasting, but unfortunately, the budget did not extend to liner notes.

Only PS 543 has some, written by our friend Mike Vernon. The major period under consideration here is 1967-1970, after all of the acts had established themselves. These discs have twelve tracks apiece, except *Power Blues*, which is mainly a set of numbers of over five minutes in duration. Recorded before 1970, this had some of the heavy metal blues, such as Keef Hartley's "Leavin' Trunk," Ten Years After's "I'm Going Home," with typical Lee-flash guitar, and a live version of Savoy Brown's recreation of Muddy Waters's "Louisiana Blues" that featured an intriguing distorted riff. The performers on all of these discs also include John Mayall with his various Bluesbreakers (Eric Clapton, Paul Butterfield, Peter Green— the latter especially fluent on the instrumental "Greeny"). The bluesmen, with their separate recordings, are represented by Champion Jack Dupree, Eddie Boyd, and Otis Spann (all pianists); Homesick James, Robert Nighthawk, and Mickey Baker (all guitarists); and harmonica player Shakey Horton.

INNOVATORS

R5.6*   **Blues Project. Projections.** Verve FTS 3008.

This group's name came from an Elektra anthology album on which the members played. They liked the resulting music so much that they formed an ensemble. Beginning members were Steve Katz (guitar), Al Kooper (organ and vocals), Tommy Flanders, and Danny Kalb. (Kooper later left to form Blood, Sweat and Tears, remaining with the Blues Project for a little more than a year.) In 1965, when this album was released, it was one of the first electric blues discs put together by a white group. The Blues Project was important for a number of reasons. First, they established themselves completely by means of albums—they did not need 45 rpm singles to survive as their elpees sold rather well. This created a new field of marketing for the rock industry and made appropriate use of the long-playing disc. Second, they established blues rock. Third, they formed the basis for the ensuing Blood, Sweat and Tears conglomeration, as the Blues Project used jazz lines and the flute in their tunes. And fourth, they were one of the first rock groups to make extensive use of the long song (beyond 200 seconds). They were thus exposed only on FM stations, as AM stations would not play longer items. Some typical good music from this, their first, album includes the slow blues "I Can't Keep from Crying," the fast dynamism of "Two Trains Running," and the boogie beat of "You Can't Catch Me." Only the Paul Butterfield Blues Band was operating in the blues mode at this time, and most of their material was a copy of the original black music. Blues Project provided its own songs.

R5.7   **Paul Butterfield. Better Days.** Bearsville BR 2119.

R5.8*   **Paul Butterfield. Golden Butter.** two discs. Elektra 7E-2005.
        Butterfield (a harp player), along with Mike Bloomfield and Elvin Bishop
(both on guitars), closely defined the white interpretation of black blues. In many
respects, particularly on their first album from 1965 (half of which is on the double
set), this material was indistinguishable from the real thing. But then the real thing
still existed and could be found in the record shops. "So what's the point?" many
critics asked. The point was that many in the potential audience didn't know this,
and as is so common in the popular music field, audiences had to be led from
grossly commercial discs to the specialized records. Besides, in its historical perspective, British blues came at least four years ahead of Butterfield or the Blues
Project. At least, Butterfield was honest about the roots of his music. Subsequent
albums featured original material and an enlarged band.
        One of the nicest works that Butterfield did was the thirteen-minute instru-
mental jam "East-West," which stressed the stylings of Eastern rhythms and jazz
before they became a widespread influence on rock. Butterfield's importance,
though, lay in bringing the electric blues to a white rock audience. His third album
introduced horns and progressive blues rock. In many respects, Butterfield was
able to enlarge upon British blues themes, so much so that when *they* went into
heavy metal using limited techniques, *he* went into progressivism. In 1973, Butterfield returned to the Chicago blues with Robert Johnson's "Walking Blues" and a
good tight group consisting of Geoff Muldaur, Amos Garrett, and Ronnie Barron.
The laid-back, updated country quality continued with Big Joe Williams's "Baby,
Please Don't Go" and the r 'n' b classic, Percy Mayfield's "Please Send Me Someone
to Love."

R5.9*   **John Mayall. Alone.** London PS 534.

R5.10*   **John Mayall. Blues Breakers.** London PS 492.

R5.11   **John Mayall. Best.** two discs. Polydor PD2-3006.
        Mayall is the godfather to the British blues groups. He had been playing the
blues since the early 1950s, being hampered only by too high and too "white"
a voice. He has never had a hit; his records only sell averagely. His work is largely
experimental within the blues framework, and in fact, he has probably done more
to advance the blues cause and new ideas in the black blues than anyone else. He
was one of the first to add horns to groups. The *Alone* album involves overdubbing;
he plays everything except drums on seven tracks. The twelve tracks were all
written by him, and he serves up liner notes describing each. There is some gospel
and a tribute to Sonny Boy Williamson, No. 2, but loneliness and sexual imageries
predominate.
        Perhaps the most influential album in blues rock is *Blues Breakers*, the
first album with the group (formed in 1962). With Eric Clapton on stunning lead
guitar (he did his best work ever in a group here), John McVie on bass, and
Hughie Flint on drums, this group captured the essence of the Chicago blues,
albeit in a derivative sense. Powerful electric renditions of Otis Rush's "All Your
Love," Ray Charles's "What I'd Say?," Freddie King's "Hideaway," Little Walter's

"It Ain't Alright," and Robert Johnson's "Ramblin' on My Mind." The Polydor double set shows his experimentation into jazz, piano, and horns to recreate the blues. Mayall's later bands have spewed forth a number of apprentices: Mick Taylor, Jack Bruce, Johnny Almond, John Mark, and Larry Taylor. Titles in this retrospective include "Room to Move," "Full Speed Ahead," and "Red Sky" from the many originals. Excellent tunes and good feeling from an uncompromising artist can be found here.

R5.12*   **Yardbirds. Featuring Eric Clapton, Jeff Beck, and Jimmy Page.** three
          discs. Charly CR 300.012/4 (British issue).
          In the wake of the Beatles and the Rolling Stones came the popular blues-
based Yardbirds. Among their innovative guitarists were Eric Clapton, Jeff Beck, and Jimmy Page. Led by Keith Relf's throaty lead vocals, this band slid over from British blues to become the forerunner of the heavy metal sound. Rock's original metallic sound has one of its roots deep in the Yardbirds, which can be heard clearly in the structured chaos of "Shapes of Things" and "Happenings Ten Years' Time Ago." A seminal early rock band that was the spawning ground for many of the superstars of the late '60s and early '70s, the Yardbirds started the "rave ups" with Clapton (long instrumental jams of recreated blues, displaying all of the musicians' virtuosity on their respective instruments). Their functioning period, 1964-1967, produced such hit gems as the popular "For Your Love," "New York City Blues," "Overundersidewaysdown," "I'm a Man," and their rendition of Howlin' Wolf's "Smokestack Lightnin'."

These three discs present a reasonable chronological progression in the history of the group. CR 300.012 features Clapton, with six hit singles on one side and five long jams from the world famous Marquee Club (London; March 1964). CR 300.013, with Beck, covers 1964-1966, from London, New York, Memphis, and Chicago; and CR 300.014 covers 1967-1968, when Page played lead guitar. In style, the early material was the best, being in the hard-nosed blues revival mold. Of the three most influential rock groups in England, the Yardbirds were the best musicians, while the Rolling Stones were the best performers and the Beatles the best singers. The Yardbirds proved to be an excellent training ground for each of its three lead guitarists, as they went on to better and bigger groups, wielding diverse influences—the rave ups of Clapton went to John Mayall, Cream, Blind Faith, etc.; the pyrotechnical virtuosity of Beck went to the Jeff Beck Group and to jazz rock fusion; while the blitzkrieg guitar notes of Page went to Led Zeppelin and heavy metal music. The problem with the Yardbirds was a series of miscalculations—they toured America too late, they had poor management, their records were poorly mixed (avoid *any* American Epic releases; prefer the three Charlys), they were too far ahead of their time (blues revival, jazz rave ups, psychedelic music) in terms of effect on the market. Yet, each and every heavy metal group has acknowledged their influence, and they are the leaders in cult followings. To put it simply, no other group has ever unleashed *three* lead guitarists of the caliber of Clapton, Beck, and Page.

STANDARDS

R5.12a*   **Allman Brothers Band. The Road Goes on Forever.** two discs. Capricorn 2CP 0164.

The Allman Brothers began, as did so many other bands, by reinterpreting the black blues. Their main distinguishing characteristic was Duane Allman's sweetly polished bottleneck guitar pointed off against Dicky Betts's hard-edged rock guitar. The seventeen selections here, from 1969-1973, were carefully chosen to reflect all aspects of the band's workings, and they are arranged in chronological order. Their first recorded song under the name Allman Brothers (they had worked a few years previously under a variety of names, such as Hourglass) was the gripping "Black Hearted Woman"; another good cut was "Whipping Post." Side two of this set reduces their *Fillmore East* album to a few notables, while side three is a condensation of the more remarkable cuts from *Eat a Peach*. The material on side four is derived from their *Brothers and Sisters* album. Their earlier work—"Statesboro Blues," "Stormy Monday," "Hoochie Coochie Man"—was all black music, and contrasts with the musical maturity of the last efforts, such as "Wasted Words," "Jessica," and "Ramblin' Man." Besides their work as a cohesive band, the Allmans also showed great ability to perform as session men on diverse albums, showing a rigor that is often lacking in other bands. A southern boogie band, they melded blues, r 'n' b, and country music into a tightly-driven musical force.

R5.13   **The Animals. Greatest Hits.** MGM SE 4602.

Formed in England in 1962, when Eric Burdon joined a group called the Alan Price Combo, the Animals, as they came to be known (possibly for their antics and dress on stage) was one of the bands from Britain that invaded the United States in the early sixties following on the bootheels of the Beatles. Burdon and boys, and Jagger and the Rolling Stones, were the first congregations to explode the pretty world of the polite British rock scene as they cavorted on stage to the raucous sounds of songs by Chuck Berry, Fats Domino, and other r 'n' b contributors. As well, the Animals utilized numerous older blues songs and can be said to have pioneered the British blues band movement that would follow. From 1962-1966, they dominated British rock in Northern England, a heavily industrialized working class area. Burdon had an exceptionally heavy black sound in his working class vocals. Their r 'n' b material included: "Bring It on Home to Me," "Don't Let Me Be Misunderstood," "We Gotta Get out of This Place," and the epic "House of the Rising Sun," a traditional blues song that they learned from Josh White's version. The material is all accurate and stands up surprisingly well, even today, as enjoyable music.

R5.14*   **Jeff Beck. Truth/Beck-Ola.** two discs. Epic BG 33779.

Beck was highly influenced by Les Paul's use of electronics, overdubs, and general explorations of the guitar's performances. He came out of the blues-based Yardbirds (replacing Clapton); and along with Rod Stewart (vocals), Ron Wood (bass) and Nicky Hopkins (piano), he projected a strong blues line in his arrangements for his new group, especially in the vocal-guitar duets. "Shape of Things" was a former Yardbirds hit; "You Shook Me" is especially loud and frenetic, and borrowed from Willie Dixon, noted Chicago bluesman. "Rice Pudding" has superb

Beck fingerwork, while "Beck's Bolero" is an engaging rendition of the Ravel classical theme. Worthwhile novelties here include "Ol' Man River" and "Greensleeves," both items showing the adaptability of rock to standards and traditional songs (refashion them with a heavy beat). Beck's work at this period gave all of rock an uplift from the trite derivative music that was then in vogue.

R5.15   **Canned Heat. Cookbook.** Liberty LST 11000.

Canned Heat was a very diversified group in its origins. Bob Hite, a big man with big vocals, actually had a collection of over 70,000 blues records; Al Wilson (who later died) played a sharp rhythmic guitar that early on established the boogie beat of their blues music; and Henry Vestine played lead guitar. They were perhaps more successful in Europe with their brand of black blues, based on boogie rhythms, John Lee Hooker-type drones, and the country blues (in an amplified sense). This album is a greatest hits compilation and includes such tunes as "Rollin' and Tumblin'," "Bullfrog Blues," "Dust My Broom," "Goin' Down Slow," "On the Road Again," and "Going up the Country." All of these items were standard black country blues turned into long, improvisational-type boogie tunes. Canned Heat was important for spreading the blues gospel in the rock idiom.

R5.16*   **Eric Clapton. History.** two discs. Atco SD2-803.

Clapton was deeply influenced by B. B. King's singing vocal lines on the guitar. He took King's techniques of playing (strike a note, hold it, bend it, quiver it, and then slide to the next note) and developed the modal riffs so commonly found in the music of his first real group, Cream. Because there is very little movement of the fingers involved in this style, Clapton soon adopted the nickname "Slowhand." King's influence was modified by the impact on Clapton of Chuck Berry, Bo Diddley, Blind Lemon Jefferson, and Skip James—all bluesmen. He essentially learned how to play his music by listening to records and imitating. This set of two discs covers his entire career. With the Yardbirds, he recorded "I Ain't Got You" (a tune by Billy Boy Arnold); with John Mayall's Bluesbreakers, he recreated Freddie King's "Hideaway" as an instrumental, plus the invigorating "Tribute to Elmore" (referring to Elmore James). From the Cream years came "Sunshine of Your Love" and the seventeen-minute live version of "Spoonful," as well as "Badge." His next group was Blind Faith, with the track "Sea of Joy." Other items here come from his associations with Delaney and Bonnie, with Derek and the Dominoes ("Layla"), and from his solo albums. All in all, this is a fairly good retrospective, much along the same lines as the Duane Allman anthology, although it does duplicate some individual items available under the names Cream, Blind Faith, and John Mayall. There is a good discussion of Clapton's history and technical expertise by Jean-Charles Costa, which can be summed up by simply saying that after his Cream years, Clapton's extended solo works were unfocused and even boring; yet because he *was* Clapton, he was still influential.

R5.17   **Electric Flag. A Long Time Comin'.** Columbia CS 9597.

The Electric Flag experimented with a riffing brass section before Blood, Sweat and Tears did, but the Flag only managed to exist for a year after 1967. Their music had been characterized by driving rhythms and the musical interplay of all eight performers, an unusually large group for the day. Some of the stars included Mike Bloomfield (a leading blues guitarist from Paul Butterfield's band), Buddy Miles (a drummer who performed with leading soul groups), Barry Goldberg (the organist from the Steve Miller band), John Simon (a personal pianist), and composer-vocalist Nick Gravenites. The Flag were firmly in the blues picture at this time, scoring with such remakes as "Killing Floor," "Sittin' in Circles," and "Over-Lovin' You."

R5.18*   **Fleetwood Mac. In Chicago.** two discs. Sire SASH 3715-2.

R5.19   **Fleetwood Mac. Vintage Years.** two discs. Sire SASH 3706-2.

Fleetwood Mac was an early British blues band that gave up on that form around 1970, when almost all of the original members had left. From 1967 through to 1969, a number of leading British bluesmen appeared with the band, notably Peter Green (who earlier replaced Clapton in Mayall's Bluesbreakers), John McVie (bass), Mick Fleetwood (drums), Jeremy Spencer (lead guitar) and Danny Kirwen (also lead guitar; added in 1968). Most of the crew had previously played with Mayall and enjoyed a successful tutelage. Also, this was the only band ever to employ three lead guitarists at one time. Mac was successful in carving a niche through doing the original blues material written by Green and Spencer, in addition to modifications of the repertoires from B. B. King, Elmore James— and even Elvis Presley when they wanted to parody something.

The better selections on their hits album include "Black Magic Woman," "Evening Boogie," "Looking for Somebody," "Shake Your Moneymaker," and "Trying So Hard to Forget." By 1970, only McVie and Fleetwood were left, and they transmuted into a pop act stressing female singers (as a heavier alternative to the Carpenters). But before the original group disbanded, they went to Chicago in 1969 to record some sessions with Chicago bluesmen, and each type of performer was feeding lines to the other. Bluesmen featured were Otis Spann on piano (who does a marvelous job of punctuating the boogie beat), Willie Dixon on bass, Shakey Horton on harmonica, drummer S. P. Leary, plus a variety of guitarists. Good feelings emanated throughout the production, and the results are really superb mixtures of white and black derivations in "Rockin' Boogie," "Everyday I Have the Blues," "Someday Soon, Baby," "Last Night," and "Hungry Country Girl."

R5.20*   **Janis Joplin. Pearl.** Columbia KC 30322.

Joplin came from Texas, where she learned to mesh herself into the roots of folk, blues, and bluegrass music. Her hoarse voice was unusual at the time (although it was merely an updating of Wanda Jackson's), as was her lifestyle. In reaction to her visual act in *Monterey Pop*, she was grossly overrated. In actuality, she was an excellent shouter in the erotic/sexual vein, full of physical pain and enthusiasm. Not only did she project the concept of a bitch in heat (right on the stage) but she simulated multiple orgasms when the song climaxed. Unfortunately, this does not come across on records. She had been served with some of the worst bands in rock history that worked at cross-purposes to her style. She had the star complex, but the bands wouldn't let her lead, taking the same attitude in employing a female singer as would a swing band leader. For her last album (above), she finally had a band she could work with, but then she died. And the band has not been heard from since. Excellent material here includes "My Baby," "Get It While You Can," "Cry Baby," and "Move Over." There is also the definitive version of "Me and Bobby McGee." This is probably one of the best albums overall in the rock genre. Richard Bell's piano, John Till's guitar, and Ken Pearson's organ are with Janis all the way.

R5.21   **Led Zeppelin.** Atlantic SD 7208.
     This early version of Led Zeppelin was blues based, being firmly in the Chicago blues school of Muddy Waters, Howlin' Wolf, and others. The main reason for this was that its founding members came from the Yardbirds, an even more blues-oriented band. The first lineup featured Jimmy Page, an ex-session man on guitar; John Paul Jones, another ex-session man who took care of keyboards and arrangements; John Bonham, drums; and Robert Plant on bluesy vocals. While Willie Dixon contributes two of the nine tracks on their first album, all of the remainder are the band's originals, and all are blues. Perhaps it was prophetic in their group name—Led Zeppelin—to lead the heavy metal attack in a few years.

R5.22   **Steve Miller. Sailor.** Capitol ST 2984.
     Steve Miller operated in the Chicago blues mold despite his Texas upbringing. He went solo after being with the Barry Goldberg Blues Band, and his career took off in 1968 after his receiving the fattest advance and contract of any American musician up to that time. Unfortunately, he burned himself out; and while this first album is very substantial, he soon became a routine rock performer, and his decline was as swift as his ascendancy. On this recording, he played lead guitar and sang; Boz Scaggs, soon to split over a personality clash, played rhythm guitar. Stress was on the blues, with some original compositions, notably: "Dear Mary," "Song for Our Ancestors," "My Friend," "Overdrive," and the incredible "Living in the U.S.A."

R5.23   **Traffic. Heavy Traffic.** United Artists UALA 421G.
     Traffic was yet another black blues-based band, featuring the talents of Stevie Winwood (vocals and keyboards), Chris Woods (reeds), Jim Capaldi (drums and piano), and Dave Mason (bass). Later, Rick Grech would join as Mason left (in 1970). Winwood was a great talent, being proficient in writing, composing, singing, and piano work. The bulk of the band came from the old Spencer Davis Group of 1966, and retained the flavor and complexities of the British blues bands through "Paper Sun," "Hole in My Shoe," "Mr. Fantasy," and "Gimme Some Lovin'."

ACID ROCK

INTRODUCTION

     Acid rock, also known as psychedelic rock, had several intents. One was to reproduce the distorted hearing of an individual under the influence of LSD or another hallucinogen. A second one was to recreate for a drugless individual the illusion of psychedelia through the music and an on-stage visual light show. A third was to create music while under the influence of drugs. Unfortunately, this third intent does not work, as drugs severely restrict one's technical abilities (as was the case with John Fahey). All of this should not be construed as condoning drugs, but merely as an effort to reproduce or recreate their effects in a musical way. Acid rock was for those *not* on drugs, but not all acid rock was suitable for those who took drugs and went on trips. Psychedelic rock was intended for listening, not for dancing. This abrupt shift in a form of music that previously had the rhythmic capabilities to produce happiness dramatically changed the whole concept of rock music.

To reproduce "disturbed" music, musicians needed electronic technology for advanced amplification and weird sounds. The music was developed mainly in San Francisco in 1965 by the Jefferson Airplane and the Grateful Dead; however, the style was developed earlier by the Beatles, who first employed structural complexities, rhythmic intricacies, and other experimentation. They composed "Norwegian Wood" and "Day in the Life" employing Indian raga music styles and the sitar (this Oriental association followed drugs around, even if the hallucinogen was marijuana). Some of this music even reflected the social themes found in folk music, especially the stream of consciousness ideas of Bob Dylan. Progression in acid rock embraces sustained and languid melodics, complex instrumentation, a variety of imaginative stylings, and imagery in lyrics. The musical phrases come in lurches of surging power, a sort of tripping, uncertain movement. As does art, acid rock deals with tone, coloration, texture, and density. Most live concerts, which went on for hours (such as those of the Grateful Dead), added improvisation for spontaneous effects. On record, the long timings of each track allow for some development of the many themes, and the variations on a chord.

The one drawback to the intellectual qualities of acid rock (but one of its attractions for the folk element) is that "finesse replaces visceral excitement." It is "head" music that needs no surging energy or buoyancy, which was the mode in regular rock music of the time. The period of acid rock extended to 1970 and included such material as Van Dyke Parks' *Song Cycle*, the Beach Boys' "Good Vibrations," the Rolling Stones' "Paint It Black," and the Byrds' "Eight Miles High." Since 1970, acid rock returned infrequently because of the expense of touring light shows and the limited scope of experimentation. Acid rock songs can also be found scattered among other categories here, especially under "Notable Experimentation."

INNOVATORS

R6.1*   **The Doors.** Elektra EKS 74007

R6.2*   **The Doors. Strange Days.** Elektra EKS 74014.

R6.3   **The Doors. Waiting for the Sun.** Elektra EKS 74024.

The Doors was one of the first groups to use the organ effectively. Robbie Krieger came to the group with a classical/flamenco guitar background. He produced long, fluid lines that ran into each other for a glass effect. John Densmore, drummer, was adept at jazz rhythms that were sharp and abrupt. Ray Manzarek's organ created many counter-melodies. Jim Morrison, who did most of the writing, was also a filmmaker and literary writer with an insolent sounding nasal voice that whined. From the 1967-1971 period, the Doors led the Los Angeles underground bands. Morrison's death in 1971 ended that. Their music promoted surrealistic violence, concentrating on evil and Satanism, and that played off the sexuality of Morrison's voice and his shrieks. The music was a basic mixture of psychedelia and hard rock, but the fame of the Doors spread when Morrison simulated masturbation on stage. From their first album came the big hit, "Light My Fire," as well as the symbolic "Break on through to the Other Side," and the sado-masochistic *long, long* tune (for its period): "The End." This 11:35 song was repeated as "When the Music's Over" on the second album, where the introspection was replaced by a call to revolution. The material on the third album is especially in the stream of consciousness mode, with "Not to Touch the Earth" (a very fast uptempo number), "The Unknown Soldier," and the flamenco "Spanish Caravan."

R6.4*   **Grateful Dead.** Warner Brothers WS 1689.

R6.5*   **Grateful Dead. Anthem of the Sun.** Warner Brothers WS 1749.

R6.6*   **Grateful Dead. Workingman's Dead.** Warner Brothers WS 1869.
    The "Dead" were a social institution. Coming together from diverse roots to work with the Ken Kesey acid tests of 1965 in San Francisco, the Dead produced some of the strangest, yet most enduring, sounds in all of rock music. Their early work as a jug band and then as the Warlocks promoted the fusion of blues and rock music. Their individualistic style came from the cooperative nature of the group, a nature that often leaned to long performances and to free performances. (Massive ten-hour sets that required four or more hours to set up the sound system and were given free in a park somewhere within the Bay Area were the rule, not the exception.) The members included Jerry Garcia on diverse guitars, Phil Lesh on bass, "Pig Pen" on drums, Bob Weir for rhythm guitar, and Bob Hunter for the vocals after the second album. Their first album introduced the blues concept with "Sitting on Top of the World" and the long improvisational lines that later became "progressive rock" as played on FM stations. Others here included "Cream Puff War," "Good Morning, Little School Girl," and "The Golden Road." *Anthem of the Sun*, their second album, was the best acid record ever released. All the selections here (from 1968) were pieced together from eighteen live performances, and they took every riff and guitar line of note to produce the classics "The Faster We Go, the Rounder We Get," "Alligator," and "Born Cross-Eyed." *Workingman's Dead* was perhaps their best all-round album, featuring the country-folk sounds then emerging in "Casey Jones," "Cumberland Blues," "New Speedway Boogie," and "Uncle John's Band." They pioneered both the loud music concept and the jam. They were always at their best live, where they created intricately changing patterns within each song as it was strung out to great lengths—the model of progressivism.

R6.7*   **Jefferson Airplane. Surrealistic Pillow. RCA LSP 3766.**

R6.8   **Jefferson Airplane. Volunteers. RCA LSP 4238.**

R6.9*   **Jefferson Airplane. Worst. RCA LSP 4459.**
    Beginning in 1967, the Jefferson Airplane was the first San Francisco group
to get national distribution, and thus, the national hits. They were the first to
be prominently displayed on posters, and their psychedelic impact was enormous.
Their strength lay in combining three streams of in-vogue fashions: acid and pill
popping; "flower power"; and the Oriental influence. Taking the folk-rock background of San Francisco as well, they melded all of these into a truly distinctive
and original American sound. The superb lineup was very cohesive as a group,
and their well-disciplined performances continued long after other similar groups
broke up. Jorma Kaukonen was lead guitarist, Paul Kantner provided rhythm
guitar, Jack Casady gave the surging bass lines, Spencer Dryden provided the early
drumming, and Marty Balin and Grace Slick did the vocal lines. Their total environment, which included the "alternative lifestyle" of living together, led them to
play all kinds of music in the areas of jazz, blues, ballads, and so forth.
    One of their finest albums is their second, from 1967, *Surrealistic Pillow*.
This album introduced "White Rabbit" (penned by Slick), a worthy song about
drugs, and the song "Somebody to Love." Through this album, Slick became the
first prominent female singer with a rock band; her shrieking voice predated Janis
Joplin's. Unfortunately, the Airplane's jams and light shows are naturally not available on album; however, they were the first group to incorporate such items in
their shows, which made them distinct from studio versions. This impact has yet
to be assessed. Other important songs include "Ballad of You and Me and Pooneil"
(written after Fred Neil), "Watch Her Ride," "Crown of Creation," and "Plastic
Fantastic Lover."

STANDARDS

R6.10   **Country Joe and the Fish. The Life and Times of Country Joe and the
        Fish from Haight-Ashbury to Woodstock. two discs. Vanguard VSD
        27/28.**
    Joe MacDonald is an enigma: he is many things to many people, and nobody
has been able to typify his music except to call it "contemporary." As the title
indicates, this set is a survey from 1965 through 1969, when the Fish split. About
half of the material is live, coming from Berkeley, the Fillmore East, the Fillmore
West, and Woodstock (the last items were not available on the Cotillion albums
documenting that concert). Country Joe's early work was a combination of blues
and electric jugband; this resulted in his first songs: the obscene "Fish Cheer" and
"I Feel-Like-I'm-Fixin'-to-Die Rag." His group was one of the first to break out of
the San Francisco area on a national basis (and to some great extent, even went
over to Europe). He was the first to produce a psychedelic light show in New York
City. His early anti-war material was actually performed on television, and at one
time, he symbolized the entire "consciousness movement" and its associations
with rock music, being influenced by Richard Farina. His good audience rapport

came because of his many free concerts at benefits. Much of his music can be categorized as personal through tender love songs; as anti-establishment, through pointed burlesques; and as political songs of outrage. In some respects, because his record company did not know how to handle him, he was in advance of those who would follow, and his fans were definitely a cult. Typical songs here include "Who Am I?," "Waltzing in the Moonlight," "Superbird (Tricky Dick)," "Marijuana," "Masked Marauder," and "Love Machine."

R6.11   **Dr. John. The Night Tripper (Sun, Moon, Herbs).** Atco SD 33-362.
    Mac Rebenneck was a studio session man in New Orleans, deep into r 'n' b material from the Crescent City (and found on his *Gumbo* album, annotated at R2.48). In addition, both cowboy songs and country blues had their influences on him. This album was his first under his pseudonym "Dr. John," and it emphasizes the "gris-gris" musical influences of the bayou and the Haitian voodoo ceremonies that found their way into Louisiana. It is a distinct music, based on the blues progression and mysticism plus dissonance from the percussion. Cajun-music-meets-voodoo is perhaps the best way to sum it up, with titles such as "Gris-gris Gumbo Ya Ya," "Croker Courtbullion," "Danse Fambeaux," and "Mama Roux." Soon, almost all music coming from the New Orleans area was wrongly characterized as "voodoo rock," yet it was simply a highly rhythmic and infectious variation of jump r 'n' b music.

R6.12   **Moby Grape. Great Grape.** Columbia CS 31098.
    From the psychedelic era of the great California bands came the Grape. They were the band that *didn't* make it, that didn't follow the Grateful Dead and the Jefferson Airplane into stardom. Pushed too quickly and over-promoted (they once had five singles and an album released all at once), they died out fast. But while they lived, they created a dense multi-guitar image with no stars or featured performers. Skip Spence, once drummer for the Jefferson Airplane, spoke for them. They were the first band to record a rock jam of any popularity ("Grape Jam," with Al Kooper and Mike Bloomfield) and they even had one track on their 33 1/3 rpm disc that had to be played at 78 rpm. The Grape tried a comeback a few years ago—but, alas. . . .

R6.13   **Quicksilver Messenger Service. Happy Trails.** Capitol ST 120.
    QMS was a San Francisco rock band following in the steps of the Grateful Dead, including all of the loud music and the drug songs. It was led by guitarist John Cipollina, who would later move on to form other groups. Their sound was characterized by good vocals for the time, as well as unexpected time changes: *Happy Trails* is a love album, but it does not always concern people. The tracks appear to form a part of a suite, but they don't. Titles include: "Who Do You Love?," "When Do You Love?," "Where Do You Love?," "How Do You Love?," and "Which Do You Love?"

R6.14   **Vanilla Fudge.** Atco SD 33-224.
    This New York City band only had its name in common with several other less notable groups with peculiar appellations. Its stars were drummer Carmine Appice and bassist Tim Bogert. It was essentially a hard rock group that interpreted

compositions of the time (this first album is derived from sessions in 1967), but their reworking was in different styles, almost as a parody. For instance, there was the exceptionally slow pacing of the Beatles' "Eleanor Rigby" and "Ticket to Ride," the dirge of the Supremes' "You Keep Me Hanging On," and the misery of Sonny and Cher's "Bang Bang." Both the overpowering organ of Mark Stein and the Hendrix-like flash guitar of Vince Martell projected slow build-ups and crescendoes of sound patterns, creating both lulls and storms.

COUNTRY/FOLK ROCK

INTRODUCTION

Country/folk rock is the fusion of material and traditions derived from the folk music idiom with the instrumentation and beat of rock. It is an amorphous combination of blues, rock and roll, country, popular music, and protest songs. Its greatest impact was in the mid-1960s, when protest songs merged with rock rhythms and this type of music found a new audience. Its next manifestation was as country rock, which meant going through the folk process from traditional sources to written materials. Country rock was favored by those who could sing; folk rock was left to those who couldn't sing, but simply growled in the time-honored folk tradition. The last permutation after country rock was the troubador or singer-songwriter, who was essentially first a folk-type and then a rock musician. At this level, the merger was not quite complete because folk-derived lyrics dominated.

INNOVATORS

R7.1   **The Band.** Capitol STAO 132.

R7.2   **The Band. Best.** Capitol ST 11553.

R7.3*   **The Band. Music from Big Pink.** Capitol SKAO 2955.

R7.4*   **The Band. Northern Lights–Southern Cross.** Capitol ST 11440.

R7.5*   **The Band. Stage Fright.** Capitol SW 425.
           The Band was a collection of obscure, anonymous men who once performed with Rompin' Ronnie Hawkins in Canada for several years; they gained good groundwork in producing musically tight, cohesive music because Hawkins would rehearse them night and day as a "bar band." Later, they became Levon and the Hawks while out on their own; and in 1965, they became the electric band behind Bob Dylan. Only Levon Helm was born in the United States (Alabama); the other four were Canadians, largely from Ontario (then equivalent to the American Midwest in its musical tastes). Dylan's influence was pronounced: they became the first piano-organ combination in rock; they developed a uniquely personal style

of singing about American life and history, merging country and folk roots into
rock music.

Overall, they have free and loose vocals, with simple, tightly constructed
music that is reproduceable in concerts. Their music, then, derives from a piano-
organ combination, with an augmented wah-wah pedal on the guitar for a country-
style steel guitar effect; four-on-four drumming that never intrudes; brief instrumental solos that stick to the melody, based on simple open progressions, often
embellished but never dominated by riffs (and given added tension through sparing
use of dissonance); and selected instrumentation for atmosphere (baritone sax,
harmonica, trumpet, tuba). Their singing style is deft: the high and lonesome
harmonies (either lending a naive and/or desperate air to the proceedings) are
perhaps the most advanced in pop music. They encompass all aspects of the human
voice with immense flexibility, and they can flit in and out of ensemble vocal
passages effortlessly (even switching from one lead to another with similarities
in timbre). This restraint and cool feeling not only prevails in the music and the
vocals but, of necessity, must match the lyrics.

Robbie Robertson, lead guitarist, writes most of the material, with occasional assistance from Rick Danko (bass), drummer Helm, and Richard Manuel,
pianist. Just about all of it is rural and religious, with references to the Bible,
historical events, the American Civil War, and so forth. The impact of country
music on the Band is so great that they have gone back in style to before the sentimental ballads of the late nineteenth century to reconstruct what *could* have
been written at that time. Such tunes as "The Weight" exhibit classic poetic sym-
bols of compassion and loneliness; "King Harvest" is pure nostalgia for the lost
rural life; "Stage Fright" is an analysis of the star performer; "The Night They Drove
Old Dixie Down" is the classic Civil War song about the South's defeat; Dylan
material includes "This Wheel's on Fire," "Tears of Rage," and "I Shall Be Released"
(some partially written by the Band). "Chest Fever" features a brilliant introduction by classically trained organist Garth Hudson. Their most rural album was their
second, the untitled set noted above, with such descriptions as "Across the Great
Divide," "Rag Mama Rag," "Up on Cripple Creek." They returned to the rural
theme in a more pronounced way with their 1975 offering, which included the
masterful stories of "Hobo Jungle" and "Acadian Driftwood."

R7.6*   **Buffalo Springfield. Again.** Atco SD33-226.

With the emergence of Buffalo Springfield in 1967, folk rock took a long
step toward maturity and even though, by the end of that year, the Springfield
no longer existed, it was to become one of the most influential sounds in American
rock. Composed of Steve Stills, Neil Young, Richie Furay, and Jim Messina, the
group had a distinctive sound of close, often harsh vocals, a touch of folk hard-
edged with rock. This, their second and most important album, featured Young's
"Broken Arrow," an indicator of where the group was headed. Unable to relate
to each other, the band's members fragmented, with Stills and Young joining
Dave Crosby and Graham Nash to form yet another well known and distinctive
group, and with Messina and Furay putting together Poco. By 1974, the original
members of the Buffalo Springfield had formed groups, left groups, recorded solo,
recorded as session men, and generally spread the "Springfield sound." Throughout, there was a definite Canadian bias. Half of the group was from Canada, but

in summary, all members were individuals (which is why they split). Their excellent compositions and melodies made this group perhaps the best American group ever, with such items as "Bluebird" and "Rock 'n' Roll Woman."

R7.7*   **Byrds. Greatest Hits.** Columbia CS 9576.

R7.8*   **Byrds. Sweetheart of the Rodeo.** Columbia CS 9670.
          Jim McGuinn was a twelve string guitarist caught up in the folk revival; he changed his first name to Roger, formed the Byrds, and hit on the happy combination of "folk rock." The idea was to take contemporary folk songs (derived from the folk tradition but not "purist" folk music because they were composed [see the "Troubador" section of the *Grass Roots Music* volume]) and give them a rock beat, while still maintaining the folk-based twelve string acoustic guitar. Later, the Byrds were to produce a steady rhythm with four-part harmonies, sometimes overdubbed several times, accompanied by folk stylings on the electric guitar but with a straight bass guitar line (that is, minus the surging power then in evidence with rock music and soul music). They preceded Dylan with this concept by producing, early in 1965, the memorable "Mr. Tambourine Man," one of Dylan's minor songs up to that point. At the same time, their steady rhythm made them one of the first rock groups to create music solely for the listener.
          Despite this cohesion on disc, the Byrds were fraught with personnel difficulties; McGuinn remained the sole constant as Clarence White, Gene Parsons, Gram Parsons, Gene Clark, David Crosby (who played with the sitar at this stage in his development), and Chris Hillman passed through. The spin-off bands alone would require a book to annotate, but apart from solo careers, several groups predominated in the folk rock tradition, including the Dillard and Clark Expedition; Crosby, Stills, Nash and Young; and the Flying Burrito Brothers.
          Columbia released the *Greatest Hits* album in 1967, and it contained the folk sounds of "Turn, Turn, Turn," "The Bells of Rhymney," "Mr. Tambourine Man," and what was hailed as the classic drug song, "Eight Miles High" (which was actually about an airplane trip after a disastrous British tour; "Seven" would be more appropriate for the height of around 35,000 feet, but it didn't scan). Despite a poor British tour, they were very influential on the then-emerging electric folk groups in the British Isles, particularly Fairport Convention, then a rock group beginning to employ folk rhythms.
          The most dramatic change in music to affect a rock group—even a folk rock ensemble—came about through the influence of Gram Parsons. Parsons persuaded McGuinn to get into country music as a logical extension of folk music (for modern country music does have its roots in folk music). *Sweetheart of the Rodeo* was the resulting album, and Parsons (although he didn't sing here for contractual reasons) contributed two originals. One was "Drugstore Truck Driving Man." Its lyrics were aimed at hypocritical attitudes, and thus it qualified as a protest song; but its melody and accompaniment had every country lick and rhythm possible à la Nashville sound, and introduced the pedal steel guitar. They continued with Dylan material, but this time chose "You Ain't Going Nowhere," which easily qualified as country music. The sweet harmonies, which harkened back to those of the Louvin Brothers and the Blue Sky Boys, predominated on such country classics as "Blue Canadian Rockies" and "I Am a Pilgrim." Other songs included

"Sing Me Back Home," "Hickory Wind," and Woody Guthrie's "Pretty Boy Floyd."

As an aside, their music was also to have dramatic impact on the bluegrass field, creating "newgrass," which is really bluegrass with added rock rhythms and contemporary lyrics. Several of the Byrds had played in bluegrass-style bands, notably Clarence White; and the country Flying Burrito Brothers (with Gram Parsons) transmuted later into Country Gazette when the Brothers partially reunited the Kentucky Colonels. Follow? Thus, the Byrds were instrumental in promoting several distinct types of rock music: folk rock, country rock, newgrass, and even acid music, as they turned country harmonies into acid rock through the (mistakenly titled) "Eight Miles High." The Byrds were one of the most significant ensembles in rock music—ever.

STANDARDS

R7.9 **Crosby, Stills and Nash.** Atlantic SD 8229.

R7.10* **Crosby, Stills, Nash and Young. Déjà Vu.** Atlantic SD 7200.

R7.11 **Crosby, Stills, Nash and Young. Four Way Street.** two discs. Atlantic SD2-902.

David Crosby came from the Byrds; Graham Nash came from the Hollies; and both Stephen Stills and Neil Young came from the Buffalo Springfield. All four were country-influenced through the use of part-harmonies, and all four had achieved their aims of putting country-derived music into the rock world before assembling as an ad hoc group (Young was added later, after the first record cited above). The first album was unamplified, and it enjoyed terrific critical and popular success, especially Stills's "Suite: Judy Blue Eyes," a seven minute picture dedicated to Judy Collins, and "Helplessly Hoping," also dedicated to Judy Collins. "Long Time Coming" is Crosby's lament for the late Robert Kennedy. The more dreamy material came from Nash ("Lady of the Island" and "Marrakesh Express").

The songs on the *Déjà Vu* album came from their Woodstock period, when they devoted more time to their harmonic development in four parts, with the addition of Young as the fourth person. This was a blending of folk and rock (words and music) with country overtones through the part singing. This unamplified return to simplicity was really discovered by the group accidentally, as they originally formed just to play together for fun. But by doing so, they became one of the first "supergroups," the graduates of current groups (as in a sports playoff). *Four Way Street* is really a showcase of solo materials by each of the four; it does not emphasize harmonic developments as did the other album. Indeed, some of the material here is re-recorded from Young's *After the Gold Rush* album, as well as older Buffalo Springfield tunes. Young and Stills collaborate on the thirteen-minute "Southern Man," Crosby sings "Triad," the lightweight Nash performs "Right between the Eyes" and "Teach Your Children," while Stills works alone on "America's Children."

R7.12* **Eagles. Desperado.** Asylum SD 5068.

R7.13 **Eagles. Their Greatest Hits, 1971-1975.** Asylum 7ES-1052.
The Eagles are the leading country rock band, better overall than Poco,
the Dillard and Clark Expedition, or the Flying Burrito Brothers. All personnel
had previously played in rock bands or in those other bands just mentioned. Their
soft-rock good harmonies tell of love, existence, and loneliness in the true country
fashion. Their overall best album is *Desperado*, featuring "Saturday Night" as a
waltz, with well-pitched and mellow harmonies, and the wild "Out of Control,"
which shows that the team can handle basic rock rhythms. Bernie Leadon came
from Dillard and Clark and the Flying Burrito Brothers; Randy Meisner came
aboard from Poco; and Don Henley had vast experience with Linda Ronstadt's
working group. The ten tracks on the hits album capture their singles successes,
and includes the Jackson Browne tune "Take It Easy," which was their first big
seller with its danceable rhythms, catchy melodies, sensible lyrics, and four part
harmony. Other tunes include "Lyin' Eyes," "One of These Nights," "Tequila
Sunrise," and "Take It to the Limit."

R7.14 **The Flying Burrito Brothers. The Gilded Palace of Sin.** A & M SP 4175
The Burritos were the direct stepchild of the Byrds and featured the particular
genius and smooth vocals of Gram Parsons and Chris Hillman, as well as a host
of other country/folk rock stalwarts who were to record under the Burrito banner.
This, the first of six fine albums, features such Parsons   compositions as "Hot
Burrito, No. 1" as well as Dan Penn's "Do-Right Woman." There is a hint of the
direction that the Burritos (and later, the Eagles) would take with the slightest
sounds of bluegrass sneaking in by the back door. But for 1969, at the height
of the country rock fervor, this album is a good indication of the hippies and
the hillbillies getting it together. The country rock "Sin City" and "My Uncle"
were handled with no nasal whines and without any Nashville sweetness, but
with the distinctive pedal steel guitar of session man Sneaky Pete.

R7.15 **Gram Parsons. G. P.** Reprise MS 2123.

R7.16 **Gram Parsons. Grievous Angel.** Reprise MS 2171.
Parsons was largely responsible for introducing country rock to the masses
of youth culture in the 1960s. His brand of country music was the achingly sweet
and sad hurting music, emphasizing high harmonies rather than honky-tonk swing.
He joined the Byrds (1967-1969), and although he never sang on their *Sweethearts
of the Rodeo* album, he helped to construct it, contributing two fine songs and
the sailing, mournful steel pedal guitars that emulated vocal harmonies. With
Chris Hillman, he formed the Flying Burrito Brothers, and they advanced the
country rock mode even further. He fell out with the group when they became
too rock-oriented.
In the year before he died (1973), he crafted two excellent country rock
albums, noted above. He brought in contemporary bluegrass-country performers
(Alan Munde, banjo; Byron Berline, fiddle; and Buddy Emmons, pedal steel guitar)
and found Emmylou Harris, whose high, soaring voice was what he needed to com-
plement his singing to produce that important traditional sound. The material

on these two albums is about half Parsons originals and half country songs by others. George Jones's "That's All It Took" is a breathy number; "We'll Sweep out the Ashes in the Morning" has his characteristic high vocal (showing roots in Roy Acuff) and an excellent Dobro accompaniment; and there is also "Streets of Baltimore." The second album features Tom T. Hall's "I Can't Dance," the Louvin Brothers' "Cash on the Barrelhead," and Boudleaux Bryant's "Love Hurts." Pretentious as it may sound, one critic noted that Parsons' style was "the innocence of youth with past traditions instilled into him, while fighting a morally ambiguous world."

R7.17   **New Riders of the Purple Sage. Powerglide.** Columbia KC 31284.
        This country rock group was brought together and sponsored by Jerry Garcia of the Grateful Dead (he played pedal steel on their first, awkward album). Bluegrass and folk come easy to this mellow city-bred group. Spencer Dryden is the drummer, from the older Jefferson Airplane; Buddy Cage is the star on pedal steel guitar and Dobro. John Dawson, David Nelson, and Dave Torbert are the writers, vocalists, and guitar trio. And in case you are interested, yes, there was a group called Riders of the Purple Sage, which once concentrated on commercial western swing. And that is just about what this group does. Joe Maphis's "Dim Lights, Thick Smoke" leads off the first side, and Johnny Otis's "Willie and the Hand Jive" closes the second side. In between, most of this material is their own, stressing such elements of country songs as love, loose living, and the event. "Contract" is absolutely the best country rock tune ever made: listen.

R7.18   **Poco. The Very Best of.** two discs. Epic PEG 33537.
        Poco formed as a spinoff band from Buffalo Springfield, with Richie Furay (rhythm guitarist) bringing over the conceptions of harmony singing by joining Jim Messina. The band was characterized by its tight coordination and good arrangements. The twenty tracks here certainly are pioneer works in the history of country rock and the songs of sad stories and heartaches. Typical tracks include "A Good Feelin' to Know," "Grand Junction," "Rocky Mountain Breakdown," "Here We Go Again," and "Pickin' up the Pieces." Liner notes covering each of the group's previous eight albums were written by Pete Fornatale.

R7.19*   **Neil Young. After the Gold Rush.** Reprise RS 6383.

R7.20   **Neil Young. Harvest.** Reprise MS 2032.
        Canadian-born Young started out with the Buffalo Springfield as lead guitarist and composer. After they broke up, he began a solo career that also involved a floating group variously known as Crosby, Stills, Nash and Young (who sang all together or as duos, trios, and even solo). Most of Young's music is essentially of the soft ballad type, a gentle rock with acoustic guitar, but he can extend himself to heavy amplification and heavy rock music. Basically, he is a romantic whose lyrics dominate the music. He has been successful in combining rock and roll with folk music as an instrumental blend for the background to his poetic lyrics. Tracks on these two discs include "Southern Man," "Only Love Can Break Your Heart," "I Believe in You," "Heart of Gold," "Old Man," and "Don't Let It Bring You Down."

R7.21   **Youngbloods. Best.** RCA LSP 4399.

The Youngbloods were the last of the popular folk groups to gather together before the end of the folk boom; they may even have helped to prolong it. Their leader was Jesse Colin Young, a bass player who also handled most of the vocals. He was a former blues folk singer with an exceptionally good voice (pleasant, for a blues singer). The group rehearsed for a year before recording and arrived at some curious amalgam of country-blues-jazz-rock music. Tracks included "Grizzly Bear" (done in ragtime), Dino Valenti's "Get Together," "Four in the Morning," "See See Rider," "Statesboro Blues," and "All over the World."

HEAVY METAL (HARD ROCK)

INTRODUCTION

Heavy metal music seemed to take the worst offerings of acid rock and blues rock. The music played by groups here demanded an extraordinary volume, distortion, and mechanical riffing. Keyboards and electric basses were added to the music of lead guitarists and some rather pedestrian drummers. Much of the music deliberately disregarded dancing and rhythmic aspects, sticking with the propensity of acid rock towards "non-swing" music (e.g., Led Zeppelin's "Dazed and Confused"). Much of the singing/lyrics were subordinated to the instrumental sound, which preferred "chaos over coherence." Thus, within a relatively easy blues progression, there appears to be a jackhammer approach for solos rather than a developed set of thematic variations. This was called "blitzkrieg obbligatos," and a typical example can be found by listening to Eric Clapton on Cream's "Spoonful." The basic elements of this music were very monotonous, but to be successful, heavy metal relied on imaginative performers to project a unique sound, and they thereby become "stylists" through technical tricks.

When innovations ceased to exist (or when they were never there), then the lack of imagination quickly forced bands to become exponents of "punk rock." This term describes "trash with flash," wherein everything is thrown at an audience except good music. Punk rock is mainly done by those who wanted to play the blues—an easy medium—but couldn't. They thus evolved a style that didn't require great virtuosity. The guitar solo was dropped (as the guitarist was deficient) in favor of the insistent riff being played by *all* instruments at once. The lyrical quality changed to reflect weird violence, madness, drugs, disease, and pestilence. Not only are some of these groups dull, but they are also short on ideas. They all begin to sound alike and are appreciated by an audience who largely can't keep pace with musical development. Their few redeeming values lie in stageshows featuring themes, lights, and stories—such as those contributed by Alice Cooper, David Bowie, and Lou Reed. These are enjoyable in themselves, but they fall flat on discs, which transmit only the aural portion.

Older groups from the past included MC5, Iggy Pop and the Stooges, Blue Cheer, Iron Butterfly, Velvet Underground, and Grand Funk Railroad. Influences back and forth across the Atlantic follow the route of, for example, the Chicago blues to British blues to Grand Funk Railroad to Black Sabbath to the Blue Oyster

Cult, with each emulating the sound of its immediate predecessor. Other heavy metal offerings can be located in the "Notable Experimentation" section.

INNOVATORS

R8.1*   **Cream. Best.** Atco SD33-291.

R8.2   **Cream. Heavy Cream.** two discs. Polydor PD2-3502.

R8.3*   **Cream. Wheels of Fire.** two discs. Atlantic SD2-700.
       Cream was formed in the summer of 1966 by three musicians who considered themselves to be the "cream" of the then-existing British rock performers. Eric Clapton (lead guitar) came from John Mayall's Bluesbreakers, the Yardbirds, the Roosters, Powerhouse, and Casey Jones and the Engineers. Jack Bruce (bassist) had been with Manfred Mann, Graham Bond's Organization, Powerhouse, John Mayall's Bluesbreakers, and Alexis Korner's Blues Incorporated. Ginger Baker (drummer) came from Korner, Bond, and similar blues-oriented groups. They wanted to eliminate the usual barriers and restrictions of conventional groups by forming the first of the "power trios"—with extended solos on guitar, drums, and bass, plus the newly developing triple-speed improvisational reworking of blues classics from the 1950s. Not only did they spawn imitators in the trio format (such as Mountain and Grand Funk), but also they were one of the few groups to credit their blues sources.
       One of their classics was a long version of Willie Dixon's "Spoonful" (on the *Wheels of Fire* set), lifted from a live performance. Their most popular hit, though, was the more lyrical "Sunshine of Your Love." Although the band occasionally indulged in exhibitionistic solos at their concerts (and hence on their "live" tracks), some of the headier moments in all of rock are to be found on their records. Among these is Clapton's floating guitar on "I Feel Free" and other fluid lines (he is called "Slowhand"); the interplay on "I Feel Fine" or "Politician"; and the competition on "N.S.U." The nature of the trio was such that they competed with each other quite a lot. Their main belief in improvisation made them three soloists. Clapton's blue lines were equalized with Baker's frenetic drumming, as was Bruce's use of the bass for its own lines (not just for rhythm or the beat). Bruce had an effect on the use of the bass in rock, as Blanton did in jazz.
       All three musicians produced music that was prominent and could be recognized. They played loud music but never distorted it solely for the sake of distortion. Despite the volume, the drum solos and each note (or slurring of notes) of the guitars came through crisp and clear. They strove for satisfying, non-commercial music. In effect, they played for themselves in the competing sense; and along with the Grateful Dead and the Jefferson Airplane, they produced some of the first rock music used for FM airplay. They were one of the first groups to find success with albums rather than with singles, in much the same manner as the Kingston Trio of a decade earlier. Soon, other rock groups would lean to the "album only" concept, as well as to the innovative technique of rock solos for everybody in the band. Heavy metal music began, augmented by Led Zeppelin, who also were blues-derived. Cream moved several steps further along in the blues

vein than Paul Butterfield did; Butterfield stuck too close to the originals for the white audience (beyond a minority of fans). Cream progressed through the blues spectrum and thereby created a revival for the blues music of Muddy Waters, Howlin' Wolf, Jimmy Reed, etc. Clapton, by acknowledging B. B. King as his "main man," promoted King to star status. Cream existed for two years, from 1966 to 1968. It is to their credit that they did the honest thing and split when they felt that they could advance no more.

R8.4*   **Jimi Hendrix. Are You Experienced?** Reprise RS 6261.

R8.5*   **Jimi Hendrix. Electric Ladyland.** two discs. Reprise 2RS 6307.

R8.6*   **Jimi Hendrix. Greatest Hits.** Reprise MS 2025.

R8.7   **Jimi Hendrix. Soundtrack Recordings from the Film "Jimi Hendrix."** Reprise 2RX 6481.
          Hendrix was one of the greatest rock instrumentalists of the 1960s. His blunt attack and the resulting angry metallic whine stressed emotional rawness and rough complexions; he can be contrasted to the other great rock instrumentalist from the same time period, Eric Clapton, and the latter's virtuosity with sustained notes. Much of Hendrix's music was frankly experimental; he continued to innovate and garner new techniques right up to the time he died. He was dramatically influenced by Dylan's lifestyle, but he produced what can be termed as "reactive music." He took Phil Spector's "wall of sound" approach on his guitar, to shut out the world by enveloping himself in sound. At the same time, he was one of the few blacks working in the rock field; he went to England for several years and acquired "seasoning," as well as picking up two English sidemen (Mitch Mitchell, drums, and Noel Redding, bass) for the power trio format.
          Musically, Hendrix was an excellent writer who sang his own material, although he did do some Dylan tunes from time to time such as the until-then-overlooked "All along the Watchtower" that Hendrix brought into prominence. Technically, his guitar work was superb. He made masterful use of the wah-wah pedal plus tremolo, reverb, and feedback to embellish his essentially blues guitar licks and the guitar runs. In doing this, he ran through a lot of equipment. His amplifiers were always at full volume; he jumped on the wah-wah pedals and crushed fuzztone boxes. His greatest contribution to the guitar lay in his bending the strings out of place and promoting distortion to start feedback with the tremolo bar; thus, pickups in the guitar amplify all of the bending strings, and the resultant whine is a roaring noise. This distortion plus slow lines cleverly sustained through wah-wah and feedback had a pronounced influence on white guitarists and their acid music (Hendrix's music *wasn't* acid music). His stage act, unfortunately not available on disc, was explicitly sexual and erotic. He caressed his guitar, rubbed his thighs, licked his strings, jabbed at the guitar, and set it afire. A showman who created some of the greatest rock music ever, such as "Purple Haze," "Foxy Lady," "Crosstown Traffic," the Troggs' "Wild Thing," B. B. King's version of "Rock Me Baby," "Hey Joe," and the stunning version of "Star Spangled Banner" (heard here from Woodstock Festival but in a truncated form). The *Soundtrack* album has excerpts

from his appearances at Monterey, Berkeley, Woodstock, Isle of Wight, and the Fillmore East.

R8.8*   **Led Zeppelin. II.** Atlantic SD 8236.

R8.9   **Led Zeppelin. IV.** Atlantic SD 7208.
     Led Zep leads the heavy metal parade. One of the most popular bands in rock today, they were the heirs apparent to the throne left vacant by the Yardbirds. Founded by Jimmy Page (the brilliant guitarist from the Yardbirds), they hit their stride with their second album, which has become a prototype for the many imitators that have followed. Page is a master of the machine gun guitar style popularized by Jimi Hendrix; and Robert Plant's screaming vocals, while not exactly blues, are often models of exciting frenzy.   Among their many metal masterpieces are "Whole Lotta Love" and "Stairway to Heaven." The yelling and moaning in Plant's vocals were capitalized upon, to the extent that their attack (on the latter album) now resembled Little Richard's rather than that of Howlin' Wolf or Muddy Waters on the first album. Despite this action, to the extent that they parody themselves as on "Whole Lotta Love," they are definitely adventuresome within limits. They have carefully cultivated an audience by releasing records only occasionally, rather than on a regular basis. A little bit of Led Zep goes a long way. Although their later albums contain more than a taste of hackneyed formula rock, Led Zep remains the best loved and longest-lived of all of the "dynamite" bands, and it attracted a following from all levels of rock fandom, including not only the Hendrix-Clapton fanatics but today's teeny boppers.

STANDARDS

R8.10   **Alice Cooper. Greatest Hits.** Warner Brothers BS 2803.
     The resident bizarro in rock was Alice Cooper (a male). The progenitor of the dada rock movement presented a totally outrageous stage show complete with boa constrictors, a fake hanging, chickens, and mock slaughter of toy dolls. In the flotsam and jetsam of the deco-rock movement, Alice stands head and shoulders over Marc Bolan, Iggy Pop, David Bowie, and a host of bespangled icons of youth. Is it music? This collation comes as close to being a listenable rock sound as any of dear Alice's efforts. If you can forgive the guitar gimmicks, the organ wallowings, and the fuzztone explosions, *and* decipher the lyrics (which are often puerile)—yes! This album perhaps best represents all of the trash and glitter rock of "sex and violence" records. Indeed, Cooper has been recognized as the "patron saint of trash." His material is clearly aimed at exposing the emasculation of society by the forces of authority; and if one thinks that this is a strong statement, then consider his stage act, where Alice gets executed as retribution for "her" sins. To further document the "emasculation," consider a man calling himself Alice. In many ways, as a native of Detroit, Alice Cooper is following in the footsteps of the old MC5 to create radical music. Tracks here include some of the biggest selling singles: "School's Out," "Billion Dollar Babies," the erotic "Muscle of Love," and "No More Mr. Nice Guy."

R8.11*   **Bachman-Turner Overdrive. Best.** Mercury SRM1-1101.

Randy Bachman split from the Guess Who over musical differences, a common event for other groups as well. With two brothers and C. F. Turner, he formed Brave Belt, recorded two albums that failed to sell, and then reorganized them into a heavy metal group that stressed Bachman's riff and raw shouting vocals. The driving beat is the secret behind the music, and while there is simplicity here, there is never any real repetition. It sells, and after four albums, Mercury collated some top selling singles ("Let It Ride," "Lookin' out for Me," "Blue Collar," "Take It Like a Man," "Hey You") in addition to new live recordings of "Takin' Care of Business" (eight minutes in duration) and "Gimme Your Money."

R8.12*   **Blind Faith.** RSO 3016.

If Cream was the rock world's first supergroup, then Blind Faith must be the first super-supergroup. It only lasted about six months—just enough time to put out an album and do a few concerts—and then it was on to other things. Ginger Baker, Eric Clapton (both from Cream), Stevie Winwood (from Traffic) and Rick Grech (from Family) came aboard for progressive rhythms in 1969, and they left behind them several intelligent songs from the post-blues days. Winwood's crying voice was emphatic on "Can't Find My Way Home" or "Had to Cry Today." The instrumental work seems to fall on Clapton's shoulders, but in essence this is the same lineup as in Cream, except that they had a good vocalist (nobody in the Cream days could really sing well, let alone sing and play at the same time). Jack Bruce's wandering but improvisational bass was replaced by rhythm master Grech. It all does sound like Cream, but without the blues. The highlight—definitely— of the record is Clapton's mystical "Presence of the Lord" (he was entering a religious period here, in a time of fast changes), which features a superb wah- wah electric guitar solo plus crying lines. Nobody at this time could use the wah- wah as effectively as Clapton (except maybe Hendrix). The wah-wah in this tune comes out as JHWH or jaw-wah, an obvious reference to Jehovah and the religious element: God speaks to Clapton through his guitar.

R8.13   **Blue Oyster Cult.** Columbia C 31063.

Although the decibel level of this band's first and best album ascends above the level of human pain, they are America's most competent exponents of British- based virtuoso heavy metal music. Lead guitarist Buck Dharma's "auto factory" guitar sounds employ every trick developed by earlier practitioners of amplified music. This excellent derivative band started out making music the basis of their show rather than glitter.

R8.14   **Captain Beefheart and His Magic Band. Trout Mask Replica.** two
          discs. Reprise MS-2027.

Over the past half dozen years, C. B. has released an equal number of albums, through which he has slowly crept to the stage of becoming a cult figure in rock. Often called the only true dadaist in rock, his music crackles with African chant rhythms, free jazz, Delta blues, and arhythmic patterns. This double disc release of 1969 remains the outstanding tribute to the inventiveness and imagination that is possible in this genre of popular music. The 27 cuts range from the Albert Ayler-influenced "Hair Pie: Bake One," with its wrangling horns, to some of the most maniacal lyrics on vinyl. Beefheart's influence is far greater in Europe, but he has attracted a vocal following in the United States.

R8.15*   **Deep Purple. Purple Passages.** two discs. Warner Brothers 2LS 2644.

R8.16   **Deep Purple. In Rock.** Warner Brothers WS 1877.

R8.17*   **Deep Purple. Machine Head.** Warner Brothers BS 2607.

Deep Purple arose in 1968 from the ashes of Episode Six, a classically-inclined experimental group. The three original members were Jon Lord (keyboards), Ian Paice (drummer), and Ritchie Blackmore (lead guitar), the latter leaving in 1975. However, for seven years, this basic trio always had as well a bassist and a vocalist that seemed to change every eighteen months or so. With bassist Roger Glover and singer Ian Gillian, they began their "heavy metal" phase of originally-written material credited to the entire band (not just to a few members, like Lennon-McCartney or Richards-Jagger). Before that time, for Tetragrammaton Records, they covered many solid tunes such as Joe South's "Hush," Neil Diamond's "Kentucky Woman," and an eleven-minute version of Phil Spector's "River Deep, Mountain High." They are a touring band and have made a bigger success outside of their native land. Their essential work, on the two separate albums, is indicative of a blues band but with surrealistic rhythms to create an ebb and flow. For instance, there are Blackmore's incisive guitar obbligatos balanced by Lord's classically-inclined keyboards, as on "Highway Star." One critic called this "baroque instrumental interludes." Their heavy metal sound comprises effective riffs that vary from number to number (as in "Smoke on the Water" or "Living Wreck"). This is the hook that grabs the listener. Then the riff gets permutated in the Lord-Blackmore combinations, quite effectively, to become, as the critic says, "art heavy metal with superfluous harmonics." The electronics of the two leads were an immediate predecessor to those of Yes and other synthesized bands.

R8.18   **Grand Funk Railroad. Mark, Don and Mel, 1969-1971.** two discs. Capitol SABB 11042.

This trio was undoubtedly the most commercially popular of the heavy metal rock groups, although the critics hated their repetitious, loud, derivative music. Still, they sold exceptionally well. This highly arranged and overproduced band did achieve some respectability with "Gimme Shelter" (the Rolling Stones song), "Feelin' Alright," "Mean Mistreater" (the common blues line), "Time Machine," and "Mr. Limousine Driver."

R8.19   **Iron Butterfly. In-a-Gadda-da-Vida.** Atco SD33-250.

Iron Butterfly was born under the influence of such British heavy rock bands as Cream and the Who. Los Angeles based, they were the first of the American electronic elephants and competed with Blue Cheer, another thunderous American rock ensemble, for the title "world's loudest rock band" (currently held by Deep Purple, according to the Guinness Book of World Records). For sheer volume, the seventeen-minute side of this album, "In-a-Gadda-da-Vida [In the Garden of Eden]," is recommended. "Iron Butt" flys no longer, but in their wake have followed countless sound-alike bands, each one more momentarily popular than the last.

R8.20   **The Move. Best of the Move.** two discs. A & M SP 3625.
Originally formed in the mid-60s and featuring lead guitarist Roy Wood, the Move was one of the original heavy metal bands. Producers of a series of invigorating singles such as "Night of Fear," the band went through an unending series of personnel changes, feeding other new musical entourages or reincarnating as the Electric Light Orchestra and Wizzard. Even if there was never, due to the constant changes the band went through, a "Move sound," they did create inventive music. This 25-cut reissue (nineteen composed by Wood) features early, middle, and late Move music—including their boisterous "Brontosaurus" and the original version of their classic "Cherry Blossom Clinic" (based on Wood's visit to a mental hospital). Virtually unknown in the United States, the Move were an important chapter in the development of rock music in Great Britain. Other tracks here include "I Can Hear the Grass Grow" and "Flowers in the Rain," both done in their typically aggressive four-part harmonies.

R8.21   **Steppenwolf. 16 Greatest Hits.** Dunhill DSX 50135.
With John Kay and Jerry Edmonton, the Steppenwolf group combined rock, soul, and blues into a hard edge put out by means of fuzztone guitar, organ, and grating vocals. They were one of the first of the heavy groups, and they were also some of the most competent instrumental players around (perhaps reflecting on their Canadian upbringing?). "Born to Be Wild" was the definitive motorbike song and was used in the film *Easy Rider*; "The Pusherman" was one of the very first anti-drug songs. Overall, this is a very enjoyable and consistent album.

R8.22   **Velvet Underground. Velvet Underground and Nico.** Verve 65008.
The New York based Velvets were discovered by Andy Warhol, who told them to freak out. Many were classically-trained child prodigies, such as Lou Reed (guitars) and John Cale (keyboards). They made their first impressions by touring with Warhol's total environment show (light, noise, films, dance, etc.), adding their own dimensions through on-stage whippings and so forth, which makes them one of the first of the rock theater acts. For their time, along with sob vocalist Nico, they were very musically advanced. Songs dealt with death ("Black Angel's Death"), drugs ("Heroin"), violence (the sado-machoism of "Venus in Furs"), and themes of sexual perversions. Other tracks here include "Sunday Morning," "I'm Waiting for the Man," and "Run, Run, Run."

NOTABLE EXPERIMENTATION

INTRODUCTION

Experimentation is not always successful, but in the rock music world it did help to pave the way for derivative and pop groups. As rock music producers are pragmatic, then "whatever sells must be good," and the whole industry begins emulation of anything good (that is, selling). Most rock experiments are done by reasonably proficient groups who can convince recording companies that their work should be made available to the masses who so rarely buy this type of music anyway. Much of the experimentation is contrived and self-conscious; most of it is simple, derived in turn from the classics or from jazz. Some strength does come from underground or counter-culture fans (usually a loyal cult), but usually such records go through the mainstream of records unnoticed until some other musician tries a simple modification and succeeds.

Worthy experiments listed on the following pages have won critical acclaim, which is the sole basis for their inclusion here. Their sources are mainly acid rock and the new electronic instrumentation. Heavy metal groups did contribute "theater rock," where the music is presented as a whole concept involving light, sound, story, and performance. But they are a failure on disc because the albums are very incomplete, containing aural information only. Jim Morrison of the Doors started it all with long, improvised concert renditions of his ten-minute album songs. The latest extension of the show tunes has been by such groups as Queen, Kiss, and the New York Dolls. All of the albums listed here are about equal in intent; thus, no indication has been given to rank one over another by means of asterisks.

RECORDINGS

R9.1   **Beach Boys. Pet Sounds.** Capitol DT 2458.
With this album, the Beach Boys moved away from basic rock and roll. They used Phil Spector's "wall-of-sound" approach to accompany their harmonized falsetto singing. Such titles as "Wouldn't It Be Nice?," "God Only Knows," and "I Know There's an Answer" reflect the southern California involvement with drugs and offbeat religions. This album is well-orchestrated with polyrhythms.

R9.2   **The Beatles. Sgt. Pepper's Lonely Hearts Club Band.** Capitol ST 2653.
When this record arrived in 1967, the critics could not contain themselves. Everything—including the kitchen sink—was read into the album and its photographs. (What were the Beatles up to? Was Paul McCartney dead and buried under the wreaths? Nothing could be further from the truth.) This album is a logical extension of *Revolver* and *Rubber Soul*. It is not a concept album, for the tunes are fragmented and not related to one another in the slightest. This was one more album in the life of the Beatles, and not a departure. [It is in this section only because this is where most people will begin to look for it.] Some good stories are told here, such as the maudlin "She's Leaving Home," George Harrison's introspective sitar-based "Within You without You," the music hall shows of "Being for the Benefit of Mr. Kite," "When I'm Sixty-Four," "Sgt. Pepper's Lonely Hearts Club Band," and so forth, climaxing with "A Day in the Life"—its allusions and the long, forty second final chord. We suspect that the reason for the treatment by the critics and others is because this was the first and only Beatles record to have the lyrics printed on the cover, and everyone (who could) read them.

R9.3   **Deep Purple. In Live Concert: Concerto for Group and Orchestra.**
Warner Brothers WS 1860.
Jon Lord had classical roots, and in the early days of Episode Six and Deep Purple, the group had classical allusions scattered throughout their work. With time, maturity, and money, Lord was able to fulfill his dream of a merger between rock and classical music. The three movements here exhibit typical concerto forms.

The group and orchestra (the Royal Philharmonic, led by Marcolm Arnold) are antagonistic, but perhaps overly so. Deep Purple is the master of the blues riff. They have the orchestra play one, led by the clarinet and permutated into all sorts of variations. The group then takes over, and in essence, begins a contest or match with the other sections to determine who can play the riff best of all. In line with other concertos, there is a break for the guitar cadenza. The second movement utilizes two tunes, one for the cor anglais and the other for the flute, again being taken over by the rock band and made into a pop item, followed by an organ cadenza. The third movement harkens back to the 6/8 structure of the first, before moving on into 2/4 and the drum cadenza. This was a free-for-all. It is interesting, though, and one of the few fusion pieces that came from a rock group (usually the approach is made by the orchestra or classical composer).

R9.4   **Emerson, Lake and Palmer. Pictures at an Exhibition.** Cotillion ELP 66666.

Greg Lake is the lead vocalist here, playing bass and guitars in a blues mold fashioned after much time with King Crimson. Carl Palmer is the drummer, again from the blues world of Arnold Brown. Keith Emerson plays electric organ and synthesizer (plus any other keyboards), and he was formerly with the Nice, a classically-oriented rock band. Beginning in 1970 as a supergroup along the lines of Cream, ELP became a pre-Yes cult group that specialized in loud noises. They related rock to the classics, often borrowing and not bothering to credit sources (public domain material does not pay a cent, but *arrangements* of such material do), and permutating different stylings in a variety of settings. This 45-minute program is derived from a 1971 concert at Newcastle, England, and is based for the most part on Mussorgsky's epic, with some original material. Heard are the "Promenade" from picture to picture, "The Gnome," "The Old Castle," "The Hut of Baba Yaga," and "The Great Gates of Kiev." A worthwhile effort, even if a little noisy, but sure to turn off serious listeners.

R9.5   **Focus. Dutch Masters (A Selection of Their Finest Recordings, 1969-1973).** Sire SASD 7505.

Focus is a classically-oriented Dutch band that gives more emphasis to instrumental music than to vocals (indeed, some of the vocals are merely inspired yodeling). Leader Thijs Van Leer (classic piano and flute) called his group's music "evolutionary rock," in the sense that they went back to pre-Baroque music for their musical inspiration. Jan Akkerman provides a classically-inspired guitar, and both soloists also have a number of single albums under their own names. Titles here include "Hocus Pocus" (in two versions: one fast, the other slow), "Making Waves," "Sylvia," and a brief exploration into a suite through "Focus, II, and III."

R9.6   **Fugs. First Album.** ESP 1018.

R9.7   **Fugs. Virgin.** ESP 1028.

The original Fugs were poets who decided to sing their own poetry; in this respect, they predated Leonard Cohen. Since the intent of popular music is subverted by the creation of music after lyrics have been carefully crafted through poetic feelings, the effect here is one of stiltedness and half-talking rather than singing. The Fugs were the very first underground rock group, basically a group of outrageous freaks who were highly offensive to most people at that time. Their mode of comedy was satire, with such ribald tunes as "Coca Cola Douche," "Saran Wrap," and "Boobs a Lot." The two leaders were Tuli Kupferberg and Ed Sanders, both of whom struck out on their own after the Fugs broke up. It may be difficult to be both political and pornographic at the same time, but the Fugs achieved it with "Slum Goddess," "I Couldn't Get High," and "CIA Man." Highly irreverent.

R9.8   **Incredible String Band. The Big Huge/Wee Tam.** two discs. Elektra EKS 74036/7.

Mike Heron and Robin Williamson are multi-instrumentalists who were leading Scottish folksingers in the early 1960s. They are at once both eccentric and eclectic. Their combined thirty or so instruments are exotic (gimbri, sarangi, kazoo, etc.) and are of necessity overdubbed, which precludes stage appearances recreating their records. Their weird lyrics are augmented by juxtaposition, such as "Air," which relates the story of the blood's taking in oxygen. This is only on one level; there could be sexual images here, as well as contrasts with the astral and mundane levels. Their music is filled with imagery, poetry, and mysticism, and quite often, it is difficult to sort them all out. They are one of the few groups able to successfully set free verse to music. They have good voice as well as excellent harmonies from the folk tradition. Titles on these two discs relate to myths, witchcraft, philosophy, and the church, through such items as "Maya," "Mountain of God," "Circle Is Unbroken," "Job's Tears," "Ducks on a Pond," and so forth. Most of their material is overly long, being pictures strung together and, contrary to popular music form, the choruses never return.

R9.10   **Jethro Tull. Aqualung.** Reprise MS 2035.

Aqualung was one of the few successful concept-story albums in rock music. Side one is a series of vignettes drawn from modern secular "seedy" English life, such as the shabby "Cross-Eyed Mary the Slut." The lead character, with a persistent hacking cough, looks for God in any man, whether tramp or Pope, in Ian Anderson's paean to spiritual equality. A variety of rock styles are employed in order to get across the philosophic and religious feeling. Side two concerns Christian hypocrisy, and it is a blues rock suite of five parts. "My God" is a soulful blues commentary on the overabundance of social services offered through religions, at the price of a loss of spiritual services. "Hymn 43" is a blues for Jesus, referring to "gory glory seekers" that use His name in vain. "Slipstream" concerns dying, with a hint of an afterlife; "Locomotive Breath" is again about dying, but the allegory is of a train ride where the passenger has no way of stopping the careening locomotive. "Wind Up" is a summation. Throughout, Anderson's electric flute is very tasteful but raw when needed. The printed lyrics that accompany the album are in Gothic lettering, which obviously suggests the liturgical nature of the album.

R9.11   **King Crimson. Young Person's Guide.** two discs. Atlantic 2SDS-900.

This group emerged from Great Britain in the late 1960s with an awesome sound made up of three/fifths mysticism and two/fifths budding prodigies. The mysticism soon faded, but the personnel did not. From King Crimson came

Greg Lake, first to leave (to form the influential ensemble, Emerson, Lake and Palmer). After Lake, Robert Fripp and Pete Sinfield departed to make several excellent albums. Groups such as King Crimson, Yes, the Nice, and Genesis have, for the past half decade, gathered coteries of fans and have become the staple fare of FM progressive rock radio. This "best" collection of Crimson had been selected by the band members themselves from their nine albums. Each of the fifteen tracks comes with complete discographic information, and there is a lavish twenty-page booklet giving dates of tours, excerpts from rock press coverage, photos, etc. The songwriting team of Sinfield (lyrics) and Ian MacDonald (classical compositions), together with an excellent light show, contributed to their early manic successes in "Red," "Moonchild," "Starless," "The Court of the Crimson King," and "Epitaph." King Crimson was the first rock group to make real use of the violin, and to employ weird, freaky lyrics—now called progressive rock.

R9.12   **Kinks. Arthur (or, The Decline and Fall of the British Empire).** Reprise RS 6360.
The transition of the Kinks from rockers to music hall emulators came about with this epic poem from 1969. All of it was scored by their phenomenal leader, Ray Davies. Arthur of the title is a middle-class, middle-aged English workman expressing the frustrations, problems, and the effects of our world on the next generation. "Victoria" explores the topic of England's past glory and her traditions; "Yes Sir, No Sir" refers to military service restrictions; "Mr. Churchill Says" is about World War II; "Australia" details a new start by Arthur's children; "Shangri-La" is basically about escapism; and "Nothing to Say" relates the sad tale of the generation gap.

R9.13   **MC5. Kick out the Jams.** Elektra EKS 74042.
For Chicago's 1968 Democratic Convention, the MC5 (Motor City Five) came together as a political singing group. Agitators for revolution, they produced some of the first hard rock music from white Detroit. Their association with the White Panthers made them a guerrilla rock band, and their live performances were very energetic with their brusque instrumental approach. They had to be seen to be believed, and only a fraction of their total involvement in the performance comes across on this 1969 disc. Norman Mailer heard them in 1968, as described thus: "There was the sound of mountains crashing in this holocaust of the decibels, hearts bursting . . . as if this were the sound of death by explosion within, the drums of physiological climax . . . smashing down a rapids . . . electric crescendo screaming." Titles here include the feature track, "Come Together," "Motor City Is Burning," and "Starship."

R9.14   **Moody Blues. Days of Future Passed.** Deram DES 18012.
One of the longest surviving of the British rock bands is the Moody Blues. At first closely related to the music of the Hollies, Beatles, and Kinks, the "Moodies" have moved away into classical rock, a sub-genre of rock inhabited by the likes of Procol Harum. Their use of the Mellotron, a sort of mutant organ, symbolizes their search for new sounds in a rapidly aging musical genre. They have attracted an immense following since 1967, and although the rock press tends to satirize them as "pretentious," this album has survived and contains some of the most

lyrically beautiful moments in rock. "Nights in White Satin" holds somewhat the same place of distinction in rock's history as Procol Harum's "A Whiter Shade of Pale." This loosely put together series of images begins with the day (and dawn) and goes well into the night. It is not a fusion of rock with classical music, since it borrows several classical devices for its own unique ends. Peter Knight conducted the London Festival Orchestra. On their next album, the Moodies played all 33 instruments themselves (overdubbing); this, of course, led to problems of public performance. The music here is very melodic in tone, with enigmatic, highly rhythmic tunes, and eerie, spacey lyrics for both desolation and inspiration.

R9.15   **Mothers of Invention. Absolutely Free.** Verve V6-5013X.

R9.16   **Mothers of Invention. Freak Out.** two discs. Verve V6-5005-2X.
        Frank Zappa assembled a group of retreaded musicians in the early 1960s and whipped them into shape, to cover rock music, jazz, blues, the classics and serialism (mainly Varèse). They were one of the first groups to use props and visual aids in their concerts: they combined music, art, theater, and audience participation. Zappa's cynical personal philosophy (which runs throughout all of his music) is that the "ugliest part of a person's body might very well be his mind"—thus such songs as "Who Are the Brain Police?," "Plastic People," and "Soft-Sell Conclusions." The early group (around 1966-1967) were the best assembled, with Ray Collins and Zappa on vocals, Ian Underwood playing piano and sax, Motorhead Sherwood on sax, and Bunk Gardner on sax and drums. All of their material is ugly satire, and for this, they developed a large underground following.
        In addition to the lyrics, Zappa (who would probably be the best lead guitarist in the world, *if* he applied himself) introduced time changes on such items as "Call Any Vegetable" and "Invocation and Ritual Dance of the Young Pumpkin" that were exceptionally difficult to play, and riffs that were disarmingly simple. The "Invocation" number has Dunbar on a wah-wah pedal for his sax, one of the first uses of this pedal for non-stringed instruments. The bitingly satiric "America Drinks and Goes Home" (as well as its predecessor, and related song, "America Drinks") comments on the cocktail lounge existence. "Hungry Freaks, Daddy" is about the opposite life. Throwaway lines, sarcasm, religious iconoclasm—all forms are used and discarded. Zappa has pure genius for using the rock venue.

R9.17   **The Nice. The Immediate Story, v.1.** two discs. Sire SASH 3710-2.
        The Nice were together for three years, 1968-1970, with Brian Davison (drums), Keith Emerson (organ), David O'List (lead guitar), and Lee Jackson (bass). Their music was some of the first in the theatrical mode and evolved into "shock rock"—full of burnings, whippings and stabbings. As such, they preceded Alice Cooper and David Bowie. Their influences, though, were from the classical world (mainly Schoenberg), the Oriental world, plus some jazz. When they split for greener pastures, only Keith Emerson emerged as a giant (with Emerson, Lake and Palmer). Their direct descendent in the rock music world is the band called Yes (the aural evidence for this is presented on the absolutely first-rate rendition of Bernstein's "America" from *West Side Story*). Other popular items included the classically-derived "Rondo," "Flower King of Flies," and the collectively-improvised jazz-like "Thoughts of Emerlist Davjack."

R9.18   **Mike Oldfield. Tubular Bells. Virgin VR 13-105.**

This is a light, pleasant album. Oldfield has taken 32 instruments and created an aural pastiche through electronics. Much time was spent in the studios to play all of the instruments and overdub them, plus to do the inevitable mixdown onto two or four tracks. Most of the best "mood" music is on side one; on side two, far too much time is taken up with introducing the sounds of each instrument.

R9.19   **Pink Floyd. The Dark Side of the Moon. Harvest SMAS 11163.**

R9.20   **Pink Floyd. A Nice Pair. two discs. Harvest SABB 11257.**

If there is to be any rock group performing the clichéed "Avant Garde Rock," then it must be Pink Floyd, the best of the electronically-oriented bands. Keyboardist Rick Wright, lead guitarists Dave Gilmore or (earlier) Syd Barrett, bassist Roger Waters, and drummer Nick Mason created the first British light show and British psychedelic rock. But they were more than just a band striving for effects. They moved mostly into electronics (such as keyboards and fuzztones) at a time when nobody else was doing this, except in jazz. The tone of their music is decidedly jazz with a humorous twitch.

The double album presents selections from their first three records, from a period that emphasized their spacey music ("Interstellar Overdrive" and its disjointed sounds; "Saucerful of Secrets," a twelve-minute imaginative piece that makes effective use of stereo dynamics). Their success derives primarily from their ability to control the flow of the music, and to allow certain fluctuating levels of softer music rather than endlessly beating listeners over the head with the maximum of decibels. This is intellectual music for listening, as in "Let There Be More Light" or "Set the Controls for the Heart of the Sun," both of which illustrate their organizational skills in letting introductions slowly build up to a crescendo and then to a dramatic ending. *The Dark Side of the Moon* was their ninth album, but the first one to travel effectively across the Atlantic to the U.S. market. On this disc, they explore the expansion and the contraction of time and space, where the explosive "On the Run" is killed by a ticking clock that leads into "Time." Pink Floyd also enjoyed some success with film scoring.

R9.21   **Rolling Stones. Their Satanic Majesties Request. London NPS 2.**

This album was thought of as the Stones' response to the Beatles' *Sgt. Pepper* album (see entry R9.2); yet, as they both came out at the same time and both projects were done in secret, this does not seem likely. At any rate, this album was loudly booed by the critics at that time as being pretentious schlock. However, it is more of a unified conception than *Sgt. Pepper*. The Beatles' album was a logical extension of *Revolver*, but it was not a concept album. The tunes were fragmented, not related, so *Sgt. Pepper* was actually one more album in the life of the Beatles. The Rolling Stones, on the other hand, had made a success of their rough-and-ready negativism, their primitive sexuality. *Their Satanic Majesties Request* is the complete opposite of this, being very positive and quite tender and lyrical; a radical departure, it should have been more startling than *Sgt. Pepper*. With the perspective of time, we can see that *Satanic Majesties* is a far superior album to *Sgt. Pepper* (which had no hit or otherwise superior songs). The conception of the Stones is the future, and they feel that, despite disturbing tendencies ("Sing This All

Together," "On with the Show"), the future is bright indeed ("She's a Rainbow," "The Lantern"). Excellent rhythms and lyrics abound in "2000 Man" with its unsubtle, heavy metal time change in the middle; and in the whimsically light and airy "2000 Light Years from Home." And, of course, there is that fantastic psychedelic cover.

R9.22   Soft Machine. Third. two discs. Columbia CG 30339.

This group comprises Michael Rutledge on keyboards, Robert Wyatt on bass, and Kevin Ayers with vocals and guitars. (Ayers has since pursued a solo career.) They were the first to come up with the jazz rock fusion, predating Yes and Pink Floyd. At the same time, they developed a light show, the only English group doing this. They were introduced to the United States at the Museum of Modern Art's 1968 jazz series. The music is basically jazz with all of the (few) features of extended rock solos: melody, fuzz tone bass, incessant riffs, repetitious sounds, noise, repetitive drumming—all strung together into "improvised" sets. The rhythms, construction, material, interpretation, and so forth all favor a pronounced rock emphasis and exhibit rock characteristics, but at such a level that they do not project in the so-called surrealistic vein in which Yes and Pink Floyd do. While not as successful as, say, Weather Report (their nearest competitors), they were first into this area and no doubt influenced Miles Davis (who, in turn, influenced Weather Report).

R9.23   United States of America. Columbia CS 9614.

R9.24   Joe Byrd and the Field Hippies. The American Metaphysical Circus. Columbia MS 7317.

The first disc is one of two of the most influential experimental avant garde rock albums created in the United States (R9.25 is the other). Electronics are introduced here, far in advance of their general employment in the rock world. This was 1968, and keyboardist Joe Byrd (who fell under the spell of John Cage) here has assembled a group of classically-trained musicians: Rand Forbes (who plays an unfretted electric bass for greater range), Dorothy Moskowitz (vocals), plus violins and a wide range of percussion from Africa. Byrd wrote, conducted, arranged, and produced this album. Despite the fact that it took seven hours for the group to set up its keyboards, amps, transformers, and diverse electric gadgets (distortion amplifiers, ring modulators, tape echo units, etc.), all of the music on this album *could* be played "live"; there is no overdubbing. Byrd uses the Durrell synthesizer to initiate the melody; he does not alter it. This gives him power and space to create densities and textures around the melody, to point off Moskowitz's high vocals. Using wah-wah devices, the violins could be raised or dropped an octave. The opening track of U.S.A. (entitled "American Metaphysical Circus") introduces the insensibilities of American life: "the price is right/the cost of one admission is your mind"; the last track, "The American Way of Love," is mainly about a Broadway hooker. In between are more songs dealing with death, violence, love, and dreams.

The second album continues the first, but Joe Byrd has an entirely new team here, and most of the instrumentation is traditional. The electronics have been superseded by reed instruments (except for synthesizer). The themes are a development of the first track on the previous album, and include bitter material (war, inner city decay) about the departure of Lyndon Johnson from the Presidency and surrealistic fantasies on old age and dreams. Good head material.

R9.25 **Van Dyke Parks. Song Cycle.** Warner Brothers WS 1727.

This is one of the two most influential experimental avant garde rock albums created in the United States (R9.23 is the other). Parks is an entirely creative person. He works at Warner Brothers as a composer, a lyricist, a skillful arranger, and a producer. The experiment here was an intellectual endeavor; it lost a bundle of money for the company. He had worked on it since 1964; it was released in the fall of 1968. All the material is his except for "Vine Street" (by Randy Newman) and an instrumental version of Donovan's "Colours." Complex Joycean insights abound in musical puns; some allusions borrowed from Debussy, Mahler, Stravinsky, and Ives; and others from Broadway or the Andrews Sisters. There is no central theme, but many are impressionistic songs (like monologues) containing puns ("dreams are still born in Hollywood"), anagrams, and metaphorical mazes. The tone poem framework extends to Hollywood themes, war, civil rights, education systems, and so forth—all punctuated by understatement and scored with orchestral textures and harmonic changes. For instance, "Vine Street" opens with a country/bluegrass flavor before moving on to violin strings, and so forth.

R9.26 **Rick Wakeman. Six Wives of Henry VIII.** A & M SP 4361.

"This album is based around my interpretations of the musical characteristics of the wives of Henry VIII. Although the style may not always be in keeping with their individual history, it is my personal conception of their characters in relation to keyboard instruments"—Rick Wakeman, keyboardist for the rock group Yes. Very brief historical notes are given on the jacket of this album, but they are meaningless in the context of the impressionistic music. And the running order of the selections does not match the women's "wife order" with Henry. Nevertheless, this was a valiant attempt to project images and pastiches through the keyboard. Assisting are the other members of Yes. The selections "Catherine of Aragon" and "Anne Boleyn" have vocal tracks added. (For those interested, the keyboards used included Mini-Moog synthesizers, Mellotrons, grand pianos, organs, harpsichords, electric pianos, ARP synthesizers, oscillators, fuzz and wah-wah pedals—plus echo units.) Wakeman would later go on to create *Journey to the Center of the Earth* and *Myths of King Arthur and the Knights of the Round Table*, both pretentious stage shows as well as albums, but both had to be seen in addition to being heard.

R9.27 **Who. Tommy.** two discs. Decca DXSW 7205.

The Who's first concept album was produced in 1968. Because of their name and the music world's involvement with rock musicals such as *Hair* and later *Godspell*, *Tommy* was swept up into the musical theater, and ultimately it became a movie and a ballet. It was highly influential for its time, but its main impact now appears to have blown over. This is primarily due to the weak story line and the tenuous relationship that some of the songs have to this story. Basically, a boy overcomes his deaf, blind, and dumb condition by learning how to manipulate a pinball machine. He then becomes idolized beyond belief and is regarded as a messianic figure. Tiring of all this, he rejects his followers, for he feels that they must go through what he has gone through in order to learn. Some of his fans won't let him go; others turn on him for his "hypocrisy" towards them. "Pinball Wizard" sums it up rather well.

R9.28   Yes. Close to the Edge. Atlantic SD 7244.

Yes's ancestor was the Nice. Chris Squires (bass), Steve Howe (guitar), and Rick Wakeman (organist) continued the innovative use of classical themes when the Nice broke up in 1970. In addition to what this latter band did, Yes contributed the harmonic shifts later so vital to electronic rock music. The bassist often played a top lead, with the drummer improvising the beat. This inversion of the rhythm section made it necessary for the "front line" to continue the ebb and flow of the pulse, which included Howe's flowing melodies and Wakeman's fluid touch. This 1972 album is probably their zenith: a collection of suites of detached music, emphasizing electronic manipulations to create moods. Side one has the long title track, a stylized instrumental with the diverse themes expanding and synthesized in dialectic fashion. The two tracks "Total Mass Recall" and "And You and I" are basically sound paintings, which are difficult to describe.

Citations,
Directories,
Indexes

🌷🌷🌷🌷🌷🌷🌷🌷🌷

BOOK CITATIONS

Most of the material in this book is based on a combination of readings from both book and periodical sources. In the listing that follows, the key books of concern to students of contemporary popular music are listed alphabetically. Taken together, the books cited in the four volumes would constitute a library detailing popular music in America. We have excluded two categories of books. Generally, *biographies* have been omitted unless they deal substantially with an innovator, concentrate on his/her stylings, and show that artist's impact and influence on other performers in the same genre. Thus, for example, we list here Gray's book on Bob Dylan rather than Scaduto's largely biographical offering. Second, we have omitted *songbooks* and instructional materials that look like songbooks, unless they deal substantially with the impact and influence of the music, such as Lomax's book.

It is very difficult to separate books about different musical genres, for there is much overlapping; thus, we discuss titles in the literature survey preceding each section by referring to a designated number, which then can be followed up here for source data and comment. At the same time, many books are called "reference works" (bibliographies, discographies) and "monographic surveys." To the student of music, these terms are meaningless. In consideration of all of the above, an alphabetical reference listing seems the best way to handle the matter. At any rate, this is just a source list; please refer to the musical section for comments on the literature.

1 Annual Index to Popular Music Record Reviews, 1972- . Compiled by
   A. Armitage and D. Tudor. Metuchen, NJ: Scarecrow, 1973- .
   This annual provides location to about 15,000 record reviews in about
55 magazines, noting for each review the reviewer's evaluation of the record. It provides a synoptic report on the year's music, pre-selecting the "best of the year" and indicating the length of each review.

2 Baral, Robert. Revue: The Great Broadway Period. Rev. ed. New York:
   Fleet Press Corp., 1970. 296p.

3 Barnes, Ken, ed. Sinatra and the Great Song Stylists. London: Allan, 1972.
   illus. discog.

4 Batcheller, John. Music in Recreation and Leisure. Dubuque, IA: W. C.
   Brown Co., 1972. 135p. paper.
   A short treatise on the importance of music as a social function, with
chapters on how to relax through music.

5 Belz, Carl. The Story of Rock. 2nd ed. New York: Oxford University Press,
   1972. 286p. discog. illus. bibliog.
   This is a scholarly, chronological survey of a "sociological folk art," covering
origins, style, influences, and the media. No musical analysis.

6 Berendt, Joachim Ernst. The Jazz Book; From New Orleans to Rock and
   Free Jazz. Rev. ed. New York: Lawrence Hill, 1975. 480p. discog.
   The most popular jazz book in the world (several translations; millions of
copies sold).

7 Bluestein, Gene. The Voice of the Folk; Folklore and American Literary
   Theory. Amherst: University of Massachusetts Press, 1972. 170p. bibliog.
   Half of this book is devoted to folk music, and includes a study of blues
as a literary tradition, the black influence, and rock as poetry.

8 Boeckman, Charles. And the Beat Goes On; A Survey of Pop Music in
   America. Washington: R. B. Luce, 1972. 224p. illus.

9 Brand, Oscar. The Ballad Mongers; Rise of the Modern Folk Song. New York:
   Funk and Wagnalls, 1967. 240p.

10 Bronson, Bertrand Harris. The Ballad as Song. Berkeley: University of
    California Press, 1969. 324p.

11 Brown, Len, and Gary Friedrich. Encyclopedia of Rock and Roll. New
    York: Tower Publications, 1970. 217p.
    This book covers 1954-1963, and as such, it predates and extends Roxon's
encyclopedia [No. 103].

12 Burt, Jesse, and Bob Ferguson. So You Want to Be in Music! Nashville,
    TN: Abingdon Press, 1970. 175p.
    This career-oriented handbook does a good job of explaining the mechanics
behind breaking into the business—songwriting, studio techniques, and so forth.
Glossary of recording terms.

13 Burton, Jack. The Blue Book of Broadway Musicals. 3rd ed. Watkins Glen,
    NY: Century House, 1976. 358p. illus. bibliog. discog.
    This aims to cover all 1,500 or so musical productions that have appeared
on Broadway since 1900: operetta, musical comedy, and revues. Historical summaries precede complete listings for each production.

14 Burton, Jack. The Blue Book of Hollywood Musicals. Watkins Glen, NY:
    Century House, 1953. 296p. bibliog. discog.
    The period covered is 25 years: 1927-1952. Information on historical matters
and a survey precede the listings of all musical films from Hollywood.

15 Burton, Jack. The Blue Book of Tin Pan Alley; A Human Interest Encyclo-
    pedia of American Popular Music. 2nd ed. Watkins Glen, NY: Century House,
    1962-1965. 2v. illus. discog.
    Volume one covers up to 1910; volume two continues to 1950, with a
supplement by Larry Freeman to 1965. Here is biographical information on composers and singers, plus listings of their major songs (with discographical information).

16 Chasins, Abram. Music at the Crossroads. New York: Macmillan, 1972.
    240p.
    An appraisal of the current state of instrumental music, both classical and
popular, with consideration of the effects of jazz-rock-folk on "serious" music.

17 Christgau, Robert. Any Old Way You Choose It; Rock and Other Pop Music, 1967-1973. Baltimore: Penguin Books, 1973. 330p. paper only.
Reprints of his volumns for Village Voice and Newsday, involving much serious and personal criticism of American rock music.

18 Cohn, Nik. Rock from the Beginning. New YOrk: Stein and Day, 1969. 238p.
Originally published in England as "Pop from the Beginning," this book investigates the working-class, youth aspects of rock music. Particularly valuable for early elements of British pop.

18a Connor, D. Russell, and Warren W. Hicks. BG: On the Record; A Bio-discography of Benny Goodman. New Rochelle, NY: Arlington House, 1969. 691p. illus. bibliog. discog.
Connor published "BG: Off the Record" privately in 1958; this retitled effort is an immense updating that contains a tremendous amount of data about Goodman's recordings, his sidemen, etc.

19 Cummings, Tony. The Sound of Philadelphia. London: Methuen, 1975. 157p. illus. paper only.
Traces the roots of rock and roll, r 'n' b, and modern soul that developed in one city.

20 Denisoff, R. Serge. Great Day Coming; Folk Music and the American Left. Urbana: University of Illinois Press, 1971. 220p.
Traces the use of folk music for socio-political ends from 1930 to the present.

21 Denisoff, R. Serge. Sing a Song of Social Significance. Bowling Green, OH: Bowling Green University Popular Press, 1972. 229p. illus. tables.
A series of papers about songs of persuasion and protest in American life.

22 Denisoff, R. Serge. Solid Gold; The Record Industry, Its Friends, and Enemies. New York: Transaction Books; distr. by Dutton, 1976. 350p.
Traces the steps through which a song goes to reach the public.

23 Denisoff, R. Serge. Songs of Protest: War and Peace; a Bibliography and Discography. Santa Barbara, CA: American Bibliographical Center-Clio Press, 1973. 88p. paper only.
Scope covers books, periodicals, songbooks, songs, and country and western music in the discography. This leads to a preliminary assessment of the role of music in American anti-war movements from the Revolutionary War to the present.

24 Denisoff, R. Serge, comp. The Sounds of Social Change; Studies in Popular Culture. Chicago: Rand McNally, 1972. 332p.

25 Dilello, Richard. The Longest Cocktail Party; A Personal History of Apple. Chicago: Playboy, 1972. 336p. discog.
An inside view of Apple Records, the former business venture of the Beatles.

26 Dimmick, Mary Laverne. The Rolling Stones; An Annotated Bibliography. Pittsburgh, PA: Graduate School of Library and Information Science, University of Pittsburgh, 1972. 73p.
This appears to be the only example of a bibliographical source book for rock groups.

27 Dutton, David, and Lenny Kaye. Rock 100. New York: Grosset and Dunlap, 1977. 278p. illus.
   About 100 influential rock and soul artists are discussed along with commentaries on various styles and sounds (e.g., Motown sound, disco).

28 Eisen, Jonathan, ed. The Age of Rock. New York: Random House, 1969. 388p.
   The first of three books edited by Eisen, this anthology comes from the pop press, rock journals, and so forth. It includes Tom Wolfe's 1965 article on Phil Spector and some of the early writings of Jon Landau.

29 Eisen, Jonathan, ed. The Age of Rock, 2. New York: Random House, 1970.

30 Engel, Lehman. The American Musical Theater. Rev. ed. New York: Macmillan, 1975. 266p. bibliog. discog.
   A brief survey/overview.

31 Escott, Colin, and Martin Hawkins. Catalyst; The Story of Sun Records. London: Aquarius, 1975. 173p. illus.

32 Ewen, David. All the Years of American Popular Music. Englewood Cliffs, NJ: Prentice-Hall, 1977. 850p.
   A comprehensive one-volume survey of all aspects of popular music, 1620-1975.

33 Ewen, David. Great Men of American Popular Song. Englewood Cliffs, NJ: Prentice-Hall, 1970. 387p.
   Mainly historical and biographical, this book does not attempt analysis. Its subtitle is: the history of American popular song told through the lives, careers, achievements, and personalities of its foremost composers and lyricists. There are 28 composers and thirteen lyricists covered.

34 Ewen, David. History of Popular Music. New York: Barnes and Noble, 1961. 229p. bibliog. paper only.
   A brief introductory text to popular songs, the musical theater, and jazz in America from Colonial times to 1960.

35 Ferlingere, Robert D. A Discography of Rhythm and Blues and Rock and Roll Vocal Groups, 1945-1965. Pittsburg, CA: The Author (P.O. Box 1695), 1976. 600p.
   20,000 song titles are listed in chronological order by master number, covering the output (78, 45, 33 1/3 rpm speeds, plus long-playing and extended playing formats) of over 2,600 groups and single artists with groups. Unreleased titles are also included, as well as recording dates.

36 Field, James J. American Popular Music, 1875-1950. Philadelphia, PA: Musical Americana, 1956.

37 Flattery, Paul. The Illustrated History of British Pop. New York: Drake, 1975. 126p. illus.
   This mainly deals with the 1950s and early 1960s.

38 Flower, John. Moonlight Serenade; A Bio-discography of the Glenn Miller
    Civilian Band. New Rochelle, NY: Arlington House, 1972. 554p. illus.
    discog.
    A virtually day-by-day account of the performances and recordings of the
band. Index to song titles and personnel.

39 Fuld, James J. The Book of World Famous Music: Classical, Popular and
    Folk. Rev. and enl. ed. New York: Crown, 1971. 688p. bibliog.
    A discussion of 1,000 songs, primarily through tracing their roots.

40 Gabree, John. The World of Rock. Greenwich, CT: Fawcett Publications,
    1968. 176p. paper only.
    In addition to "rock," coverage is also extended to related musical styles
of soul, rhythm 'n' blues, country, blues, and folk.

41 Gillett, Charlie. Making Tracks; The Story of Atlantic Records. New York:
    Outerbridge and Lazard, 1973.
    This is probably the only book on the history of music recording, as it is
a corporate history of Atlantic Records. This company was the most influential
of the early r 'n' b labels—and still is.

42 Gillett, Charlie, ed. Rock File. London: New English Library, 1972. 156p.
    discog.
    Includes a list of the English Top Twenty hits from 1955 through 1969.
Includes various "playlists" of critics' choices for album samplings.

43 Gillett, Charlie. The Sound of the City; The Rise of Rock 'n' Roll. New
    York: Dell Publishing, 1972. 343p. discog. bibliog.
    Originally published in 1970, this "second" edition contains a general updating
and revised discography. Of all the rock books, this is the most important and
scholarly. Gillett knows what he is talking about, a trait often found among British
writers. United Artists in England released an album to accompany the book,
covering New Orleans from 1951 to 1962.

44 Gillett, Charlie, and Stephen Nugent. Rock Almanac. Garden City, NY:
    Anchor Press/Doubleday, 1976. 464p. illus. discog. paper only.
    Top twenty American and British singles and albums of the 50s, 60s and 70s.

45 Gleason, Ralph J. The Jefferson Airplane and the San Francisco Sound.
    New York: Ballantine Books, 1969. 340p. paper only.
    The first half covers history from 1965 through 1969; the second half is
mainly interview material with the Airplane, Bill Graham, and Jerry Garcia.

46 Goldstein, Richard. Goldstein's Greatest Hits. Englewood Cliffs, NY: Prentice-
    Hall, 1970. 258p.
    His collected writings from 1966-1968, originally published in the Village
Voice, the New York Times, and New York Magazine.

47 Gray, Michael. Song and Dance Man; The Art of Bob Dylan. London: Abacus,
    1973. 332p. illus. discog. paper only.
    An analysis of Dylan's songs, lyrics, music—placed in the context of his
time (impact and influence).

48 Green, Stanley. The World of Musical Comedy; The Story of the American Musical Stage as Told through the Careers of Its Foremost Composers and Lyricists. 3rd ed. Cranbury, NJ: A. S. Barnes, 1974. 556p. illus. discog.
From 1893-1972, with details of stage performances and various OC, ST, and studio recordings.

49 Guralnick, Peter. Feel Like Goin' Home; Portraits in Blues and Rock 'n' Roll. New York: Outerbridge and Dienstfrey, 1971. 224p. illus. bibliog. discog.
Interviews with and perceptive comments on both black and white bluesmen.

50 Herdeg, Walter, ed. Graphics/Record Covers. New York: Hastings House, 1974. 192p. illus.
History and illustrations of record jacket designs.

51 Hoare, Ian, ed. The Soul Book. London: Methuen, 1975. 206p. illus. discog. paper only.
Traces the development of gospel, r 'n' b, Motown, Memphis, and New Orleans styles, plus blue-eyed soul and modern funk.

52 Hoover, Cynthia. Music Machines—American Style; A Catalog of an Exhibition. Washington: Smithsonian Institution Press; distr. by Govt. Print. Off., 1971. 139p. illus. bibliog.
The exhibition portrayed the development of music machines from cylinders and player pianos to Moog synthesizers, and the effect of technology on performers and audiences.

53 Hopkins, Jerry. The Rock Story. New York: Signet/New American Library, 1970. 222p. discog. paper only.
The first section details a history of rock; the balance is a collection of reprinted essays by Hopkins.

54 Horn, David. The Literature of American Music in Books and Folk Music Collections: A Fully Annotated Bibliography. Metuchen, NJ: Scarecrow, 1977. 556p.
A detailed listing of 1,696 books considered essential for a library on all aspects of American music: folk, country, blues, rock, musical stage, soul, jazz etc. Strong annotations.

55 Howard, John Tasker, and George Kent Bellows. A Short History of Music in America. New York: Crowell, 1967. 496p. illus. bibliog. notes.
A brief history that surveys folk, classical, spirituals, recorded music, and musical comedy.

56 Hughes, Langston, and Milton Meltzer. Black Magic; A Pictorial History of the Negro in American Entertainment. Englewood Cliffs, NJ: Prentice-Hall, 1967. 375p.

57 Jahn, Mike. Rock; From Elvis Presley to the Rolling Stones. New York: Quadrangle/New York Times Book Co., 1973. 326p. illus. discog.

58 Jasper, Tony. Understand Pop. London: S.C.M. Press, 1972. 192p. illus. bibliog.

59 Kinkle, Roger D. The Complete Encyclopedia of Popular Music and Jazz, 1900-1950. New Rochelle, NY: Arlington House, 1974. 4v. (2644 pages). discog.

60 Laing, David, ed. The Electric Muse; The Story of Folk into Rock. London: Methuen, 1975. 182p. illus. discog. paper only.
Coverage of the folk revivals in both England and the United States, plus the electric folk of Dylan, the Byrds, Fairport Convention, and Steeleye Span.

61 Laing, David. The Sound of Our Time. Chicago: Quadrangle Books, 1970. 198p. bibliog.
Another general history of popular rock music, by a British critic and editor. He emphasizes contexts and relationships, providing a theoretical framework for the subject.

62 Landau, Jon. It's Too Late to Stop Now; A Rock 'n' Roll Journal. San Frandisco: Straight Arrow Books, 1972. 227p.
Similar to other books (notably Williams or Goldstein) this is a collection of writings from Rolling Stone, Crawdaddy, and the Boston Phoenix.

63 Larson, Bob. Rock & Roll; The Devil's Diversion. McCook, NE: The Author, 1970. 176p. illus.
A fundamentalist's view of rock and roll as a satanic plot.

64 Laufe, Abe. Broadway's Greatest Musicals. New York: Funk & Wagnalls, 1973. 502p. illus. bibliog.
The period covered is 1884 through 1971. Facts and figures as they relate to the shows' productions are mixed with plot summaries, costume and set descriptions, and excerpts from reviews.

65 Lee, Edward. Music of the People; A Study of Popular Music in Great Britain. London: Barrie & Jenkins, 1970. 274p. illus. bibliog. music.
A discussion of folk roots, the impact of American pop music, the mid-Atlantic sounds, and the British influence on U.S. music.

66 Lewine, Richard, et al. Songs of the American Theater; A Comprehensive Listing of More Than 12,000 Songs. New York: Dodd, Mead, 1973. 820p.
From 1925 through 1971, plus a selection of important songs from 1900 through 1924. Film and television songs are also included, along with original cast album details, vocal scores, and composer data.

67 Lewine, Richard and Alfred Simon. Encyclopedia of Theatre Music. New York: Random House, 1961.

68 Lieber, Leslie. How to Form a Rock Group. New York: Grosset & Dunlap, 1968. 128p.

69 Limbacher, James L. Film Music: From Violins to Video. Metuchen, NJ: Scarecrow, 1974. 835p. bibliog. discog.
A fairly comprehensive aid that includes reprints of definitive or explanatory articles, plus various indexes by titles of films, composers, years, and certain discographical detail for each film.

70 Logan, Nick, and Bob Woffinden. The Illustrated Encyclopedia of Rock.
   New York: Harmony Books, 1977. 254p. illus. discog.
   650 entries; 300 record jacket photos in color; 150 photos of assorted
"nothing special."

71 Lydon, Michael. Boogie Lightnin'. New York: Dial, 1974. 229p. illus.
   These reprints from his magazine articles stress the contribution of black
music through rhythm 'n' blues and the blues to American culture. There are
histories and profiles of John Lee Hooker, Bo Diddley, the Chiffons, Aretha
Franklin, Ray Charles, and so forth, as well as a section on the development and
use of the electric guitar.

72 Lydon, Michael. Rock Folk; Portraits from the Rock 'n' Roll Pantheon.
   New York: Dial, 1971. 200p.
   Interviews (mostly from the New York Times magazine) with Janis Joplin,
B. B. King, Chuck Berry, the Grateful Dead, the Rolling Stones, and others.

73 Mabey, Richard. The Pop Process. London: Hutchinson, 1969. 190p. bibliog.
   Coverage of English rock and pop groups, from the late fifties to the early
sixties.

74 McCarthy, Albert. Big Band Jazz. New York: G. P. Putnam's, 1974. 368p.
   illus. (chiefly black and white photos). bibliog. discog.
   This is a definitive history of the origins, progress, influence, and decline
in the United States and elsewhere of big band and swing jazz units. Coverage
extends to 550 bands plus a superb discography of over 325 records. All examples
are taken from recorded material.

75 McCarthy, Albert. The Dance Band Era; The Dancing Decades from Ragtime
   to Swing, 1910-1950. Philadelphia: Chilton, 1972. 176p.
   This is a large format book, with copious black and white photographs of
the bands that English people danced to—Ray Noble, Fox, Ambrose, etc. Swing
is deliberately played down, as the emphasis is on dancing. The discography is
excellent and comprehensive.

76 Marcus, Greil. Mystery Train; Images of America in Rock 'n' Roll Music.
   New York: Dutton, 1975. 275p. illus.
   Sociological and political ramifications of rock and rolk rock music.

77 Marcus, Greil, comp. Rock and Roll Will Stand. Boston: Beacon Press,
   1969. 182p. discog.
   Selected articles from underground rock papers. Each emphasizes a subjective involvement in the music, and each has a discography at the end of the
article.

78 Mattfield, Julius. Variety Music Cavalcade. 3rd ed. Englewood Cliffs, NJ:
   Prentice-Hall, 1971.

79 Mellers, Wilfrid. Music in a New Found Land. London: Barrie and Rockliff,
   1964.
   Here is wide coverage of the American musical tradition, relating classics
to blues to jazz to pop.

80 Melly, George. Revolt into Style; The Pop Arts in Britain. London: Allen Lane, The Penguin Press, 1970. 245p.
Largely based on Melly's periodical articles, this is an analytic history of popular culture in Britain in the 1960s. Its scope is wider than music and includes television, films, stage, the press, and writings.

81 Meltzer, Richard. The Aesthetics of Rock. New York: Something Else Press, 1970. 346p.
Personal reflections and analysis of contemporary rock music, as seen by a reviewer and critic who has his own unique, and sometimes difficult, writing style and vocabulary.

82 Millar, Bill. The Drifters; The Rise and Fall of the Black Vocal Group. New York: Macmillan, 1972. 180p. illus.
Coverage is extended to many other black vocal groups of the 1950s.

83 Morse, David. Motown and the Arrival of Black Music. New York: Macmillan, 1972. 144p. illus.
Examines the impact of the softer, urban sounds of black music.

84 The Music Yearbook: A Survey and Directory with Statistics and Reference Articles. 1972- . New York: St. Martin's Press, 1973- . 750p. average length.
This annual is the most up-to-date source of information on British music and musicians. Survey articles cover all aspects of classical and popular music, with lists of books and periodicals, addresses of relevant record companies, associations, halls, museums, etc. The American equivalent is The Musician's Guide, from Music Information Service.

85 The Musician's Guide. 1954- . New York: Music Information Service, 1954- . (available every four years. Last edition: 1976).
The basic directory of music information for the United States. Sections include data on record collections, various recording awards such as the "Grammies," addresses of groups, books to read, and so forth. The British equivalent is The Music Yearbook.

86 Nanry, Charles, ed. American Music; From Storyville to Woodstock. New Brunswick, NJ: Transaction Books, 1972. 288p.
This collection of reprinted articles covers only jazz and rock.

87 National Portrait Gallery. "A Glimmer of Their Own Beauty; Black Sounds of the Twenties." Washington: Govt. Print. Off., 1971. 32p., chiefly illus. bibliog.
A catalog of an exhibition of pictures of Negro musicians.

88 New York Library Association. Children's and Young Adult Services Section. Records and Cassettes for Young Adults; A Selected List. New York, 1972. 52p. paper only. discog.
Categories include rock, roul, blues, jazz, country and western, and various non-musical records and cassettes. Useful for the "now" sounds of 1972.

89 Nite, Norm N. Rock On; The Illustrated Encyclopedia of Rock 'n' Roll for the Solid Gold Years. New York: Thomas Y. Crowell, 1974. 676p.
Includes all relevant pop material from the fifties.

90 Nite, Norm N. Rock On: The Illustrated Encyclopedia of Rock n' Roll;
Vol. II: The Modern Years: 1964-Present. New York: Thomas Y. Crowell,
1978. 590p. illus. index.
Continues the above, and it has a list of hit sellers from the period.

91 Passman, Arnold. The Dee Jays. New York: Macmillan, 1971. 320p.
He traces the evolution of the "disc jockey" from 1909 to the underground
FM stations in San Francisco, with good detail on how songs are selected for airplay.

92 Paul, Elliot. That Crazy American Music. Port Washington, NY: Kennikat
Press, 1970. 317p. bibliog.
Originally published by Bobbs-Merrill in 1957.

93 Pleasants, Henry. The Great American Popular Singers. New York: Simon
and Schuster, 1974. 384p. illus.
The author examines the vocal tradition in popular music, the phenomenon
of imitation breeding imitation, the meaning of "art" as applied to popular music,
and various evaluations of 22 innovators in the fields of jazz, musical stage, blues,
gospel, country, soul, and so forth.

94 Popular Music Periodicals Index, 1973- . Comp. by Dean Tudor and Andrew
Armitage. Metuchen, NJ: Scarecrow, 1974- .
An annual author-subject index to sixty or so periodicals utilizing a special
thesaurus involving musical genres.

95 Propes, Steve. Golden Goodies; A Guide to 50s and 60s Popular Rock and
Roll Record Collecting. Philadelphia, PA: Chilton, 1975. 185p. discog.

96 Propes, Steve. Golden Oldies; A Guide to 60s Record Collecting. Philadelphia, PA: Chilton, 1974. 240p. discog.

97 Propes, Steve. Those Oldies but Goodies; A Guide to 50's Record Collecting.
New York: Macmillan, 1973. 192p. bibliog. discog.
A guide to current prices, sources, and reading material devoted to collecting
78 and 45 rpm phonodiscs from the 1950-1960 period.

98 Recording Industry Association of America. The White House Record
Library. Washington: White House Historical Association, 1973. 105p.
A catalog of 2,000 records presented to the White House in March 1973.
Categories include popular, classical, jazz, folk, country, gospel, and spoken word.

99 Redd, Lawrence N. Rock Is Rhythm and Blues; The Impact of Mass Media.
East Lansing: Michigan State University Press, 1974. 167p. illus.

100 Rhode, H. Kandy. The Gold of Rock & Roll, 1955-1967. New York: Arbor
House, 1970. 352p. bibliog.
This is a listing of the Top Ten songs, week by week, for 1955-1967. Infor-
mation includes: the song title, performer, record number, lyricist, and publisher.
There are yearly summaries, and information on sales records, chart listings, and
radio logs.

101 Rivelli, Pauline, and Robert Levin, eds. The Rock Giants. New York: World,
1971.
These articles have been collected from the magazine Jazz & Pop, which has
since ceased publishing.

102 Rolling Stone Magazine. The Rolling Stone Record Review. New York: Pocket Books, 1961. 556p. paper only.

Rolling Stone Magazine. The Rolling Stone Record Review. v.2. New York: Pocket Books, 1974. 599p. paper only.

103 Roxon, Lillian. Rock Encyclopedia. New York: Grosset & Dunlap, 1969. 611 illus. discog.

Despite obvious defects, this remains the basic work for details on the big rock stars of the mid-sixties and types of musical expression, such as the San Francisco sound. Concludes with top elpees from Cashbox, 1960-1968; top singles from Cashbox, 1949-1968; and Billboard's number one weekly hits, 1950-1967.

104 Rublowsky, John. Popular Music. New York: Basic Books, 1967. 164p.
Emphasis is on country and western, rock, and current popular materials.

105 Rust, Brian. The American Dance Band Discography, 1917-1942. New Rochelle, NY: Arlington House, 1975. 2v. (2066 pages).

Some 2,373 white bands are covered (except Glenn Miller and Benny Goodman, who have their own books); 7,141 entries in the index.

106 Rust, Brian. The Complete Entertainment Discography; From the Mid-1890s to 1942. With Allen G. Debus. New Rochelle, NY: Arlington House, 1973. 677p.

This listing, in performer order by alphabetical arrangement, is similar to other genre "discographies," except that its criteria for inclusion are based on exceptions: anybody that does not fit into existing or contemplated listings. Thus, most popular singers and all of vaudeville are here.

107 Rust, Brian. The Dance Bands. London: Ian Allan, 1972. 160p. illus.
Mainly British, from 1919-1944, with many rare photographs.

107a Rust, Brian. Jazz Records, A-Z, 1897-1942. 4th ed. New Rochelle, NY: Arlington House, 1978. 2v.

Similar to Jepsen's discography, this is an alphabetically arranged list of a jazz artist's records within the specified time period. Updated in a variety of sources including Jazz Journal and Storyville.

108 Rust, Brian. The Victor Master Book, v.2 (1925-1936). Hatch End, Middlesex: The Author, 1969. 776p.

A complete listing, in numerical order, of every popular music record issued by RCA Victor between 1925-1936.

109 Salem, James M. A Guide to Critical Reviews, Part II: The Musical from Rodgers-and-Hart to Lerner-and-Loewe. Metuchen, NJ: Scarecrow, 1967. 353p.

110 Sarlin, Bob. Turn It Up (I Can't Hear the Words); The Best of the New Singer/Songwriters. New York: Simon and Schuster, 1974. 222p. illus.
A critique of the lyrics of troubador singing from the early 1970s.

111 Schafer, William J. Rock Music; Where It's Been, What It Means, Where It's Going. Minneapolis, MN: Augsburg Pub., 1972. 128p. illus. bibliog. discog. paper only.

Discussion in terms of youth culture.

112 Schicke, C. A. Revolution in Sound: A Biography of the Recording Industry. Boston: Little, Brown, 1974. 238p.
  A history of the recording industry, covering all forms of influences and manipulation.

113 Scott, John Anthony. The Ballad of America; The History of the United States in Song and Story. New York: Grosset & Dunlap, 1967. 403p.

114 Shaw, Arnold. The Rock Revolution. New York: Crowell-Collier, 1969. 215p. discog. glossary.
  Shaw presents good information on the recording industry and on the music business.

115 Shaw, Arnold. The Rockin' 50s; The Decade That Transformed the Pop Music Scene. New York: Hawthorn, 1974. 296p. illus. bibliog. discog.
  The origins of rock and roll are covered by examining trends, personalities, issues, and so forth through exhaustive interviews.

116 Simon, George T. The Big Bands. 2nd ed. New York: Macmillan, 1971. 584p. illus.
  A complete survey of the big bands and the big names; the first edition had a three record set (one each from Decca, RCA, and Columbia) to accompany it.

117 Simon, George T. Simon Says; The Sights and Sounds of the Swing Era, 1935-1955. New Rochelle, NY: Arlington House, 1971. 476p. illus.
  This is an anthology of reviews and critical pieces originally published in Metronome, where the author was editor for twenty years.

118 Smith, Cecil. Musical Comedy in America. New York: Theatre Arts Books, 1950.
  A straight-forward historical account through the first half of this century.

119 Smolian, Steven, comp. A Handbook of Film, Theatre, and Television Music on Record, 1948-1969. New York: Record Undertaker (P.O. Box 437, New York City 10023), 1970. 64p. paper only.

120 Somma, Robert, ed. No One Waved Goodbye; A Casualty Report on Rock and Roll. New York: Outerbridge and Dienstfrey, 1971. 121p.
  A discourse on the deaths of Janis Joplin, Jimi Hendrix, Brian Jones, and Brian Epstein.

121 Stambler, Irwin. Encyclopedia of Pop, Rock and Soul. New York: St. Martin's Press, 1975. 609p. illus.

122 Stambler, Irwin. Encyclopedia of Popular Music. New York: St. Martin's Press, 1965. 359p. discog. bibliog.
  380 entries cover songs, musicals, singers and styles. The period is largely 1925-1965, and various musical awards are listed.

123 Stambler, Irwin. Guitar Years; Pop Music from Country and Western to Hard Rock. Garden City, NY: Doubleday, 1970. 137p.
  This short book is actually a compendium of bits and pieces dealing with guitar influences on music of the sixties.

124 Stearns, Marshall, and Jean Stearns. Jazz Dance; The Story of American Vernacular Dance. New York: Macmillan, 1968. 464p. illus. bibliog. filmog.

125 Taubman, Howard, ed. The New York Times Guide to Listening Pleasure. New York: Macmillan, 1968. 328p. discog.

This is mainly a how-to guide for the novice record collector. A good two-thirds of the book deals with classical music; the balance concentrates on folk, jazz, Latin America, and the musical theater.

126 Taylor, John Russell. The Hollywood Musical. New York: McGraw-Hill, 1971. 278p. illus.

Discusses 275 major films and gives brief details on 1,443 others. There is a biographical index and an index to 2,750 songs. Cross-referenced and profusely illustrated.

127 Thomas, Tony. Music for the Movies. New York: A. S. Barnes, 1973. 270p.

Subjects covered include scoring for the silent film, and film music from 1929 to date. There are biographical chapters for 24 top names.

128 Tudor, Dean, and Andrew Armitage. "Best of the Year." LJ/SLJ Previews, April and May issues, 1974-1976.

A round-up of those years' best records, as reflected by the reviewing media.

129 U.S. Library of Congress. Reference Department, Music Division. Sousa Band: A Discography. Comp., James R. Smart. Washington: Govt. Print. Off., 1970. 123p. discog.

Purpose is to present in one source the recording history of the Sousa Band. Foreign releases are excluded.

130 Whitburn, Joel. Top Easy Listening Records, 1961-1974. Menomenee Falls, WI: Record Research, 1975.

Alphabetically arranged by artist and title, from the Billboard "Top 50 Easy Listening" charts. Also included are a Trivia section and photos.

131 Whitburn, Joel. Top LP Records, 1945-1972. Menomenee Falls, WI: Record Research, 1974.

Artist arrangement and broad subject categories based on the Billboard charts of jazz, rock, pop, r 'n' b, etc.

132 Whitburn, Joel. Top Pop Records, 1940-1955. Milwaukee, WI: Haertlineghn Graphics, 1973.

Arrangement is alphabetical by artist, and all 1,760 selections are taken from Billboard.

133 Whitburn, Joel. Top Pop Records, 1955-1970. Detroit, MI: Gale Research, 1972. 236p.

Facts about 9,800 recordings listed in Billboard's "Hot 100" Charts, grouped under the names of the 2,500 or so recording artists. Annual supplements are available from the compiler.

134 Whitcomb, Ian. After the Ball. London: Allen Lane, The Penguin Press, 1972. 312p.

The author, a singer, explores the phenomenon of popular music, from "After the Ball" (written in 1892) through Tin Pan Alley to the Beatles. Concentration is mostly on British pop.

135 Whitcomb, Ian. Tin Pan Alley; A Pictorial History, 1919-1939. New York: Paddington Press/Two Continents, 1975. 251p. illus. music.

136 Wilder, Alec. American Popular Song; The Great Innovators, 1900-1950. New York: Oxford University Press, 1972. 536p. illus.
A study of important songs, grouped by their composers. Wilder believes that songwriting has deteriorated since 1950.

137 Wilk, Max. They're Playing Our Song. New York: Atheneum, 1973. 295p.
The stories behind the words and music of songwriters from Jerome Kern through Fields, Ruby, Gershwin, Comden, Mercer, Arlen, Berlin, etc. to Sondheim.

138 Williams, Paul. Outlaw Blues; A Book of Rock Music. New York: Dutton, 1969. 191p. bibliog. discog.
This is a collection of articles from Williams's years at Crawdaddy. It became the prototype for books of this genre, and radically changed moods of rock criticism.

139 Williams, Richard. Out of His Head; The Sound of Phil Spector. New York: Outerbridge and Lazard, 1972. 206p. illus.
Includes the history of recent record business and introduction to the Los Angeles pop music scene.

140 Wise, Herbert H., ed. Professional Rock and Roll. Hew York: Collier Books, 1967. 94p. paper only.
Emphasizes different aspects of performing, along with instrumentation, equipment, lead singing, touring, agents, roadies, managers, publishers, etc.

141 Wood, Graham. An A-Z of Rock and Roll. London: Studio Vista, 1971. 128p.
Covers about 100 British and American artists who worked in the 1955-1961 period.

PERIODICAL CITATIONS

For many of the same reasons as in the Book Citations section, periodical titles here are listed alphabetically, sequentially numbered, and keyed to references in the section discussing musical genres. Periodicals come and go in the popular music world, depending on interests, finances, and subscriptions sold, and much valuable information is thereby lost. The following twelve periodicals show some stability and should at least be around when this book is two years old; consequently, prices are not noted, nor are street addresses given for foreign publications that tend to move around. The annotations give a physical description of their contents, but please refer to the music genre for more complete details on specific articles or discussions. In addition to periodicals listed, about forty more are printed in the English language (all are indexed in *Popular Music Periodicals Index, 1973-* ; Scarecrow Press), about 75 more in non-English languages, and countless scores of fanzine and very specialized publications.

1 Circus. 1966- . Semi-monthly. 866 United Nations Plaza, New York, NY 10017.
   A rock fan magazine, with lots of color pictures and interviews/biographies; intended for the younger audience.

2 Contemporary Keyboard. 1975- . Bimonthly. P.O. Box 907, Saratoga, CA 95070.
   Emphasizes all aspects of keyboards (piano, organ, electronic music synthesizers, etc.) with reviews, articles on personalitites in both popular and classical modes of music, plus performance tips and instructions.

2a Country Music People. 1970- . Monthly. Sidcup, Kent, England.
   A British magazine that presents critical reviews and articles on all aspects of country music, including old time, western swing, instruments, etc.

2b Country Music Review. 1973- . Monthly. London, England.
   A British magazine that concentrates on the historical development of modern country music, with many articles on personalities from the 1930s, 40s, and 50s.

3 Creem. 1969- . Monthly. Birmingham, Michigan.
   Calls itself "America's only rock 'n' roll magazine." Articles deal with music exclusively. Good reviews.

4 Downbeat. 1934- . Biweekly. 222 W. Adams St., Chicago, IL 60606,
   The oldest continuing jazz magazine, now spreading its coverage to progressive rock music and the new jazz personalities. Good record reviews, transcriptions of improvised jazz solos.

5 Guitar Player. 1967- . Monthly. 348 North Santa Cruz, Los Gatos, CA 95030.
   Emphasizes all aspects of guitars (bass, pedal, acoustic, electric, etc.) with reviews, articles on personalities in both popular and classical modes of music, plus performance instructional guidance.

6 High Fidelity. 1951- . Monthly. P.O. Box 14156, Cincinnati, OH 45214.
   A general magazine with slight coverage of popular music.

7 Melody Maker. 1931- . Weekly. Sutton, Surrey, England.
The best of the five British weeklies devoted to popular music. News, views, and articles on rock, jazz, folk, blues, soul, reggae, country, etc. Unusually good record reviews.

8 Popular Music and Society. 1971- . Quarterly. 318 South Grove Street, Bowling Green, OH 43402.
An interdisciplinary journal "concerned with music in the broadest sense of the term." Scholarly articles.

9 Rolling Stone. 1968- . Biweekly. 625 Third Street, San Francisco, CA 94107.
America's strongest youth culture magazine, describing music as a way of life. Very opinionated, but only about one-third of it is now solely music.

10 Stereo Review. 1958- . Monthly. P.O. Box 2771, Boulder, CO 80302.
A general magazine favoring audio equipment, classical music, and popular music about equally.

DIRECTORY OF LABELS AND STARRED RECORDS

This directory presents, in alphabetical order, the names and addresses of all the American manufacturers of long-playing records cited in this set of books. Similarly, the starred records from all four volumes are listed here, not simply those for the present volume. British, Japanese, Swedish, French, Danish, etc., records can be obtained from specialist stores or importers. Other information here includes some indication of the types of popular music that each firm is engaged in and a listing in label numerical order of all the starred (special importance) records as indicated in the text, along with the entry number for quick reference. For this reason, starred foreign discs are also included in this directory/listing. This directory notes the latest **issuance** of a disc. Some albums may have been reissued from other labels, and they will be found under the label of the latest release. **In all cases, please refer to the main text.** Cross-references are made here where appropriate, especially for "family" names within a label's corporate ownership. To expedite filing and ease of retrieval, this listing of records follows the **numerical order of each label's issues**, ignoring the alphabetical initialisms.

A & M, 1416 North LaBrea Avenue, Hollywood, CA 90028
    specialty: general rock and pop

    SP 4245—Herb Alpert. Greatest Hits. P3.1
    SP 4251—Jimmy Cliff. Wonderful World, Beautiful People. B5.7a
    SP 4257—Fairport Convention. Liege and Lief. F2.49
    SP 4519—Cat Stevens. Greatest Hits. F10.90

ABC, 8255 Beverly Blvd., Los Angeles, CA 90048
    specialty: general

    S 371—Paul Anka. R2.15
    490X—Ray Charles. A Man and His Soul. two discs. B2.40
    654—Impressions. Best. B4.9
    724—B. B. King. Live at the Regal. B1.296
    780—Curtis Mayfield. His Early Years with the Impressions. two discs. B4.11
    781/2—Ray Charles. Modern Sounds in Country and Western Music.
        2 discs. B4.26
    ABCX 1955-1963—Rock 'n' Soul; The History of the Pre-Beatle Decade
        of Rock, 1953-1963. 9 discs. R2.12

Ace of Clubs (English issue)
    specialty: older popular music, jazz

    ACL 1153—Spike Hughes and His All-American Orchestra. J4.47
    ACL 1158—Django Reinhardt and Stephane Grappelli. J6.113

Ace of Hearts (English issue). recently deleted
    specialty: MCA reissues (all forms of popular music)

        AH 21—Andrews Sisters. P2.145
        AH 28—Jack Teagarden. Big T's Jazz. J3.91
        AH 58—Carter Family. A Collection of Favourites. F5.108
        AH 112—Carter Family. More Favourites. F5.111
        AH 119—Jimmy Rushing. Blues I Love to Sing. B1.426
        AH 135—Uncle Dave Macon. F5.31
        AH 168—Jack Teagarden. "J.T." J3.92

Adelphi, P. O. Box 288, Silver Spring, MD 20907
    specialty: blues, folk

Advent, P. O. Box 635, Manhattan Beach, CA 90266
    specialty: blues music

    2803—Johnny Shines. B1.359

Ahura Mazda (c/o Southern Record Sales)
    specialty: blues

    AMS 2002—Robert Pete Williams. B1.130

All Platinum, 96 West Street, Englewood, NJ 07631
    specialty: blues and soul, mainly from the Chess catalog which it
      purchased; see also CHESS records

    2ACMB 201—Howlin' Wolf. A.K.A. Chester Burnett. two discs. B1.284
    2ACMB 202—Little Walter. Boss Blues Harmonica. two discs. B1.297
    2ACMB 203—Muddy Waters. A.K.A. McKinley Morganfield. two discs.
      B1.303

Alligator, P.O. Box 11741, Fort Dearborn Station, Chicago, IL 60611
    specialty: blues

    AL 4706—Koko Taylor. I Got What It Takes. B1.407

Angel, 1750 N. Vine Street, Hollywood, CA 90028
   specialty: classical and classical interpretations of popular music

   S 36060—New England Conservatory Ragtime Ensemble. Scott Joplin:
   The Red Back Book. J2.28

Antilles, 7720 Sunset Blvd., Los Angeles, CA 90046
   specialty: folk and pop

   AN 7017—Shirley Collins and the Albion Country Band. No Roses. F2.47

Apple, 1750 N. Vine Street, Hollywood, CA 90028
   specialty: rock

   SKBO 3403/4—The Beatles. 1962-1970. four discs. R4.3/4.

Argo (English issue)
   specialty: folk (British), classical, spoken word

   ZDA 66-75—Ewan MacColl and Peggy Seeger. The Long Harvest. ten discs.
   F2.23

Arhoolie, 10341 San Pablo Avenue, El Cerrito, CA 94530
   specialty: blues, old time music, ethnic music

   1001—Mance Lipscomb, Texas Sharecropper and Songster. B1.213
   1007—Mercy Dee Walton. B1.369
   1008—Alex Moore. B1.228
   1021—Fred McDowell. Delta Blues. B1.120
   1027—Fred McDowell. volume 2. B1.119
   1028—Big Mama Thornton. In Europe. B1.408
   1036—Juke Boy Bonner. I'm Going Back to the Country Where They Don't
   Burn the Buildings Down. B1.146
   1038—Clifton Chenier. Black Snake Blues. B1.324
   1066—Earl Hooker. His First and Last Recordings. B1.279
   2003—Lowell Fulson. B1.332
   2004—Joe Turner. Jumpin' the Blues. B1.431
   2007—Lightnin' Hopkins. Early Recordings, v.1. B1.182
   2010—Lightnin' Hopkins. Early Recordings, v.2. B1.182
   2011—Robert Pete Williams. Angola Prisoner's Blues. B1.131
   2012—Prison Worksongs. B1.55
   2015—Robert Pete Williams. Those Prison Blues. B1.134
   5011—Snuffy Jenkins. Carolina Bluegrass. F6.82

Arista, 6 West 57th St., New York, NY 10019
  specialty: rock, jazz, pop

  B 6081—The Monkees. Re-Focus R3.20

Asch *See* Folkways

Asylum, 962 N. LaCienega, Los Angeles, CA 90069

  SD 5068—Eagles. Desperado. R7.12
  7E-1017—Jackson Browne. Late for the Sky. F10.3

Atco, 75 Rockefeller Plaza, New York, NY 10019
  specialty: blues, rock, soul, rhythm 'n' blues

  SD 33-226—Buffalo Springfield. Again. R7.6
  SD33-259—Jerry Jeff Walker. Mr. Bojangles. F10.92
  SD33-266—King Curtis. Best. B4.44
  SD33-291—Cream. Best. R8.1
  SD33-292—Bee Gees. Best, v.1. R4.22
  SD33-371—The Coasters. Their Greatest Recordings: The Early Years. B2.27
  SD33-372—LaVern Baker. Her Greatest Recordings. B2.71
  SD33-373—Chuck Willis. His Greatest Recordings. B2.70
  SD33-374—The Clovers. Their Greatest Recordings. B2.26
  SD33-375—The Drifters. Their Greatest Recordings: The Early Years. B2.31
  SD33-376—Joe Turner. His Greatest Recordings. B1.430
  2SA-301—Otis Redding. Best. two discs. B4.28
  SD2-501—Wilson Pickett. Best. two discs. B4.27
  SD2-803—Eric Clapton. History. two discs. R5.16

Atlantic, 75 Rockefeller Plaza, New York, NY 10019
  specialty: jazz, blues, rock, soul, rhythm 'n' blues

  1224—Lennie Tristano. Line Up. J5.87
  1234—Joe Turner. The Boss of the Blues. B1.428
  1237—Charles Mingus. Pithecanthropus Erectus. J5.128
  1238—Jimmy Giuffre. Clarinet. J5.90
  1305—Charles Mingus. Blues and Roots. J5.125
  1317—Ornette Coleman. The Shape of Jazz to Come. J5.112
  1327—Ornette Coleman. Change of the Century. J5.108

Atlantic (cont'd)

1353—Ornette Coleman. This Is Our Music. J5.113
1357—Lennie Tristano. New. J5.88
1364—Ornette Coleman. Free Jazz. J5.109
1378—Ornette Coleman. Ornette. J5.110
SD 1429—Modern Jazz Quartet and Laurindo Almeida. Collaboration. P3.15
SD 1588—Ornette Coleman. Twins. J5.150
S 1594—Roberta Flack. Quiet Fire. B4.64
SD 1598—Gary Burton. Alone at Last. J5.143
SD 1613—Turk Murphy. The Many Faces of Ragtime. J2.26
SD 1614—Billie Holiday. Strange Fruit. J6.123
SD 1639—Art Ensemble of Chicago. J5.136
SD 1652—Modern Jazz Quartet. Blues on Bach. P3.14
SD 7200—Crosby, Stills, Nash and Young. Déjà Vu. R7.10
SD 7213—Aretha Franklin. Young, Gifted and Black. B4.67
SD 7224—Blind Willie McTell. Atlanta Twelve String. B1.125
SD 7225—Professor Longhair. New Orleans Piano. B2.67
SD 7262—Willie Nelson. Shotgun Willie. F8.119
SD 7271—Roberta Flack. Killing Me Softly. B4.63
SD 7291—Willie Nelson. Phases and Stages. F8.118
SD 8004—Ruth Brown. Rock & Roll. B2.73
SD 8020—T-Bone Walker. T-Bone Blues. B1.315
SD 8029—Ray Charles. What'd I Say. B2.41
SD 8054—Ray Charles. Greatest. B2.39
SD 8153—The Drifters. Golden Hits. B2.30
SD 8161/4—History of Rhythm 'n' Blues, v.1-4. four discs. B2.13
SD 8176—Aretha Franklin. Lady Soul. B4.66
SD 8193/4—History of Rhythm 'n' Blues, v. 5-6. two discs. B4.3
SD 8202—Booker T. and the MGs. Best. B4.8
SD 8208/9—History of Rhythm 'n' Blues. v. 7-8. two discs. B4.3
SD 8218—Sam and Dave. Best. B4.30
SD 8236—Led Zeppelin. II. R8.8
SD 8255—Champion Jack Dupree. Blues from the Gutter. B1.329
SD 8289—Marion Williams. Standing Here Wondering Which Way to Go. B3.66
SD 8296—John Prine. F10.82
SD 18204—Aretha Franklin. 10 Years of Gold. B4.65
SD2-305—Chick Corea. Inner Space. two discs. J6.128
SD2-306/7—The Tenor Sax: The Commodore Years. four discs. J6.8
SD2-316—Jazz Years; 25th Anniversary. two discs. J5.101

Atlantic (cont'd)
    SD2-700—Cream. Wheels of Fire. two discs. R8.3
    SD2-904—Carmen McRae. The Great American Songbook. two discs. P2.77
    SD2-906—Aretha Franklin. Amazing Grace. two discs. B3.39
    MM4-100—Mabel Mercer. A Tribute to Mabel Mercer on the Occasion of Her
        75th Birthday. four discs. P2.78

Atteiram, P.O. Box 418, 2871 Janquil Drive, Smyrna, GA 30080
    specialty: bluegrass

Audiofidelity, 221 W. 57th Street, New York, NY 10019
    specialty: folk, jazz

Basf, 221 W. 57th Street, New York, NY 10019
    specialty: jazz

Bandstand (c/o Southern Record Sales)
    specialty: big bands
    7106—Screwballs of Swingtime. P4.3

Barclay (France)
    specialty: general
    920067—Stuff Smith and Stephane Grappelli. Stuff and Steff. J4.148

Barnaby, 816 N. LaCienega Blvd., Los Angeles, CA 90069
    specialty: rock and roll
    BR 4000/1—Cadence Classics, v. 1-2. two discs. R2.3
    BR 6006—Everly Brothers. Greatest Hits. two discs. R2.18

Barnaby/Candid (recently deleted from CBS)
    specialty: jazz, blues
    Z 30246—Otis Spann. Is the Blues. B1.310
    Z 30247—Lightnin' Hopkins. In New York. B1.183
    Z 30562—Cecil Taylor. Air. J5.132
    KZ 31034—Charles Mingus. The Candid Recordings. J5.126
    KZ 31290—Otis Spann. Walking the Blues. B1.311

Bear Family (West Germany)
    specialty: old time music
    FV 12.502—Jules Allen. The Texas Cowboy. F7.19
    FV 15.507—Dock Walsh. F5.79

Bearsville, 3300 Warner Blvd., Burbank, CA 91505
    specialty: rock

Bell, 6 West 57th Street, New York, NY 10019
  specialty: general pop

  1106—The Fifth Dimension. Greatest Hits on Earth. P2.137

Biograph, 16 River Street, Chatham, NY 12037
  specialty: jazz, blues, popular

  BLP C3—Boswell Sisters. 1932-1935. P2.135
  BLP C4—Mississippi John Hurt. 1928: His First Recordings. B1.190
  BLP C7/8—Ted Lewis. 1926-1933, v. 1-2. two discs. P5.13
  BLP 1008Q—Scott Jopkin. Ragtime, v. 2. J2.10
  BLP 12003—Blind Blake. v.1. B1.145
  BLP 12005—Chicago Jazz, 1923-1929, v. 1. J3.63
  BLP 12022—Ethel Waters. Jazzin' Babies Blues, v. 1. B1.411
  BLP 12023—Blind Blake. v.2. B1.145
  BLP 12026—Ethel Waters. v.2. B1.411
  BLP 12029—Skip James, Early Recordings. B1.198
  BLP 12031—Blind Blake. v.3. B1.145
  BLP 12037—Blind Blake. v.4. B1.145
  BLP 12043 Chicago Jazz, 1923-1929, v.2. J3.63
  BLP 12050—Blind Blake. v.5. B1.145

Birchmount (Canada)
  specialty: country and popular

  BM 705—Hank Williams. In the Beginning. F8.41

Black Lion, 221 West 57th Street, New York, NY 10019
  specialty: jazz and blues

  BL 173—Barney Kessel and Stephane Grappelli. Limehouse Blues. J6.106

Black Lion (England)
  specialty: jazz and blues

  BLP 30147—Jimmy Witherspoon. Ain't Nobody's Business! B1.433

Blue Goose, 245 Waverly Place, New York, NY 10014
  specialty: blues, jazz

Blue Horizon (England) recently deleted
  specialty: blues

  7-63222—Otis Rush. This One's a Good 'Un. B1.357
  7-63223—Magic Sam. 1937-1969. B1.346

Blue Note, 6920 Sunset Blvd., Hollywood, CA 90028
  specialty: jazz and blues

  BST 81201/2—Sidney Bechet. Jazz Classics, v.1-2. two discs. J3.20
  BST 81503/4—Bud Powell. Amazing, v.1-2. two discs. J5.31
  BST 81505/6—J. J. Johnson. The Eminent, v.1-2. two discs. J5.64

Blue Note (cont'd)
>BST 81518—Horace Silver with the Jazz Messengers. J5.36
>BST 81521/2—Art Blakey. A Night at Birdland. two discs. J5.9
>BST 84003—Art Blakey. Moanin'. J5.8
>BST 84008—Horace Silver. Finger Poppin'. J5.35
>BST 84067—Jackie McLean. Bluesnik. J5.66
>BST 84077—Dexter Gordon. Doin' All Right. J5.56
>BST 84163—Eric Dolphy. Out to Lunch. J5.155
>BST 84194—Wayne Shorter. Speak No Evil. J5.161
>BST 84237—Cecil Taylor. Unit Structures. J5.135
>BST 84260—Cecil Taylor. Conquistador. J5.133
>BST 84346—Thad Jones—Mel Lewis Orchestra. Consummation. J4.171
>BNLA 158/160—Blue Note's Three Decades of Jazz, v.1-3. six discs. J1.6
>BNLA 401-H—Sonny Rollins. 2 discs. J5.76
>BNLA 456—H2—Lester Young. Aladdin Sessions. two discs. J4.124
>BNLA 507—H2—Fats Navarro. Prime Source. two discs. J5.26
>BNLA 533—H2—T-Bone Walker. Classics of Modern Blues. two discs. B1.313
>BNLA 579—H2—Thelonious Monk. Complete Genius. two discs. J5.24

Blues Classics, 10341 San Pablo Ave., El Cerrito, CA 94530
>specialty: blues, gospel

>BC 1—Memphis Minnie, v.1. B1.388
>BC 2—The Jug, Jook and Washboard Bands. B1.414
>BC 3—Sonny Boy Williamson, No. 1., v.1. B1.136
>BC 4—Peetie Wheatstraw. B1.253
>BC 5/7—Country Blues Classics, v.1-3. B1.14
>BC 9—Sonny Boy Williamson, No. 2. The Original. B1.318
>BC 11—Blind Boy Fuller. B1.168a
>BC 12—Detroit Blues: The Early 1950s. B1.58
>BC 13—Memphis Minnie, v.2. B1.388
>BC 14—Country Blues Classics, v.4. B1.14
>BC 16—Texas Blues: The Early 50s. B1.101
>BC 17/19—Negro Religious Music, v.1-3. three discs. B3.17
>BC 20—Sonny Boy Williamson, No. 1., v.2. B1.136
>BC 24—Sonny Boy Williamson, No. 1., v.3. B1.136

Blues on Blues (c/o Southern Records Sales) recently deleted
>specialty: blues

Bluesville (recently deleted)
>specialty: blues

>BV 1044—Lonnie Johnson and Victoria Spivey. Idle Hours. B1.208

Bluesway *See* ABC

Boogie Disease, Box 10925, St. Louis, MO 63135
>specialty: blues

Boogie Woogie (c/o Southern Records Sales)
　　specialty: jazz and blues

　　BW 1002—Meade Lux Lewis. J6.94

Brunswick (recently deleted); see also MCA
　　specialty: jazz and soul

　　BL 754185—Jackie Wilson. Greatest Hits. B4.32

Buddah, 810 Seventh Ave., New York, NY 10019
　　specialty: pop, soul, gospel

　　2009—Staple Singers. Best. B3.54
　　BDS 5070—Edwin Hawkins Singers. Oh Happy Day. B3.40
　　BDS 5665-2—Steve Goodman. Essential. two discs. F10.58

CBS, 51 West 52nd Street, New York, NY 10019
　　specialty: general; formerly known as Columbia

　　CL 997—Count Basie. One O'Clock Jump. J4.17
　　CL 1098—The Sound of Jazz. J1.22
　　CL 1228—Jo Stafford. Greatest Hits. P2.79
　　CL 1230—Rosemary Clooney. Rosie's Greatest Hits. P2.96
　　CL 1780—James P. Johnson. Father of the Stride Piano. J6.30
　　CL 2604—Sophie Tucker. The Last of the Red Hot Mamas. P2.130.
　　CL 2639—Chick Webb. Stompin' at the Savoy. J4.52
　　CL 2830—Paul Whiteman. P5.19
　　CS 1065—Bill Monroe. 16 All Time Greatest Hits. F6.41
　　CS 1034—Roy Acuff. Greatest Hits. F8.17
　　CS 8004—Mitch Miller. Sing Along with Mitch. P2.139
　　CS 8158—Marty Robbins. Gunfighter Ballads and Trail Songs. F7.30
　　PC 8163—Miles Davis. Kind of Blue. J5.151
　　PC 8271—Miles Davis. Sketches of Spain. J5.85
　　CS 8638—Mitch Miller. Mitch's Greatest Hits. P2.138
　　CS 8639—Marty Robbins. Greatest Hits. R1.17
　　CS 8807—Barbra Streisand. P2.126
　　CS 8845—Lester Flatt and Earl Scruggs. Carnegie Hall. F6.28
　　KCS 8905—Bob Dylan. The Times They Are A-Changin'. F10.19
　　PC 9106—Miles Davis. My Funny Valentine. J5.153
　　KCS 9128—Bob Dylan. Bringing It Back Home. F10.14
　　PC 9428—Miles Davis. Milestones. J5.152
　　KCS 9463—Bob Dylan. Greatest Hits, v.1. F10.16
　　CS 9468—18 King Size Country Hits. F8.11
　　CS 9478—Johnny Cash. Greatest Hits, v.1. F8.19
　　G 31224—Count Basie. Super Chief. two discs. J4.18
　　KG 31345—Johnny Mathis. All Time Greatest Hits. two discs. P2.13
　　PC 31350—Simon and Garfunkel. Greatest Hits. F10.46
　　KC 31352—Weather Report. I Sing the Body Electric. J6.138
　　KG 31361—Marty Robbins. All Time Greatest Hits. two discs. F8.78
　　KG 31364—Ray Price. All Time Greatest Hits. two discs. F8.76

CBS (cont'd)

KG 31379—Mahalia Jackson. Great. two discs. B3.42

KG 31547—Benny Goodman. All Time Hits. two discs. J4.58

KG 31564—Eddie Condon's World of Jazz. two discs. J3.66

KG 31571—Ethel Waters. Greatest Years. two discs. P2.86

KG 31588—Percy Faith. All Time Greatest Hits. two discs. P5.79

KG 31595—The Gospel Sound, v.2. two discs. B3.9

G 31617—Teddy Wilson All Stars. two discs. J4.122

KC 31758—Earl Scruggs. Live at Kansas State. F6.124

KG 32064—Duke Ellington. Presents Ivie Anderson. two discs. P5.10

KG 32151—Precious Lord; Gospel Songs of Thomas A. Dorsey. two discs. B3.19

KC 32284—Clifford Brown. The Beginning and the End. J5.38

KG 32338—Luis Russell. His Louisiana Swing Orchestra. two discs. J4.85

KG 32355—A Jazz Piano Anthology. two discs. J6.12

KG 32416—Bob Wills. Anthology. two discs. F7.48

G 32593—Cab Calloway. Hi De Ho Man. two discs. P5.23

KG 32663—Gene Krupa. His Orchestra and Anita O'Day. two discs. P5.36

KC 32708—The Original Boogie Woogie Piano Giants. J6.91

KG 32822—Benny Goodman and Helen Forrest. two discs. P5.11

KG 32945—The World of Swing. two discs. J4.11

CG 33639—Johnny Cash. At Folsom Prison and San Quentin. two discs. F8.18

C2-33682—Bob Dylan. Basement Tapes. two discs. F10.12

C 33882—Lefty Frizzell. Remembering the Greatest Hits. F8.57

CS 9533—Leonard Cohen. Songs. F10.6

CS 9576—The Byrds. Greatest Hits. R7.7

KCS 9604—Bob Dylan. John Wesley Harding. F10.18

PC 9633—Miles Davis. Miles Ahead. J5.83

CS 9655—Art Tatum. Piano Starts Here. J6.38

CS 9660—Ballads and Breakdowns of the Golden Era. F5.1

CS 9670—The Byrds. Sweetheart of the Rodeo. R7.8

KCS 9737—Laura Nyro. New York Tendaberry. F10.80

LE 10043—Lester Flatt and Earl Scruggs. Foggy Mountain Banjo. F6.29

LE 10106—Little Jimmie Dickens. Greatest Hits. F8.53

G 30008—The Story of the Blues, v.1. two discs. B1.17

G 30009—Big Bands Greatest Hits, v.1. two discs. P5.2

C 30036—Bukka White. Parchman Farm. B1.257

G 30126—Bessie Smith. Any Woman's Blues. two discs. B1.394

KC 30130—Santana. Abraxas. R4.42

KC 30322—Janis Joplin. Pearl. R5.20

G 30450—Bessie Smith. Empty Bed Blues. two discs. B1.395

C 30466—Maynard Ferguson. M. F. Horn. J4.168

C 30496—Leroy Carr. Blues Before Sunrise. B1.107

G 30503—Great Hits of R & B. two discs. B2.12

C 30584—Earl Scruggs. Family and Friends. F6.122

G 30592—The Fifties Greatest Hits. two discs. P1.5

G 30628—Charles Mingus. Better Get It in Your Soul. two discs. J5.124

G 30818—Bessie Smith. The Empress. two discs. B1.396

CBS (cont'd)

    KC 30887—Johnny Cash. Greatest Hits, v.2. F8.19

    KC 31067—John McLaughlin. The Inner Mounting Flame. J6.137

    G 31086—The Gospel Sound, v.1. two discs. B3.9

    G 31093—Bessie Smith. Nobody's Blues But Mine. two discs. B1.397

    KC 31170—Blood, Sweat, and Tears. Hits. R4.9

    KG 31213—Big Bands Greatest Hits, v.2. two discs. P5.2

    KC 33894—George Morgan. Remembering. F8.103

    PC 34077—Leonard Cohen. Best. F10.5

    KG ———Robert Johnson. Complete. three discs. B1.110 (to be released).

    C4L 18—Thesaurus of Classic Jazz. four discs. J3.86

    C4L 19—Fletcher Henderson. A Study in Frustration, 1923-1938. four discs. J4.41

    C3L 21—Billie Holiday. Golden Years, v.1. three discs. J6.121

    C3L 22—Mildred Bailey. Her Greatest Performances, 1929-1946. three discs. P2.87

    C2L 24—Joe Venuti and Eddie Lang. Stringing the Blues. two discs. J3.98

    C3L 25—Woody Herman. The Thundering Herds. three discs. J4.46

    C2L 29—Gene Krupa. Drummin' Man. two discs. J4.71

    C3L 32—Jazz Odyssey: The Sound of Chicago. three discs. J3.67

    C3L 33—Jazz Odyssey: The Sound of Harlem. three discs. J3.83

    C3L 35—Original Sounds of the 20s. three discs. P1.9

    C3L 40—Billie Holiday. Golden Years, v.2. three discs. J6.121

    GP 26—Miles Davis. Bitches Brew. two discs. J6.131

    GP 33—Bessie Smith. The World's Greatest Blues Singer. two discs. B1.393

    O2L 160—Benny Goodman. Carnegie Hall Concert. two discs. J4.38

    C2S 823—Tony Bennett. At Carnegie Hall. two discs. P2.2

    C2S 841—Bob Dylan. Blonde on Blonde. two discs. F10.13

    C2S 847—Eubie Blake. The Eighty-Six Years of Eubie Blake. two discs. J2.9

CBS Canada

    specialty: general; formerly known as Columbia

CBS (England)

    specialty: general

    52538—Charlie Christian, v.1. J5.10

    52648—Big Bill Broonzy. Big Bill's Blues. B1.152

    52796—Blacks, Whites and Blues. F3.32

    52797—Recording the Blues. B1.20

    52798—Ma Rainey and the Classic Blues Singers. B1.375

    63288—Screening the Blues. B1.36

    66232—The Story of the Blues, v.2. two discs. B1.17

CBS (France)

    specialty: general

    62581—Charlie Christian, v.2. J5.10

    62853—Benny Goodman. Trio and Quartet, v.1. J4.96

CBS (France) (cont'd)
 62876—Teddy Wilson. Piano Solos. J6.41
 63052—Django Reinhardt. Paris, 1945. J6.116
 63086—Benny Goodman. Trio and Quartet, v.2. J4.96
 63092—Clarence Williams Blue Five, with Louis Armstrong and Sidney
  Bechet. J3.50
 64218—Rare Recordings of the Twenties, v.1. B1.381
 65379/80—Rare Recordings of the Twenties, v.2-3. B1.381
 65421—Rare Recordings of the Twenties, v.4. B1.381
 66310—Miles Davis. Essential. three discs. J5.122
 67264—Duke Ellington. Complete, v.1. two discs. J4.27
 68275—Duke Ellington. Complete, v.2. two discs. J4.27
 80089—Roy Eldridge. Little Jazz. J4.25
 88000—Duke Ellington. Complete, v.3. J4.27
 88001/4—Louis Armstrong. Very Special Old Phonography. eight discs.
  J3.17
 88031—Buck Clayton. 1953-1955. two discs. J4.157
 88035—Duke Ellington. Complete, v.4. two discs. J4.27
 88082—Duke Ellington. Complete, v.5. two discs. J4.27
 88129—Erroll Garner. Play It Again, Erroll. two discs. P3.8
 88137—Duke Ellington. Complete, v.6. two discs. J4.27
 88140—Duke Ellington. Complete, v.7. two discs. J4.27
 J 27—New York Scene in the 1940s. J3.85

CBS (Japan)
 specialty: general

 20 AP 13/4—Stanley Brothers, v.1-2. F6.54 and F9.73

Cadence (recently deleted); most available on *Barnaby* label.
 specialty: pop

 3061—Andy Williams. Million Seller Songs. P2.67

Cadet (recently deleted); see All Platinum
 specialty: rhythm 'n' blues and soul

 S 757—Ramsey Lewis. The "In" Crowd. B4.53

Caedmon, 505 Eighth Avenue, New York, NY 10018
 specialty: spoken word, educational, folk music

 TC 1142/6—Folksongs of Britain, v.1-5. five discs. F2.9
 TC 1162/4—Folksongs of Britain, v.6-8. three discs. F2.9
 TC 1224/5—Folksongs of Britain, v.9-10. two discs. F2.9

Camden *See* RCA

Cameo (recently deleted)
 specialty: pop, rock and roll

 P 7001—Chubby Checker. Twist. R2.16

Canaan, 4800 W. Waco Drive, Waco, TX 76703
    specialty: sacred

Capitol, 1750 N. Vine Street, Hollywood, CA 90028
    specialty: general (country, rock, mood)
    SKAO 143—Ferlin Husky. Best. F8.64
    SKAO 145—Buck Owens. Best, v.3. F8.75
    ST 294—Fred Neil. Everybody's Talkin'. F10.36
    DTBB 264—Jim and Jesse. 20 Great Songs. two discs. F6.33
    DKAO 377—Peggy Lee. Greatest. three discs. P2.75
    SW 425—The Band. Stage Fright. R7.5
    SM 650—Merle Travis. The Merle Travis Guitar. F8.37
    SM 756—Tennessee Ernie Ford. Hymns. F9.39
    ST 884/6—Country Hits of the 40s, 50s, and 60s. three discs. F8.9
    SM 1061—Louvin Brothers. The Family Who Prays. F9.49
    ST 1253—Jean Shepard. This Is F8.146
    ST 1312—Rose Maddox. The One Rose. F8.140
    ST 1380—Tennessee Ernie Ford. Sixteen Tons. F8.56
    ST 1388—Les Baxter. Best. P5.78
    T 1477—Ray Anthony. Hits. P5.77
    SWBO 1569—Judy Garland. At Carnegie Hall. two discs. P2.69
    SWCL 1613—Nat "King" Cole. Story. three discs. P2.5
    ST 2089—Hank Thompson. Golden Hits. F7.47
    ST 2105—Buck Owens. Best, v.1. F8.75
    ST 2180—Kingston Trio. Folk Era. three discs. F4.11
    ST 2373—Merle Haggard. Strangers. F8.111
    ST 2422—Beatles. Rubber Soul. R4.7
    ST 2576—Beatles. Revolver. R4.6
    ST 2585—Merle Haggard. Swinging Doors. F8.112
    DT 2601—Dean Martin. Best. P2.54
    SM 2662—Merle Travis. Best. F8.36
    STFL 2814—Frank Sinatra. Deluxe Set. six discs. P2.16
    ST 2897—Buck Owens. Best, v.2. F8.75
    SKAO 2939—Cannonball Adderley. Best. J6.126
    SKAO 2946—Al Martino. Best. P2.58
    DTCL 2953—Edith Piaf. Deluxe Set. P2.113
    SKAO 2955—The Band. Music from Big Pink. R7.3
    STCL 2988—Judy Garland. Deluxe Set. three discs. P2.70
    T 10457—Django Reinhardt. Best. J6.110
    M 11026—Miles Davis. Birth of the Cool. J5.82
    M 11029—Gerry Mulligan. Tentette. Walking Shoes. J5.97
    M 11058—Duke Ellington. Piano Reflections. J6.17a.
    M 11059—Tadd Dameron. Strictly Bebop. J5.14
    M 11060—Lennie Tristano. Crosscurrents. J5.86
    ST 11082—Merle Haggard. Best of the Best. F8.110
    ST 11177—Supersax Plays Bird. J5.5
    ST 11193—Louvin Brothers. The Great Gospel Singing of the Louvin
        Brothers. F9.50
    SKC 11241—Tex Ritter. An American Legend. three discs. F7.13

Capitol (cont'd)
> ST 11287—Gene Vincent. The Bop That Just Won't Stop (1956). R1.18
> ST 11308—Les Paul and Mary Ford. The World Is Still Waiting for the Sunrise. P2.112
> SVBO 11384—Beach Boys. Spirit of America. two discs. R3.3
> ST 11440—The Band. Northern Lights. R7.4
> SKBO 11537—The Beatles. Rock 'n' Roll Music. two discs. R3.4
> ST 11577—Glen Campbell. Best. F8.98

Capitol (Japan)
> ECR 8178—Rose Maddox. Sings Bluegrass. F6.87

Capricorn, 3300 Warner Blvd., Burbank, CA 91505
> specialty: rock

> 2CP 0108—Duane Allman. An Anthology, v.1. two discs. R4.20
> 2CP 0139—Duane Allman. An Anthology, v.2. two discs. R4.20
> 2CP 0164—Allman Brothers Band. The Road Goes On Forever. two discs. R5.12a

Charisma (England)
> specialty: folk, rock

> CS 5—Steeleye Span. Individually and Collectively. F2.58

Charly (England)

> CR 300-012—Yardbirds, Featuring Eric Clapton. R5.12
> CR 300-013—Yardbirds, Featuring Jeff Bech. R5.12
> CR 300-014—Yardbirds, Featuring Jimmy Page. R5.12

Checker (recently deleted); see All Platinum
> specialty: rhythm 'n' blues, soul

> 3002—Little Milton. Sings Big Blues. B2.60

Chess (recently deleted, but many copies still available); see All Platinum and Phonogram
> specialty: blues

> 1483—Muddy Waters. Folk Singer. B1.302
> 1514—Chuck Berry. Golden Decade, v.1. two discs. B2.37
> 1553—Muddy Waters. They Call Me Muddy Waters. B1.304
> 2CH 50027—Sonny Boy Williamson, No. 2. This Is My Story. two discs. B1.319
> 2CH 50030—The Golden Age of Rhythm 'n' Blues. two discs. B2.10
> 60023—Chuck Berry. Golden Decade, v.2. two discs. B2.37
> 60028—Chuck Berry. Golden Decade, v.3. two discs. B2.37

Chiaroscuro, 221 W. 57th Street, New York, NY 10019
> specialty: jazz

> CR 101—Earl Hines. Quintessential Recording Sessions. J6.26

Chiaroscuro (cont'd)
　　CR 106—Don Ewell. A Jazz Portrait of the Artist. J6.53
　　CR 108—Eddie Condon. Town Hall Concerts, 1944/5. J3.71
　　CR 113—Eddie Condon. Town Hall Concerts, 1944/5. J3.71
　　CR 120—Earl Hines. Quintessential Continued. J6.25

Chrysalis, 1750 N. Vine Street, Hollywood, CA 90028
　　specialty: folk, rock

　　CHR 1008—Steeleye Span. Below the Salt. F2.57
　　CHR 1119—Steeleye Span. Please to See the King. F2.59

Classic Jazz, 43 W. 61st Street, New York, NY 10023
　　specialty: jazz

Classic Jazz Masters (Denmark)
　　specialty: jazz

　　CJM 2/10—Jelly Roll Morton. Library of Congress Recordings. nine discs.
　　　J3.27

Collectors Classics (c/o Southern Record Sales)
　　specialty: bluegrass

　　CC 1/2—Stanley Brothers, v.1-2. two discs. F6.55
　　CC 3—Lonesome Pine Fiddlers. F6.85
　　CC 6—Banjo Classics. F6.2

Columbia *See* CBS

Columbia (England)
　　specialty: pop, mood

　　SCX 6529—Shirley Bassey. Very Best. P2.90

Concert Hall (France)
　　specialty: jazz, pop

　　SJS 1268—Tribute to Fletcher Henderson. J4.12

Concord Jazz, P.O. Box 845, Concord, CA 94522
　　specialty: jazz

Contact (recently deleted)
　　specialty: jazz

　　LP 2—Earl Hines. Spontaneous Explorations. J6.27

Contemporary, 8481 Melrose Place, Los Angeles, CA 90069
　　specialty: jazz

Contour (England)
   specialty: pop, rock

   2870.388–Dell-Vikings. Come and Go With Me. R2.31

Coral, 100 Universal City Plaza, Universal City, CA 91608
   specialty: reissues of MCA material; general

   CXB 6–McGuire Sisters. Best. P2.151

Coral (England)
   specialty: reissues of MCA material; general

   COPS 7453–Gospel Classics. B3.7
   CDMSP 801–Bing Crosby. Musical Autobiography. five discs. P2.11

Coral (West Germany)
   specialty: reissues of MCA material; general

   COPS 6855–Roy Eldridge. Swing Along with Little Jazz. two discs. J4.26
   COPS 7360–The Bands Within the Bands. two discs. J4.91

Cotillion, 75 Rockefeller Plaza, New York, NY 10019
   specialty: rock, contemporary folk

   SD2-400–Woodstock Two. two discs. R4.2
   SD3-500–Woodstock Three. three discs. R4.2

Country Music History (West Germany)
   specialty: old time music

   CMH 211–Jenks "Tex" Carman. The Dixie Cowboy. F7.24

County, Box 191, Floyd, VA 24091
   specialty: old time music, bluegrass

   402–Delmore Brothers. Brown's Ferry Blues, 1933-1941. F8.21
   404–Wade Mainer. F5.90
   405–The Hillbillies. F5.85
   505–Charlie Poole, v.1. F5.69
   506–Gid Tanner, v.1. F5.76
   509–Charlie Poole, v.2. F5.69
   511–Mountain Blues, 1927-1934. F5.15
   515–Mountain Banjo Songs and Tunes. F5.19
   516–Charlie Poole, v.3. F5.69
   518/20–Echoes of the Ozarks, v.1-3. three discs. F5.21
   521–Uncle Dave Macon. Early Recordings, 1925-1935. F5.35
   524–DaCosta Woltz's Southern Broadcasters. F5.61
   526–Gid Tanner, v.2. F5.76
   536–Kessinger Brothers. 1928-1930. F5.114
   540–Charlie Poole, v.4. F5.69
   541/2–Grand Ole Opry Stars. two discs. F8.13
   714–Kenny Baker and Joe Greene. High Country. F6.67
   729–Lilly Brothers. Early Recordings. F6.35

County (cont'd)
       733—Clark Kessinger. Legend. F5.62
       738—Stanley Brothers. That Little Old Country Church House. F9.76
       742—Lilly Brothers. What Will I Leave Behind. F9.48
       749—Springtime in the Mountains. F6.18

Creative World, 1012 S. Robertson Blvd., Los Angeles, CA 90035
       specialty: progressive jazz, Stan Kenton

       ST 1030—Stan Kenton. The Kenton Era. four discs. J4.173

Davis Unlimited, Route 11, 16 Bond Street, Clarksville, TN 37040
       specialty: country, bluegrass, old time music

       DU 33015—Fiddlin' Doc Roberts. Classic Fiddle Tunes Recorded during the
          Golden Age. F5.99
       DU 33030—Vernon Dalhart. Old Time Songs, 1925-1930, v.1. F5.29a

Dawn Club (c/o Southern Record Sales)
       specialty: jazz reissues

       DC 12009—Bud Freeman. Chicagoans in New York. J3.72

Debut (Denmark)
       specialty: modern jazz

       DEB 144—Albert Ayler. Ghosts. J5.140

Decca *See* MCA

Delmark, 4243 N. Lincoln, Chicago, IL 60618
       specialty: jazz, blues

       201—George Lewis. On Parade. J3.15
       202—George Lewis. Doctor Jazz. J3.12
       203—George Lewis. Memorial Album. J3.14
       212—Earl Hines. At Home. J6.23
       DS 420/1—Anthony Braxton. For Alto. two discs. J5.105
       DS 605—Curtis Jones. Lonesome Bedroom Blues. B1.338
       DS 612—Junior Wells. Hoodoo Man Blues. B1.370

Deram (England)
       specialty: rock, folk, pop

       SMK 1117—Shirley Collins. A Favourite Garland. F2.14

Dot, 8255 Beverly Blvd., Los Angeles, CA 90048
       specialty: country, pop

       ABDP 4009—Mac Wiseman. 16 Great Performances. F6.112
       25071—Pat Boone. Pat's Greatest Hits. R2.26
       25201—Billy Vaughan. Golden Hits. P5.91
       25820—Original Hits—Golden Instrumentals. R2.10

Duke, 8255 Beverly Blvd., Los Angeles, CA 90048
    specialty: blues, soul

    DLP 71—Johnny Ace. Memorial Album. B2.48
    DLP 83—Junior Parker. Best. B1.352
    DLP 84—Bobby "Blue" Bland. Best, v.1. B2.49
    DLP 86—Bobby "Blue" Bland. Best, v.2. B2.49

Dunhill, 8255 Beverly Blvd., Los Angeles, CA 90048
    specialty: rock, folk

    DSD 50132—Jimmy Buffett. A White Sport Coat and a Pink Crustacean.
        F10.54
    DXS 50145—Mamas and Papas. 20 Golden Hits. two discs. R3.19

ECM, 810 Seventh Avenue, New Yorkl NY 10019
    specialty: modern jazz
    1014/6—Chick Corea. Piano Improvisations, v.1-3. three discs. J6.130
    1018/9—Circle. Paris Concert. two discs. J5.149
    1035/7—Keith Jarrett. Solo Concerts: Bremen and Lausanne. J6.64

EMI (Denmark)
    specialty: general

    EO 52-81004—Session at Riverside: New York. J4.164
    EO 52-81005—Bobby Hackett and Jack Teagarden. Jazz Ultimate. J4.142
    EO 52-81006—Session at Midnight: Los Angeles. J4.163

EMI (England)
    specialty: general

    Odeon CLP 1817—Django Reinhardt. Legendary. J6.111
    One Up OU 2046—Big 'Uns from the 50s and 60s. R2.2
    Starline SRS 5120—Wanda Jackson. R2.20
    Starline SRS 5129—Johnny Otis. Pioneer of Rock. B2.64

EMI (France)
    specialty: French music, general

    Pathe CO 54-16021/30—Swing Sessions, 1937-1950. ten discs. J1.5
    Pathe SPAM 67.092—Edith Piaf. Recital, 1962. P2.115
    CO 62-80813—Jay McShann's Piano. J6.67

ESP, 5 Riverside Drive, Krumville, NY 12447
    specialty: jazz

    1014—Sun Ra. Heliocentric Worlds, v.1. J5.130
    1017—Sun Ra. Heliocentric Worlds, v.2. J5.130

Eclipse (England)
    specialty: reissues of jazz and nostalgia

    ECM 2051—Django Reinhardt. Swing '35-'39. J6.112

Elektra, 962 N. LaCienega, Los Angeles, CA 90069
  specialty: folk, rock

  EKS 7217—Folk Banjo Styles. F3.30
  EKS 7239—Bob Gibson. Where I'm Bound. F4.9
  EKS 7277—Tom Paxton. Ramblin' Boy. F10.44
  EKS 7280—Judy Collins. Concert. F4.6
  EKS 7287—Phil Ochs. I Ain't Marching Anymore. F10.41
  EKS 7310—Phil Ochs. In Concert. F10.42
  EKS 74007—The Doors. R6.1
  EKS 74014—The Doors. Strange Days. R6.2
  EKS 75032—David Ackles. American Gothic. F10.48
  EKS 75035—Judy Collins. Colors of the Day: Best. R4.27
  EKL-BOX—The Folk Box. four discs. F3.7
  ELK 271/2—Woody Guthrie. Library of Congress Recordings. three discs.
      F10.20
  EKL 301/2—Leadbelly. Library of Congress Recordings. three discs. Bl.209
  7E-2005—Paul Butterfield. Golden Butter. two discs. R5.8

Elektra (England)
  specialty: folk, rock

  K 52035—Dillards. Country Tracks: Best. F6.120

Enterprise, 2693 Union Avenue, Memphis, TN 38112
  specialty: soul, gospel

  1001—Isaac Hayes. Hot Buttered Soul. B4.51

Epic, 51 W. 52nd Street, New York, NY 10019
  specialty: general

  EE 22001—Johnny Hodges. Hodge Podge. J4.109
  EE 22003—Bobby Hackett. The Hackett Horn. J4.140
  EE 22005—The Duke's Men. J4.133
  EE 22007—Chuck Berry and His Stomping Stevedores. J4.131
  EE 22027—Gene Krupa. That Drummer's Band. J4.75
  BN 26246e—The Yardbirds. Greatest Hits. R5.12
  BN 26486—Tammy Wynette. Greatest Hits, v.1. F8.133
  KE 30325—Sly and the Family Stone. Greatest Hits. B4.31
  EG 30473—Johnny Otis Show Live at Monterey. two discs. B4.4
  E 30733—Tammy Wynette. Greatest Hits, v.2. F8.133
  KE 31607—Johnny Nash. I Can See Clearly Now. B4.56
  KE 33396—Tammy Wynette. Greatest Hits, v.3. F8.133
  PE 33409—Jeff Beck. Blow by Blow. R4.8
  BG 33752—George Jones and Tammy Wynette. Me and the First Lady/We
      Go Together. two discs. F8.151
  BG 33779—Jeff Beck. Truth/Beck-Ola. two discs. P5.14.
  BS 33782—Bob Wills/Asleep at the Wheel. Fathers and Sons. two discs.
      F7.49
  B2N 159—Those Wonderful Girls of Stage, Screen and Radio. two discs. P6.86

Epic (cont'd)
B2N 164—Those Wonderful Guys of Stage, Screen and Radio. two discs.
P6.87
CE2E-201/2—Bing Crosby. Story. four discs. P2.8
SN 6042—Swing Street. four discs. J4.10
SN 6044—Jack Teagarden. King of the Blues Trombone. three discs. J3.93
L2N 6072—Encores from the 30s, v.1 (1930-1935). two discs. P1.4 [v.2
never released]

Epic (France)
specialty: general

LN 24269—Johnny Dodds and Kid Ory. J3.24
66212—Count Basie with Lester Young. two discs. J4.19

Eubie Blake Music, 284A Stuyvesant Ave., Brooklyn, NY 11221
specialty: ragtime and reissues

Euphonic, P.O. Box 476, Ventura, CA 93001
specialty: piano jazz, blues

Everest, 10920 Wilshire Blvd. West, Los Angeles, CA 90024
specialty: reissues in folk, blues, and jazz

FS 214—Charlie Parker. v.1. J5.71
FS 216—Otis Spann. B1.305
FS 217—Champion Jack Dupree. B1.327
FS 219—Charlie Christian. At Minton's. J5.11
FS 232—Charlie Parker. v.2. J5.71
FS 253—Fred McDowell. B1.118
FS 254—Charlie Parker. v.3. J5.71
FS 293—Al Haig. Jazz Will O' the Wisp. J6.56

Excello, 1011 Woodland St., Nashville, TN 37206
specialty: blues

DBL 28025—Excello Story. two discs. B4.2

Extreme Rarities, c/o Ken Crawford, 215 Steuben Ave., Pittsburgh, PA 15205
specialty: jazz and soundtrack reissues

Fantasy, 10th and Parker Sts., Berkeley, CA 94710
specialty: blues, jazz

9432—Woody Herman. Giant Step. J4.170
9442—Staple Singers. The Twenty-Fifth Day of December. B3.57
CCR-2—Creedence Clearwater Revival. Chronicle. two discs. R3.6
F 24720—Jack Elliott. Hard Travellin': Songs by Woody Guthrie and Others.
two discs. F4.30

Fat Cat's Jazz, Box 458, Manassas, VA 22110
specialty: jazz

Flying Dutchman, 1133 Avenue of the Americas, New York, NY 10036
specialty: jazz

FD 10146—Coleman Hawkins. Classic Tenors. J4.99

Flying Fish, 3320 N. Halstead, Chicago, IL 60657
specialty: bluegrass and Western swing, blues

101—Hillbilly Jazz. two discs. F7.38

Flyright (England)
specialty: blues, r'n'b

LP 108/9—Memphis Minnie. 1934-1949. two discs. B1.389

Folk Legacy, Sharon Mt. Rd., Sharon, CT 06069
specialty: folk

FSB 20—Harry Cox. Traditional English Love Songs. F2.18
FSA 26—Sarah Ogan Gunning. A Girl of Constant Sorrow. F3.66
FSA 32—Hedy West. Old Times and Hard Times. F3.93
FSI 35—Michael Cooney. The Cheese Stands Alone. F3.62

Folklyric, 10341 San Pablo Avenue, El Cerrito, CA 94530
specialty: blues and folk reissues

9001—Son House. Legendary, 1941/42 Recordings. B1.189

Folkways, 43 W. 61st Street, New Yorkl NY 10023
specialty: folk, blues, jazz

2301/2—Jean Ritchie. Child Ballads in America. two discs. F3.84
2314—American Banjo Tunes and Songs in Scruggs Style. F6.1
2315—Stoneman Family. Banjo Tunes and Songs. F5.74
2316—Ritchie Family. F3.85
2318—Mountain Music Bluegrass Style. F6.17
2320/3—Pete Seeger. American Favorite Ballads. four discs. F4.65
2351—Dock Boggs. v.1. F5.45
2356—Old Harp Singing. F9.11
2392—Dock Boggs. v.2. F5.45
2395/9—New Lost City Ramblers. v.1-5. five discs. F5.66
2409—Country Songs—Old and New. F6.25
2426—Doc Watson and Jean Ritchie. F4.20
2431/2—Newport Folk Festival, 1959/60. v.1-2. two discs. F3.15
2433—Lilly Brothers. Folksongs from the Southern Mountains. F6.36
2445—Pete Seeger. American Favorite Ballads. F4.65

Folkways (cont'd)

    2456—Pete Seeger. Broadsides. F3.89

    2480—Cisco Houston. Sings Songs of the Open Road. F10.67

    2492—New Lost City Ramblers. Play Instrumentals. F5.67

    2501/2—Pete Seeger. Gazette, v.1-2. two discs. F3.89

    2641/5—New Orleans, v.1-5. five discs. J3.2

    2801/11—Jazz, v.1-11. eleven discs. J1.9

    2941/2—Leadbelly. Last Sessions, v.1-2. four discs. B1.115

    2951/3—Anthology of American Folk Music. six discs. F3.4

    3527—Little Brother Montgomery. Blues. B1.223

    3562—Joseph Lamb. A Study in Classic Ragtime. J2.11

    3575—Irish Music in London Pubs. F2.35

    3810—Buell Kazee. His Songs and Music. F3.71

    3903—Dock Boggs. v.3. F5.45

    5212—Woody Guthrie. Dust Bowl Ballads. F10.61

    5264—New Lost City Ramblers. Songs of the Depression. F5.95

    5272—Harry K. McClintock. Haywire Mac. F10.70

    5285—Almanac Singers. Talking Union. F4.1

    5801/2—American History in Ballads and Songs. six discs. F3.21

    FTS 31001—Woody Guthrie. This Land Is Your Land. F10.22

    FTS 31021—Watson Family. F4.19

Fontana, 1 IBM Plaza, Chicago, IL 60611

    specialty: general

    27560—New Vaudeville Band. P2.153

Fontana (England)

    specialty: general

    STL 5269—Martin Carthy. F2.13

Fountain (England)

    specialty: jazz and blues reissues

    FB 301—Ida Cox, v.1. B1.401

    FB 304—Ida Cox, v.2. B1.401

Freedom (England)

    specialty: modern jazz

    FLP 40106—Cecil Taylor. D Trad That's What. J5.134

GHP (West Germany)

    specialty: old time music

    902—Riley Puckett. Old Time Greats. F5.39

    1001—Dock Walsh. F5.81

GNP Crescendo, 9165 Sunset Blvd., Hollywood, CA 90069

    specialty: jazz

GNP Crescendo (cont'd)
    S18—Max Roach-Clifford Brown. In Concert. J5.33
    9003—Coleman Hawkins. The Hawk in Holland. J4.101

Gannet (Denmark)
    specialty: jazz

    GEN 5136/7—Jimmy Yancey, v.1-2. two discs. J6.96

Good Time Jazz, 8481 Melrose Place, Los Angeles, CA 90069
    specialty: dixieland jazz, piano jazz

    10035—Luckey Roberts/Willie "The Lion" Smith. Harlem Piano. J6.34
    10043—Don Ewell. Man Here Plays Fine Piano. J6.50
    10046—Don Ewell. Free 'n' Easy. J6.49
    12001/3—Lu Watters. San Francisco Style, v.1-3. three discs. J3.59
    12004—Kid Ory. 1954. J3.42
    12022—Kid Ory. Tailgate! J3.46
    12048—Bunk Johnson. Superior Jazz Band. J3.10

Gordy, 6464 Sunset Blvd., Hollywood, CA 90028
    specialty: soul, blues

Greene Bottle (c/o Southern Record Sales)
    specialty: blues

Groove Merchant, Suite 3701, 515 Madison Avenue, New York, NY 10022
    specialty: jazz, blues

Gusto, 220 Boscobel Street, Nashville, TN 37213
    specialty: reissues of Starday and King records

Halcyon, Box 4255, Grand Central Station, New York, NY 10017
    specialty: jazz

Halcyon (England)
    specialty: reissues of jazz and nostalgia items

    HAL 5—Annette Hanshaw. Sweetheart of the Thirties. P2.104

Harmony (recently deleted); see also CBS
    specialty: budget line reissues of Columbia and Brunswick items

    HL 7191—Harry James. Songs That Sold a Million. P5.83
    HL 7233—Wilma Lee and Stoney Cooper. Sacred Songs. F9.30
    HL 7290—Bill Monroe. Great. F6.39
    HL 7299—Molly O'Day. Unforgettable. F8.131
    HL 7308—Johnny Bond..Best. F7.6
    HL 7313—Bob Atcher. Best Early American Folksongs. F7.22
    HL 7317—Sons of the Pioneers. Best. F7.16
    HL 7340—Lester Flatt and Earl Scruggs. Great Original Recordings. F6.30
    HL 7382—Gene Autry. Great Hits. F7.4

Harmony (cont'd)

> HL 7396—Carter Family. Great Sacred Songs. F9.26
> HL 7402—Lester Flatt and Earl Scruggs. Sacred Songs. F9.37
> HS 11178—Wilma Lee and Stoney Cooper. Sunny Side of the Mountain. F6.73
> HS 11334—Roy Acuff. Waiting for My Call to Glory. F9.15
> H 30609—Johnny Ray. Best. R2.22

Harmony (Canada)

> HEL 6004—Jazzmen in Uniform, 1945, Paris. J1.4

Herwin, 45 First Street, Glen Cove, NY 11542
> specialty: jazz and blues reissues

> 101—Freddie Keppard. J3.6
> 106—King Oliver. The Great 1923 Gennetts. J3.7
> 202—Bessie Johnson. 1928-29. B3.43
> 203—Sanctified, v.2: God Gave Me the Light, 1927-1931. B3.5
> 204—Blind Joe Taggart. B3.61
> 207—Sanctified, v.3: Whole World in His Hands, 1927-1936. B3.27
> 208—Cannon's Jug Stompers. two discs. B1.419
> 401—They All Played the Maple Leaf Rag. J2.8

Hi, 539 W. 25th Street, New York, NY 10001
> specialty: soul

> XSHL 32070—Al Green. Let's Stay Together. B4.48

Hilltop (recently deleted)
> specialty: Mercury budget reissues of country material through Pickwick records

> JS 6036—Louvin Brothers. F8.29
> JS 6093—Lester Flatt and Earl Scruggs. F6.27

Historical, P.O. Box 4204, Bergen Station, Jersey City, NJ 07304
> specialty: reissued jazz, blues, and country materials

> HLP 9—Benny Moten. Kansas City Orchestra, 1923-29. J4.83
> HLP 10—Chicago Southside, 1926-1932, v.1. J3.64
> HLP 24—The Territory Bands, 1926-1931, v.1. J3.103
> HLP 26—The Territory Bands, 1926-1931, v.2. J3.103
> HLP 30—Chicago Southside, 1926-1932, v.2. J3.64
> HLP 8001—Fields Ward. Buck Mountain Band. F5.101
> HLP 8004—Stoneman Family. 1927-1928. F5.73

Imperial (recently deleted); see United Artists
> specialty: blues and soul

> LP 9141—Smiley Lewis. I Hear You Knocking. B2.58

Impulse, 8255 Beverly Blvd., Los Angeles, CA 90048
   specialty: jazz (modern and mainstream)

   AS 6—John Coltrane. Africa Brass. J5.115
   AS 10—John Coltrane. Live at the Village Vanguard. J5.120
   AS 12—Benny Carter. Further Definitions. J4.24
   AS 77—John Coltrane. A Love Supreme. J5.121
   AS 95—John Coltrane. Ascension. J5.116
   AS 9108—Earl Hines. Once Upon a Time. J4.69
   AS 9148—John Coltrane. Cosmic Music. J5.117
   AS 9183—Charlie Haden. Liberation Suite. J5.156
   AS 9229-2—Pharoah Sanders. Nest. two discs. J5.158
   ASH 9253-3—The Saxophone. three discs. J6.5
   ASY 9272-3—The Drum. three discs. J6.2
   ASY 9284-3—The Bass. three discs. J6.1

Increase (recently deleted); see All Platinum
   specialty: rock and roll and rhythm 'n' blues in a disc jockey simulation

   2000/12—Cruisin', 1955-1967. thirteen discs. R2.4

Island, 7720 Sunset Blvd., Los Angeles, CA 90046
   specialty: folk and reggae music

   SW 9329—The Wailers. Catch a Fire. B5.9
   ILPS 9330—Toots and the Maytals. Funky Kingston. B5.8
   ILPS 9334—The Chieftains. 5. F2.39

Island (England)
   specialty: folk and reggae music

   FOLK 1001—The Electric Muse. four discs. F2.45
   HELP 25—Albion Country Band. F2.46a

Jamie (recently deleted)
   specialty: rock and roll

   S 3026—Duane Eddy. 16 Greatest Hits. R2.17

Jazum, 5808 Northumberland St., Pittsburgh, PA 15217
   specialty: jazz and nostalgia reissues

   21—Boswell Sisters. P2.136
   30/1—Boswell Sisters. two discs. P2.136
   43/4—Boswell Sisters. two discs. P2.136

Jazz Archives, P.O. Box 194, Plainview, NY 11805
   specialty: jazz

   JA 6—Charlie Christian. Together with Lester Young, 1940. J5.12
   JA 18—Lester Young. Jammin' with Lester. J4.127
   JA 23—Charlie Christian, with Benny Goodman's Sextet, 1939/41. J5.13

Jazz Composers' Orchestral Association, 6 West 96th Street, New York, NY 10024
specialty: modern jazz

JCOA 1001/2—Jazz Composers' Orchestra. two discs. J5.123

Jazzology, 3008 Wadsworth Mill Place, Decatur, GA 30032
specialty: jazz

Jazz Piano (Denmark)
specialty: piano jazz reissues

JP 5003—Library of Congress Sessions. J6.84

Jim Taylor Presents, 12311 Gratiot Ave., Detroit, MI 48205
specialty: mainstream jazz and blues

JTP 103—Olive Brown and Her Blues Chasers. B1.398

John Edwards Memorial Foundation, c/o Center for Study of Folklore &
Mythology, UCLA, Los Angeles, CA 90024
specialty: reissues of blues, and country and western material

Kama Sutra, 810 Seventh Ave., New York, NY 10019
specialty: rock and roll

KSBS 2010—Sha Na Na. Rock & Roll Is Here to Stay! R2.51
KSBS 2013—Lovin' Spoonful. Very Best. R3.18

Kapp (recently deleted); see also MCA
specialty: mood

3530—Roger Williams. Gold Hits. P3.24
3559—Jack Jones. Best. P2.48

Kent, 96 West Street, Englewood, NJ 07631
specialty: blues

KST 533—B. B. King. From the Beginning. two discs. B1.294
KST 534—Johnny Otis. Cold Shot. B1.351
KST 537—Jimmy Reed. Roots of the Blues. two discs. B1.232
KST 9001—Elmore James. Legend, v.1. B1.286
KST 9010—Elmore James. Legend, v.2. B1.286
KST 9011—B. B. King. 1949-1950. B1.291

Kicking Mule, P.O. Box 3233, Berkeley, CA 94703
specialty: blues, folk, and guitar albums

106—Rev. Gary Davis. Ragtime Guitar. J2.25

King, 220 Boscobel St., Nashville, TN 37213
specialty: blues, bluegrass and country music, soul

541—Hank Ballard. Greatest Jukebox Hits. B2.36
552—Don Reno and Red Smiley. F6.47

King (cont'd)
> 553—Cowboy Copas. All Time Hits. F8.49
> 615—Stanley Brothers. F6.58
> 826—James Brown. Live at the Apollo, v.1. B4.24
> 848— Don Reno and Red Smiley. F6.47
> 872—Stanley Brothers. America's Finest Five String Banjo Hootenanny.
>   F6.59
> 919—James Brown. Unbeatable Sixteen Hits. B4.25
> 1022—James Brown. Live at the Apollo, v.2. B4.24
> 1059—Freddy King. Hideaway. B1.340
> 1065—Don Reno. Fastest Five Strings Alive. F6.99
> 1081—Little Willie John. Free At Last. B2.61
> 1086—Wynonie Harris. Good Rockin' Blues. B1.423
> 1110—James Brown Band. Sho Is Funky Down Here. B4.40
> 1130—Roy Brown. Hard Luck Blues. B2.38

King Bluegrass, 6609 Main Street, Cincinnati, OH 45244
> specialty: bluegrass

Kudu, 6464 Sunset Blvd., Hollywood, CA 90028
> specialty: soul

> 05—Esther Phillips. From a Whisper to a Scream. B4.74

Leader (England)
> specialty: folk

> LEAB 404—Copper Family. A Song for Every Season. four discs. F2.16

Lemco, 6609 Main Street, Cincinnati, OH 45244
> specialty: bluegrass

> 611—J. D. Crowe. The Model Church. F9.31
> 612—Red Allen and the Allen Brothers. Allengrass. F6.113

Library of Congress, Washington, D.C.
> specialty: folk and ethnic music, blues; see also Flyright

> LBC 1/15—Folk Music in America, v.1-15. fifteen discs. F3.9 [in progress]
> AAFS L 26/7—American Sea Songs and Shanties, v.1-2. two discs. F3.25
> AAFS L 62—American Fiddle Tunes. F3.16

London, 539 W. 25th Street, New York, NY 10001
> specialty: general

> NPS 4—Rolling Stones. Let It Bleed. R4.16
> PS 114—Edmundo Ros. Rhythms of the South. P5.112
> PS 483—Mantovani. Golden Hits. P5.100
> PS 492—John Mayall. Blues Breakers. R5.10
> PS 493—Rolling Stones. Got Live (If You Want It). R4.14
> PS 534—John Mayall. Alone. R5.9
> PS 539—Rolling Stones. Beggar's Banquet. R4.13

London (cont'd)
> NPS 606/7–Rolling Stones. Hot Rocks, v.1. two discs. R4.15
> XPS 610–Mantovani. 25th Anniversary Album. P5.101
> NPS 626/7–Rolling Stones. Hot Rocks, v.2. two discs. R4.15
> XPS 906–Mantovani. All Time Greatest. P5.99

MCA, 100 Universal City Plaza, Universal City, CA 91608
> specialty: general; formerly known as Decca, and consequently many older
> records were renumbered

> DL 8044–Kansas City Jazz. J3.101
> DL 8671–Gateway Singers. At the Hungry i. F4.8
> DL 8731–Bill Monroe. Knee Deep in Bluegrass. F6.45
> DL 8782–Sister Rosetta Tharpe. Gospel Train. B3.62
> DL 9034/8–Al Jolson. Story. five discs. P2.12
> DL 75326–Conway Twitty and Loretta Lynn. Lead Me On. F8.153
> DS 79175–The Who. Live at Leeds. R4.17
> DL 9221–Earl Hines. Southside Swing, 1934/5. J4.68
> DL 9222/3–Chick Webb, v.1-2. two discs. J4.51
> DL 9224–Duke Ellington, v.1: In the Beginning (1926/8). J4.28
> DL 9227/8–Fletcher Henderson, v.1-2. two discs. J4.40
> DL 9236–Jay McShann. New York–1208 Miles (1941-1943). J4.80
> DL 79237/40–Jimmie Lunceford, v.1-4. four discs. J4.77
> DL 9241–Duke Ellington, v.2: Hot in Harlem (1928/9). J4.28
> DL 9242–Big Bands Uptown, 1931-1943, v.1. J3.78
> DL 9243–Jan Savitt. The Top Hatters, 1939-1941. P5.44
> DL 9247–Duke Ellington, v.3: Rockin' in Rhythm (1929/31). J4.28
> 1–Loretta Lynn. Greatest Hits, v.1. F8.130
> 81–Jimmy Martin. Good 'n' Country. F6.38
> 86–Red Foley. Songs of Devotion. F9.38
> 104–Bill Monroe. Bluegrass Instrumentals. F6.43
> 110–Bill Monroe. The High, Lonesome Sound. F6.44
> 115–Jimmy Martin. Big 'n' Country Instrumentals. F6.37
> 131–Bill Monroe. A Voice from On High. F9.61
> 420–Loretta Lynn. Greatest Hits, v.2. F8.130
> 527–Bill Monroe. I Saw the Light. F9.60
> 2106–Neil Diamond. His 12 Greatest Hits. P2.33
> 2128–Elton John. Greatest Hits. R4.10
> DEA 7-2–Those Wonderful Thirties. two discs. P1.14
> DXS 7181–Webb Pierce. Story. two discs. F8.30
> 2-4001–Bill Anderson. Story. two discs. F8.44
> 2-4005–Inkspots. Best. two discs. B2.22
> 2-4006–Billie Holiday. Story. two discs. J6.122
> 2-4008–Fred Waring. Best. two discs. P2.141
> 2-4009–Buddy Holly. two discs. R1.8
> 2-4010–Bill Haley and His Comets. Best. two discs. R1.7
> 2-4018–A Jazz Holiday. two discs. J3.82
> 2-4019–Art Tatum. Masterpieces. two discs. J6.36
> 2-4031–Kitty Wells. Story. two discs. F8.132
> 2-4033–Four Aces. Best. two discs. P2.149

MCA (cont'd)

    2-4038—Patsy Cline. Story. two discs. F8.129
    2-4039—Mills Brothers. Best. two discs. P2.140
    2-4040—Ernest Tubb. Story. two discs. F8.38
    2-4041—Guy Lombardo. Sweetest Music This Side of Heaven. two discs.
      P5.37
    2-4043—Bert Kaempfert. Best. two discs. P5.85
    2-4047—Ella Fitzgerald. Best. two discs. P2.68
    2-4050—Count Basie. Best. two discs. J4.13
    2-4052—The Weavers. Best. F4.21
    2-4053—Red Foley. Story. two discs. F8.101
    2-4056—Carmen Cavallaro. Best. two discs. P5.106
    2-4067—The Who. A Quick One (Happy Jack). two discs. R4.19
    2-4068—The Who. Magic Bus. two discs. R4.18
    2-4071—Eddie Condon. Best. two discs. J3.68
    2-4072—Xavier Cugat. Best. two discs. P5.107
    2-4073—Jimmy Dorsey. Best. two discs. P5.26
    2-4076—Glen Gray and the Casa Loma Orchestra. Best. two discs. P5.32
    2-4077—Woody Herman. Best. two discs. J4.43
    2-4079—Louis Jordan. Best. B2.45
    2-4083—Bob Crosby. Best. two discs. J3.54
    2-4090—Bill Monroe. Best. two discs. F6.42
    2-8001—American Graffiti. two discs. R2.1
    2-11002—That's Entertainment! two discs. P6.85

MCA (England)

    specialty: general; formerly Decca American

    MCFM 2720—Dick Haymes. Best. P2.45
    MCFM 2739—Connie Boswell. Sand in My Shoes. P2.68a

MCA (France)

    specialty: general; jazz reissues from American Decca

    510.065—Lucky Millinder. Lucky Days, 1941-1945. B2.22a
    510.071—The Swinging Small Bands, v.1. J4.93
    510.085—James P. Johnson. J6.29
    510.088—The Swinging Small Bands, v.2. J4.93
    510.090—Kings and Queens of Ivory, v.1. J6.15 (set in progress)
    510.111—The Swinging Small Bands, v.3. J4.93
    510.123—The Swinging Small Bands, v.4. J4.03

MCA (West Germany)

    specialty: general; reissued Decca material

    628.334—Tex Ritter. The Singing Cowboy. two discs. F7.14

MGM, 810 Seventh Ave., New York, NY 10019
    specialty: general

    GAS 140—Osborne Brothers. F6.93
    SE 3331—Hank Williams. I Saw the Light. F9.85

MGM (cont'd)
SE 4946—Tompall and the Glaser Brothers. Greatest Hits. F8.128

MGM (England)
specialty: general; reissues of American MGM product

2353.053—Hank Williams. Greatest Hits, v.1. F8.40
2353.071—Billy Eckstine. Greatest Hits. P2.34
2353.073—Hank Williams. Greatest Hits, v.2. F8.40
2353.118—Hank Williams. Collector's, v.1. F8.39
2683.016—Hank Williams. Memorial Album. two discs. F8.42
2683.046—Hank Williams. On Stage! two discs. F8.43

MPS (West Germany)
specialty: jazz

20668—Oscar Peterson. Exclusively for My Friends, v.1. J6.69
20693—Oscar Peterson. Exclusively for My Friends, v.6. J6.69
206696—Oscar Peterson. Exclusively for My Friends, v.2. J6.69
206701—Oscar Peterson. Exclusively for My Friends, v.3. J6.69
206718—Oscar Peterson. Exclusively for My Friends, v.4. J6.69

Magpie (England)
specialty: blues

PY 18000—Robert Wilkins. Before the Reverence, 1928-1935. B1.129a

Mainstream, 1700 Broadway, New York, NY 10019
specialty: jazz and blues

MRL 311—Lightnin' Hopkins. The Blues. B1.181
MRL 316—Maynard Ferguson. Screamin' Blues. J4.169
MRL 399—Andy Kirk. March, 1936. J4.70

Mamlish, Box 417, Cathedral Station, New York, NY 10025
specialty: blues

S3804—Mississippi Sheiks. Stop and Listen Blues. B1.220

Master Jazz Recordings, 955 Lexington Avenue, New York, NY 10024
specialty: jazz

MJR 8116—Billy Strayhorn. Cue for Saxophone. J4.150

Matchbox (England)
specialty: blues

SDR 213—Little Brother Montgomery. 1930-1969. B1.222

Melodeon, 16 River Street, Chatham, NY 12037
specialty: blues, jazz, bluegrass reissues

MLP 7321—Skip James. Greatest of the Delta Blues Singers. B1.199
MLP 7322—Stanley Brothers. Their Original Recordings. F6.57

Melodeon (cont'd)
  MLP 7323—Blind Willie McTell. The Legendary Library of Congress Session, 1940. B1.127
  MLP 7324—Part Blues. B1.34
  MLP 7325 Red Allen. Solid Bluegrass Sound of the Kentuckians. F6.21

Mercury, 1 IBM Plaza, Chicago, IL 60611
  specialty: general

  MG 20323—Carl Story. Gosepl Quartet Favorites. F9.81
  60232—Dinah Washington. Unforgettable. B4.79
  60587—Frankie Laine. Golden Hits. P2.50
  60621—George Jones. Greatest Hits. F8.26
  60645—Sarah Vaughan. Golden Hits. P2.83
  SR 61268—Dave Dudley. Best. F8.121
  SR 61369—Tom T. Hall. Greatest Hits, v.1. F8.113
  SRM 1-1044—Tom T. Hall. Greatest Hits, v.2. F8.113
  SRM 1-1078—Johnny Rodriguez. Greatest Hits. F8.105
  SRM 1-1101—Bachman-Turner Overdrive. Best. R8.11
  SRM 20803—Jerry Lee Lewis. The Session. two discs. R2.49
  SRM 2-7507—Rod Stewart. Best. R4.44

Milestone, 10th and Parker Streets, Berkeley, CA 94710
  specialty: jazz and blues; reissues from the Riverside catalog

  M 2012—Earl Hines. A Monday Date, 1928. J6.21
  47002—Bill Evans. Village Vanguard Session. two discs. J6.55
  47003—Wes Montgomery. While We're Young. two discs. J6.108
  47004—Thelonious Monk. Pure Monk. two discs. J6.32
  47007—Sonny Rollins. Freedom Suite, Plus. two discs. J5.77
  47018—Jelly Roll Morton. 1923-1924. two discs. J6.33
  47019 Bix Beiderbecke and the Chicago Cornets. two discs. J3.53
  47020—New Orleans Rhythm Kings. two discs. J3.57
  47021—Ma Rainey. two discs. B1.392

Monmouth/Evergreen, 1697 Broadway, Suite 1201, New York, NY 10019
  specialty: jazz, reissued stage and show soundtracks, reissued nostalgia-pop music

  MES 6816—Ray Noble and Al Bowlly, v.1. P5.102
  MES 6917—Maxine Sullivan and Bob Wilber. The Music of Hoagy Carmichael. P2.82
  MES 7021—Ray Noble and Al Bowlly, v.2. P5.102
  MES 7024/5—Claude Thornhill. two discs. P5.89 and P5.90
  MES 7027—Ray Noble and Al Bowlly, v.3. P5.102
  MES 7033—Jack Hylton, v.1. P5.98
  MES 7039/40—Ray Noble and Al Bowlly, v.4-5. two discs. P5.102
  MES 7055—Jack Hylton, v.2. P5.98
  MES 5056—Ray Noble and Al Bowlly, v.6. P5.102

Monument, 51 W. 52nd Street, New York, NY 10019
specialty: country music

18045—Roy Orbison. Very Best. R2.21
Z 30817—Kris Kristofferson. Me and Bobby McGee. F10.24
Z 32259—Arthur Smith. Battling Banjos. F6.105

Motown, 6255 Sunset Blvd., Hollywood, CA 90028
specialty: soul

663—The Supremes. Greatest Hits. two discs. B4.12
702-S2—Gladys Knight and the Pips. Anthology. two discs. B4.68
MS5-726—Motown Story; The First Decade. five discs. B4.5
782-A3—The Temptations. Anthology. three discs. B4.18
793-R3—Smokey Robinson and the Miracles. Anthology. three discs. B4.29

Muse, Blanchris, Inc., 160 W. 71st Street, New York, NY 10023
specialty: jazz and blues

MR 5087—Elmore James/Eddie Taylor. Street Talkin'. B1.368

Muskadine, Box 635, Manhattan Beach, CA 90266
specialty: blues reissues

Nonesuch, 962 N. LaCienega, Los Angeles, CA 90069
specialty: mainly classical, but here includes ragtime music

H 71305—Joshua Rifkin. Joplin Piano Rags, v.3. J2.23
HB 73026—Joshua Rifkin. Joplin Piano Rags, v.1/2. J2.23

Ode, 1416 North LaBrea, Hollywood, CA 90028
specialty: popular

SP 77009—Carole King. Tapestry. R3.15

Odeon *See* EMI Odeon (England)

Old Homestead, P.O. Box 100, Brighton, MI 48116
specialty: bluegrass, old time music, sacred music, and reissues

OH 90001—Wade Mainer. Sacred Songs of Mother and Home. F9.54
OHCS 101—Molly O'Day. A Sacred Collection. F9.63

Old Masters, Max Abrams, Box 76082, Los Angeles, CA 90076
specialty: jazz and pop reissues

TOM 23—Ted Weems. 1928-1930. P5.46a

Old Timey, 10341 San Pablo Ave., El Cerrito, CA 94530.
specialty: reissues of old time music and western swing

OT 100/1—The String Bands, v.1-2. two discs. F5.24
OT 102—Ballads and Songs. F5.3

Old Timey (cont'd)
>OT 103/4—Cliff Carlisle, v.1-2. two discs. F8.48
>OT 105—Western Swing, v.1. F7.36
>OT 106/7—J. E. Mainer's Mountaineers, v.1-2. two discs. F5.65
>OT 112—Tom Darby and Jimmy Tarlton. F5.113
>OT 115—Allen Brothers. The Chattanooga Boys. F5.117
>OT 116/7—Western Swing, v.2-3. two discs. F7.36

Oldie Blues (Holland)
>specialty: blues reissues

>OL 2801—Pete Johnson, v.1. J6.93
>OL 2806—Pete Johnson, v.2. J6.93

Onyx, Blanchris, Inc., 160 W. 71st Street, New York, NY 10023
>specialty: jazz reissues

>ORI 204—Red Rodney. The Red Arrow. J5.75
>ORI 205—Art Tatum. God Is in the House. J6.35
>ORI 207—Hot Lips Page. After Hours in Harlem. J5.67
>ORI 208—Don Byas. Midnight at Minton's. J5.42
>ORI 221—Charlie Parker. First Recordings! J5.28

Origin Jazz Library, Box 863, Berkeley, CA 94701
>specialty: blues and gospel reissues

>OJL 12/3—In the Spirit, No. 1-2. two discs. B3.13

Pablo, 1133 Avenue of the Americas, New York, NY 10036
>specialty: mainstream jazz

>2625.703—Art Tatum. Solo Masterpieces. thirteen discs. J6.39
>2625.706—Art Tatum. Group Masterpieces. eight discs. J4.155

Paltram (Austria)
>specialty: blues and gospel

>PL 102—Texas Blues. B1.97

Paramount, 8255 Beverly Blvd., Los Angeles, CA 90048
>specialty: popular, rock

>PAS 6031—Commander Cody and His Lost Planet Airmen. Hot Licks, Cold Steel, and Truckers' Favorites. F8.108

Parlophone (England)
>specialty: general, jazz reissues

>PMC 7019—Lonnie Johnson and Eddie Lang. Blue Guitars, v.1. B1.207
>PMC 7038—The Chocolate Dandies. 1928-1933. J4.55
>PMC 7082—The Territory Bands, 1926-1929. J3.104
>PMC 7106—Lonnie Johnson and Eddie Lang. Blue Guitars, v.2. B1.207

Parrot, 539 W. 25th Street, New York, NY 10001
    specialty: general
    XPAS 71028—Tom Jones. This Is P2.49

Peacock, 8255 Beverly Blvd., Los Angeles, CA 90048
    specialty: gospel
        136—Mighty Clouds of Joy. Best. B3.48
        138—Dixie Hummingbirds. Best. B3.33
        139—Five Blind Boys of Mississippi. Best. B3.36
        140—Golden Gems of Gospel. B3.6

Philadelphia International, 51 W. 52nd Street, New York, NY 10019
    specialty: soul

Philips, 1 IBM Plaza, Chicago, IL 60611
    specialty: general; see also Phonogram
    PHS 600.298—Nina Simone. Best. B4.70

Philo, The Barn, North Ferrisburg, VT 05473
    specialty: folk music

Phoenix, 7808 Bergen Line Ave., Bergenfield, NJ 07047
    specialty: jazz and blues reissues
    LP 7—Wynonie Harris. Mister Blues Meets the Master Saxes. B1.424

Phonogram (England)
    specialty: general, reissues of Philips and Chess materials
        6414.406—Alan Stivell. Renaissance of the Celtic Harp. F2.61
        6467.013—Memphis Country. F8.12
        6467.025/7—Sun Rockabillies, v.1-3. three discs. R1.5
        6467.306—Muddy Waters. At Newport. B1.300
        6641.047—Genesis, v.1. four discs. B1.275
        6641.125—Genesis, v.2. four discs. B1.276
        6641.174—Genesis, v.3. four discs. B1.277
        6641.180—The Sun Story, 1952-1968. two discs. R1.6

Pickwick, 135 Crossways Park Drive, Woodbury, Long Island, NY 11797
    specialty: reissues of Mercury and Capitol material, all fields

Piedmont (c/o Southern Record Sales)
    specialty: blues
        PLP 13157—Mississippi John Hurt. Folksongs and Blues, v.1. B1.191
        PLP 13161—Mississippi John Hurt. Folk Songs and Blues, v.2. B1.191

Pine Mountain, Box 584, Barbourville, KY 40906
    specialty: reissues of old time material
    PM 269—The Blue Sky Boys. Precious Moments. F9.22

Polydor, 810 Seventh Avenue, New York, NY 10019
specialty: general pop and soul

PD 4054—James Brown. Hot Pants. B4.39
104.678—James Last. This Is P5.86

Polydor (England)
specialty: pop and soul

2310.293—Charlie Feathers/Mac Curtis. Rockabilly Kings. R1.14
2384.007—Oscar Peterson. Exclusively for My Friends, v.5. J6.69
2424.118—Jerry Butler. Best. B4.42

Prestige, 10th and Parker Streets, Berkeley, CA 94710
specialty: jazz, blues and folk music

7159—Thelonious Monk. Monk's Mood. J5.25
7326—Sonny Rollins. Saxophone Colossus. J5.79
7337—Stan Getz. Greatest Hits. J5.89c
7593—Dickie Wells. In Paris, 1937. J4.156
7643—Benny Carter. 1933. J4.20
7827—Lee Konitz. Ezz-thetic. J5.92
PR 24001—Miles Davis. two discs. J5.16
PR 24020—Clifford Brown. In Paris. two discs. J5.40
PR 24024—The Greatest Jazz Concert Ever. two discs. J5.6
P 24030—Dizzy Gillespie. In the Beginning. two discs. J5.22
PR 24034—Miles Davis. Workin' and Steamin'. two discs. J5.21
P 24039—Eddie "Lockjaw" Davis. The Cookbook. two discs. P3.6
P 24040—Buck Clayton and Buddy Tate. Kansas City Nights. two discs.
J4.161
P 24044—Sonny Stitt. Genesis. two discs. J5.80
PR 24045—25 Years of Prestige. two discs. J5.104
P 34001—Charles Mingus. The Great Concert. three discs. J5.127

Puritan, P.O. Box 946, Evanston, IL 60204
specialty: bluegrass

Pye (England)
specialty: general

502—Donovan. History. F10.8

RBF, 43 W. 61st Street, New York, NY 10023
specialty: jazz, blues and old time music reissues

RF 3—A History of Jazz: The New York Scene, 1914-1945. J3.80
RBF 8/9—The Country Blues, v.1-2. two discs. B1.11
RBF 10—Blind Willie Johnson. B3.45
RBF 11—Blues Rediscoveries. B1.10
RBF 15—Blues Roots: The Atlanta Blues. B1.63
RBF 19—Country Gospel Song. F9.5
RBF 51—Uncle Dave Macon. F5.32

RBF (cont'd)
>   RBF 202—The Rural Blues. two discs. B1.22
>   RBF 203—New Orleans Jazz: The Twenties. two discs. J3.5

RCA, 1133 Avenue of the Americas, New York, NY 10036
>   specialty: general; formerly known as Victor

>   LSPX 1004—Guess Who. Best. R3.10
>   LPM 1121—Rosalie Allen. Queen of the Yodellers. F8.134
>   LPM 1183—Eartha Kitt. That Bad Eartha. P2.109
>   LPE 1192—Glenn Miller. Plays Selections from "The Glenn Miller Story."
>   P5.15
>   LPM 1223—Eddy Arnold. All Time Favorites. F8.88
>   LPM 1241—Artie Shaw's Gramercy Five. J4.146
>   LPM 1246—Fats Waller. Ain't Misbehavin'. J4.117, P2.65
>   LPM 1295—Muggsy Spanier. The Great Sixteen. J3.58
>   LPM 1364—Duke Ellington. In a Mellotone. J4.32
>   LPM 1649—Jelly Roll Morton. King of New Orleans Jazz. J3.26
>   LPM 2078—Bunny Berigan. P5.5
>   LPM 2323—Bix Beiderbecke. Legend. J3.88
>   LPM 2398—Dizzy Gillespie. The Greatest. J5.53
>   LSP 2587—Lena Horne. Lovely and Alive. P2.72
>   LSP 2669—Elton Britt, v.1. F8.47
>   LSP 2887—Chet Atkins. Best. F8.90
>   LSP 2890—Jim Reeves. Best, v.1. F8.92
>   LSC 3235—Spike Jones. Is Murdering the Classics. P4.8
>   LSP 3377—Glenn Miller. Best. P5.14
>   LSP 3476—Sons of the Pioneers. Best. F7.17
>   LSP 3478—Hank Snow. Best, v.1. F8.32
>   LSP 3482—Jim Reeves. Best, v.2. F8.92
>   LSP 3766—Jefferson Airplane. Surrealistic Pillow. R6.7
>   LSP 3956—Nilsson. Aerial Ballet. F10.75
>   LSP 3957—Jose Feliciano. P2.40
>   LSP 3988—Gary Burton. A Genuine Tong Funeral. J5.144
>   LSP 4187—Jim Reeves. Best, v.3. F8.92
>   LSP 4223—Charley Pride. Best, v.1. F8.104
>   LSP 4289—Harry Nilsson. Nilsson Sings Newman. F10.77
>   LSP 4321—Porter Wagoner. Best, v.2. F8.83
>   LSP 4374—Nina Simone. Best. B4.69
>   LSP 4459—Jefferson Airplane. Worst. R6.9
>   LSP 4682—Charley Pride. Best, v.1. F8.104
>   LSP 4751—Waylon Jennings. Ladies Love Outlaws. F8.11
>   LSP 4798—Hank Snow. Best, v.2. F8.32
>   LSP 4822—Elton Britt, v.2. F8.47
>   LSP 4854—Waylon Jennings. Lonesome, On'ry, and Mean. F8.115
>   ARL1-0035—Arthur Fiedler and the Boston Pops. Greatest Hits of the 20s.
>   P5.81
>   ARL1-0041/5—Arthur Fiedler and the Boston Pops. Greatest Hits of the
>   30s, 40s, 50s, 60s, and 70s. five discs. P5.81

RCA (cont'd)
 KPM1-0153—Elvis Presley. The Sun Sessions. R1.11
 APL1-0240—Waylon Jennings. Honky Tonk Heroes. F8.116
 CPL1-0374—John Denver. Greatest Hits. F10.56
 APL1-0455—George Hamilton IV. Greatest Hits. F8.61
 APL1-0928—Neil Sedaka. His Greatest Hits. R2.42
 ANL1-1035—Spike Jones. Best. P4.7
 ANL1-1071—Carter Family. 'Mid the Green Fields. F5.110
 ANL1-1083e—The Browns. Best. F8.97
 APL1-1117—Dolly Parton. Best. F8.143
 ANL1-1137—Perry Como. I Believe. F9.28
 ANL1-1140—Vaughan Monroe, Best. P2.59
 ANL1-1213—Porter Wagoner. Best, v.1. F8.83
 CPL1-1756e—Russ Columbo. A Legendary Performer. P2.29
 CPL1-2099—Woody Guthrie. Dust Bowl Ballads. F10.62
 CPL1-5015—Cleo Laine. Live!! At Carnegie Hall. P2.74
 CPL2-0466—Stars of the Grand Ole Opry, 1926-1974. two discs. F8.8
 ADL2-0694—Wilf Carter. Montana Slim's Greatest Hits. two discs. F7.10
 VPS 6014—Hank Snow. This Is My Story. two discs. F8.33
 LSP 6016—Willie "The Lion" Smith. Memoirs. two discs. J6.74
 VPS 6027—Sam Cooke. This Is. . . . two discs. B2.42
 VPS 6032—Eddy Arnold. This Is. . . . two discs. F8.89
 VPM 6040—Benny Goodman. This Is. . . . , v.1. two discs. J4.62
 VPM 6042—Duke Ellington. This Is. . . . two discs. J4.33
 VPM 6043—This Is the Big Band Era. two discs. P5.4
 VPM 6056—Gene Austin. This Is. . . . two discs. P2.1
 VPM 6063—Benny Goodman. This Is. . . . , v.2. J4.62
 VPSX 6079—Chet Atkins. Now and . . . Then. two discs. F8.91
 VPM 6087—Tommy Dorsey. Clambake Seven. two discs. P5.9

RCA Bluebird (series devoted to reissues)
 AXM2-5501 Tampa Red. two discs. B1.242
 AXM2-5503—Bill Boyd. Country Ramblers, 1934-1950. two discs. F7.39
 AXM2-5506—Big Maceo. Chicago Breakdown. two discs. B1.283
 AXM2-5507—Fletcher Henderson. Complete, 1923-1936. two discs. J4.39
 AXM2-5508—Earl Hines. The Father Jumps. two discs. J4.65
 AXM2-5510—Monroe Brothers. Feats Here Tonight. F5.115
 AXM2-5512—Glenn Miller. Complete, v.1. two discs. P5.39 (in progress,
  about 20 discs)
 AXM2-5517—Artie Shaw. Complete, v.1. two discs. P5.45 (in progress, about
  12 discs)
 AXM2-5518—Fats Waller. Piano Solos, 1929-1941. two discs. J6.40a
 AXM2-5521—Tommy Dorsey. Complete, v.1. two discs. P5.8 (in progress,
  about 12 discs)
 AXM2-5525—Blue Sky Boys. two discs. F5.105
 AXM2-5531—The Cats and the Fiddle. I Miss You So. two discs. B2.24
 AXM2-55??—Grand Ole Opry Stars. two discs. F8.14 (forthcoming)
 AXM2-55??—Patsy Montana. two discs. F7.11 (forthcoming)
 AXM6-5536—Lionel Hampton. Complete, 1937-1941. six discs. J4.97

RCA Camden (reissues)

> 2460—Pee Wee King. Biggest Hits. F7.44

RCA Vintage (jazz and blues and folk reissues; series recently deleted)

> LPV 501—Coleman Hawkins. Body and Soul. J4.98
> LPV 504—Isham Jones. P5.12
> LPV 507—Smoky Mountain Ballads. F5.7
> LPV 513—John Jacob Niles. Folk Balladeer. F3.79
> LPV 519—The Bebop Era. J5.2
> LPV 521—Benny Goodman. Small Groups. J4.95
> LPV 522—Authentic Cowboys and Their Western Folksongs. F7.1
> LPV 532—The Railroad in Folksong. F3.40
> LPV 533—Johnny Hodges. Things Ain't What They Used to Be. J4.112
> LPV 548—Native American Ballads. F5.5
> LPV 551—Charlie Barnet, v.1. P5.21
> LPV 552—Early Rural String Bands. F5.22
> LPV 554—Fred Waring. P2.143
> LPV 555—Paul Whiteman, v.1. P5.18
> LPV 558—Johnny Dodds. J3.22
> LPV 565—Leo Reisman, v.1. P5.17
> LPV 566—Barney Bigard/Albert Nicholas. J4.132
> LPV 567—Charlie Barnet, v.2. P5.21
> LPV 569—Early Bluegrass. F6.15
> LPV 570—Paul Whiteman, v.2. P5.18
> LPV 581—Bunny Berigan. His Trumpet and Orchestra, v.1. P5.7
> LPV 582—Artie Shaw. J4.86

RCA (England)

> specialty: general

> SD 1000—Frank Sinatra, with Tommy Dorsey. six discs. P2.14
> INTS 1072—Gene Krupa. Swingin' with Krupa. J4.74
> INTS 1343—Rudy Vallee Croons the Songs He Made Famous. P2.22
> DPS 2022—Jimmy Driftwood. Famous Country Music Makers. two discs.
>   F10.9
> LSA 3180—Hoagy Carmichael. Stardust. P2.26
> LPL1-5000—Cleo Laine. I Am a Song. P2.73
> LFL4-7522—Perry Como. The First Thirty Years. four discs. P2.6

RCA (France)

> specialty: jazz and blues reissues

> 730.549—Jelly Roll Morton, v.1. J3.25
> 730.561—Boogie Woogie Man. J6.82
> 730.581—Memphis Slim. B1.349
> 730.605—Jelly Roll Morton, v.2. J3.25
> 730.703/4—Original Dixieland Jazz Band. two discs. J3.51
> 730.708—Erskine Hawkins, v.1. J4.64
> 730.710—Barney Kessel. J6.101

RCA (France) (cont'd)

    731.051/2—Louis Armstrong. Town Hall Concert, 1947. two discs. J3.38
    731.059—Jelly Roll Morton, v.3. J3.25
    741.007—Ethel Waters. 1938/1939. P2.85
    741.040—Jelly Roll Morton, v.4. J3.25
    741.044—Benny Goodman. The Fletcher Henderson Arrangements, v.1. J4.37
    741.054—Jelly Roll Morton, v.5. J3.25
    741.059—Benny Goodman. The Fletcher Henderson Arrangements, v.2. J4.37
    741.061—Don Redman. 1938/1940. J4.50
    741.070—Jelly Roll Morton, v.6. J3.25
    741.073—Benny Carter. 1940/1941. J4.21
    741.080—McKinney's Cotton Pickers. Complete, v.1. J4.48
    741.081—Jelly Roll Morton, v.7. J3.25
    741.087—Jelly Roll Morton, v.8. J3.25
    741.088—McKinney's Cotton Pickers. Complete, v.2. J4.48
    741.089—The Greatest of the Small Bands, v.1. J4.92
    741.103—The Greatest of the Small Bands, v.2. J4.92
    741.106—The Greatest of the Small Bands, v.3. J4.92
    741.107—New Orleans, v.1. J3.3
    741.109—McKinney's Cotton Pickers. Complete, v.3. J4.48
    741.116—Erskine Hawkins, v.2. J4.64
    741.117—The Greatest of the Small Bands, v.4. J4.92
    DUKE 1/4—Duke Ellington. Integrale. J4.31
    FPM1-7003—New Orleans, v.2. J3.3
    FPM1-7059—McKinney's Cotton Pickers. Complete, v.4. J4.48
    FPM1-7014—The Greatest of the Small Bands, v.5. J4.92
    FPM1-7024—Erskine Hawkins, v.3. J4.64
    FPM1-7059—McKinney's Cotton Pickers. Complete, v.5. J4.48
    FXM1-7060—Henry "Red" Allen, v.1. J3.33
    FXM1-7090—Henry "Red" Allen, v.2. J3.33
    FXM1-7124—The Greatest of the Small Bands, v.6. J4.92
    FXM1-7136—Jean Goldkette. 1928-1929. P5.28
    FXM1-7323—Big Joe Williams. B1.259
    FXM3-7143—History of Jazz Piano. three discs. J6.10
    FXM1-7192—Henry "Red" Allen, v.3. J3.33

RCA (Japan)
    specialty: jazz, blues, and country

    RA 5459/66—Jimmie Rodgers. 110 Collection. eight discs. F8.31
    RA 5641/50—Carter Family. The Legendary Collection, 1927-1934, 1941. ten discs. F5.109

RSO, 75 Rockefeller Plaza, New York, NY 10019
    specialty: rock music

    RSO 3016—Blind Faith. R8.12

Radiola Records

2MR 5051—The First Esquire All-American Jazz Concert, January 18, 1944. two discs. J1.19

Ranwood, 9034 Sunset Blvd., Los Angeles, CA 90069
specialty: mood music

Rebel, Rt. 2, Asbury, WV 24916
specialty: bluegrass

1497—Country Gentlemen. Gospel Album. F9.29
1506—Country Gentlemen. Award Winning. F6.23
1511—Seldom Scene. Act One. F6.126
1514—Ralph Stanley. Plays Requests. F6.52
1520—Seldom Scene. Act Two. F6.126
1528—Seldom Scene. Act Three. F6.126
1530—Ralph Stanley. A Man and His Music. F6.51
1547/8—Seldom Scene. Recorded Live at the Cellar Door. two discs. F6.128

Red Lightnin' (England)
specialty: blues reissues

RL 001—Buddy Guy. In the Beginning. B1.337
RL 006—When Girls Do It. two discs. B1.274
RL 007—Junior Wells. In My Younger Days. B1.371
RL 009—Earl Hooker. There's a Fungus Amung Us. B1.281
RL 0010—Clarence "Gatemouth" Brown. San Antonio Ballbuster. B1.322

Reprise, 3300 Warner Blvd., Burbank, CA 91505
specialty: general, troubador music

FS 1016—Frank Sinatra. A Man and His Music. two discs. P2.17
6199—Tom Lehrer. An Evening Wasted. P4.10
6216—Tom Lehrer. Songs. P4.11
6217—The Kinks. Greatest Hits. R4.11
6261—Jimi Hendrix. Are You Experienced? R8.4
6267—Arlo Guthrie. Alice's Restaurant. F10.60
6286—Randy Newman. F10.38
6341—Joni Mitchell. Clouds. F10.30
6383—Neil Young. After the Gold Rush. R7.19
6430—Pentangle. Cruel Sister. F2.53
2RS 6307—Jimi Hendrix. Electric Ladyland. two discs. R8.5
MS 2025—Jimi Hendrix. Greatest Hits. R8.6
MS 2038—Joni Mitchell. Blue. F10.29
MS 2064—Randy Newman. Sail Away. F10.39
MS 2148—Maria Muldaur. R4.35

Rimrock, Concord, AR 72523
specialty: sacred, bluegrass

1002—The Family Gospel Album. F9.2

Rome, 1414 E. Broad St., Columbus, OH 43205
  specialty: bluegrass

  1011—Don Reno and Red Smiley. Together Again. F6.49

Roots (Austria)
  specialty: blues and gospel reissues; old time music reissues

  RL 301—Blind Lemon Jefferson, v.1. B1.112
  RL 306—Blind Lemon Jefferson, v.2. B1.112
  RL 317—Lucille Bogan and Walter Roland. Alabama Blues, 1930-1935.
    B1.386
  RL 322—Memphis Jug Band, v.1. B1.421
  RL 330—Tommy Johnson/Ishman Bracey. Famous 1928 Sessions. B1.113
  RL 331—Blind Lemon Jefferson, v.3. B1.112
  RL 337-Memphis Jug Band, v.2. B1.421
  RL 701—Riley Pickett. Story, 1924-1941. F5.40

Roulette, 17 W. 60th Street, New York, NY 10023
  specialty: general and jazz

  RE 124—Count Basie. Echoes of an Era: Kansas City Suite/Easin' It. two
    discs. J4.166

Roulette (England)
  specialty: general and jazz

  SRCP 3000—Count Basie. The Atomic Mr. Basie. J4.165

Rounder, 186 Willow Avenue, Somerville, MA 02143
  specialty: blues, old time music, bluegrass

  001—George Pegram. F5.96
  0011—Tut Taylor. Friar Tut. F5.44
  0014 Don Stover. Things in Life. F6.109
  0017—Almeda Riddle. Ballads and Hymns from the Ozarks. F3.83
  1001—Blind Alfred Reed. How Can a Poor Man Stand Such Times and Live?
    F5.41
  1002—Aunt Molly Jackson. Library of Congress Recordings. F3.68
  1003—Fiddlin' John Carson. The Old Hen Cackled and the Rooster's Gonna
    Crow. F5.29
  1004—Burnett and Rutherford. A Rambling Reckless Hobo. F5.118
  1005—Gid Tanner. "Hear These New Southern Fiddle and Guitar Music."
    F5.78
  1006—Blue Sky Boys. The Sunny Side of Life. F5.106
  1007—Frank Hutchison. The Train That Carried My Girl from Town. F5.30
  1008—Stoneman Family. 1926-1928. F5.72
  1013/20—Early Days of Bluegrass, v.1-8. eight discs. F6.16
  2003—Martin, Bogan and Armstrong. Barnyard Dance. B1.218
  3006—Boys of the Lough. Second Album. F2.10

Rural Rhythm, Box A, Arcadia, CA 91006
    specialty: bluegrass

Sackville (Canada)
    specialty: jazz

    2004—Willie "The Lion" Smith and Don Ewell. Grand Piano Duets. J6.76

Savoy, 6 West 57th Street, New York, NY 10019
    specialty: jazz; in the process of being reissued by Arista

    MG 12020—Dizzy Gillespie. Groovin' High. J5.54
    MG 12106—J. J. Johnson. Boneology. J5.63
    MG 14006—Clara Ward Singers. Lord Touch Me. B3.64
    MG 14014—Great Golden Gospel Hits, v.1. B3.11
    MG 14019—Sonny Terry and Brownie McGhee. Back Country Blues. B1.248
    MG 14069—Great Golden Gospel Hits, v.2. B3.11
    MG 14076—James Cleveland, v.1. B3.29
    MG 14131—James Cleveland, v.2. B3.29
    MG 14165—Great Golden Gospel Hits, v.3. B3.11
    MG 14252—James Cleveland, v.3. B3.29
    SJL 2201—Charlie Parker. Bird: The Savoy Recordings. two discs. J5.30
        [in progress]
    SJL 2202—Lester Young. Pres. two discs. J4.126
    SJL 2211—Dexter Gordon. Long Tall Dexter. two discs. J5.55
    SJL 2214—Billy Eckstine. Mr. B and the Band. two discs. P2.35
    SJL 2216—Fats Navarro. Savoy Sessions: Fat Girl. two discs. J5.27

Scepter, 254 W. 54th Street, New York, NY 10019
    specialty: pop

Shandar (France)
    specialty: modern jazz

    SR 10000—Albert Ayler, v.1. J5.139
    SR 10004—Albert Ayler, v.2. J5.139

Shelter, 100 Universal City Plaza, Universal City, CA 91608
    specialty: rock

    SW 8901—Leon Russell. R4.41

Sire, 8255 Beverly Blvd., Los Angeles, CA 90048
    specialty: rock

    SAS 3702—The History of British Rock, v.1. two discs. R4.1
    SAS 3705—The History of British Rock, v.2. two discs. R4.1
    SAS 3712—The History of British Rock, v.3. two discs. R4.1
    SASH 3715—Fleetwood Mac. In Chicago. two discs. R5.18

Solid State, 6920 Sunset Blvd., Hollywood, CA 90028
    specialty: jazz
    18048—Thad Jones-Mel Lewis Orchestra. Monday Night. J4.172

Sonet (Sweden)
    specialty: jazz and blues

    SLP 2547—Barney Kessel and Red Mitchell. Two Way Conversation. J6.107

Sonyatone Records (c/o Southern Record Sales)

    STR 201—Eck Robertson. Master Fiddler, 1929-1941. F5.41a

Smithsonian Classic Jazz, P.O. Box 14196, Washington, D.C. 20044
    specialty: jazz reissues

Speciality, 8300 Santa Monica Blvd., Hollywood, CA 90069
    specialty: rhythm 'n' blues, blues, soul, gospel music

    2113—Little Richard. Greatest 17 Original Hits. B2.46
    2115—Ain't That Good News. B3.1
    2116—Soul Stirrers and Sam Cooke, v.1. B3.53
    2126—Percy Mayfield. Best. B2.62
    2128—Soul Stirrers and Sam Cooke, v.2. B3.53
    2131—Don and Dewey. B2.53
    2177/8—This Is How It All Began, v.1-2. two discs. B2.4

Spivey, 65 Grand Ave., Brooklyn, NY 11205
    specialty: blues

    2001—Victoria Spivey. Recorded Legacy of the Blues. B1.405

Spotlite (England)
    specialty: reissues of bop jazz

    100—Billy Eckstine. Together. J5.49
    101/6—Charlie Parker. On Dial. six discs. J5.29
    119—Coleman Hawkins and Lester Young. J4.106
    131—Howard McGhee. Trumpet at Tempo. J5.23

Springboard, 947 U.S. Highway 1, Rahway, NJ 07601
    specialty: reissues of jazz and rock 'n' roll

Stanyan, 8440 Santa Monica Blvd., Hollywood, CA 90069
    specialty: mood

    SR 10032—Vera Lynn. When the Lights Go On Again. P2.76

Starday, 220 Boscobel St., Nashville, TN 37213
    specialty: country and western, bluegrass and sacred materials

    SLP 122—Stanley Brothers. Sacred Songs from the Hills. F9.75
    SLP 146—Bill Clifton. Carter Family Memorial Album. F6.71
    SLP 150—George Jones. Greatest Hits. F8.28
    SLP 161—Lewis Family. Anniversary Celebration. F9.46
    SLP 174—Country Gentlemen. Bluegrass at Carnegie Hall. F6.24
    SLP 250—Diesel Smoke, Dangerous Curves, and Other Truck Driver
        Favorites. F8.10

Starday (cont'd)
    SLP 303—Preachin', Prayin', Singin'. F9.14
    SLP 398—Moon Mullican. Unforgettable Great Hits. F8.72
    SLP 482—New Grass Revival. F6.121
    SLP 772—Stanley Brothers. Sing the Songs They Like Best. F6.61
    SLP 953—Stanley Brothers. Best. F6.60
    SLP 956—Carl Story. Best. F9.80
    SLP 961—Don Reno and Red Smiley. Best. F6.48

Starline *See* EMI Starline (England)

Stash, Record People, 66 Greene Street, New York, NY 10012
    specialty: jazz and blues reissues [thematic: drugs and alcohol]
    100—Reefer Songs. P4.4

Stax, 2693 Union Ave., Memphis, TN 38112
    specialty: soul

Storyville (Denmark)
    specialty: jazz and blues
    670.184—Boogie Woogie Trio. J6.83
    671.162—Lonnie Johnson. B1.203

Strata East, 156 Fifth Avenue, Suite 612, New York, NY 10010
    specialty: modern jazz

String (England)
    specialty: old time music, western swing
    801—Beer Parlor Jive. F7.33

Sun, 3106 Belmont Blvd., Nashville, TN 37212
    specialty: rock 'n' roll, rhythm 'n' blues, blues, country; see also Phonogram
        and Charly for English reissues
    100/1—Johnny Cash. Original Golden Hits, v.1-2. two discs. R1.13
    102/3—Jerry Lee Lewis. Original Golden Hits, v.1-2. two discs. R1.9
    106—Original Memphis Rock & Roll. R1.4
    128—Jerry Lee Lewis. Original Golden Hits, v.3. R1.9

Sunbeam, 13821 Calvert St., Van Nuys, CA 91401
    specialty: big band reissues, Benny Goodman
    SB 101/3—Benny Goodman. Thesaurus, June 6, 1935. three discs. J4.61

Sussex, 6255 Sunset Blvd., Suite 1902, Hollywood, CA 90028
    specialty: soul

Swaggie (Australia)
    specialty: jazz and blues reissues

Swaggie (cont'd)
    S 1219/20—Sleepy John Estes, v.1-2. two discs. B1.164
    S 1225—Lonnie Johnson. B1.204
    S 1235—Cripple Clarence Lofton/Jimmy Yancey. B1.216, J6.98
    S 1242—Bix Beiderbecke. Bix and Tram, 1927/8, v.1. J3.87
    S 1245—Bob Crosby's Bob Cats. 1937-1942, v.1. J3.56
    S 1251/2—Django Reinhardt. two discs. J6.114/5
    S 1269—Bix Beiderbecke. Bix and Tram, 1927/8, v.2. J3.87
    S 1275—Count Basie. Swinging the Blues, 1937/39. J4.14
    S 1288—Bob Crosby's Bob Cats. 1937-1942, v.2. J3.56

Swing Era (c/o Southern Record Sales)
    specialty: reissues of big band material
    LP 1001—Themes of the Big Bands. P5.3

Takoma, P.O. Box 5369, Santa Monica, CA 90405
    specialty: folk guitar and blues
    B 1001—Bukka White. Mississippi Blues. B1.256
    C 1002—John Fahey, v.1: Blind Joe Death. F4.32
    C 1024—Leo Kottke. 6 and 12 String Guitar. F4.37

Tamla, 6464 Sunset Blvd., Hollywood, CA 90028
    specialty: soul
    S 252—Marvin Gaye. Greatest Hits, v.1. B4.46
    S 278—Marvin Gaye. Greatest Hits, v.2. B4.46
    S 282—Stevie Wonder. Greatest Hits, v.1. B4.62
    T 308—Stevie Wonder. Where I'm Coming From. B4.34
    T 313—Stevie Wonder. Greatest Hits, v.2. B4.62
    T 326—Stevie Wonder. Innervisions. B4.37

Tangerine, 8255 Beverly Blvd., Los Angeles, CA 90048
    specialty: soul

Tax (Sweden)
    specialty: jazz reissues
    m8000—Lester Young. The Alternative Lester. J4.125
    m8005—Cootie Williams. The Boys from Harlem. J4.87
    m8009—The Territory Bands. J3.107
    m8011—Cootie Williams. The Rugcutters, 1937-1940. J4.88

Testament, 577 Lavering Avenue, Los Angeles, CA 90024
    specialty: blues
    T 2207—Chicago Blues: The Beginning. B1.270
    T 2210—Muddy Waters. Down on Stovall's Plantation. B1.301
    T 2211—Otis Spann. Chicago Blues. B1.307
    T 2217—Johnny Shines and Big Walter Horton. B1.361
    T 2219—Fred McDowell. Amazing Grace. B3.46
    T 2221—Johnny Shines. Standing at the Crossroads. B1.235

The Old Masters *See* Old Masters

Tishomingo (c/o Southern Record Sales)
specialty: western swing

2220—Rollin' Along. F7.34

Topic (England)
specialty: folk music

12 T 118—Bert Lloyd. First Person. F2.21
12 T 136—The Watersons. Frost and Fire. F2.31

Tradition, 10920 Wilshire Blvd., Los Angeles, CA 90024
specialty: folk

2050—The Clancy Brothers and Tommy Makem. Best. F2.40
2053—Oscar Brand. Best. F4.5

Trip, 947 U.S. Highway 1, Rahway, NJ 07065
specialty: reissues of Emarcy jazz catalog (Mercury)

TLP 5501—Sarah Vaughan. 1955. P2.84

Truth (Austria)
specialty: gospel music

1002/3—Guitar Evangelists, v.1-2. two discs. B3.12

Twentieth Century, 8255 Sunset Blvd., Los Angeles, CA 90046
specialty: general

Union Grove (c/o Southern Record Sales)
specialty: material from the Union Grove Fiddlers' Convention

United Artists, 6920 Sunset Blvd., Hollywood, CA 90028
specialty: general

UAS 5596—Country Gazette. A Traitor in Our Midst. F6.117
UAS 5632—Duke Ellington. Money Jungle. J6.18
UA 6291—George Jones. Best. F8.23
UAS 9801—Will the Circle Be Unbroken? three discs. F8.16
UAS 9952—Miles Davis. two discs. J5.15
UALA 089-F2—Vicki Carr. The Golden Songbook. two discs. P2.93
UALA 127-J3—John Lee Hooker. Detroit. three discs. B1.175
UALA 233G—Fats Domino. two discs. B2.44
UALA 243-G—Gordon Lightfoot. The Very Best. F10.27

United Artists (England)
specialty: general

UAS 29215—Sound of the City: New Orleans. B2.19
UAS 29898—Slim Whitman, Very Best. 2 discs. F8.94

United Artists (England) (cont'd)
  UAD 60025/6–The Many Sides of Rock 'n' Roll, v.1. two discs. R2.8
  UAD 60035/6–The Many Sides of Rock 'n' Roll, v.2. two discs. R2.8
  UAD 60091/2–Lena Horne. Collection. two discs. P2.71
  UAD 60093/4–The Many Sides of Rock 'n' Roll, v.3. two discs. R2.8

Vanguard, 71 W. 23rd Street, New York, NY 10010
  specialty: folk music and blues

  2053/5–Newport Folk Festival. three discs. F3.15
  2087/8–Newport Folk Festival. two discs. F3.15
  6544–Bert Jansch and John Renbourn. Jack Orion. F2.50
  VSD 79144/9–Newport Folk Festival. six discs. F3.15
  VSD 79180/6–Newport Folk Festival. seven discs. F3.15
  VSD 79216/8–Chicago/The Blues/Today! three discs. B1.266
  VSD 79219/25–Newport Folk Festival. seven discs. F3.15
  VSD 79306/7–Joan Baez. Any Day Now. two discs. F10.1
  VSD 79317–Greenbriar Boys. Best. F6.80
  VSD 5/6–Ian and Sylvia. Greatest Hits, v.1. two discs. F4.35
  VSD 9/10–Doc Watson. On Stage. two discs. F4.18
  VSD 15/16–The Weavers. Greatest Hits. two discs. F4.22
  VSD 23/24–Ian and Sylvia. Greatest Hits, v.2. two discs. F4.35
  VSD 35/36–The Greatest Songs of Woody Guthrie. two discs. F3.37
  VSD 39/40–Max Morath. The Best of Scott Joplin and Other Rag Classics.
    two discs. J2.17
  VSD 41/42–Joan Baez. Ballad Book. two discs. F4.3
  VSD 43/44–Odetta. Essential. two discs. F4.45
  VSD 47/48–From Spirituals to Swing, 1938/39. two discs. J4.2
  VSD 49/50–Joan Baez. Contemporary Ballad Book. two discs. F10.2
  VSD 65/66–Jimmy Rushing. Best. two discs. B1.425
  VSD 79/80–Joan Baez. Lovesong Album. two discs. F4.4
  VSD 99/100–Vic Dickenson. Essential. two discs. J4.137
  VSDB 103/4–Buck Clayton. Essential. two discs. J4.158

Vanguard (England)
  specialty: jazz, blues and folk

  VRS 8502–Mel Powell. Thingamagig. J4.114
  VRS 8528–Mel Powell. Out on a Limb. J4.113

Verve, 810 Seventh Ave., New York, NY 10019
  specialty: jazz

  FTS 3008–Blues Project. Projections. R5.6
  VC 3509–Charlie Parker. J5.69
  V6-8412–Stan Getz. Focus. J5.89b
  V6-8420–Oscar Peterson. Trio Live from Chicago. F6.71
  V6-8526–Bill Evans. Conversations with Myself. J6.54
  V6-8538–Oscar Peterson. Night Train. J6.72
  V6-8808–Billie Holiday. Best. J6.120

Verve (England)
>specialty: jazz, reissues of American Verve

>2304.074–Stan Getz. Greatest Hits. P3.9
>2304.169–Coleman Hawkins and Ben Webster. Blue Saxophones. J4.105, J4.119
>2317.031–Woody Herman. At Carnegie Hall, March 25, 1946. J4.42
>2610.020–Jazz at the Philharmonic, 1944-1946. two discs. J1.12
>2682.005–Johnny Hodges. Back to Back/Side by Side. two discs. J4.107
>2683.023–Ben Webster and Oscar Peterson. Soulville. two discs. J4.120
>2683.025–Teddy Wilson and Lester Young. Prez and Teddy. two discs. J4.123, J4.128
>2683.049–Ben Webster. Ballads. two discs. P3.21

Vetco, 5828 Vine Street, Cincinnati, OH 45216
>specialty: old time music reissues

>101–Uncle Dave Macon. The Dixie Dewdrop, v.1. F5.33
>105–Uncle Dave Macon. The Dixie Dewdrop, v.2. F5.33

Vocalion, 100 Universal City Plaza, Universal City, CA 91608
>specialty: reissues of MC material

>VL 3715–Sons of the Pioneers. Tumbleweed Trails. F7.18
>VL 73866–Jo Stafford. Sweet Singer of Songs. P2.80

Virgin, 75 Rockefeller Plaza, New York, NY 10019
>specialty: rock

Viva, 6922 Hollywood Blvd., Hollywood, CA 90028
>specialty: reissues of nostalgia materials

Vogue (France)
>specialty: reissues of jazz and blues

>SB 1–Sidney Bechet. Concert à l'Exposition Universelle de Bruxelles, 1958. J3.19
>LAE 12050–Gerry Mulligan. J5.95

Volt, 2693 Union Ave., Memphis, TN 38112
>specialty: soul

Voyager, 424 35th Avenue, Seattle, WA 98122
>specialty: old time music

>VRLP 303–Gid Tanner. A Corn Licker Still in Georgia. F5.77

Wand (recently deleted)
>specialty: rhythm 'n' blues

>653–Isley Brothers. Twist and Shout. B2.34

Warner Brothers, 3300 Warner Blvd., Burbank, CA 91505
   specialty: general

   2WS 1555—Peter, Paul and Mary. In Concert. two discs. F4.13
   WS 1749—Grateful Dead. Anthem of the Sun. R6.5
   WS 1765—Petula Clark. Greatest Hits. P2.95
   WS 1835—Van Morrison. Moondance. F10.33
   WS 1843—James Taylor. Sweet Baby James. F10.47
   WS 1869—Grateful Dead. Workingman's Dead. R6.6
   BS 2607—Deep Purple. Machine Head. R8.17
   BS 2643—Bonnie Raitt. Give It Up. R4.39
   2LS 2644—Deep Purple. Purple Passages. two discs. R8.15
   BS 2683—Eric Weissberg. Dueling Banjos. F6.63
   3XX 2736—Fifty Years of Film Music. three discs. P6.79
   2SP 9104—Phil Spector's Greatest Hits. two discs. R2.11a

World Jazz, 221 West 57th Street, New York, NY 10019
   specialty: jazz

World Pacific Jazz (recently deleted)
   specialty: jazz

   1211—Cy Touff and Richie Kamuca. Having a Ball. J4.115

World Records (England)
   specialty: nostalgia, jazz, British dance bands; formerly World Record Club

   F 526—The Anatomy of Improvisation. J5.1
   SH 118/9—Golden Age of British Dance Bands. two discs. P5.93
   SH 146—Al Bowlly. P2.4
   SH 220—Original Dixieland Jazz Band. London Recordings, 1919-1920.
      J3.52
   SHB 21—Ambrose. two discs. P5.94

Xanadu, 3242 Irwin Ave., Knightsbridge, NY 10463
   specialty: reissues of jazz

Yazoo, 245 Waverly Place, New York, NY 10014
   specialty: blues

   L 1001—Mississippi Blues, 1927-1941. B1.84
   L 1002—Ten Years in Memphis, 1927-1937. B1.76
   L 1003—St. Louis Town, 1927-1932. B1.94
   L 1005—Blind Willie McTell. The Early Years, 1927-1933. B1.126
   L 1011—Big Bill Broonzy. Young. B1.155
   L 1013—East Coast Blues, 1926-1935. B1.65
   L 1016—Guitar Wizards, 1926-1935. B1.41
   L 1017—Bessie Jackson and Walter Roland. 1927-1935. B1.387
   L 1020—Charley Patton. Founder of the Delta Blues. two discs. B1.129
   L 1022—Ten Years of Black Country Religion, 1926-1936. B3.23
   L 1023—Rev. Gary Davis. 1935-1949. B3.31

Yazoo (cont'd)
>L 1024—Mister Charlie's Blues. F5.14
>L 1025—Cripple Clarence Lofton/Walter Davis. B1.215
>L 1033—Roosevelt Sykes. The Country Blues Piano Ace. B1.238
>L 1036—Leroy Carr. Naptown Blues, 1929-1934. B1.108
>L 1037—Blind Willie McTell. 1927-1935. B1.124
>L 1041—Georgia Tom Dorsey. Come on Mama, Do That Dance. B1.162
>L 1050—Furry Lewis. In His Prime, 1927-1929. B1.211

DIRECTORY OF SPECIALIST RECORD STORES

The record stores listed here handle orders for hard-to-find and rare items (primarily covering blues, country, ethnic, folk, and jazz). In fact, where many labels are concerned, record stores will be the only means of distribution. The following stores are highly recommended because of the superior service they give in obtaining issues from small, independent labels. Request a current catalog. (Note: These stores *may* offer library discounts, but since they are *not* library suppliers per se, this should be clarified at the outset of any transaction.)

UNITED STATES

County Sales
Box 191
Floyd, VA 24091

Rare Record Distributing Co.
417 East Broadway
P.O. Box 10518
Glendale, CA 91205

Roundup Record Sales
P.O. Box 474
Somerville, MA 02144

Southern Record Sales
5101 Tasman Drive
Huntington Beach, CA 92649

CANADA

Coda Jazz and Blues Record Centre
893 Yonge Street
Toronto M4W 2H2

GREAT BRITAIN (INCLUDING EUROPE)

Dave Carey—The Swing Shop
18 Mitcham Lane
Streatham, London SW16

Collet's Record Centre
180 Shaftesbury Ave.
London WC2H 8JS

Dobell's Record Shop
75 Charing Cross Road
London WC 2

Flyright Records
18 Endwell Rd.
Bexhill-on-Sea
East Sussex

Peter Russell Record Store
24 Market Avenue
Plymouth PL1 1PJ

MAINSTREAM POPULAR
ARTISTS' INDEX

Every performing artist in the **Mainstream Popular** section of this book is listed alphabetically, and immediately following the name is a series of alphanumeric codes referring the reader to the appropriate annotation in the main text. Included are references to those annotations in which the artist is noted as having been influential or influenced but does not necessarily appear on the relevant phonodisc. Also, in the case of annotations covering several offerings by one performer or group, the alphanumeric code here listed refers only to the *first* code of a series in which that first code is obviously the first entry of a combined review. The code numbers in boldface type refer to an artist or group's major main entry phonodiscs (those items starred in text).

Almeida, Laurindo, **P3.15**
Alpert, Herb, **P3.1**
Ambrose, P1.7, **P5.94**
Ames, Ed, **P2.23**
Ames Brothers, P2.23, **P2.144-44a**
Anderson, Ivie, **P5.10**
Anderson, Leroy, **P3.2**, P6.108
Andrews, Julie, P6.9, P6.38, P6.69, P6.90, P6.99
Andrews Sisters, P1.3, **P2.145**
Anthony, Ray, **P5.77**
Arlen, Harold, P1.4, P5.12, P6.109
Armstrong, Louis, P1.4, P1.9, P1.16, **P5.5**
Arnheim, Gus, **P5.20**
Arnold, Eddy, **P2.24**
Astaire, Adele, P6.3, P6.55, P6.59
Astaire, Fred, P5.17, P6.3, P6.55, P6.59, P6.85, P6.87, **P6.103-4, P6.123**
Austin, Gene, P1.4, P1.8, **P2.1**

Bacharach, Burt, P1.15, **P2.133**, P6.110
Bagley, Ben, **P6.1**
Bailey, Mildred, P1.4, P1.11, **P2.87**, P5.18
Bailey, Pearl, **P2.88**, P6.26, P6.45
Baker, Josephine, **P6.124**
Ballard, Kaye, P6.1, P6.21, P6.68, P6.90
Barnet, Charlie, P4.2, **P5.21-22**
Basie, Count, P1.16, P2.87, **P5.4**
Bassey, Shirley, **P2.89-90**, P6.71
Baxter, Les, **P5.78**
Beatles, The, P1.40
Beiderbecke, Bix, P1.9, P2.26, P5.5, P5.18, P5.28
Bellson, Louis, P2.88
Beneke, Tex, P5.39-41
Bennett, Tony, P1.5, **P2.2-3**, P2.66, **P6.109**
Berigan, Bunny, P2.7, P2.135, P5.4, **P5.5-7**, P6.168

Berlin, Irving, **P6.111**
Bibb, Leon, P6.2
Bigard, Barney, P4.4
Bikel, Theodore, P6.46
Black, Stanley, **P5.106**
Blake, Eubie, **P6.166**
Blue Sky Boys, P1.10
Bolcom, William, **P1.1**
Bonfa, Luis, P3.10
Boswell, Connee, P1.11, P2.68a
Boswell Sisters, P2.68a, **P2.135-6, P2.145**, P5.29, P6.86
Bowlly, Al, **P2.4**, P5.102
Brewer, Teresa, **P2.91**
Brice, Fanny, P6.84, **P6.125**
Brown, Clifford, P2.84
Brown, Les, P2.97, **P5.47-48**
Browne, Sam, P1.7, **P5.94**
Brubeck, Dave, **P6.119**
Brunis, George, P5.13
Bryant, Anita, **P2.92**
Brynner, Yul, P6.29
Butler, Jerry, P1.15
Byrd, Charlie, P3.10
Byrd, Jerry, P1.6

Calloway, Cab, P1.14, **P5.23**, P6.33, P6.87, P6.102a
Cantor, Eddie, P1.12, **P2.25**, P6.87
Carle, Frankie, P1.3a
Carmichael, Hoagy, P1.10, **P2.26-7**, P2.82
Carpenters, The, **P2.146**
Carr, Vicki, **P2.93-4**
Carroll, Diahann, P6.26
Carter, Benny, P2.85, P3.21
Cash, Johnny, P1.17
Cassidy, Jack, P6.63, P6.65, P6.68
Cavallaro, Carmen, **P5.106a**

Chacksfield, Frank, **P6.115**, **P6.119**, **P6.121**, **P6.126**
Channing, Carol, P6.25
Cherry, Don, **P2.28**
Chevalier, Maurice, P6.84, **P6.128-9**, P6.94
Chordettes, The, **P2.147**
Clark, Petula, **P2.95**
Clinton, Larry, P5.4
Clooney, Rosemary, P1.5, **P2.96**
Cole, Nat "King," **P2.5**
Columbo, Russ, P2.7, **P2.29**
Como, Perry, **P2.6**, P2.54
Condon, Eddie, P6.169
Conniff, Ray, **P2.148**
Coon-Sanders Nighthawks, **P5.24**
Coward, Noël, **P6.112**, **P6.130-1**
Cramer, Floyd, **P3.3**
Crawford, Jesse, P1.8, **P3.4**
Crosby, Bing, P1.4, P1.9-10, P2.4, **P2.7-11**, P2.29, P2.63, P2.68a, P2.87, P2.145, P5.18, P6.96, **P6.132**
Crosby, Bob, P2.68a
Cugat, Xavier, P2.120, **P5.107-9**
Cutshall, Cutty, P5.44

Damone, Vic, **P2.30**, P6.57
Dankworth, Johnny, **P2.73-4**
Davis, Eddie "Lockjaw," **P3.6a**
Davis, Sammy, Jr., **P2.31-2**
Dawn, Dolly, P5.34
Day, Doris, **P2.97-8**, P6.79
Dee, Lenny, **P3.5**
Del Rio, Delores, P6.84
Denny, Martin, **P5.49**
De Vol, Frank, **P6.113**
Diamond, Neil, **P2.33**
Dietrich, Marlene, P6.86
Dorsey, Jimmy, P1.3, P5.13, **P5.25-6**, P5.28
Dorsey, Tommy, P1.10, **P2.14**, P2.87, P4.2, P5.1, P5.5, **P5.8-9**
Dorsey Brothers, P1.4, P1.9, P2.7, P2.85, P2.135, P5.18
Douglas, Mike, P5.36a
Drake, Alfred, P6.30-1, P6.39
Duchin, Eddy, P1.4, P5.17, **P5.27**
Durante, Jimmy, P1.14
Durbin, Deanna, **P6.133**

Eberle, Ray, P5.33, P5.39-41
Eberly, Bob, P5.26
Eckstine, Billy, **P2.34-5**
Eddy, Nelson, **P6.134-5**
Edison, Harry "Sweets," P2.26, P3.21
Edwards, Cliff, P1.9
Edwards, Darlene, **P4.4a-4b**
Edwards, Jonathan, **P4.4a-4b**

Edwards, Tommy, **P2.39**
Edwards, Webley, **P5.50-51**
Eldridge, Roy, P2.34, P2.87, P5.36
Elgart, Les, **P5.52**
Elliman, Yvonne, P6.28
Ellington, Duke, P1.8-9, P1.16, P2.7, P5.2, **P5.10**, P6.33
Elman, Ziggy, P5.4
Elwin, Maurice, P1.7, P5.95
Etting, Ruth, P1.9, P1.11-12, **P2.99**
Evans, Gil, P5.89-90

Faith, Percy, P1.5, **P5.79**, **P6.114-16**, **P6.121**
Faye, Alice, **P6.136**
Faye, Francis, P1.14
Feliciano, José, **P2.40**
Ferera, Frank, P1.6
Ferrante and Teicher, **P5.53**
Fiedler, Arthur, **P5.80-81**, **P6.108**, **P6.110**, **P6.120**
Fifth Dimension, The, **P2.137**
Firman, Bert, P1.7, **P5.95**
Fisher, Eddie, **P2.41**
Fisher, Tom, P1.17
Fitzgerald, Ella, P1.16, **P2.68**, P4.4, P5.30, **P6.109**, **P6.111**, **P6.114**, **P6.119-20**, **P6.137-43**
Ford, Mary, **P2.112**
Formby, George, **P2.42**
Forrest, Helen, **P5.10**, P5.45
Foster, Stuart, P5.8
Four Aces, **P2.149**
Four Lads, **P2.150**
Fox, Roy, P5.93, **P5.96**
Freberg, Stan, **P4.5**
Freeman, Bud, P4.2
Friml, Rudolf, **P6.113**
Froman, Jane, P1.11, P1.14

Gardner, Kenny, P5.37
Garland, Judy, P2.45, **P2.69-70**, P6.79, P6.85, P6.101, P6.106, **P6.144-46**
Garner, Erroll, **P3.7-8**
Gershwin, Frances, **P6.114**
Gershwin, George, **P6.114**
Getz, Stan, P1.10, **P3.9-10**
Gibbons, Carroll, P2.4, **P5.97**
Gibbs, Georgia, **P2.100**
Gibbs, Parker, P5.46a
Gilberto, Astrid, P3.10
Gilberto, Joao, P3.10
Gingold, Hermione, P6.94
Gleason, Jackie, **P5.54**
Glenn, Tyree, P2.85
Goldkette, Jean, **P5.28**
Goldsboro, Bobby, P2.43
Gonella, Nat, P5.102

Goodman, Benny, P2.85, P2.87, **P5.11,** **P5.**13, **P5.29-31,** P5.45
Gordon, Dexter, P2.35
Gorme, Eydie, **P2.101**
Gould, Morton, **P5.55, P6.116, P6.119**
Goulet, Robert, **P2.44,** P6.9
Grant, Earl, **P3.11**
Grant, Gogi, P1.17
Gray, Glen, P5.2, **P5.32-33**
Grey, Joel, P6.8
Griffin, Ken, **P3.6**

Hale, Binnie, P6.62
Hall, Adelaide, P6.33
Hall, George, **P5.34**
Hall, Juanita, **P2.102,** P6.26, P6.45, P6.47
Hammerstein, Oscar II, **P6.120**
Hampton, Lionel, P5.2
Haney, Carol, P6.42
Hanshaw, Annette, **P2.103-4,** P5.29
Harris, Barbara, P6.40
Harrison, Rex, P6.38
Hart, Lorenz, **P6.120**
Hawkins, Coleman, P1.16, P4.2
Hawkins, Erskine, P5.4
Haymes, Dick, **P2.45**
Heath, Ted, **P5.56,** P5.95, P5.98
Herbert, Victor, **P6.115**
Herman, Woody, P5.2, P5.12
Heywood, Eddie, **P5.57**
Hildegarde, P1.13
Hilliard, Harriet, P5.42
Himber, Richard, **P5.35**
Hines, Earl, P1.9, P5.4
Hinton, Milt, P2.85
Ho, Don, **P2.45a**
Hodges, Johnny, P1.16, P5.10
Holiday, Billie, P1.16, P5.45
Holliday, Judy, P6.4
Holman, Libby, P1.14
Homer and Jethro, **P4.6**
Hoopii, Sol, P1.6
Horne, Lena, **P2.71-2,** P5.45, P6.102a
Humperdinck, Engelbert, **P2.46**
Hunt, Pee Wee, P5.32
Hutton, Betty, P5.38
Hutton, Marion, P5.39-41
Hyland, Brian, P4.1
Hylton, Jack, P1.7, **P5.98,** P6.122

Indios Tabajaras, Los, **P3.12**
Ishkabibble, P5.36a
Ives, Burl, **P2.47**

Jackie and Roy, P2.155
Jackson, Milt, **P3.14-17**

James, Harry, P2.15, **P5.82-84**
James, Joni, **P2.106, P6.122**
Jenkins, Gordon, P2.14, P2.45, P5.12, P5.58
Jessel, George, P6.84
Jobim, Antonio Carlos, P3.10
Johnson, J. J., P4.2
Jolson, Al, P1.4, P1.12, **P2.12, P6.147-8**
Jones, Isham, P1.3a-4, **P5.12**
Jones, Jack, **P2.48**
Jones, Spike, **P4.7-8**
Jones, Tom, **P2.49**
Joplin, Janis, P1.17
Jordan, Duke, P3.9

Kaempfert, Bert, **P5.85**
Kaminsky, Max, P6.168
Kane, Helen, P1.12
Kaye, Danny, P6.159
Kaye, Sammy, **P5.59-60**
Kaye, Stubby, P6.22
Keeler, Ruby, P6.79-80
Keller, Greta, P1.13, P2.107
Kelly, Gene, P6.85, P6.144
Kemp, Hal, **P5.61**
Kenton, Stan, **P6.77**
Kiley, Richard, P6.35
King, Pee Wee, **P5.62**
King, Wayne, **P5.63-64**
Kirby, John, P2.87
Kitt, Eartha, P1.13, **P2.108-9**
Klein, Mannie, P2.85
Kostelanetz, Andre, **P5.65-66, P6.115-6, P6.119**
Krupa, Gene, P1.16, **P5.36**
Kyser, Kay, P5.2, **P5.36a**

Laine, Cleo, **P2.73-4**
Laine, Frankie, P1.5, **P2.50-1**
Lang, Eddie, P2.85, P2.135, P5.18, P5.28
Langford, Frances, P1.11, P6.86
Lanza, Mario, **P6.141**
Last, James, **P5.86**
Lawrence, Carol, P6.50
Lawrence, Gertrude, P6.29, P6.32, P6.63, P6.112, **P6.131, P6.150-52**
Lee, Peggy, **P2.75**
Lehrer, Tom, **P4.10-12**
Lenya, Lotte, P6.8, P6.49, P6.58
Leonard, Jack, P5.8
Lerner, Allan Jay, **P6.117**
Lewis, Ted, P1.4, P1.9, **P5.13**
Light, Enoch, **P5.67**
Lillie, Beatrice, **P6.153**
List, Liesbeth, P1.13
Loewe, Frederick J., **P6.117**
Lombardo, Guy, P5.2, P5.36a, **P5.37**
Lopez, Vincent, P5.3, **P5.38**
Lynn, Vera, **P2.76**

Macdonald, Jeanette, P6.84, **P6.134-5**
McGuire Sisters, **P2.151**
McKuen, Rod, **P2.52**
MacMurray, Fred, P5.43
McRae, Carmen, P1.13, **P2.77**
MacRae, Gordon, **P2.53**, P6.60-61
Mallory, Eddie, P2.85
Mancini, Henry, **P6.154**
Manne, Shelly, **P3.13**
Mantovani, **P5.99-101**, **P6.111**, **P6.113**, **P6.115**, **P6.121**
Marmarosa, Dodo, P5.22
Martin, Dean, **P2.54-55**
Martin, Freddy, **P5.87-88**
Martin, Mary, P1.14, **P6.46-47**, **P6.52**, P6.56, P6.159
Martin, Tony, **P2.56-7**, P6.57
Martino, Al, **P2.58**
Mathews, Jessie, **P6.155**
Mathis, Johnny, P1.17, **P2.5**, **P2.13**
Mauriat, Paul, **P5.68**
May, Billy, P2.14, P5.21, **P5.69**, P6.137
Melachrino, **P6.120-21**
Mendes, Sergio, **P2.152**
Mercer, Johnny, P5.30, **P6.118**
Mercer, Mabel, P1.13, **P2.78**
Merman, Ethel, P1.14, P6.2, P6.23, **P6.156-7**, P6.159
Miley, Bubber, P5.12
Miller, Glenn, P2.145, P5.1, **P5.14-16**, P5.38, **P5.39-41**
Miller, Mitch, P1.5, **P2.138-9**
Mills Brothers, P1.3, **P2.140**, P2.149, P6.33
Miranda, Carmen, **P6.158**
Mitchell, Guy, P1.5
Modern Jazz Quartet, **P3.14-17**
Modernaires, The, P5.39-41
Mole, Miff, P1.9
Monroe, Vaughan, **P2.59**
Montgomery, Wes, P1.16
Morgan, Helen, P1.8-9, P1.11, **P6.125**
Morgan, Jane, **P2.110**
Morgan, Russ, **P5.70**, **P6.122**
Morris, Joan, **P1.1**
Morse, Lee, P5.29
Mostel, Zero, P6.17
Moten, Bennie, P5.4

Nash, Joey, P5.35
National Lampoon, **P4.9**
Navarro, Fats, P2.35
Nelson, Ozzie, **P5.42**
New Vaudeville Band, **P2.153**
Newton, Wayne, **P2.59a**
Nichols, Red, P5.18
Noble, Ray, P2.4, P5.2, P5.93, **P5.102**
Norvo, Red, P2.87

O'Day, Anita, P5.36
Oliver, Sy, P5.8
Olsen, George, P1.3a, P1.8, P5.43
Orlando, Tony, **P2.154**

Page, Patti, **P2.111**
Paige, Janis, P6.42
Pass, Joe, P2.77
Pastor, Tony, P5.2, P5.45
Paul, Les, **P2.112**
Payne, Jack, **P5.103**
Pepper, Art, P2.26
Peterson, Oscar, P1.16, P3.21, P4.2
Phillips, Sid, P5.94
Piaf, Edith, **P2.113-115**
Piazza, Marguerite, P6.60
Pied Pipers, P4.2
Pinza, Ezio, P6.47
Pitney, Gene, P1.15, **P1.60**
Pollack, Ben, P2.68a
Porter, Cole, **P6.119**, **P6.159**
Pourcel, Frank, **P5.71**
Powell, Baden, P6.98
Powell, Dick, P1.10, P6.79-80, P6.87, **P6.160-1**
Powell, Jane, P6.57
Prado, Perez, **P5.110**
Presley, Elvis, P2.49
Preston, Robert, P6.37
Previn, Andre, P3.13
Prima, Louis, **P2.155**

Raitt, John, P6.11, P6.42
Raney, Jimmy, P3.9
Rawls, Lou, **P2.61**
Ray, Johnny, P1.5, P1.17
Redman, Don, P2.88, P6.33
Reddy, Helen, **P2.116**
Reese, Della, **P2.117**
Reisman, Leo, P1.8, **P5.17**
Reynolds, Debbie, P1.3, P6.57
Richman, Harry, P6.87
Riddle, Nelson, P2.14, P5.72, P6.139
Rivera, Chita, P6.7, P6.50
Roach, Max, P2.34
Robey, Art, P5.22
Robinson, Bill "Bojangles," P1.14, P6.33, P6.102a
Rodgers, Richard, **P6.120**
Rogers, Buddy, P1.9
Rogers, Ginger, P6.103-4
Rollini, Adrian, P2.85
Ros, Edmundo, **P5.111-2**
Rose, David, **P5.73-74**
Rowles, Jimmy, P2.77
Roy, Harry, P5.93
Rushing, Jimmy, P5.30

Sandpipers, **P2.156**
Sargent, Kenny, P5.32
Savitt, Jan, P5.3, P5.44
Scranton Sirens, P1.3a
Seekers, **P2.157**
Seely, Blossom, P1.9
Shavers, Charlie, P4.2
Shaw, Artie, P5.1, P5.38, **P5.45-46**
Shaw, Robert, **P6.115**
Sherwood, Madeleine, P6.14
Shirelles, P1.15
Shore, Dinah, **P2.118-20**, P5.18
Short, Bobby, **P6.112, P6.114, P6.119,**
    P6.162-65
Simon and Garfunkel, **P6.95**
Sims, Sylvia, P1.13
Sinatra, Frank, **P2.14-18**, P2.54, P5.8,
    P6.79, P6.96, P6.118, **P6.120**
Sissle, Noble, **P6.166**
Smith, Bessie, P1.9
Smith, Jimmy, **P3.20**
Smith, Kate, P1.4, P1.9, **P2.121-22**
Smith, Keely, **P2.155**
Smith, Stuff, P4.4
Smith, Trixie, P4.4
Smithsonian Social Orchestra, **P1.2**
Smeck, Roy, P1.6
Smoothies, **P2.158**
Sonny and Cher, **P2.159**
Spanier, Muggsy, P5.13
Springfield, Dusty, **P2.123**
Spivak, Charlie, P5.2, P5.38
Stafford, Jo, **P2.79-80**, P4.2, **P4.4a-b**, P5.8
Starr, Kay, **P2.124**, P5.22
Stewart, Rex, P5.10
Stone, Elly, P6.27
Stone, Lew, P5.93, P5.94, **P5.104-105**
Storm, Gale, **P2.125**
Streisand, Barbra, **P2.126-27**, P6.19
Sullivan, Maxine, **P2.81-82**
Swingle Singers, **P2.160**

Teagarden, Jack, P5.18
Temple, Shirley, **P6.167**
Terry, Clark, P4.2
Thomas, B. J., P1.15, **P2.62**
Thompson, Kay, P6.86
Thornhill, Claude, P5.2, **P5.89-90**
Tilton, Martha, P5.30
Tiomkin, Dimitri, **P6.127**
Todd, Dick, **P2.63**
Tucker, Sophie, P1.9, P1.14, **P2.128-130,**
    P6.84
Trotter, John Scott, P2.68a
Trumbauer, Frankie, P1.4

Vale, Jerry, **P2.64**
Valente, Caterina, **P2.131-32**
Valentine, Jerry, P2.35
Vallee, Rudy, P1.9, **P2.22**
Van Dyke, Dick, P6.7, P6.99
Vaughan, Billy, **P5.91-92**
Vaughan, Sarah, **P2.83-84**
Venuti, Joe, P1.9, P2.85, P2.135, P5.18, P5.28
Verdon, Gwen, P6.13, P6.48
Vinton, Bobby, P1.15

Waller, Fats, **P2.65**, P5.13, P6.102a
Ward, Helen, P5.30
Waring, Fred, P1.8, **P2.141-3**
Warren, Fran, P5.22
Warwicke, Dionne, P1.15, **P2.133**
Waters, Ethel, P1.4, P1.9, P1.14, **P2.85-86,**
    P5.29, P6.33, **P6.170**
Webster, Ben, **P3.21**, P5.10
Weems, Ted, P1.3a, P2.6, P5.46a
Welcome, Ruth, **P3.22**
Welk, Lawrence, **P5.75**
West, Mae, P6.86
Weston, Paul, **P4.4a-4b**, P6.116, P6.138, P6.168
Whiteman, Paul, P1.4, P1.9-10, P1.12, P2.7,
    P5.18-19, P6.114
Wiley, Lee, P1.4, P1.11, P5.17, P6.86, **P6.109,**
    P6.114, P6.119-20, P6.168-69
Wilber, Bob, **P2.81-82**
Williams, Andy, **P2.66-67, P6.120**
Williams, Cootie, P5.10
Williams, Mary Lou, P2.87
Williams, Roger, **P3.23**
Wilson, Dooley, P6.5, P6.79
Wilson, Nancy, **P2.134**
Wilson, Teddy, P2.34, P2.87, P3.21
Winterhalter, Hugo, **P5.76**
Wright, Edythe, P5.8

Young, Lester, P2.34
Young, Victor, P2.7, P2.45

Every performing artist in the **Rock** section of this book is listed alphabetically, and immediately following the name is a series of alphanumeric codes referring the reader to the appropriate annotation in the main text. Included are references to those annotations in which the artist is noted as having been influential or influenced but does not necessarily appear on the relevant phonodisc. Also, in the case of annotations covering several offerings by one performer or group, the alphanumeric code here listed refers only to the *first* code of a series in which that first code is obviously the first entry of a combined review. The code numbers in boldface type refer to an artist or group's major main entry phonodiscs (those items starred in text).

Ace, Johnny, R2.12
Adams, Faye, R2.5
Alice Cooper, **R8.10**
Allman, Duane, **R4.20**, R5.12
Allman Brothers, **R4.20**, R5.12a
Anderson, Ian, **R9.10**
Animals, **R5.13**
Anka, Paul, **R2.15**
Appice, Carmine, R6.14
Argent, **R4.21**
Argent, Rod, R4.47
Association, The, **R3.2**
Atkins, Chet, R2.18, R3.10, R4.3
Avalon, Frankie, R2.8, **R2.23**
Ayers, Kevin, **R9.22**
Ayler, Albert, R8.14

Bachman, Randy, R3.10, **R8.11**
Bachman-Turner Overdrive, **R8.11**
Baez, Joan, R4.2
Baker, Ginger, R5.1, **R8.1-3**
Baker, Mickey, R5.1
Baldry, Long John, R5.1
Ballard, Hank, R2.4, R2.16
Band, The, R4.43, **R7.1-5**
Barber, Chris, R1.1
Bay City Rollers, R3.4, R4.3
Beach Boys, The, R3.3, R3.13, **R9.1**
Beatles, The, R3.3, **R3.4**, R3.18, R4.1, **R4.3-7**, R4.11, R4.13, R4.22, **R9.2**
Beck, Jeff, **R4.8**, R4.44, R5.12, **R5.14**
Bee Gees, The, R4.1, **R4.22**
Bell, Richard, R5.20
Berline, Byron, R7.15
Berry, Chuck, R2.13, R3.3, R3.4, R3.17, R4.3, R4.11, R4.13, R4.43
Betts, Dicky, R5.12
Big Bopper, The, R2.51
Bishop, Elvin, R5.8

Black, Bill, R2.10, **R2.24**
Blackmore, Ritchie, **R8.15**
Blackwell, Otis, R3.6
Blind Faith, **R8.12**
Blood, Sweat and Tears, **R4.9**, R4.25
Bloomfield, Mike, R5.7, R5.17
Blue Oyster Cult, **R8.13**
Blues Project, The, R5.6
Blue Sky Boys, R2.18, R7.7
Blunstone, Colin, R4.47
Bob B. Soxx and the Blue Jeans, R2.11-11a
Bogert, Tim, R6.14
Bond, Graham, R5.1
Bonds, Gary U.S., **R2.25**
Bonnie and Delaney
    See Delaney and Bonnie
Bonzo Dog Band, **R4.23**
Booker T., R2.1
Boone, Pat, R2.2, R2.9, **R2.26**
Bostic, Earl, R2.10
Bowie, David, R4.1, **R4.24**
Boyd, Eddie, R5.1
Bread, R3.2, **R3.5**
Brown, Buster, R2.1
Bruce, Jack, R5.1, **R8.1-3**
Burdon, Eric, **R5.13**
Buffalo Springfield, R3.11, R4.3, **R7.6**
Burlison, Paul, R1.12
Burnette, Dorsey, R1.12
Burnette, Johnny, **R1.12**
Butterfield, Paul, R4.2, R5.1, **R5.7-8**, R8.1
Byrd, Joe, **R9.23-24**
Byrds, The, R3.18-19, **R7.7-8**

Cadets, The, R2.8
Cadillacs, The, R2.12
Cage, Buddy, R7.17
Cale, John, R8.22
Canned Heat, R4.2, **R5.15**

Cannon, Freddy, **R2.27**
Captain Beefheart and His Magic Band, **R8.14**
Carroll, Johnny, R1.2
Carter, Clarence, R4.20
Cash, Johnny, **R1.13**, R1.15
Chad and Jeremy, R4.1
Champs, The, R2.10
Chandler, Gene, R2.12
Charles, Ray, R2.4
Checker, Chubby, **R2.16**
Chicago, **R4.25**
Chordettes, R2.3
Cipollina, John, R6.13
Clapton, Eric, R4.20, R4.30, R5.1, R5.9, R5.12, **R5.16**, **R8.1-3**, **R8.12**
Clark, Dave, R4.1
Clark, Dee, R2.5, R2.12
Clark, Gene, R7.7
Clark, Petula, R4.1
Clayton-Thomas, David, R4.4
Cochran, Eddie, **R2.28**
Cocker, Joe, R4.2, **R4.26**
Cohen, Leonard, R4.27
Collins, Albert, R4.31
Collins, Judy, **R4.27-29**
Cooke, Sam, R4.43-44
Cooper, Alice
    See Alice Cooper
Cortez, Dave "Baby," R2.10
Country Joe and the Fish, R4.2, **R6.10**
Covay, Don, R2.20
Cream, R4.1, R5.16, **R8.1-3**
Creedence Clearwater Revival, **R3.6**
Crescendos, R2.8
Crewcuts, The, R2.14
Crosby, David, R7.7, **R7.9-11**
Crosby, Stills, Nash and Young, R3.3, R4.2-3, **R7.9-11**
Crystals, The, R2.11-11a
Cummings, Burton, R3.10
Curtis, King, R4.20
Curtis, Mac, **R1.14**

Daltry, Roger, R4.17-19
Darin, Bobby, **R2.30**
Davies, Ray, R4.11-12
Davis, Miles, R9.22
Davis, Spencer, R5.1
Deep Purple, R4.1, **R8.15-17**, **R9.3**
Delaney and Bonnie, R4.20, **R4.30**, R5.16
Dell-Vikings, R2.2, **R2.31**
Derek and the Dominoes, R5.16
Diamond, Neil, R3.1, R3.20
Diamonds, R2.14
Diddley, Bo, R2.5, R4.13
Dillard and Clark Expedition, R7.12
Dinning, Mark, R2.51

Dion and the Belmonts, **R2.32**
Dr. John, **R2.48**, **R6.11**
Doggett, Bill, R2.10, **R2.33**
Domino, Fats, R2.2, R2.26
Donegan, Lonnie, R1.1, R2.9, R2.13
Donovan, R4.1
Doors, **R6.1-3**
Dunbar, Aynsley, R5.1, R9.15
Duncan, Johnny, R1.1
Dupree, Champion Jack, R5.1
Dylan, Bob, R4.3, R4.43, R7.1, R7.7, **R8.4-7**

Eagles, The, **R7.12-13**
Eddy, Duane, R2.4, **R2.17**, R4.3
Electric Flag, **R5.17**
Elliot, Cass, R3.19
Emerson, Lake and Palmer, **R9.4**
Emmons, Buddy, R7.15
Everly Brothers, R2.3, **R2.18-19**, R4.3

Fabian, **R2.34**
Faces, R4.44
Faith, Adam, R2.13
Feathers, Charlie, **R1.14**
Five Satins, R2.8
Fleetwood Mac, **R5.18-19**
Fleetwoods, R2.8
Flying Burrito Brothers, R7.12, **R7.14**
Focus, **R9.5**
Fogerty, John, R3.6
Four Lads, R2.22
Four Seasons, **R3.7**
Frampton, Peter, R2.49
Francis, Connie, **R2.35**, R3.9
Franklin, Aretha, R4.20
Franklin, Erma, R3.1
Freeman, Bobby, R2.1
Fripp, Robert, R9.11
Frost, Frank, R1.6
Fugs, R2.50, **R9.6-7**
Furay, Richie, R7.6, R7.18

Gallagher, Rory, R2.49, R3.1
Garcia, Jerry, **R6.4-6**
Garrett, Amos, R5.7
Gates, David, R3.5
Gaylords, R2.14
Geils, J., **R4.31**
Glaser, Tompall, R1.15
Goldberg, Barry, R5.17
Goldsboro, Bobby, **R3.8**
Gore, Lesley, **R3.9**
Grand Funk Railroad, **R8.18**
Grateful Dead, The, **R6.4-6**
Greer, Peter, R5.1, R5.18

Guess Who, The, **R3.10**
Guthrie, Arlo, R4.2

Haley, Bill, **R1.7**, R2.1, R4.3
Hall, Roy, R1.2
Hammond, John, R4.20
Harris, Emmylou, R7.15
Harrison, George
  See Beatles
Harris, Thurston, R2.8
Hartley, Keef, R5.1
Havens, Richie, R4.2, R4.44
Hawkins, Dale, R3.6
Hawkins, Ronnie, R7.1
Hazlewood, Lee, R3.24
Helms, Bobby, **R2.36**
Hendrix, Jimi, R4.1-2, **R8.4-7**, R8.8
Hermans Hermits, R4.3
Hillman, Chris, R7.7, R7.14
Hilltoppers, R2.9
Hodges, Eddie, R2.3
Hollies, **R3.11**, R4.3
Holly, Buddy, **R1.8**, R1.14, R2.1, R2.45,
  R4.43
Homesick James, R5.1
Hooker, John Lee, R4.31, R5.15
Hopkins, Nicky, R5.14
Horton, Shakey, R5.1
Horton, Walter, R1.6
Hunter, Tab, R2.2

Incredible String Band, **R9.8**
Iron Butterfly, **R8.19**
Isley Brothers, R3.4

Jackson, Wanda, **R2.20**, R2.38
Jagger, Mick, R4.13
James, Elmore, R5.18
James, Tommy, **R3.12**
Jan and Dean, **R3.13**
Jay and the Americans, **R3.14**
Jefferson Airplane, R4.2, **R6.7-9**
Jennings, Waylon, R1.15
Jethro Tull, R4.32, **R9.10**
John, Elton, R4.1, **R4.10**
Johnson, Robert, R4.13
Johnny and the Hurricanes, R2.8
Jones, Davy, R4.24
Jones, Joe, R2.5
Jones, Paul, R4.33
Joplin, Janis, **R5.20**
Jordan, Louis, R2.10
Justis, Bill, R1.4, **R2.37**

Kaukonen, Jorma, R6.7-9
Kay, John, R8.21
King, Albert, R3.17
King, B. B., R5.16, R5.18, R8.1
King, Ben E., R2.11a
King, Carole, **R3.15**
King Crimson, R9.4, **R9.11**
Kirks, R4.1, **R4.11-12**, **R9.12**
Kirwen, Danny, R5.18
Knechtel, Larry, R3.5
Knox, Buddy, R2.5
Kooper, Al, R4.9, R5.6
Korner, Alexis, R5.1
Kweskin, Jim, R4.35

Lake, Greg, R9.4
Led Zeppelin, **R5.21**, **R8.8-9**
Lee, Alvin, R2.49
Lee, Brenda, **R2.38**
Lennon, John
  See Beatles
Lewis, Gary, **R3.16**
Lewis, Jerry Lee, R1.4, R1.5, **R1.9-10**, R1.14,
  R2.49, R4.10
Lewis, Joe Hill, R1.6
Lewis, Smiley, R2.8
Little Caesar and the Romans, R2.12
Little Eva, R2.5
Little Richard, R2.2, R2.13, R2.20, R3.4, R8.8
Lord, Jon, **R8.15**
Louvin Brothers, R2.18, R7.7
Love, Darlene, R2.11-11a
Lovin' Spoonful, The, R3.5, **R3.18**
Lowe, Jim, R2.2

MC5, R8.10, **R9.13**
McCartney, Paul
  See Beatles
McCoy, Charlie, R2.3
McCoys, The, R3.1
McDowell, Fred, R4.38
Mack, Lonnie, R2.10
McPhee, T. S., R5.1
McGuinn, Roger (Jim), R7.7
McVie, John, R5.9, R5.18
McVoy, Carl, R1.4
Mamas and the Papas, The, R3.11, R3.18, **R3.19**
Mann, Manfred, R4.1, **R4.33**
Martindale, Wink, R2.2
Mason, Dave, **R4.34**, R5.23
Mathis, Johnny, R4.10
Mayall, John, R5.1, **R5.9-11**, R5.16
Melanie, R4.2
Messina, Jim, R7.6, R7.18
Milburn, Amos, R2.8
Miles, Buddy, R5.17
Miller, Mitch, R2.39

Miller, Steve, **R5.22**
Mitchell, Guy, R1.17, **R2.39**
Mitchell, Joni, R4.27
Moby Grape, **R6.12**
Monkees, The, **R3.20**
Monotones, The, R2.51
Monroe Brothers, R2.18
Moody Blues, The, **R9.14**
Morrison, Jim, **R6.1-3**
Morrison, Van, R3.1, R4.1, R4.43
Moskowitz, Dorothy, R9.23
Mothers of Invention, The, **R2.50**, **R9.15-16**
Mountain, R4.2
Move, **R8.20**
Muldaur, Geoff, R5.7
Muldaur, Maria, **R4.35-36**

Nash, Graham, R3.11, **R7.9-11**
Nash, Johnny, R3.17
Nelson, Rick, **R2.40**
Nelson, Sandy, R2.8, R2.10
Nelson, Willie, R1.15
Nervous Norvus, R2.2
New Riders of the Purple Sage, **R7.17**
Newley, Anthony, R4.24
Nice, R9.4, **R9.17**
Nighthawk, Robert, R5.1

Oldfield, Mike, **R9.18**
Olympics, R2.8
Orbison, Roy, R1.4, R1.6, **R2.21**, R4.43
Orioles, R2.12

Page, Jimmy, R5.1, R5.12, R5.21, **R8.8-9**
Palmer, Carl, R9.4
Paris Sisters, The, R2.11a
Parker, Junior, R1.6, R2.12
Parks, Van Dyke, **R9.25**
Parsons, Gram, R7.7, R7.14, **R7.15-16**
Penguins, The, R2.8
Perkins, Carl, R1.4, R1.5, R1.6, **R1.15**, R2.20, R3.4
Peter and Gordon, R4.1
Phillips, John, R3.19
Pickett, Wilson, R4.20
Pierce, Webb, R1.2
Pink, Floyd, **R9.19-20**
Pitney, Gene, R2.11a
Plant, Robert, R5.21, **R8.8-9**
Platters, The, R2.14
Poco, R7.12, **R7.18**
Presley, Elvis, **R1.11-11a**, R1.15, R1.16, R1.18, R2.27, R4.43, R5.18
Price, Alan, R5.13
Procol Harum, **R4.37**

Professor Longhair, R2.48
Puckett, Gary, **R3.21**

Quicksilver Messenger Service, **R6.13**

Raitt, Bonnie, **R4.38-39**
Rascals, The, **R4.40**
Ray, Johnny, **R2.22**
Reed, Jimmy, R2.49, R4.13
Reed, Lou, R8.22
Regents, The, R2.1, R3.3
Relf, Keith, R5.1, R5.12
Reparata and the Delrons, R2.8
Reuben and the Jets, **R2.50**
    See also Mothers of Invention
Rich, Charlie, R1.4, R1.6, **R1.16**
Richard, Cliff, R2.13
Richards, Keith, R4.13
Righteous Brothers, The, R2.11a, **R3.22**
Rivers, Johnny, **R3.17**
Robbins, Marty, **R1.17**
Robertson, Robbie, R7.1
Robinson, Fenton, R4.20
Rodgers, Jimmy, R2.5
Rolling Stones, The, R3.3, R4.11, **R4.13-16**, R4.31, **R9.21**
Ronettes, The, R2.11-11a
Royal Teens, The, R2.4
Rush, Otis, R4.31
Russell, Leon, **R4.41**
Rydell, Bobby, **R2.41**

Sam and Dave, R3.22
Santana, R4.2, **R4.42**
Santo and Johnny, R2.10
Savoy Brown, R5.1
Scaggs, Boz, R4.20, R5.22
Sebastian, John, R3.18, R4.2
Sedaka, Neil, **R2.42**
Shadows, The, R2.12
Sha Na Na, **R2.51**
Shannon, Del, R2.1, R2.8
Shirley and Lee, R2.12
Shirelles, **R2.43**
Silhouettes, R2.8
Simmonds, Kim, R5.1
Simon, Carly, **R3.23**
Sinatra, Nancy, **R3.24**
Sinfield, Pete, R9.11
Slick, Grace, **R6.7-9**
Smith, Huey, R2.48
Smith, Warren, R1.4, R1.6
Soft Machine, **R9.22**
Spann, Otis, R5.1, R5.18
Spector, Phil, R2.8, R2.11-11a, R3.22, R4.11, R8.4, R9.1
Spencer, Jeremy, R5.18

Springfield, Dusty, R4.1
Springsteen, Bruce, **R4.43**
Steppenwolf, **R8.21**
Stewart, Rod, R4.1, **R4.44,** R5.1, **R5.14**
Stills, Stephen, R7.6, **R7.9-11**
Stone, Sly, R4.2
Storm, Gale, R2.2
Surfaris, The, R2.10
Swinging Blue Jeans, The, R4.1

Taupin, Bernie, R4.10
Teddy Bears, R2.8
Ten Years After, R4.2, **R4.45**, R5.1
Thomas, B. J., **R3.25**
Thomas, Rufus, R1.6
Thornton, Big Mama, R2.12
Three Dog Night, **R4.46**
Till, John, R5.20
Tillotson, Johnny, R2.3
Tornadoes, The, R2.13
Townshend, Peter, R4.17-19
Traffic, R4.34, **R5.23**
Troggs, The, R4.1
Trower, Robin, R4.37
Tubb, Ernest, R1.13
Turbans, The, R2.12
Turner, Ike and Tina, R2.11a
Twitty, Conway, **R2.44**

United States of America, The, **R9.23**

Valli, Frankie, R3.7
Van Dyke, Leroy, R2.2
Vanilla Fudge, **R6.14**
Vaughan, Billy, R2.9, R2.26
Vee, Bobby, R2.8, **R2.45**
Velvet Underground, The, **R8.22**
Ventures, The, R2.8, **R2.46**
Vincent, Gene, **R1.18**, R2.18
Vinton, Bobby, **R2.47**
Voorman, Klaus, R2.49

Wakeman, Rick, **R9.26**, R9.28
Wallace, Sippi, R4.38
Wells, Mary, R2.5
White, Clarence, R7.7
Who, The, R4.1, R4.2, **R4.17-19,** R9.27
Williams, Hank, R1.13
Williams, Larry, R2.8, R3.4
Wilson, Brian, R3.3
Winwood, Stevie, R4.34, R5.1, R5.23,
    R8.12
Wood, Ron, R5.14
Wood, Roy, R8.20

Woody, Don, R1.2
Wray, Link, R2.3

Yardbirds, The, R5.1, **R5.12,** R5.16, R5.21
Yes, R9.26, **R9.28**
Young, Jesse Colin, R7.21
Young, Neil, R7.6, **R7.10-11,** **R7.19-20**
Youngbloods, The, **R7.21**

Zappa, Frank, **R2.50,** R4.23, **R9.15-16**
Zombies, The, R4.21, **R4.47**